D1550078

Essential Readings in Nursing Managed Care

Editor

Susan Odegaard Turner, RN, MN, MBA, PhD
Chief Executive Officer
Turner Healthcare Associates, Inc.
Thousand Oaks, California

Project Staff
California Strategic Planning Committee for Nursing
Irvine, California

Assistant Clinical Professor
UCLA School of Nursing
Los Angeles, California

and

Aspen Reference Group

AN ASPEN PUBLICATION®
Aspen Publishers, Inc.
Gaithersburg, Maryland
1999

The author has made every effort to ensure the accuracy of the information herein. However, appropriate information sources should be consulted, especially for new or unfamiliar procedures. It is the responsibility of every practitioner to evaluate the appropriateness of a particular opinion in the context of actual clinical situations and with due considerations to new developments. The author, editors, and the publisher cannot be held responsible for any typographical or other errors found in this book.

Library of Congress Cataloging-in-Publication Data

Essential readings in nursing managed care / editor, Susan Odegaard Turner and Aspen Reference Group.
p. cm.
Collection of previously published articles.
Includes bibliographical references and index.
ISBN 0-8342-1326-5
1. Nursing—Effect of managed care on. 2. Nursing services—Administration. 3. Managed care plans (Medical care) I. Turner, Susan Odegaard. II. Aspen Reference Group (Aspen Publishers) [DNLM: 1. Nursing Services—organization & administration collected works. 2. Case Management—organization & administration collected works. 3. Managed Care Programs—organization & administration collected works. WY 100 E78 1999]
RT42.E86 1999
362.1'73'068—dc21
DNLM/DLC
for Library of Congress
98-50336
CIP

Copyright © 1999 by Aspen Publishers, Inc.
All rights reserved.

Aspen Publishers, Inc., grants permission for photocopying for limited personal or internal use. This consent does not extend to other kinds of copying, such as copying for general distribution, for advertising or promotional purposes, for creating new collective works, or for resale.

For information, address Aspen Publishers, Inc., Permissions Department, 200 Orchard Ridge Drive, Suite 200, Gaithersburg, Maryland 20878.

Orders: (800) 638-8437
Customer Service: (800) 234-1660

About Aspen Publishers • For more than 35 years, Aspen has been a leading professional publisher in a variety of disciplines. Aspen's vast information resources are available in both print and electronic formats. We are committed to providing the highest quality information available in the most appropriate format for our customers. Visit Aspen's Internet site for more information resources, directories, articles, and a searchable version of Aspen's full catalog, including the most recent publications: **http://www.aspenpublishers.com**

Aspen Publishers, Inc. • The hallmark of quality in publishing
Member of the worldwide Wolters Kluwer group.

Editorial Services: Denise H. Coursey
Library of Congress Catalog Card Number: 98-50336
ISBN: 0-8342-1326-5

Printed in the United States of America

362.173068
E78

1 2 3 4 5

Table of Contents

Contributors

Sara E. Barger, DPA, RN, FAAN
Dean and Professor
Capstone College of Nursing
The University of Alabama
Tuscaloosa, AL

James W. Begun, PhD
Professor and Director
Doctoral Program in Health Services Organizations and Research
Department of Health Administration
Medical College of Virginia Campus
Virginia Commonwealth University
Richmond, VA

Judith G. Berg, RN, MS
Senior Vice President
Nursing Services
Cottage Health System
Santa Barbara, CA

Norman E. Bolus, BS, CNMT
Graduate Student
School of Public Health
University of Alabama at Birmingham
Birmingham, AL

Kenneth Brownson, EdD, PhD, RN, C
President
Adult Education Resource
Newark, DE

Mary Ellen Clyne, MSN, RN, CNAA
Director of Nursing
Departments of Orthopaedics, Same-Day Surgery, Admitting, and Rehabilitation Services
Hospital Center at Orange
Orange, NJ

Linda Cole, MSN, RN, CCRN
Outcomes Manager/Clinical Nurse Specialist
Outcomes Management Department
St. Luke's Episcopal Hospital
Houston, TX

Catherine E. Cooke, PharmD
Assistant Professor
Department of Pharmacy Practice and Science
University of Maryland at Baltimore
Baltimore, MD

Gregory Crow, EdD
Professor, Graduate Coordinator and Program Director of Leadership and Case Management Programs
Department of Nursing
Sonoma State University
Rohnert Park, CA
Senior Consultant
Tim Porter-O'Grady Associates, Inc.
Atlanta, GA

Steve Davis
Editor, *Reengineering the Hospital*
Aspen Publishers, Inc.
Gaithersburg, MD

Satish P. Deshpande, PhD
Professor of Management
Haworth College of Business
Western Michigan University
Kalamazoo, MI

Jeanne Donlevy, BSPA, RN
Senior Vice President for Nursing Service
The Good Samaritan Hospital
Lebanon, PA

Steven B. Dowd, EdD, RT (R) (QM) (MR)
Associate Professor and Program Director
Radiography
University of Alabama at Birmingham
Birmingham, AL

Joan Marie Flynn, MA, RN, C
Patient Service Nurse Educator
Department of Veterans Affairs Medical Center
New York, NY

Mary Forlenza, MSN, RN
Staff Nurse
Department of Critical Care
Hospital Center at Orange
Orange, NJ

Harriet S. Gill
Principal
Gill/Balsano Consulting, LLC
Atlanta, GA

Linda McGillis Hall, RN, MSc, PhD Candidate
Lecturer
Faculty of Nursing
University of Toronto
Toronto, Ontario
CANADA

C. David Hardison, PhD
Vice President
First Consulting Group
Long Beach, CA

Marjorie M. Heinzer, PhD, RN, CS, CRNP
Assistant Professor of Nursing
La Salle University
Associate Director of Nursing for Research
Albert Einstein Medical Center
Philadelpha, PA

Debra Bumsted Hernandez, MSN, RNC, CCRN
Director
Care Management/Delivery
Veterans Memorial Medical Center
Meriden, CT

Susan Houston, PhD, RN
Director
Outcomes Measurement and Research
St. Luke's Episcopal Hospital
Houston, TX

Diane Schaming Hupp, RN, MSN, CNA
Patient Service Manager
Children's Hospital of Pittsburgh
Pittsburgh, PA

Gladys L. Husted, RN, PhD
Professor
School of Nursing
Duquesne University
Pittsburgh, PA

James H. Husted
Served as Philosophy Editor for Integra
Expert in philosophy for Dial-An-M, the information network of American Mensa
Pittsburgh, PA

Jacob Joseph, PhD
Assistant Professor of Management
University of Alaska at Fairbanks
Fairbanks, AK

David Keepnews, JD, MPH, RN
Director
Office of Policy
American Nurses Association
Washington, DC

JoEllen Goertz Koerner, PhD, RN, FAAN
Vice President of Patient Services
Sioux Valley Hospital
Sioux Falls, SD

Rosemarie M. Kolker, RRA, MS
Assistant Quality Officer
Office of Clinical Practice Evaluation
Strong Memorial Hospital
Rochester, NY

Vicki D. Lachman, RN, PhD, CS, CNAA
President
V.L. Associates
Philadelphia, PA

Elizabeth R. Lenz, PhD, FAAN
Professor and Associate Dean
Columbia University School of Nursing
New York, NY

Margaret M. Mahon, PhD, RN, CPNP
Assistant Professor
University of Pennsylvania
School of Nursing
Philadelphia, PA

Paula Marchionno, RN, MSN
Vice President for Nursing
Niagara Falls Memorial Medical Center
Niagara Falls, NY

Geri Marullo, MSN, RN
Executive Director
American Nurses Association
Washington, DC

Kathryn J. McDonagh, MSN, RN, CNAA, CHE, FAAN
President/Chief Executive Officer
Northwest Covenant Medical Center
Denville, NJ

Terry McGoldrick, MSN, RN
Director of Nursing for Professional Development
Albert Einstein Medical Center
Philadelphia, PA

Sharon McLane, RN, MBA, CNAA
Associate Director of Critical Care Services
M.D. Anderson Cancer Center
University of Texas
Houston, TX

D. Kathy Milholland, PhD, RN
Senior Policy Fellow, Nursing Practice Health Policy
Department of Nursing Practice
American Nurses Association
Washington, DC

Elvira Miller, EdD, RN
Associate Medical Center Director for Patient Services
Department of Veterans Affairs Medical Center
New York, NY

Kathleen Mitchell, MA, RN
Director of Medicine, Neurology, Oncology, and Psychiatry Nursing Services
Georgetown University Medical Center
Washington, DC

Wanda K. Mohr, PhD, RNC
Assistant Professor
University of Pennsylvania
School of Nursing
Philadelphia, PA

Mary O. Mundinger, DrPH, FAAN
Dean and Centennial Professor in Health Policy
Columbia University School of Nursing
New York, NY

Kyoko Nagaike, RN, MPH, BSN
Manager
Executive Health Program
Kuakini Medical Center
Honolulu, HI

Janet Owen, MS, RNC, CPHQ
Clinical Educator
Pediatric/Perinatal and Dialysis Services
Georgetown University Medical Center
Washington, DC

Robert J. Panzer, MD
Associate Medical Director for Clinical Services
Chief Quality Officer at the University of Rochester Medical Center/Strong Memorial Hospital
Rochester, NY

Bonnie Pietruch, MSN, RN
Director
CDM/Special Projects
The Good Samaritan Hospital
Lebanon, PA

Tim Porter-O'Grady, EdD, PhD, FAAN
President and Senior Partner
Tim Porter-O'Grady Associates, Inc.
Atlanta, GA

Susan Jo Roberts, DNSc, RNCS
Associate Professor
Northeastern University
College of Nursing
Boston, MA

Michael Rovinsky
Senior Manager
Gill/Balsano Consulting, LLC
Atlanta, GA

Patricia A. Rowell, PhD, RN
Senior Policy Fellow, Nursing Practice Health Policy
Department of Nursing Practice
American Nurses Association
Washington, DC

Susan Warner Salmond, EdD, RN
Professor of Nursing
Graduate Program Director
Department of Nursing
Kean College of New Jersey
Union, NJ

Linda Berger Spivack, MSN, RN
Director
Transition Planning
Veterans Memorial Medical Center
Meriden, CT

Vivian S. Sternweiler, MS, RN
Medical-Surgical Clinical Nurse Specialist
Division of Nursing
Beth Israel Deaconess Medical Center
Boston, MA

Deborah A. Straka, MSN, RN, CNS
Associate Editor of *Advanced Practice Nursing Quarterly*
Senior Nursing Director at Allegheny General Hospital
Pittsburgh, PA
Consultant
The Hay Group, Inc.
New York, NY

Diana Taylor, RN, PhD, FAAN
Associate Professor
Department of Family Health Care Nursing
School of Nursing
University of California-San Francisco
San Francisco, CA

Annette M. Totten, MPA
Project Director
Columbia University School of Nursing
New York, NY

Deborah N. Tuttle, RN, MPS
Associate Director
Office of Clinical Practice Evaluation
Associate Quality Officer
Strong Memorial Hospital
Rochester, NY

Katherine Cardone Uehlinger, MS, RN
Nursing Coordinator
Mental Health Services
Georgetown University Medical Center
Washington, DC

Juliet Umadac, MS, RN, CCRN
Patient Services Nurse Educator
Department of Veterans Affairs Medical Center
New York, NY

Marianne E. Weiss, RN, CNS, DNSc
Associate Professor
College of Nursing
Marquette University
Milwaukee, WI

Kenneth R. White, MPH, PhD, RN, FACHE
Instructor and Assistant Director
Professional Graduate Programs
Department of Health Administration
Medical College of Virginia Campus
Virginia Commonwealth University
Richmond, VA

Maureen Whitman, MN, RN
Deputy Title V Director
Center for Child and Family Health
Oregon Health Division
Portland, OR

Cheryl Zwingman-Bagley, MSN, RN, CNAA
Transition Leader
Hartford Hospital
Hartford, CT

Preface

This collection of selected readings is a companion to *The Nurse's Guide to Managed Care,* a text designed to provide a broad overview of the managed health care system as it relates to nursing. *The Nurse's Guide to Managed Care* is limited in scope because it is a single text. However, this selection of readings has been assembled to bring additional breadth to the original text.

The articles included in this collection have been selected for several reasons. An article may present more depth to a subject worth future discussion. In some cases, the article may present a point of view not found in the text or not shared by the author. Other articles are included simply to provoke discussion in the classroom.

I may not agree with the perspective or points made by the authors of these readings, but the reader can be exposed to an alternate point of view and interpretation. I am appreciative of the valuable contributions made by the authors of these articles.

The readings were selected to parallel the chapters in the text. They are not exhaustive and represent only a sampling of available literature on nursing and managed care. Each chapter in the text contains additional references and other readings that may be of value. Students are encouraged to find other sources to enrich their knowledge of the field.

It is my hope that these companion texts used as adjuncts to academic courses and literature will continue to enhance the scope and influence of nursing in the managed health care environment.

1

Nursing at the Crossroads

Profession Building in the New Health Care System

Kenneth R. White and James W. Begun

Deeply rooted in their historical context, nurses have struggled to achieve credibility, autonomy, and power on a par with physicians and other health professionals. Not only have nurses had to prove themselves as legitimate professionals, but they also have had to fight the battle for women's equal rights. Although nursing has had a long history of oppression,[1] great strides have been made in attaining legitimacy and power for professional nursing. In the last 100 years, nursing has transitioned from a blue-collar, domestic servant class to a knowledge-based discipline linked to every aspect of the health care system. Nursing has long since rejected the handmaiden role and has assertively redefined the nurse as a leader who may best guide the total care of the patient.[2]

Yet much remains to be accomplished. To further the goals of greater legitimacy and power, it is necessary for nursing to revise many of the strategies that made sense prior to the 1990s. With health care changing at a galloping pace, it follows that the sources of power in the health care system, and the mechanisms for achieving power, would change also. Nursing must transform its strategies for achieving power in order to keep pace.

NURSING AS A COMPLEX ADAPTIVE SYSTEM

In order to view the profession of nursing as a whole, it is useful to visualize the profession as a complex adaptive system, with the properties of such systems. An economy, a fern, a city, a society—all are examples of complex adaptive systems. As a system, the nursing profession includes both professional organizations and individual practitioners united by the pursuit of common goals, such as legitimacy and market power.[3] The nursing profession supplies nursing services to consumers, employers, and other purchasers of its services. Even limited to RNs, the system of nursing is still huge, encompassing some 2.2 million individuals and hundreds of professional organizations.

Complex adaptive systems generally seek to adapt to their environment, and they do so within the constraints of their historical context, unless radical transformations can be achieved.[4] The systems attempt to respond to changes in their environments and shape the environments in their own interests. This is analogous to saying that complex adaptive systems have a strategy. Strategies can be de-

Nurs Admin Q, 1996, 20(3): 79–85
© 1996 Aspen Publishers, Inc.

fined as patterns in the goal-directed plans and activities of professionals and their associations that position the profession in relation to external demands.[3] For example, the American Nurses Association (ANA) has attempted to represent the position of nursing (although only 10% of the nation's RNs are members) through its formalized policy statements and political activities. With any system as large and complex as nursing, strategic direction often is implicit rather than explicit, and emergent, only becoming apparent in retrospect, rather than planned.

As a complex adaptive system, nursing will attempt to deal with the quickening pace of change in the environment. To survive, the system will need to balance its efforts to shape the health care environment with its efforts to react to or cope with (or ignore) external forces. A new framework for profession building must be adopted in order to transform nursing into a profession that continues to serve the needs of society. In order to understand changes that are needed, it is important to summarize the traditional approach to profession building in nursing and to elucidate a more contemporary model.

TRADITIONAL PROFESSION BUILDING IN NURSING

As a result of strategic activity and social, political, and economic conditions, nursing has evolved from a powerless class of domestic servants to a much more powerful segment of health care professionals today. What strategic directions have characterized this evolutionary process of profession building?

In the fairly stable health care environment of the post-World War II period through the 1980s, nursing was able to enhance its professional power through standardization of nursing curricula, licensure, and development of nursing science. During this time, several themes emerged that we characterize as the traditional framework for profession building in nursing.

Independent vs. Dependent Roles

To increase nursing autonomy, nursing has concentrated on identifying and distinguishing independent and dependent nursing actions. To enhance legitimacy, nursing has wanted to maximize independent actions and minimize dependent actions, or transfer the dependent actions to lesser-educated workers, such as licensed practical nurses or aides. Carving out activities unique to nursing has been the quest of nursing leaders and theorists. For example, nursing diagnosis is an attempt to standardize nursing language pertaining to actions within the domain of nursing (independent) and distinct from the medical model used by physicians (dependent).

Professional Self-Regulation

Concurrent with the drive to achieve independence and uniqueness, nursing has focused on the need for self-regulation. This has resulted in an educational accreditation structure controlled within the profession (the National League for Nursing [NLN]) and licensing boards in each of the states, independent of medicine. Recently, nursing created its own specialty certification structure, the American Board of Nursing Specialties, again on the premise that self-regulation is key to controlling its destiny. The emphasis in nursing on formal credentialing is illustrated by the alphabet soup of credentials that has represented the hundreds of specialty and honorary designations.

Rigid Professional Boundaries

Nursing professional socialization has emphasized structure and rigid boundaries between the domain of nursing and that of other health professionals. Grounded in the historical context wherein nurses had to maintain flawless social and personal respectability, a set of rules about professional boundaries proliferated. Nurse practice acts carefully delimit activities that fall within the purview of the credentialed nurse. Lesser-credentialed nursing personnel or other professionals are discouraged or prohibited from participating as team members in delivering such nursing care.

Focus on Nursing as "Caring"

The underpinning of many of the theories and models of nursing is that nursing's uniqueness stems from the caring component. This typically is contrasted to the curing focus of medicine. Ray,[5] for example, argues that caring in the human health experience is the unifying focus of nursing and nursing inquiry. In the ANA's *Nursing's Social Policy Statement*,[6] caring is included in the listing of four essential features of contemporary nursing practice.

Nursing as an Oppressed Profession

Nursing has been described by Roberts[1] as exhibiting oppressed group behavior. She describes this as subtle self-hatred and dislike for other nurses that has been evident in the divisiveness and lack of cohesiveness observed in nursing groups. The conflict over moving nursing away from hospital training programs to university education models probably is rooted in the belief that caregivers should stay oppressed by the maintenance of the dominant form (i.e., hospitals, paternalism). The fact that the ANA represents only 10 percent of nurses can be viewed as evidence of lack of pride in one's group.

Nursing as a Female Profession

The fact that nursing has predominantly been a female profession has been ignored as a strategic issue by most of nursing. The roots of nursing in Florence Nightingale, the caring and sensitivity of women, and the service orientation emphasized in nurse socialization all result in female-ness being seen as a special, distinguishing characteristic of nursing. Consistent with rigid professional boundaries, men were viewed as representatives of the male-dominated medical and administrative "oppressors." Although unintentional, Porter-O'Grady believes that reverse discrimination (discrimination toward men) has existed in nursing. He believes that particularly in leadership roles it is "very challenging for men to break into what could be irreverently called the 'old girls club.'"[7(p.58)]

Focus on Job Security

As nursing began the transition from domestic servitude to hospital worker, along with the rise in industrial workers and labor unions, nurses came to believe that they had a right to job security on the basis of longevity of employment with an organization. The role of the ANA as a collective bargaining organization was established then. Many of the recent arguments from organized nursing groups purport that declining quality and outcomes are results of poor staffing levels and skill mix patterns and hospitals' plans to maximize profits at the expense of quality. In fact, fear of job loss may well underlie these expressions of concern, as well.

Development of Nursing Science

Since the 1950s, a focus of nursing has been the definition and development of nursing science. A huge body of literature has developed around the label ***nursing theory***. Meleis[8] describes this literature as including identification of nursing's domain, the mechanics of theory development, development of concepts, and philosophical debates.

Focus on Acute Care

Nurses were educated for acute care settings. Nursing school curricula focused on technical procedures, nursing process (which is the same as the scientific method), and the disease-oriented medical model. Implicit in acute care is episodic and fragmented patient care.

Standardized Entry to Practice

Consistent with the quest for the profession's self-regulation, nursing has argued for a one-size-fits-all approach. This perennial controversy focused on having the right degree or lobbying for all nurses to have the same degree as sources of power. Although the one-size-fits-all argument has not triumphed, curricula in nursing are highly standardized and subject to extensive, formalized accreditation criteria of the NLN.

Centralized Professional Organization

Nursing has pursued the traditional model of professionalization in which one dominant professional association represents the profession, in this case the ANA. Pressures to maximize the membership in the central professional association have been intense. The ANA has been expected to provide a unified voice for all of nursing.

The nursing profession historically has pursued an inward-directed set of activities to build the strength of nursing, using professionalization tactics that have been successful for medicine and some of the other health professions. The profession has tried to create a "closed" system in order to build strength to face the external environment.

CONTEMPORARY PROFESSION BUILDING IN NURSING

The traditional framework has served nursing reasonably well. However, the magnitude of change in health care is demanding that nurses look to a new framework for achieving professional power. What follows is a description of themes of the new framework for profession building in nursing.

Interdependence

It is no longer germane to focus only on independent and dependent nursing actions. Nursing does not need to prove that it is important. It is beyond that. Nurses need to work collaboratively with physicians and other health professionals. Armed with broad-based primary care clinical knowledge, nursing is positioned to be the ideal leader in a managed care environment. Nurses all across the country are leading organizational changes in hospitals and their integrated delivery networks by implementing creative and innovative approaches to improving quality and lowering costs.

The interdependence and collaborative efforts with others will result in increased emphasis on teamwork. Organizations will devote more resources to enhancing teamwork. There will not be as much use for the strict distinction between "insiders" and "outsiders." The insiders' aim should be to learn how they are perceived by others when they are compared with many other output producers.[9] Nurses should work with administrators to inform them of the various options so far as internal practices are concerned and to help design evaluative criteria that will enable administrators to make assessments that are fair and just to all producers while getting the best available outputs.

Accountability to Stakeholders

No longer is the focus on profession self-regulation. In a buyer's market, nursing must be accountable to its key stakeholders. This means that purchasers of nursing services, as well as other interdependent professions, should be partners in ensuring the quality of nursing care. Self-regulation will be transformed into shared regulation with key stakeholders.

Flexible Boundaries

The powerful profession of the future will respond to the needs of its stakeholders by continuously redesigning and reengineering the profession. This will result in greater splintering of the profession as new types of workers emerge to meet new market niches or serve new societal needs. For example, nursing education curricula will be redesigned to respond to the demands of managed care and systems integration, and specialists to serve those markets will emerge. To facilitate this process, concerns about boundary-setting that have characterized the history of nursing will need to be resisted.

Focus on Nursing as Possessing Skills and Knowledge

Nursing will not be considered unique by virtue of its being a caring profession. Purchasers of health care cannot put a price on caring. They can, however, put a price on skills and knowledge that contribute to patient outcomes. Nurses need to take their basket of goods to the market with a price tag. "Value-added" is an important commodity and what nurses contribute to improved quality and decreased costs must be measured and included in the price tag. It may mean that nursing's stakeholders will demand fewer RNs at the bedside and more RNs in advanced practice roles functioning as "knowledge workers" who delegate more of the nonprofessional routine duties to unlicensed caregivers. The time is right for nursing research to assess the impact nurses have on quality and outcomes.

Nursing as Partners in Prevention and Treatment

Yesterday's focus on nurses as oppressed women who are handmaidens to physicians is over. Nursing leaders are in positions of executive decision making. Nurses will no longer say "This can't be done" but they will ask "How can we deliver the best care at the lowest cost?" Along with physicians and allied health professionals, nurses will be functioning in advance practice roles for primary care delivery.[10] Concerns about oppressed group status will pale in importance as criteria for effectiveness become more universal and public.

Recruitment of More Men

To increase creativity and innovation for problem solving, the profession will have to seek more diversity in its members. Of acute significance is the small proportion of nurses who are men. Any strategic advantages of gender homogeneity become irrelevant in a market-driven health care system where outcomes of care and innovation are determinants of success.

Job Security Based on Contribution to Organization

Job security is no longer a right but a privilege that comes with professional accountability. Continuing education takes on an entirely new meaning. To keep pace with rapid change, nurses will have to spend more time in life-long self-learning. Organizations will spend fewer resources on defining work tasks for nurses and more time in evaluating nursing outcomes. Organizations will be less inclined to reward longevity than contributions to the organization's bottom line.

Development of Multidisciplinary Theories

As Meleis[8] believes, nursing theory development in the 21st century will be concerned less with the domain of nursing. Growing collaboration will result in "health care theories" based on the needs of populations that will be used by all members of the health care team. This requires that efforts to develop a unique nursing science be secondary to the search for theory that can guide practitioners in producing healthy patients.

Increased Corporatization

Decisions affecting the bedside nurse no longer are made locally. The consolidation of health care providers into integrated delivery networks changes the locus of power. Although local organization politics and personal power will always pervade, nursing will have more legitimate power in executive decision making at top levels of organizations. More nurses will seek graduate education in business and health administration to keep pace with job demands.

Diverse Settings of Nursing Care

Acute care is no longer the focus of nursing practice. Hospitals are merely intensive care units. Care will be delivered in the communities and nurses will need to have knowledge of the continuum of care, including preventive, home, day, hospice, and respite care. From this vantage point, nurses are ideally suited for leadership roles in case management and advanced practice roles in population-based primary care.

Multiple Entry Pathways

To satisfy the needs of the stakeholders and the new wave of social transformation[11] nursing education will be reengineered and reformed. It will be more and more difficult to standardize curricula and entry requirements, resulting in a proliferation of pathways to highly differentiated arenas of nursing practice. In making this transition, the profession can benefit by encouraging diversity in profiles of those entering the profession.

Decentralized Professional Organization

Profession building in nursing increasingly will occur in the differentiated segments of nursing. While new segments will arise, current examples include nurse midwives, nurse anesthetists, nurse executives, and the different nurse practitioner specialties. These segments will be more in touch with stakeholder needs and demands, and it will be less feasible for one single organization, such as the ANA, to attempt to assume a coordinating role.

CONCLUSION

There are signs that nursing is beginning the transition from traditional to contemporary forms of profession building. The ANA's 1995 Nursing's Social Policy Statement, for example, states that "Nursing is not separated from other professions by rigid boundaries. Nursing's scope of practice has a flexible boundary that is responsive to the changing needs of society."[6(p.12)] The recognition of the need for flexibility is an important step in strategic adaptation.

Ruminations about power and politics have occupied the minds and resources of nursing to an unusual degree. Profession building at both the local and national levels has involved a high degree of political activity within hospitals and government policy making settings. While these traditional profession building activities will continue to influence the lives of all nurses, important decisions about roles and income and other rewards are more and more likely to be based on measurable contributions. Contemporary nursing must seize this opportunity to create new pathways for strategic adaptation.

REFERENCES

1. Roberts, S.J. "Oppressed Group Behavior: Implications for Nursing." *Advances in Nursing Science* 5, no. 4 (1983): 21–30.
2. Heide, W.S. *Feminism for the health of it.* Buffalo, N.Y.: Margaretdaughters, 1985.
3. Begun, J.W., and Lippincott, R.C. *Strategic Adaptation in the Health Professions: Meeting the Challenges of Change.* San Francisco, Calif.: Jossey-Bass, 1993.
4. Begun, J.W., and White, K.R. "Altering Nursing's Dominant Logic: Guidelines from Complex Adaptive Systems Theory." *Complexity and Chaos in Nursing* 2, no. 1 (1995): 5–15.
5. Ray, M.A. "Complex Caring Dynamics: A Unifying Model of Nursing Inquiry." *Theoretic and Applied Chaos in Nursing* 1, no. 1 (1994): 23–32.
6. American Nurses Association. *Nursing's Social Policy Statement.* Washington, D.C.: American Nurses Publishing, 1995.
7. Porter-O'Grady, T. "Reverse Discrimination in Nursing Leadership: Hitting the Concrete Ceiling." *Nursing Administration Quarterly* 19, no. 2 (1995): 56–62.
8. Meleis, A.I. "Directions for Nursing Theory Development in the 21st Century." *Nursing Science Quarterly* 5, no. 3 (1993): 112–17.
9. Dunbar, R.L.M., and Ahlstrom, D. "Seeking the Institutional Balance of Power: Avoiding the Power of a Balanced View." *Academy of Management Review* 20, no. 1 (1995): 171–92.
10. Appleby, C. "Boxed In?" *Hospitals and Health Networks* 69, no. 18 (1995): 28–34.
11. Drucker, P.F. "The Age of Social Transformation." *The Atlantic Monthly* 274 (1994): 53–80.

Nursing and Threats to Patient and Nurse Safety and Quality of Patient Care

Patricia A. Rowell and D. Kathy Milholland

The current restructuring of the health care system has resulted in a greater emphasis on cost-cutting measures, leading to a reduction in the numbers and mix of registered nurses utilized to provide patient care services. As state nurses associations reported growing problems in patient care resulting from reductions in registered nurse (RN) staffing at the same time that increasing profits were recorded in the health care industry[1], the American Nurses Association (ANA) Board of Directors initiated work in a number of areas to highlight: 1) the problems of decreased RN staffing, and 2) the link between RN staffing and patient care safety and quality. These efforts have included far-reaching public relations efforts such as the "Every Patient Deserves a Nurse" campaign, public testimony, work with public officials and policy makers, and political efforts.

A critical and pioneering component of this work has been initiating data-based efforts to document linkages between RN staffing and patient outcomes. Although it is clear that care can be delivered in a manner that is both cost-effective and of high quality, the changes occurring in our health care system currently are being made without adequate understanding of their impact on patient care. While a body of literature, much of it produced during the nursing shortage of the 1980s, demonstrated some important linkages between RN staffing and length of stay, lowered mortality rates and other outcomes, there is a great need for ongoing, comprehensive, broad-based research efforts to establish and quantify linkages between RN staffing, quality of nursing care, and patient outcomes. The Board of Directors recognized this need and in March 1994, commissioned the development of a nursing report card for acute care settings, resulting in ANA's *Nursing's Safety and Quality Initiative.* This major multi-phase project has been undertaken to address the multiple challenges arising in the current health care environment and to implement multiple projects that will address those challenges.

Since the inception of the *Initiative*, much work has been done to educate the public and nurses, and develop/expand our understanding of nursing's impact on patient care. Starting with the "Every Patient Deserves a Nurse" campaign, significant investments have provided educational products and other tools for the consumer and for nurses about nursing care. Three publications on nursing's quality indicators provided impetus for continuing the science-based approach to the issue of patient safety and quality: *Nursing Care Report Card For Acute Care*[2], *Nursing Quality Indicators: Definitions and Implications*[3], *and Nursing Quality Indicators: Guide for Implementation.*[4]

J Nurse Care Qual, 1998, 12(4): 9–13
© 1998 Aspen Publishers, Inc.

The work to date was summarized in an ANA Fact Sheet: *Nursing's Quality Indicators for Acute Care Settings and ANA's Safety and Quality Initiative.*[5]

QUALITY INDICATOR VALIDATION PROJECTS

Funding from the American Nurses Foundation provided generous support to establish an approach to validate the quality indicators. The Nursing Quality Report Card Request for Proposals (RFP) was established for the state nurses associations (SNAs) to plan for projects to implement pilot studies to explore the utility and efficacy of the definitions of the quality indicators in environments of nursing practice. That work built a foundation for partnerships with service institutions to obtain data across settings. The SNAs of Arizona, California, North Dakota and Texas were funded $10,000.00 each for one year planning projects beginning in June 1996. Similar awards were made in November 1996 to SNAs in Minnesota and Virginia.

As a continuation of the work begun in 1996 with the SNA quality indicator planning grants, the six original SNA planning grant projects will receive $20,000 each in 1997 to begin the work needed to implement the use and collection of nursing's quality indicators in acute care settings.

As an extension of the initial quality indicator work, an advisory committee, chaired by Linda Sawyer, PhD, RN, CS, has been appointed and is in the process of identifying indicators which reflect the input of nursing practice in settings other than acute care. That work will continue into 1998.

EDUCATING STAFF NURSES ABOUT QUALITY INDICATORS

There clearly is a need to educate all nurses about national and local efforts involving quality initiatives, to provide them with the resources necessary to collect data in the workplace, and to keep them involved in research efforts. The *Nursing's Quality Report Card OUTCOMES* Project was developed with consultants and an ANA Congress of Nursing Practice Advisory Committee as an educational program designed to inform nurses about health care quality outcomes measurement and nursing's quality indicators. An extensive set of continuing education materials was prepared to assist nurse participants and trainers of nurse participants in the *OUTCOMES* Project workshops. Crafted around nursing's quality indicators, the program is based on the premise that nurses, in every role and setting, must acquire knowledge related to the measurement, improvement, and bench marking of nursing-sensitive clinical cost, quality, and outcomes. Train-the-trainer workshops have been offered by ANA staff in more than fifteen SNAs to date, as well as at the Centennial Convention in June 1996. SNA requests for programs continue on an ongoing basis. In addition, ANA will present a total of four regional continuing education sessions by the end of 1997. A continuing education presentation was given at the International Council of Nursing's June 1997 Quadrennial. Additionally, the SNA resource book, *Restructuring Survival Kit*[6], has a new chapter designed to assist nurses, whether in collective bargaining units or not, in the use of formal data collection projects to leverage control over inappropriate staffing and skill mix.

SKILL MIX AND OUTCOME ANALYSIS

ANA contracted with Network, Inc. (a consulting firm) in 1995 to examine the feasibility of conducting a secondary data analysis of existing large data sets to determine relationships between nursing skill mix and nursing's quality indicators in hospital settings. Health-related state data sets for 1992 and 1994 from Massachusetts, New York, and California were selected for this study. The six specific adverse patient outcomes studied were:

1. pressure ulcers
2. nosocomial infections
3. post-operative infections
4. urinary tract infections
5. pneumonia
6. patient falls

The study results fully support that registered nurse provided care has a positive impact on patient's well being during hospitalization in an acute care facility. The study results were released on Nurses Day 1997 and are published in *Implementing Nursing's Report Card: A Study of RN Staffing, Length of Stay and Patient Outcomes*.[7]

POLITICAL ACTIVITIES IN THE PROTECTION OF HEALTH CARE QUALITY

Another critical piece of ANA's public policy agenda on patient care and quality and safety has been, and will continue to be, its work to safeguard appropriate funding levels for public insurance programs, chiefly Medicare and Medicaid. In the 104th Congress, both of these programs faced massive cutbacks under budgetary proposals of the Congressional majority. ANA has been concerned about budget driven changes in health care services since health care institutions and systems, when faced with an imperative to cut costs, have to date targeted their labor costs and, in particular, nursing staffing. ANA has reiterated this concern in light of the Clinton Administration's fiscal year 98 proposal for cuts in Medicare, which would impact all hospital patients since Medicare provides a large proportion of hospital revenue. ANA lobbied intensively in the 105th Congress for a number of issues around protecting the public's health and achieved great success in a number of areas, especially in the Budget Reconciliation Act.

ANA is again using the Patient Safety Act as a legislative vehicle to carry nursing's quality indicators into the Congressional arena for debate. The bill was originally introduced in May 1996 by Representative Maurice Hinchey (D-NY) during the 104th Congress. In the 105th Congress, the bill was reintroduced and has gathered a number of cosponsors in both political parties and both houses of Congress. With this legislation as a specific rallying point for politically concerned nurses, considerable attention was drawn to the issue of patient safety and quality. N-STAT (Nursing Strategic Action Team, ANA's grassroots political action network) has been employed to generate additional cosponsors for the new bill, and to continue to bring these issues into the Congressional debate.

Legislative activity in the states is extensive. Numerous pieces of legislation which include some or all of the concepts of the Patient Safety Act have been introduced in legislatures around the country. In addition, some or all of the concepts within the Patient Safety Act have been adopted through regulation both at the Federal and state levels.

NATIONAL DATABASE OF NURSING QUALITY INDICATORS

The National Database of Nursing Quality Indicators (NDNQI) is the first component of the ANA's National Nursing Data Center. The NDNQI is the repository for the data resulting from the national quality indicator implementation projects. This database is being constructed and will be maintained by a contract vendor; however, all of the data are the property of ANA and its use is determined by the Association.

Initially, the database contains the first set of quality indicators selected for implementation and testing, as well as additional data elements which describe characteristics of a participating health care facility. Data from each participating institution will be collected monthly by the institution and reported to the NDNQI on a quarterly basis. Each participating health care facility will receive, in turn, analytical reports of their performance on the selected indicators, including comparisons from month to month, quarter to quarter, and year to year. The identity of each institution is protected and the initial performance comparisons will be only within an institution. As the database grows, comparisons among facilities will be possible with strict adherence to protecting the identities of the compared institutions.

Policies regarding research access to the NDNQI will be developed and implemented by ANA. As noted above, the NDNQI is the first component of a larger Data Center. As other databases are developed, integration of data from these internal sources as well as from external sources will be an essential and critical component of the database design and the supporting software. This integration of nursing data, as well as other related data, will enable the empirical exploration of nursing practice and policy issues to a degree not previously attainable.

ONGOING ACTIVITIES

Since research and demonstrations of effectiveness in health care occurs in other areas of activity, ANA continues to work with the National Nursing Research Round table (NNRR) and the community of nurse researchers toward a more unified emphasis on health systems and health outcomes research. Continued strong collegial relationships have been maintained with the National Institute of Nursing Research (NINR) and the major federal funder of health systems and health outcomes research, the Agency for Health Care Policy and Research (AHCPR).

ANA has also worked to influence standard-setting organizations and activities in other areas. ANA supports active liaison with the Joint Commission on Accreditation of Healthcare Organizations (Joint Commission), especially within each of the Joint Commission Professional, Technical Advisory Committees (PTACs), the Performance Measures project, and the Indicator Development project. Nursing's Quality Indicators have been shared with the Joint Commission, formally and informally. Active liaison is also maintained with the National Committee for Quality Assurance (NCQA), another organization involved in establishing standards for managed care organizations and other entities. Nursing's Quality Indicators have been shared with NCQA formally and informally. Additionally, the ANA Institute of Constituent Member Collective Bargaining Programs Task Force on Collective Bargaining Strategies for Quality Indicators continues to advocate for collection of data nursing's quality indicators in employment settings.

ANA AND SAFETY AND QUALITY—THE FUTURE

For many years, ANA has had a significant organizational commitment to advocating for safety and quality of patient care and nurse safety in the workplace. This commitment has taken on additional dimensions as the health care environment has focused on cost savings with a concomitant decline in quality of patient care and in safety for both patients and registered nurses. Of critical importance in Nursing's Safety & Quality Initiative is the focus on providing opportunities for registered nurses to gain the knowledge needed to provide leadership in the evaluation of the quality of care. Although registered nurses have advocated for patients for many years, today's environment demands that advocacy be based on facts and figures which flow from the care setting. Those facts and figures can then be used as powerful tools in pushing the industry to refocus on its reason for being—the health care of human beings.

REFERENCES

1. Lutz, S. "Providers, Suppliers Report Double-Digit Earnings Growth." *Modern Healthcare* 25 (1995): 50, 52.
2. American Nurses Association, *Nursing Care Report Card for Acute Care*. Washington, DC: American Nurses Publishing, 1995.
3. American Nurses Association, *Nursing Quality Indicators: Definitions and Implications*. Washington, DC: American Nurses Publishing, 1996.
4. American Nurses Association, *Nursing Quality Indicators: Guide for Implementation*. Washington, DC: American Nurses Publishing, 1996.
5. American Nurses Association, *Nursing's Quality Indicators for Acute Care Settings and ANA's Safety and Quality Initiative,* Washington, DC: American Nurses Publishing, 1996.
6. American Nurses Association, *Restructuring Survival Kit*. Washington, DC: American Nurses Publishing, 1996.
7. American Nurses Association, *Implementing Nursing's Report Card: A Study of RN Staffing, Length of Stay and Patient Outcomes*. Washington, DC: American Nurses Publishing, 1997.

2

Nursing and Managed Care: A Reality Check

Is It Design or Decline? Conflicts in Re-engineering

Tim Porter-O'Grady

By now, almost everyone who ever provided a health care service in America has been the subject of re-engineering. There should not be a corner of the health care system that has not had experience with redesigning and restructuring its part of the health care system at some level.

Many of the re-engineering efforts have yielded some necessary economies and efficiencies that have been long overdue.[1] Clearly, a system that uses as much of the nation's resources as does health care needed a firm dose of accountability and efficiency.

Every aspect of the health care system reflected the fact that there were few constraints on choices—promulgating the most lavish use of resources for health care of any nation in the world. Although such resources created a level of technology that was the envy of the world, it did precious little to create a higher level of social well-being.[2]

WHOLE SYSTEMS PRINCIPLES

Now, health care is on a road to higher levels of accountability and effectiveness. Many of the changes brought about to respond to the need to tighten belts have produced the conditions that require a much more substantive response to the need for real health in the United States.

Several realities have emerged to exemplify a different set of rules from those most often in evidence in the United States. Some of the emerging realities now confronting the provision of health care and the structuring of service are as follows:

- It is not possible to alter one part of the system without having a direct and dramatic impact on every other component of the system.
- Whatever is done to the point-of-service is done to the whole system because the system essentially lives at its point-of-service.
- Decisions cannot simply and forever be made on the basis of cost alone without negatively impacting the system's ability to obtain sustainable value.
- Moving people around the organizational map does not necessarily result in an improvement of service or create a more efficient organization.
- Shifting the lines and boxes on the organizational chart does nothing to create meaningful or sustainable outcomes.
- Failing to include key providers in changes that affect what they do assures that either the changes won't work or the people won't.
- Not moving decisions (that means power) to where the roles are moving

Aspen's Advisor for Nurse Executives, 1997, 12(7): 1–4
© 1997 Aspen Publishers, Inc.

assures that neither the roles nor the work will produce anything meaningful.

- Failure to involve nurses and doctors in the changes that affect what they do assures that they will neither like what is happening (even if it is good), nor will they commit their energies to its success.
- Designing anything from the "top" down in an organization never works, is never permanent, and is always inadequate to the task of creating viable and lasting change.

Time and experience have shown that these "rules" consistently apply to any changes that occur at any level in any organizational shift or redesign.[3] What is terribly surprising is the number of systems that either are unaware of them or act in total disregard of their veracity.

In many organizations, much of redesign is imposed rather than composed. The stakeholders find themselves making changes over which they had no control, indeed with which they played no role. Leadership is then somehow astonished when it does not go well or when many people oppose what appears to be an obviously wise change. Wise or not, if it isn't owned by those who implement the change, it looks surprisingly like someone else's wisdom.

STAFF VIEW OF RE-ENGINEERING

What is most disconcerting to nurse leaders is the dissonance many of them currently sense with regard to nurses' lack of enthusiasm for re-engineering issues. Let us enumerate the perspective of re-engineering from the viewpoint of most staff nurses:

1. The organization is going to change my role without asking me anything about what I think it should become.
2. The leadership is requesting that I give over what I know and do to others who can do it cheaper and better than I can now.
3. We are going to cross-train others to do pieces of what I do in order to "free me up" to do more significant things.
4. We are now to do more significant, knowledge-based, judgment-driven activities, but with one or more fewer fully skilled professional people than we had before.
5. The per unit of cost is reduced by hiring more "on-the-job" trained functionaries with a limited skill base at the time that length of stay, acuity, and performance expectation is intensifying the need for high level skills.
6. After all this redesign is done, I am the one left doing more with less.

While these paraphrased perceptions may or may not be entirely accurate, they have at some time or other been in the minds and hearts of the staff nurse. It is true that health care demand is changing and that the role of the nurse must shift toward newer roles and expectations. That cannot occur in any meaningful way without the full investment and ownership of the very nurses who are affected by these shifts and changes.

In a number of organizations that decimated the ranks of nurses in their lust for re-engineering, nurses are being recruited back to the organization to fill demands that simply went unmet by lesser trained task-based service assistants.[4]

A part of getting buy-in for change in the nurse's role is the need to help the nurse confront the vagaries of change and the shift in role and performance expectation that will invariably be a component of the new role. That means including time to mourn and grieve the loss of old functions, positions, skill expectations, and securities.

To do this requires full engagement and investment on the part of the leadership and the staff in the process of creating meaningful and sustainable change. Laying the changes on the staff and the organization simply because they are necessary is not the way to get the staff to embrace the behaviors that are essential to successful transformation.

FEW NURSES LEADING RE-ENGINEERING

What seems so common and readily apparent in this time of great change is how few nurses are involved in the myriad of patient care design changes and service shifts. It seems incongruous that the largest single provider of health services could be so absent from the planning and design tables that were constructed ostensibly to design the future models of health service delivery.

One wonders that if nurses are not leading the design of patient care, who with any competence to do so is leading it? Perhaps that explains why so few models are working, and why there is so much reaction to the methods chosen to implement them.

There is always a high cost to the system that fails to remember the underlying principles of any human-driven enterprise—make no change without involving those upon whom the change will impact.[5] Those who attempt change in this circumstance should not be surprised if it is contested and ultimately not sustained.

Sound and good re-engineering is no more difficult to implement than is bad and uninformed change. It takes the same time and commitment up front, but it happens a whole lot better and lasts a lot longer when it is done the right way. The signposts of some organizations' successes are beginning to show which factors are most often at work in organizations that undertake re-engineering well. Some key elements are:

- Begin at the point-of-service with the staff leadership working there and create as much ownership with them up front.
- Reduce the number of managers to the lowest possible number of competent managers possible—just enough to maintain the integrity and cohesiveness of the system and not a manager more than necessary.
- Have the implementers design the approach by simply sharing the cost, service parameters, and requirements the system must confront with them and challenge them to build a sustainable solution.
- The real challenge of the time is building an effective information infrastructure for the point-of-service. Information management at the point-of-service is the most critical component of successful, continuum-based, horizontally linked health systems.
- Evaluate the choices made for change in a way that allows for maximum flexibility in making adjustments or shifts in the approach or model of service.
- Nothing is cast in stone, and it is wise to change directions or processes when the early evidence suggests that the strategy is not working well. Don't commit the organization to permanent decline simply because the culture doesn't fit some predetermined notion of success or model of design.
- The knowledge worker is at the point-of-service and is a major stakeholder in the outcomes of any change. All change efforts should ultimately benefit his or her

relationship to the patient and facilitate interaction.[6]

These principles and process elements are very simple and relatively straightforward. The tragedy is not so much in the fact that they are so obvious, but in the fact that their being obvious does not seem to guarantee their being consistently applied. How many tragedies in redesign, integration, systems building, and future making could have been avoided if these principles had simply been applied as a part of the implementation process?

One final thought. How many efforts at team building, integration, re-engineering, and renewal have been capsized and sacrificed on the altar of administrative ego? It is overwhelming to see the number of change processes that fail simply because ego got in the way of effectiveness.

Individual and unilateral notions of change and success are simply not enough of a foundation for meaningful change. Diversity of view, breadth of dialogue, commitment of stakeholders, and gathering of investors in the processes of change are essential constituents of sustainable change.

No real or lasting change was ever obtained through the efforts of any one individual. Rather, success is sustained through the confluence of the action of all on whom the results depend. Each individual is an essential star in the array of stars that are critical to creating light in the universe; no one star generates all the light. Those who try do nothing but diminish the light rather than extend it.

Much effort and relationship is necessary to create meaningful and viable renewal in health care. It will take the efforts of all the various constituencies. The role of leadership is to make sure they are all at the table and that the dialogue there results in the creation of a viable and meaningful future for patient care services.

Let us hope that when it comes time to provide good service in the emerging context for patient care, we have made sure someone competent is there to do the work.

REFERENCES

1. Doerge, J., & Hagenow, N. 1995. "Management restructuring: Toward a leaner organization," *Nursing Management, 26*(12), 32–36.
2. American Nurses Association (and 42 Endorsers). 1991. *Nursing's agenda for health care reform.* Washington, DC: American Nurses Association.
3. Argyris, C. 1993. *Knowledge for action.* San Francisco, CA: Jossey-Bass.
4. Shindul-Rothschild, J., Berry, D., & Long-Middleton, E. 1996. "Where have all the nurses gone?" *American Journal of Nursing, 96*(11), 25–39.
5. Mintzberg, H. 1990. "The manager's job: Folklore and fact," *Harvard Business Review, 48*(2), 163–176.
6. Porter-O'Grady, T., & Krueger-Wilson, C. 1995. *The leadership revolution in healthcare: Altering systems, changing behavior.* Gaithersburg, MD: Aspen Publishers.

The Entrepreneurial Personality: Building a Sustainable Future for Self and the Profession

Gregory Crow

Traditional career expectations for nurses are unraveling. There was a time when nurses could count on *employment* when, where, and often on what terms they wished to be employed. We worked per diem, short hour, part time, full time, seasonally, and could manage to somehow fit nursing into our lives. We are beginning to realize that our "employee" status brought us a false sense of security.

Today we find that our confidence in an organization's ability to provide a livelihood is eroding. This eroding confidence, while familiar to many sectors of the American work force, has caught many nurses off guard and unprepared, producing anger, and leading to the futile search for predictability in a world that does not have it to offer.

Entrepreneurs live very different lives. They look to the future and see opportunity where others see barriers. They listen to the future and devise a plan to arrive there, fully equipped to flourish.

HISTORICAL CONTEXT

Entrepreneurs have been showing the way since the dawn of human history. They are proactive with the never-ending cycle of change, recognizing that change relocates opportunity. The tools of the entrepreneur have not changed throughout time. Entrepreneurs demonstrate insight, simplistic use of language, continuous expansion of their world view, informed risk taking, multiple foci, maximizing energy more than power, thriving on discovery, creativity, absorbing and integrating stimuli via a permeable mental model, accepting that there is no right way, continuous learning, and adaptability.

Over two million years ago when our ancestors made the first tools, those who could take advantage of change and use it for their benefit profited, while those who could not, became dependent on the emerging change masters.[1,2] As humans began to exert more and more control over their environment, any new ability or knowledge could spell the difference between success and failure.[2,3]

The masterful use of language is our greatest technological advance.[1,3,4] Those who mastered language, using it to sequence thought and action in simplistic and accessible ways, improving the quality of life, and influencing others toward cooperative efforts of survival, were celebrated.[1,4] The gap widened between the entrepreneurs who adapted and mastered language, and those who did not.[1]

Burke and Ornstein,[1] and Van Doren[5] note that the desire for knowledge and power over its content and distribution was realized by the invention of the printing press. This newfound power was used by those situated to take advantage of the new technology, namely the church, aristocracy, and entrepreneurial merchants.[5]

Nurs Admin Q, 1998, 22(2): 30–35
© 1998 Aspen Publishers, Inc.

Between 1455 and 1500, a span of just 45 years, Europe went from no printed texts to 20 million which were printed on presses in 245 cities. By the early 17th century, 400,000 copies of the English almanac were sold annually.[1,5] The invention of the printing press freed up the future of most of the scribes in Europe,[5] causing one of the first major waves of unemployment. This change provided options for those entrepreneurial scribes who could see that this massive change created opportunity. Entrepreneurs of the time became printers, typesetters, book sellers, editors, or better yet—best selling authors.

In 1780 there were 1.7 million person-powered cloth spinning machines in England. By 1812, a mere 32 years later, there were 5 million. Employment opportunities came with this growth; however, change was just around the corner. In 1791 the steam-powered spinner was introduced which allowed one person to operate multiple spinning machines. These new machines increased productivity and, consequently, reduced the cost of producing cloth, making it more accessible to a wider market, thereby increasing demand. By 1850 there were 250,000 steam-powered spinning machines in England alone.[1,5] The displaced spinners who acquired and used entrepreneurial skills in the application of steam power to other industries were able to take advantage of this technological change, and created and secured their future.

Throughout human history we have been faced with innovation and change that simultaneously closed and opened doors. Sometimes the new doors were obvious and sometimes they were more cryptic, requiring one to search out opportunity. Those with permeable mental models were able to see the wave, prepare for it, and enjoy success. Entrepreneurs simultaneously see the forest and the trees, while others see either. Seeing either, instead of both, narrows options and leads to stress.

OPPORTUNITY AND VIABILITY

Often the result of rapid and unrelenting change is a sense of powerlessness. Powerlessness prevents us from adapting adequately and making sound decisions about opportunity.[1,6–13] As opportunity diminishes, stress increases.

Stress, unchecked and ever-increasing, can cause us to deviate further and further from opportunity. Rather than beginning a journey that has unlimited possibilities, we may find ourselves on a journey in a cul-de-sac, continuously covering old and familiar territory.

Nurse entrepreneurs use stress to heighten their awareness and continuously monitor and adapt their roles with organizations[6,11,13] and the health care industry at large. They take advantage of shifting relationships and flourish as a result of it. This requires a shift in how we view ourselves, the profession of nursing, our education, patterns of employment, and the changing health care environment.

As individuals, and as a profession, we must realize that our viability with organizations, health care, and the public depends on whether or not we contribute essential core competencies that allow these entities to realize some gain that is important to them.[6–10] Entrepreneurs continuously demonstrate, through action, that they are essential to the organization's mission, and consequently find they have a more stable career trajectory than those whose skills are either no longer needed or can be subsumed by another group. Entrepreneurs focus their attention on industry trends and consider how these trends relate to changing roles, educational preparation, lifelong learning, personal development, and fulfilling a need that people or organizations are willing to purchase.[8–11,13]

Trends shed light onto the changing paradigm. Trends orient us to the coming wave and how to prepare for it, outline the boundaries, and indicate how to be successful in the new age.[14,15] Barker[16] informs us that paradigms provide useful information about how to take advantage of change. Individuals and systems can only respond to stimuli that fall within their world view; all other stimuli may as well be nonexistent.[17] Therefore, entrepreneurs continually expand their world view to be able to detect and integrate important changes. Entrepreneurs are able to absorb the new world view because they keep their mental models in a perpetual permeable state.

For many nurses, one source of anger and frustration with the changing system is our ignorance regarding where the world in general, and health care in particular, are going. By being unaware of emerging trends, we are surprised and angry when the bus has already left for the journey, or simply does not stop where we are waiting. Entrepreneurs do not wait for the new paradigm to crash into them; they seek it out, become familiar with the new demands, acquire the skills demanded by the new paradigm, and then let it carry them into the future.

THE NEW DEMAND

The health care environment is demanding a shift from industrial to knowledge-based nursing. Knowledge professionals own the means of production, their intelligence.[3,6,8,9] To keep abreast of the changing role of the knowledge professional, Drucker[8–10] informs us that we will have to periodically return to some form of education and training to acquire new knowledge and skills.

We are increasingly becoming the professional who interacts with data gathered from a variety of sources to turn them into information in an effort to coordinate and manage patient care through direct and indirect action. Drucker[9] tells us that data, regardless of how much we have or how often we receive them, are not information. Data must be interpreted into useful information, and this process, done thoroughly, takes considerable analytical skill.

Naisbitt[18] noted that we drown in data yet are starved for information. Entrepreneurs are able to sift through data and extract usable information. They know that information has become the energy that individuals, organizations, and systems take in from the environment to fuel their systems. Systems and organizations, like individuals, must be able to "feed" upon available data resources in order to survive and flourish. Identifying which data we will use to inform our future has become a life sustaining skill of the entrepreneur.

To step up to this new and exciting role we have to shift our thinking. Rather than conformity, which diminishes creativity, entrepreneurs cultivate a tolerance for variation and the ambiguity that naturally arises from variance. Variant thinking forces us to use our imagination in creating new systems. Entrepreneurs develop an appreciation of, and the ability to work with, non-linear models. Next-in-line (linear) thinking is not robust enough to keep pace with fast paced innovation. The move away from "either/or" models of thinking to a synthesis model allows the entrepreneur to consider multiple options. Multiple option thinking goes beyond the straight jacket of "A or B" to "nonA/nonB" models.[19]

Finally, entrepreneurs understand co-evolution. In co-evolutionary models, all participants gain from the interaction, and are able to jointly travel to new levels of performance and cooperation in a complex and ever-changing world.[19,20] Co-evolution transcends and includes.[15] It incorporates the past and the present and goes beyond them. It is always a struggle to establish new limits, and just as much a struggle to break them. Each step in the co-evolutionary process will eventually bring us to new limitations which act as triggers. These triggers act as stimuli for the entrepreneur to transcend to new levels of functioning.[14,15,20]

SUMMARY

Throughout human history, those equipped with a more acute mental model enjoyed greater social success. Over and over again we have learned that in constantly changing environments, we only survive if we can take energy from the environment.[1] Darwin[21] noted that those who cannot adapt, go the way of anything in nature that stands still or doesn't adapt: they die.

Paradigm shifts cause everything to change.[16,17] We can rely on present skills only to the extent that they are platforms for gaining skills demanded by the new paradigm. If we do not make this transition, we begin a downward spiral that removes us farther from the general direction of the new paradigm. As the spiral takes us farther from the goal, it is more difficult to get back (Figure 1).

Many feel that the pace of change has steadily accelerated and is about to out-strip

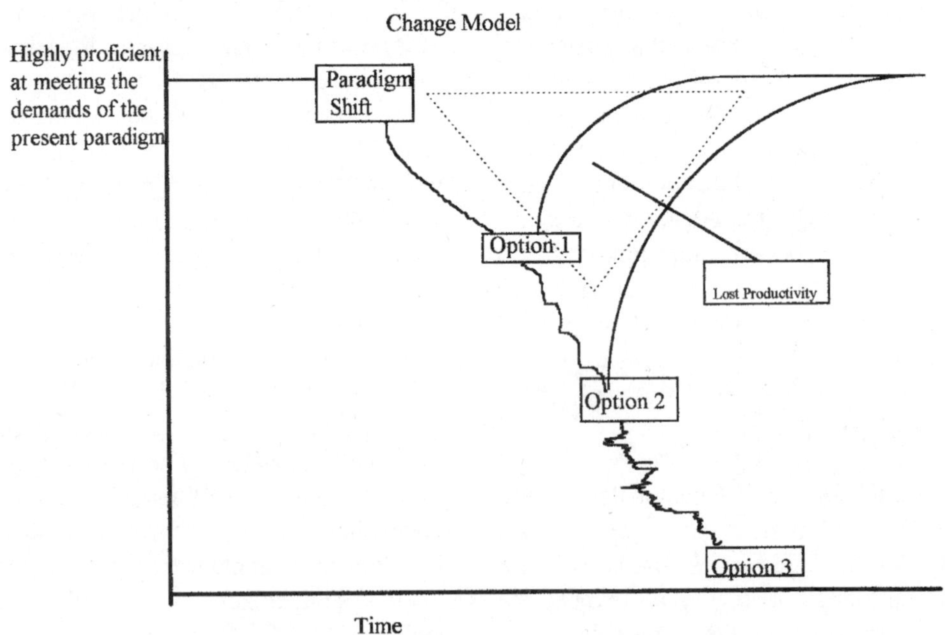

Figure 1. Highly proficient at meeting the demands of the present paradigm. *Option 1:* Recognizes paradigm shift, takes necessary action, maximal change effort. Stress is low to moderate. Recognizes that multiple options are available because opportunity is not hidden by stress. *Option 2:* Recognizes paradigm shift and ignores it for as long as possible with marginal or pseudochange effort. Stress is chronically moderate with increasing episodes of high stress. It is increasingly more difficult to get excited about the future. Develops plan to return to optimal level of functioning but takes more energy, time, and stress to do so. There are diminished options because stress has further narrowed opportunity. *Option 3:* Either recognizes and continues "as is" or misses the shift altogether, entropy sets in, and there is chronic high stress. It takes maximal effort for minimal returns; options are so narrowed that any effort to change seems futile.

our capacity to adapt. How did our ancestors think and act when change, innovation, and technological advancements challenged their very existence? We may never know the answer to this question, but two things are certain: Change is the only constant we will ever know, and security does not reside in a "job" or "place"; it resides inside each of us.

There are some general guidelines that entrepreneurs use to secure their future. They see change as opportunity, and, as a consequence, actually have more opportunity. They take accountability to investigate trends and to hear what the trend(s) are telling them. They do not wait for their profession or organization to tell them where it is going—they take it with them. They become interdependent with their organizations and continually strive to possess the core competencies that contribute to organizational success. Their mental models are permeable, because they know that they cannot prepare for what they do not see. They deeply understand that each new paradigm shift presents new limitations, and that these limitations will one day need to be breached.

The future of nursing is not in holding onto the past and attempting to protect discrete "tasks." Our future will be dependent upon us, individually and collectively, to stop feeding off the problems of the day and, instead, turn our attention to what opportunity the future is offering us.

The nurse entrepreneur accepts that the future is where opportunity resides. Nursing's history is one for us all to be proud. Our forebears were entrepreneurial stewards for all that we enjoy today. Leaders like Florence Nightingale and Lavinia Dock were not hampered with the past. They did not dwell in what was, but imagined what could be, and began that journey against odds that few of us could imagine. Let us not disappoint their spirit by doing less.

REFERENCES

1. J. Burke, and R. Ornstein, *The Axemaker's Gift* (New York: Grosset/Putnam, 1995).
2. R. Leakey, *The Origin of Humankind* (New York: Basic Books, 1994).
3. W. Knoke, *Bold New World: The Essential Road Map to the Twenty First Century* (New York: Kodansha, 1996).
4. S. Pinker, *The Language Instinct: How the Mind Creates Language* (New York: Harper, 1994).
5. C. Van Doren, *A History of Knowledge: The Pivotal Events, People, and Achievements of World History* (New York: Ballantine Books, 1991).
6. W. Bridges, *Job Shift: How to Prosper in a Workplace without Jobs* (New York: Addison Wesley, 1993).
7. W. Bridges, *Stewardship: Choosing Service Over Self-Interest* (New York: Berrett Koehler, 1993).
8. P.E. Drucker, *Managing for the Future* (New York: Truman Talley Books, 1993).
9. P.E. Drucker, *Post-Capitalist Society* (New York: Harper, 1993).
10. P.E. Drucker, *Managing in a Time of Great Change* (New York: Harper, 1995).
11. C. Handy, *The Age of Paradox* (Boston: Harvard Press, 1994).
12. Price Waterhouse, *Better Change* (New York: Irwin, 1995).
13. J. Rifkin, *The End of Work: The Decline of the Global Labor Force and the Dawn of the Post-Market Era* (New York: Tarcher/Putnam, 1995).
14. K. Wilber, *A Brief History of Everything* (Boston: Shambhala Publications, 1996).
15. K. Wilber, *Up From Eden: A Transpersonal View of Human Evolution* (Wheaton, IL: Quest Books, 1996).
16. J.A. Barker, *Paradigms: The Business of Discovering the Future* (New York: Harper Business, 1982).
17. T.S. Kuhn, *The Structure of Scientific Revolutions* (Chicago: University of Chicago Press, 1962).
18. J. Naisbitt, *Megatrends: Ten Directions Transforming Our Lives* (New York: Warner Books, 1982).
19. B. Kosko, *Fuzzy Thinking: The New Science of Fuzzy Logic* (New York: Hyperion, 1993).
20. K. Kelly, *Out of Control: The New Biology of Machines, Social Systems, and the Economic World* (New York: Addison-Wesley, 1995).
21. C. Darwin, *The Origin of Species* (London: Penguin Books, 1985).

3

The Evolving Health Care System

Strategic Implications of Developing Integrated Levels of Care

Harriet S. Gill and Michael Rovinsky

In response to the introduction of the acute care prospective payment system (PPS) for Medicare patients in 1983, acute care hospitals quickly learned to decrease average length of stay by developing and utilizing alternative, less restrictive, and theoretically less costly care delivery settings. By transferring patients to these postacute care settings, health systems were able to continue the course of patient treatment and tap into new payment streams for that care while avoiding losses incurred for extended inpatient stays under PPS. However, since postacute care settings are generally reimbursed based on costs, there was no incentive for health systems to provide integrated care across those settings. So while most health care systems spoke of providing integrated care, few actually did. As a result, although health systems were providing care in "less costly" settings, the total cost of care continued to increase.

Several market forces are now making health systems reexamine how care is provided across the continuum. The implementation of PPS for postacute care settings by the Health Care Financing Administration (HCFA), the development of provider sponsored networks (PSNs), and the growth of Medicare managed care created the necessary incentives for health systems not only to have or have access to the entire continuum of care, but also to integrate care across the continuum.

This article will focus on the development of integrated levels of care. First, the various levels of care in an integrated system will be described, including the "fit" of each level within an integrated system. Various mechanisms for putting an integrated system together will then be discussed. Once the components are assembled, patients must be managed from a levels-of-care perspective. This change of organizational perspective and its impact on the medical staff will be explored. Key challenges to and critical factors required for successful implementation will then be described. Finally, common pitfalls in the development of an integrated system of care will be identified.

THE DRIVING FORCES FOR INTEGRATION

The current Medicare PPS for acute care hospitals created incentives for hospitals and health systems to develop and gain access to various levels of care across the continuum. Patients have been transferred from one setting to another to enhance clinical outcomes and reduce the cost of care. While such motives sound good, the realities may not.

Many changes in health care are implemented with an expressed purpose of improving clinical outcomes. The reality is that improved clinical quality, although a noble

Managed Care Quarterly, 1998, 6(2): 21–35
© 1998 Aspen Publishers, Inc.

goal, is still extremely difficult to measure. Clinical quality is evaluated by the market on a pass/fail basis with a passing grade being an A. Few providers are included in managed care plans because they provide significantly better quality of care than other providers. On the other hand, poor quality of care, as evidenced by even a single aberrational incident, is newsworthy. Because of the difficulty in measuring quality improvement, the desire to enhance clinical outcomes has not motivated health systems to provide integrated levels of care.

The other reason to develop integrated levels of care is to reduce the overall cost of care. Indeed, most health systems can and do provide evidence that each successive care setting within their continuum is less costly. In fact, on a per-day or per-visit basis, each setting usually is less costly, as illustrated in Table 1.

However, since most postacute care services are reimbursed on a per-diem or per-visit basis without direct limits on the length of stay within each care setting, the aggregate cost of care per stay in a "less costly" setting may actually be higher. Recent trends in Medicare payments per discharge for postacute care services not limited in terms of overall length of stay confirm this possibility.

Medicare payments per discharge for acute care hospitals and acute rehabilitation programs (settings for which reimbursement is capped) increased by a modest 4.4 percent and 2.3 percent per year between 1991 and 1996. However, Medicare payments per discharge for skilled nursing programs and home care (settings for which there are no direct limits in terms of overall length of stay) increased by 26.4 percent and 16.8 percent per year over the same period. As a result, care settings further down the continuum which are supposed to be less costly than the more restrictive care settings may be more costly, depending on the length of stay within a particular setting.

Under current Medicare reimbursement methodologies, there is no incentive for providers to truly integrate care across the continuum to reduce the overall cost of care, for to do so would be to leave money on the table. Accordingly, most health systems have not developed truly integrated levels of care.

Several impending market shifts will force health systems to not just have access to the various components but to integrate care across the continuum as well. These changes include the implementation by HCFA of PPSs for postacute care services, the development of PSNs, and the growth of Medicare managed care.

Based on the apparent success of PPS in controlling the rise in acute care costs, Con-

Table 1 Average Cost of Care

Patient setting	*Parameter*	*Direct cost*	*Total cost*
Acute care	Per day	$600–900	$1,000–1,500
Acute rehab	Per day	500–700	800–1,200
Subacute care	Per day	250–400	400–600
Skilled nursing	Per day	100–150	200–350
Day hospital	Per day	150–250	250–400
Home care	Per visit	40–90	70–150
Ambulatory	Per visit	25–50	40–80

Source: Data from estimates by Gill/Balsano Consulting, LLC.

gress now considers PPS to be a valuable mechanism to control costs in other health care delivery settings. Specifically, HCFA plans to implement PPS for skilled nursing facilities (SNFs) on July 1, 1998, for home health in fiscal year 1999, and for acute rehabilitation in fiscal year 2000. Since Medicare beneficiaries represent 80 percent to 90 percent of subacute care patients (treated in licensed SNF beds), 65 percent to 75 percent of home health patients, and 70 to 80 percent of acute rehabilitation patients, the implementation of PPS in these settings will have a profound effect on the way care is provided within each setting. For the first time, the incentive for providers will be similar to managed care incentives, that is, to minimize the cost and the length of stay within each care setting. To do so, providers will have to carefully coordinate care within each setting and closely monitor the types of patients admitted to each program. In addition, to optimize reimbursement, providers will need to have or have access to the entire continuum of care and to coordinate care so that it is provided in the least costly, most appropriate setting available.

However, even under PPS, an incentive still exists to admit a patient to a new care setting, regardless of the overall cost of care for the episode of illness. It is only when providers are at risk for the overall cost of patient care that they have incentives to develop truly integrated levels of care. The increasing development of PSNs and the continued growth of Medicare managed care with the potential for full-risk contracting provide these incentives. Under full-risk scenarios, the importance of developing integrated levels of care increases because of the way health care resources are utilized. Approximately 41 percent of health care expenditures are for care provided to the 16 percent of patients with chronic conditions. The way care is provided to these (typically Medicare) patients can either generate a profit on a full-risk contract or result in a significant loss on the contract.

An integrated levels of care system allows health systems to control all aspects of patient flow and optimize care management. Although full-risk contracting is not yet a reality in most markets, providers must begin the process of developing an integrated levels of care system now in order to set the stage for future success.

Finally, once an organization has truly integrated its services, episodic outcome and cost data become critical. However, the value of such data should be based on their utility as predictive tools. That is, depending upon how a patient presents clinically and functionally, the data should be able to be used to develop the most cost-efficient plan of care to achieve a predicted or targeted outcome.

LEVELS OF CARE IN AN INTEGRATED SYSTEM

An integrated levels of care system may include the following components:

- Acute care hospital
- Acute rehabilitation
- Long-term hospital
- Subacute care (medical/rehabilitation)
- Traditional skilled nursing care
- Home services
- Outpatient care
- Assisted living

In general, local physician practice patterns and Certificate of Need restrictions to service development determine exactly how the system is put together.

A description of each level of care and how it fits into the integrated system follows.

Acute Care Hospital

Acute hospital care has been driven by prospective payment systems for more than a decade. The goals of PPSs were to decrease the length of stay and the cost per day. In general, those goals have been met. The average length of stay in acute care hospitals has decreased significantly over the past 10 years. This decrease has resulted in significant excess capacity in acute care hospitals. The decision for health systems today in the development of integrated levels of care is whether to develop the other levels of care in partnership with existing facilities or in existing underutilized space. Given the opportunity to cover additional overhead, many health systems opt for the latter approach.

Under a full-risk contract, the dilemma facing the health system is not so much where to transfer the patient from the acute care hospital, but whether to transfer the patient. Under current payment mechanisms, transfer of a patient to another care setting owned by the system allows a health system to tap into a new revenue stream, which serves as a financial incentive to transfer the patient from one setting to another. However, acute care hospital costs are not linear during the stay. The majority of cost is typically incurred during the early portion of the stay. Accordingly, near the end of an acute care hospital stay, the cost of transferring a patient to another setting may be higher than the actual cost of maintaining the patient in the hospital. Therefore, under a full-risk contract, providing integrated levels of care may mean not utilizing those levels of care or skipping certain levels in order to minimize the overall cost of care to the patient.

Similar thinking on the part of acute care hospitals will have to occur because of the new definition of a transfer that is included in the Balanced Budget Act of 1997. Under the act, hospitals that discharge patients to a postacute care setting (within the 10 diagnosis-related groups [DRGs] most often discharged to a postacute care setting) will receive a decrease in payment. The decrease will be based on the number of days prior to the geometric mean of the DRG that the patient is moved to another setting. This ruling creates another incentive to develop an integrated levels-of-care system. Those hospitals that do not have each of the levels of care may find themselves with increasing lengths of stay, poor profiles with managed care companies, and an inability to recoup any losses through additional revenue streams, such as SNF or home care services.

Acute Rehabilitation Hospitals and Units

Prior to the implementation of acute care PPS, the number of acute rehabilitation hospitals and units had remained relatively stable for many years. Given the need of acute care hospitals to discharge patients earlier under PPS, the number of acute rehabilitation hospitals and units increased significantly after its implementation. However, the way that acute rehabilitation programs are reimbursed creates problems in identifying their appropriate fit within an integrated system of care.

Acute rehabilitation facilities and distinct-part units are PPS-exempt and paid under the Tax Equity and Fiscal Responsibility Act (TEFRA) reimbursement system. Under this system, a TEFRA rate is determined based on the actual cost of care for Medicare patients in the first years of operation of the facility or unit. This TEFRA limit is then updated in each successive year by the health care market basket index. Reimbursement under TEFRA is like a facility-specific prospective payment. However, the TEFRA rates vary significantly among facilities, ranging from as low as $6,000 to as high as $40,000 per case. This disparity causes an enormous difference in the types of patients that can be treated in each facility. Within an integrated system, it is critical for the health system to understand the acute rehabilitation facility's

TEFRA rate and to manage admissions accordingly. For instance, if the facility's TEFRA limit is relatively low, transfer of a fairly sick patient from the acute care hospital can result in a significant loss to the health system. Alternately, if the facility's TEFRA rate is relatively high, the health system has much more flexibility in the types of patients admitted to the facility and may even be able to change the types of patients served over time, depending on the needs of the acute care hospital.

Patients admitted to an acute rehabilitation facility must meet certain requirements in order for their care to be reimbursed by Medicare. First, 75 percent of cases treated in an acute rehabilitation facility must fall within 11 diagnostic categories identified by HCFA. Second, each patient must undergo a minimum of three hours of therapy per day. Third, patients must be able to show significant improvement in their condition in a relatively short time frame. Finally, patients must require and receive more than one type of therapy for their treatment.

As patients are discharged earlier and sicker from the acute care hospital setting, these rules make it increasingly difficult to place patients in the acute rehabilitation setting. In addition, the rules are often interpreted differently by various fiscal intermediaries. For instance, some fiscal intermediaries are denying acute rehabilitation care for orthopaedic patients unless there are significant complications. Since orthopaedic cases often represent as much as 50 percent or more of the cases historically treated in an acute rehabilitation facility, this difference in interpretation can make a major difference in the need for acute rehabilitation services within a health system.

The 1997 Budget Bill requires that HCFA implement a case mix adjusted PPS for acute rehabilitation hospitals and units by fiscal year (FY) 2000 to be phased in over three years. While the exact methodology for payment has not yet been developed, it is highly likely that it will be a similar model to that about to be implemented for skilled nursing units. If this is the case, operating from both acute rehabilitation and skilled nursing levels of care will be required to manage patients as they move from one payment group to another.

Long-Term Hospital

A long-term hospital has an acute hospital license but is required to have an average length of stay for the entire facility of at least 25 days. These hospitals are reimbursed under the TEFRA system but have fewer restrictions placed on them than do acute rehabilitation facilities. In general, the length of stay requirement is the only restriction.

Long-term care hospitals are heterogeneous in profile. Many early long-term care hospitals were either psychiatric or rehabilitation hospitals. More recently, new long-term hospitals were developed (mainly by proprietary systems such as Vencor and American Transitional Care) to treat more intensely ill, long-term patients. Patients now typically treated in long-term hospitals include those who are ventilator-dependent, have multiple comorbidities postsurgically, or have multiple trauma or multiple system failure. In the acute care hospital, these patients typically represent less than 5 percent of the patient population but may represent more than 20 percent of patient days. Historically, many of these patients were discharged home from the acute care intensive care unit. Within an integrated system of care, those patients that do not require frequent readmission to the intensive care unit (approximately 50 percent of such patients) can be adequately treated in a long-term care hospital.

Because of the ability to achieve a second payment stream through the long-term hospital while significantly decreasing length of stay in the acute hospital, long-term hospital development has provided significant financial benefits to many organizations. However, because of the recent proliferation of long-term hospitals, the 1997 Budget Bill has directed HCFA to develop a proposal for a PPS for long-term hospitals by October of 1999. Finally, because long-term hospitals are acute care hospitals providing fairly intensive services to very ill patients, under managed care there may be little incentive to develop a separate entity, particularly if space is available in the acute care hospital.

Subacute Care

Subacute care has been the buzzword of the 1990s. Licensed and reimbursed as a skilled nursing bed, subacute care is provided to patients requiring skilled clinical care but not diagnostics or invasive procedures. The difference between a traditional SNF bed and a subacute bed is in how patient care, costs, and reimbursement are managed. As an SNF-based service, subacute care is reimbursed on a cost basis with cost limits for routine care. Routine cost limits are permitted with appropriate documentation of treatment provided to atypical patients with high resource utilization. Historically, SNF providers have had to position themselves either at the low acuity (traditional SNF) level to exist at routine cost limit rates or at the high acuity (subacute) level to justify exceptions to the routine cost limit.

In addition to routine costs, SNF providers are reimbursed for therapy costs subject to salary equivalency standards as well as all reasonable ancillary costs and capital costs. These additional reimbursements give incentives to providers to use therapies and develop subacute care.

Subacute care fits easily into an integrated system because, although Medicare participation criteria for SNF providers are relatively stringent, patient selection criteria are much less onerous than for acute rehabilitation. The main criteria for Medicare participation are that the patient requires skilled care and has been treated in an acute care hospital for a period including three midnights within 30 days of the admission to the SNF for the same diagnosis. Once these criteria are met, Medicare will pay for SNF care for 100 days.

Beginning in July 1998, reimbursement for skilled providers will be significantly changed. The prospective payment methodology to be implemented after that date will provide an all-inclusive, per diem rate adjusted by case mix. The case mix adjustments take into consideration clinical patient data and use these data to predict patient resource consumption. Resource Utilization Groups (RUGs) have been developed as the payment mechanism. These groups are subject to change during the course of a patient's stay as his or her condition warrants. As noted earlier, should this same payment system be implemented for acute rehabilitation providers, it will be critical that both levels of care be available to ensure appropriate patient placement.

Under Medicare risk arrangements, the integration of subacute care into the system becomes more important. Medicare health maintenance organizations (HMOs) do not have the three-midnight rule for payment for care provided in SNF beds. Therefore, in highly penetrated Medicare managed care markets, when the patient diagnosis is known, no surgery or invasive procedures are required, and the plan of care can be managed through the emergency department, patients can be admitted directly to the subacute unit, avoiding the acute care hospital admission entirely. Of course, in such a scenario, it is critically important for the subacute unit to be focused programmatically and for the health system case managers to fully understand the care that can be provided in the unit.

Subacute care tends to be segmented into rehabilitation and complex medical subacute care. In a subacute rehabilitation program, any service that can be delivered in an acute rehabilitation facility can be provided. Often, these programs look identical. In fact, the Commission for Accreditation of Rehabilitation Facilities (CARF) standards for acute rehabilitation and subacute rehabilitation are almost identical. Accordingly, subacute rehabilitation programs can meet the needs of patients who are denied acute rehabilitation due to the strict admission criteria (such as when a patient cannot tolerate three hours of therapy per day or does not fall into one of the required diagnostic categories). In addition, the lack of stringent admission requirements allows for the development of more creative patient programs. However, the significant overlap between acute rehabilitation and subacute rehabilitation (approximately 30 percent of cases) requires careful management to meet financial and clinical objectives. For instance, many health systems utilize the subacute rehabilitation unit to treat patients requiring significantly less care than patients treated in the acute rehabilitation program. In so doing, the acute rehabilitation hospital is often left with the extremely complex rehabilitation cases, which may place the facility in jeopardy of exceeding its TEFRA limit. Acute and subacute rehabilitation programs must be used synergistically in order to optimize both clinical and financial outcomes. In effect, the admission criteria for the two units must be built into the strategic plan of the integrated system so that patient transfers meet the strategic goals of the system.

As described above for subacute programs generally, subacute rehabilitation programs are essential under Medicare risk contracting and are highly favored by Medicare HMOs over acute rehabilitation facilities even if the overall cost of care turns out to be higher. Medicare HMOs are required to supply everything provided under traditional Medicare coverage. As in traditional Medicare, there is no direct limit on the length of stay in an acute rehabilitation facility. However, SNF care is limited to 100 days. Therefore, utilization of the subacute rehabilitation unit instead of an acute rehabilitation facility allows the HMO to reduce its financial exposure. Accordingly, subacute rehabilitation programs will become an increasingly important component of an integrated system of care as Medicare moves toward managed care.

Subacute medical units serve patients with complex medical conditions for whom diagnostics or surgery have been completed. The unit is often used to complete the medical treatment. Patients typically include those needing intravenous therapy; those with chronic obstructive pulmonary disease and other complex cardiology, pulmonary, and oncology illnesses; and other more frail elderly patients who may have specialized nursing needs.

The key to the successful development of a subacute medical unit, assuming the goal is to decrease acute length of stay and cost, is to base the planning for the unit on target critical mass patient populations rather than on the total number of beds that could be filled. If a subacute medical unit takes all patients who could potentially benefit from such care, it is likely that one or two patients could be identified on almost every acute care unit in the hospital. Transferring those one or two patients per unit to the subacute medical unit will not save the acute care hospital much money, since the decrease in staffing required in each of the acute care units will be negligible. Conversely, if one or two diagnostic categories are targeted that could result in the transfer of five or more patients from any one acute care unit, staffing and cost savings can be achieved. Therefore, as in the development of subacute rehabilitation programs, admission criteria are critical for the success of the unit and must be developed with consideration given to strategic and financial objectives of the organization.

Skilled Nursing Care

Traditional skilled nursing care uses the same platform as subacute care but represents a lower complexity and/or acuity of patient need. Patients generally have significant activities of daily living (ADL) needs such as dressing and toileting but only minimal medical needs. Medicare standards require skilled patients to receive three to five hours of nursing care per day and, out of those hours of care, a registered nurse must be present on at least one shift. In addition, each patient must be seen by a physician a minimum of one time per month. (The standard is the same for subacute care; however, physicians are free to see each patient as often as necessary. In subacute care, because patients tend to be significantly sicker, physicians typically see each patient three to five times per week.) Although Medicare pays for 100 days of care if a patient has spent three midnights in an acute care hospital in the previous 30 days for the same diagnosis, partly because beneficiaries must pay copayments after the first 20 days of care, the average length of stay in skilled nursing care tends to be 45 to 50 days (versus 12 to 15 days in subacute care).

Since subacute and skilled care are provided through the same Medicare vehicle, the payment changes noted above will apply to both levels of care after June 30, 1998. Because the payment mechanism allows for the same patient to move up and down a RUG payment scale, the availability of both levels of care will be critical to ensure continuity of care.

In addition, like subacute care, skilled nursing care becomes an increasingly important component of an integrated system under full-risk contracting. Since Medicare HMOs do not have the three-midnight rule for payment for care provided in SNF beds, patients theoretically can be admitted directly to the skilled nursing facility, avoiding other more costly levels of care entirely.

Long-Term Nursing Care

Long-term nursing care is usually referred to as intermediate care. Patients require little ongoing medical management. The patient population is typical frail elderly, 80 years of age and older, with significant ADL needs. In general, this population lives the rest of their lives under this level of care.

Long-term nursing care is not reimbursed under Medicare or most other insurance policies but is sometimes covered under special long-term care policies. The patient population is typically a self-pay and Medicaid population, although self-pay patients are increasingly opting for assisted living arrangements.

Although long-term nursing care is an important component of an integrated system of care, the traditional reimbursement situation makes it more attractive as a contracted or "accessible" component of an integrated system rather than an owned component. However, under risk contracting, health systems should clearly think through how they will be managing the health of residents in long-term care facilities. While reimbursement may be less than optimal under Medicaid, there remains a need to ensure that the patients' needs are met in the lowest cost setting and that they do not require frequent visits to the emergency department or, even worse, costly admissions to the acute care facility. Therefore, under managed care, integrating long-term care into the system should be seen as a cost prevention strategy rather than a reimbursement strategy.

Table 2 summarizes the distinguishing characteristics of the various programs that are provided in licensed SNF beds.

Home Care

Home care programs provide skilled and other services to patients who are homebound. Typically, home health agencies also provide infusion therapy, durable medical equipment (DME), and hospice services. Services are paid on a cost basis subject to a weighted average of home care visits by type of visit (nursing, social work, physical therapy, occupational therapy, etc.). While home care is somewhat evenly distributed between Medicare and non-Medicare payers, Medicare clearly pays for the lion's share of the visits. Typically, hospital-based home care providers establish two separate businesses—Medicare and private pay—so as not to dilute the hospital overhead allocation allowed to the Medicare agency.

Two key issues drive the pattern of utilization of home care services. First, in order to receive most home care services under Medicare, a patient must be homebound. However, when a patient moves through various levels of care, by definition that patient is not homebound and, therefore, cannot receive many of the home care services desired by patients, such as home health aide services. Since patients like and need such services, once referred for home care, patients typically remain in home care as long as they require additional low-intensity medical care rather than being referred for outpatient care or some other minimally restrictive care setting.

The second issue impacting the pattern of utilization of home care is the reimbursement system. As the last bastion of fee-for-service medicine, there is little incentive to discharge a patient once referred for home care. This issue reinforces the first issue in terms of reducing the likelihood that a patient will be referred for outpatient services or some other minimally restrictive care setting. Thus, while both managed care and Medicare utilize home care services, the number of visits per patient under managed care is significantly less than that for the Medicare patient.

Significant changes in reimbursement and interpretation of existing home care rules are imminent, including the implementation of home care PPS, which will minimize or eliminate the impact of these issues. Beginning in October of 1997, a significant reduction in Medicare payment has been imposed on agencies. This is the first step to a PPS that will eventually pay on a per episode basis. These changes point out again the importance of understanding the current practice patterns and incentives driving utilization within an integrated system, particularly as organizations move toward Medicare risk contracting. More than any other level of care, the financial incentives being built into home care reimbursement under the Medicare program are in concert with the goals of managed care.

Table 2 Characteristics of Nursing Facility Care

Level of care	*Nursing hours*	*MD visits*	*ALOS*	*Payer mix*
Subacute	4.5–6.5	3–5/week	10 to 30 days	Primarily Medicare
Skilled	2.5–3.5	2–4/month	30 to 90 days	Medicare/Medicaid
Intermediate	1.5–2.5	1/month	90 days to 3 years	Medicaid, self-pay

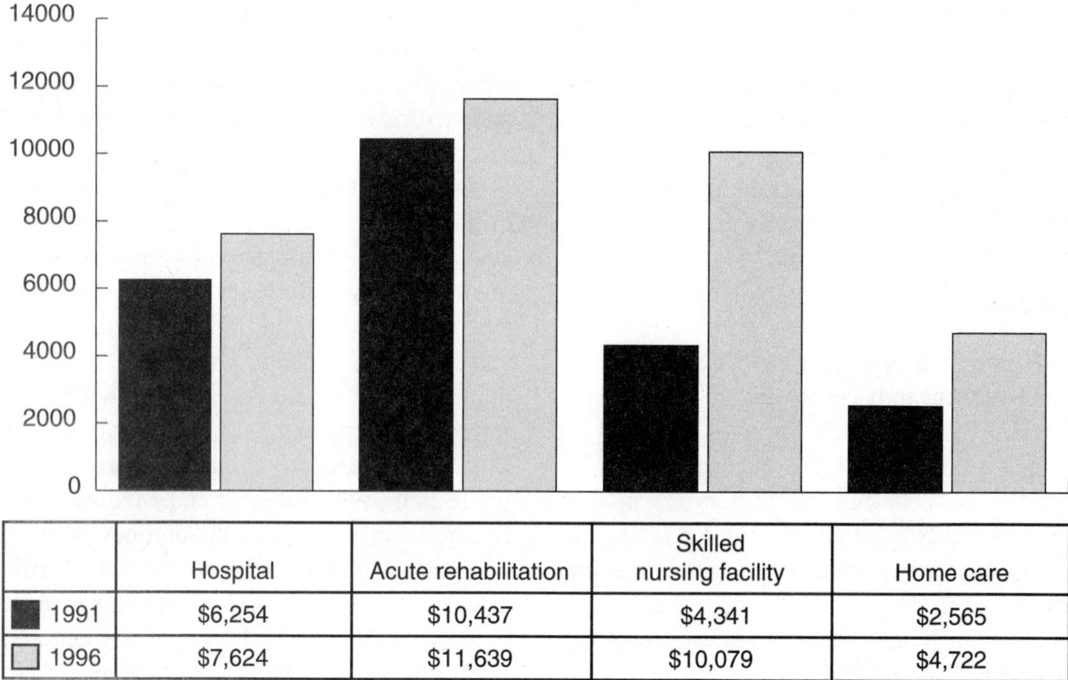

	Hospital	Acute rehabilitation	Skilled nursing facility	Home care
1991	$6,254	$10,437	$4,341	$2,565
1996	$7,624	$11,639	$10,079	$4,722

Figure 1. Medicare payments per discharge. *Source:* ProPAC Report and Recommendations to the Congress, March 1, 1997, Washington, DC: Government Printing Office, 1997.

Outpatient Care

There are as many options for outpatient care as there are inpatient settings. Outpatient services are reimbursed under Medicare Part B and by a number of other mechanisms by other payers. The key issue in the development of integrated levels of care from an outpatient care perspective is that varying levels of care can also be developed on an outpatient basis.

One relatively new outpatient level of care that can be an essential component of an integrated system is day hospital care. Basically, a day hospital program is any program whose patients would be in an acute care hospital if the program didn't exist. It is hospital care for patients who don't need to be in the hospital overnight. Day hospital programs provide physician services, nursing services, therapy services, and most other noninvasive services provided in a hospital. The important factor in the development of day hospital programs is that, by avoiding the overnight stay in the hospital, significant cost savings can be achieved. Particularly significant is the ability of the programs to decrease the cost of care for catastrophic injury patients such as spinal cord and brain injury patients. It is important to note, however, that day hospital programs are not appropriate for all patients. Successful day hospital treatment requires that the patient have an adequate support system available after the day program ends.

One option for developing a day hospital program is to establish it within a comprehensive outpatient rehabilitation facility (CORF). CORF is a Medicare designation that allows the outpatient entity to bill everything for which a hospital can bill, such as nursing, social work services, case management, and physician services. The primary requirements are that the CORF has a medical director and provides physical therapy and psychosocial services. Therefore, if the target population for day hospital treatment is primarily a Medicare population, a CORF may be an appropriate vehicle for the development of the program.

Assisted Living

The final component of an integrated system of care is assisted living. Assisted living targets the frail elderly population, typically 80 years old and older. It represents care for people with ADL needs but not much in the way of medical care. As indicated previously, it is becoming the option of choice for patients who otherwise would spend the rest of their lives in a long-term nursing care facility. It is not covered by Medicare or most other payers. However, Medicare will pay for home care services and day hospital services provided to residents of assisted living facilities under most circumstances.

Assisted living is really a blend of real estate and clinical services. Assisted living units are apartments in which primarily ADL services are provided. Accordingly, for many health systems, it makes sense to get a real estate agent to develop the building and to contract manage the clinical services for the facility. If Medicare managed care is not a significant factor in the market and assisted living facilities are available in the community, health systems may be well advised to utilize their capital resources in other ways. However, if the organization is at risk for the health of the facility residents, a more preventive approach may make the best investment.

The components of an integrated system described above are the components most prevalent today. It should be mentioned, however, that even by the time this article is published, new levels of care may exist that can be appropriately integrated into a full continuum of care. In general, the development of levels of care closely follows reimbursement activity. As reimbursement for certain levels of care is diminished and new reimbursement streams are identified, new levels of care will surely be identified that may fit within an integrated system of care.

PUTTING THE SYSTEM TOGETHER

Once all of the essential components of the integrated system are identified, a health system must determine the best way to assemble the pieces and put them together to meet its strategic and financial goals and objectives.

There are multiple mechanisms to put the integrated system together. Development options include the following:

- Shared services
- Joint ownership
- Joint operating companies
- Leasing model
- Management contract
- Bed reserve
- Managed care contract

Shared services is a fairly loose development option whereby a necessary component of the integrated system is offered or can be developed in another facility and then utilized by the health system, possibly in exchange for the purchase of services necessary to operate the program. For instance, a health system without SNF beds may work with a nursing home across the street to develop a subacute unit. The nursing home may develop the program and purchase physical therapy, laboratory, and pharmacy services required for the program from the health system. In this way, the health system receives some additional revenue and the nursing home gets a new program with a captured audience.

Sharing services is a good mechanism to use during initial phases of integrated system development to get comfortable with certain partners before developing more integrated models. However, this model does not typically provide the health system with sufficient programmatic control to truly integrate the shared service with the other levels of care provided by the health system or in the other facility.

Another option is for the health system to purchase a partial ownership stake in a nursing home, home health agency, or other facility or program. In so doing, the health system can obtain several seats on the board of the entity and some input into how things are done at the facility. However, because the health system cannot fully control patient flow, issues regarding the bottom line of the other entity have the potential to conflict with the best interests of the health system in terms of admission and discharge criteria and the flow of patients within the integrated system.

Joint operating companies work well when multiple organizations desire the same kind of patient flow. The organizations come together to form a company that then manages the entity or program. For instance, many of the components of a full continuum of care include the provision of therapy services. Typically, each entity within the system has its own therapy department, staff, equipment, space, and supplies. Since all of the components of the system require therapy services and, at least theoretically, desire the same objectives be met through patient flow through the integrated system, it may make sense to develop a joint operating company among the other entities within the system to provide therapy services and monitor patient flow throughout the system. The key to the successful development of a joint operating company is that economies of scale be achieved that better position the participating organization as a low-cost provider. Just putting services together without removing layers of management and other duplicative personnel, equipment, supplies, and services will not achieve the goals of the integrated system of care.

Leasing space in another facility works well to the degree that state regulations give the organization doing the leasing control over the operation of the program. For instance, if a health system leases space in a nursing home to develop a subacute unit and the subacute unit remains on the nursing home's cost report, the health system will have limited control over the way the program is ultimately operated since the financial liability remains with the nursing home. Alternatively, in some states, the subacute unit can be put on the health system's cost report, giving the health system ultimate control over the operation of the unit. Under this scenario, a leasing model may be a favorable development option.

Regardless of the issue of operational control, one downside to the leasing model is that it is often difficult to integrate the service developed in the leased space with the other programs provided in the facility. Therefore, potential synergies among levels of care may be lost and with them opportunities to cut more cost out of the integrated system.

Outsourcing is becoming more accepted as a way to provide services. A management contract can be an excellent way to hit the ground running and quickly develop a service that is efficient and effective. The key issue for the success of a management contract is incentive alignment. It is critical that the incentives of the management entity are aligned with those of the rest of the components of the integrated system to ensure that the component being outsourced becomes an integral part of the continuum rather than a cash cow for the management entity. For instance, the health system may want the managed program to take a patient even if money is lost in that setting as long as it represents less of a loss than would occur if the patient were treated in another setting within the system. Incentives must be aligned at the outset to make sure that the integrated system functions to reduce the overall cost of care for the system.

Another cautionary note in developing a level of care through a management contract is to make sure that what you buy is what you really want. For instance, many management companies present the ability to develop the specific program of interest as well as to implement various sophisticated medical management systems, clinical pathways, and care protocols. At first glance, access to such sophisticated care management tools from a more experienced entity is appealing. However, if the health system is developing its own systems and protocols for other components of the integrated system, the systems and protocols may be inconsistent with those provided by the management entity for the individual program. It is essential that medical management systems and protocols be consistent throughout the integrated entity. Accordingly, be careful about what you want from a management entity; you just may get it.

Another loose mechanism through which to put the pieces together is a bed reserve. As an example, if an acute care hospital is having trouble discharging patients on a timely basis and there is a subacute care unit at another facility that typically operates at full occupancy, the acute care hospital might pay the subacute facility to reserve a number of beds for its patients. There are two ways this payment is usually arranged. Either a payment is made whether or not a patient is in the bed, or a payment is made when the beds are empty. The critical issue is to make a deal that cannot be viewed as supplementing the reimbursement for Medicare or Medicaid.

Although this model does not provide the integrated system with much programmatic control, it is a viable development option when the cost of reserving the beds is less than the cost to keep the patient in an acute care bed or other component of the system.

While all of these mechanisms can serve a purpose in the development of an integrated system of care, as in most other initiatives requiring the integration of several entities or programs, the best arrangement is the one that most closely aligns the incentives of all participants. In the development of an integrated levels of care system, the only way to truly accomplish this alignment is to have each component sharing risk in a managed care contracting arrangement.

In order for all components to share risk, a new company with its own board should be established. This company can then sign managed care contracts on behalf of all of the components. The individual components may or may not be owned. The key to success is that they are all coming together to share risk and reward through the contracting entity. When the bottom line of the new company is more important than the performance of any of the individual components of care, that is the point at which the integrated system can truly provide the right care at the right time in the right setting at the right cost to the right patient.

Although the managed care contract model provides the ultimate alignment of incentives, it is not always feasible given the stage of the market and the organizational characteristics of the health system and the individual components. From a strategic perspective, the choice of mechanisms for putting the integrated system together is a three-step process: (1) determine what the system needs to look like (what entities and components need to be included), (2) determine how patients should optimally flow through the system, and (3) given regulatory and other constraints, determine how best to make the system happen. Along the way, critical decisions must be made on questions such as: what components need to be owned? If not owned, what components need to be controlled? If not controlled, what components just need to be available? If control is desired but ownership is not possible, how can a deal be cut that provides control over the clinical programs? Those decisions, made in the context of specific strategic objectives, will make a real difference in terms of how the integrated system is put together.

THE LEVELS OF CARE PERSPECTIVE

Most health systems have developed at least a few clinical pathways within the acute care hospital setting. For the chronic patient population, the most frequent utilizers of an integrated system of care, the development of acute care clinical pathways represents medical management over the first five days of what is likely to be an extended period of care. Managing patient care through the entire system over the entire course of care is much different from managing that care during an acute care stay. From a levels of care perspective, extended care management tends to require a new organizational way of thinking. This new way of thinking can be characterized as care management across the continuum as opposed to case management within components of the system. Very few health systems have achieved this new way of thinking.

First, most health systems that begin to think about care management versus case management begin by thinking about preventive care as the ultimate in care management. While this focus on decreasing admissions is noble, appropriate, and necessary in a Medicare full-risk contracting environment, it is not financially sensible given current reimbursement mechanisms of PPS. The key now is to admit the patient and then coordinate care among the levels of care to optimize clinical and financial outcomes.

In order to optimize clinical and financial outcomes, case management must be removed from the individual components of care, and elevated to care management at a macro level within the organization. This care management should be performed by an individual who understands both the clinical and financial objectives of the health system and can move patients through the system to achieve the best clinical outcome for the patient and the best financial outcome for the organization.

Efficiently and effectively moving patients across levels of care can create some concerns for the medical staff, which are important to address prior to full implementation. In general, integrated levels of care enhance efficiencies for surgeons if developed properly. Since surgeons are generally paid a global fee regardless of the number of times they round on the patient, moving the patient out of the acute care hospital setting into another level of care reduces the effort required of the surgeon to receive the same fee. However, in markets without significant managed care penetration, primary care physicians make more money the more times they round on a patient. Therefore, moving a patient from the acute care hospital setting where the physician can round on the patient seven days per week to another level of care setting where the physician can only round on the patient two to three times per week costs the physician money. (Of course, this issue is eliminated under capitation.)

The primary issue that confronts all physicians under an integrated levels of care system is that, as patients are discharged earlier from the acute care hospital, they are more seriously ill when they reach the other levels of care. As a result, physicians spend increasing amounts of time on the phone with other caregivers discussing patient care in those settings. This additional time on the phone is generally not reimbursed and takes time away from other reimbursable activities. Accordingly, in the development of integrated systems of care, health systems should be careful about what is expected from physicians and the level of cooperation anticipated.

The key to successful implementation of a levels of care system while minimizing medical staff concerns is to understand the market conditions and the various incentives for treatment that exist and to begin the education process early to identify the concerns in time to find ways to eliminate or minimize them. The integrated system must represent a win-win scenario for all constituencies.

KEY CHALLENGES TO IMPLEMENTATION

The concept of an integrated levels of care system makes intuitive sense for increasing the quality of care while decreasing its cost. Unfortunately, it is extremely difficult to implement successfully. The primary challenge to developing an integrated system of care today is a financial challenge: how to operate within the current financial incentives while transitioning to a more "at-risk" financial environment. In reality, it is very difficult for most managers to operate in a manner that is contrary to the incentives they are receiving. However, development and implementation of an integrated levels of care system takes a significant amount of time, usually between one and two years. Accordingly, providers that wait until the financial incentives encourage integrated care delivery will be significantly behind competitors who have put many of the pieces in place.

Another key challenge to implementation is having the information technology support to share clinical and financial information across care delivery sites. Again, developing the appropriate systems takes time and money. Those providers who wait to develop such systems will be at a significant disadvantage to their competitors when the first full-risk Medicare contracting opportunity arises.

Other challenges to implementing an integrated levels of care system include the following:

- Leadership: from management and the medical staff
- Process: the time to make it happen
- Organizational structure: to focus on system performance
- Clinical pathway development: to allow for care management across the continuum
- Information systems: to coordinate the various reimbursement systems
- Care management: from a clinical and a financial perspective
- Outcomes management: to measure the results

CRITICAL FACTORS FOR SUCCESSFUL IMPLEMENTATION

Every challenge is also an opportunity. Despite the significant challenges to implementation identified above, success can be achieved if appropriate planning occurs. Critical planning issues for successful implementation include the following:

Organizing for the Future

Financial goals of the integrated system will not be met if layers of management are not removed from the integrated system. The organizational structure must be flattened and incentives aligned relative to the bottom line of the system and the best clinical care of the patient in order to minimize internal competition and reduce the overall cost of care.

Developing the Right Systems

Managing patients across the continuum is a new perspective for many health care personnel. Understanding how patients flow through the system, where care management exists within the organization, and which clinical pathways have been developed across the continuum are essential for the integrated operation of the various levels of care.

Defining the Right Products

It is important to understand not only what licensed bed categories are needed, but what programs and products must go into each licensed bed category to best meet the needs of the system and the covered lives anticipated to be served in the future. Defining the right products is a strategic process that entails identifying the target patients, determining patient flow, and identifying products to meet patient needs while positioning the organization as a low-cost provider.

Eliminating Internal Competition

As long as disparate incentives exist within the organization, individual managers will continue to build their own business to the detriment of others and possibly the system. Aligning incentives is easy to discuss but difficult to achieve. Alignment must be created at the board level for the entire organization. It cannot be accomplished solely at the postacute level.

Creating a Cost-Competitive Delivery System

Putting together a cost-competitive delivery system requires an understanding of the costs and a willingness to organize so as to eliminate duplication of facilities, management, equipment, and supplies. In essence, the integrated entity must eliminate all of the overhead supporting the old individual service/silo mentality.

Identifying Good Partners

Freestanding providers of individual components of care are at risk for being cut off from their referral sources as health systems move to develop integrated systems of care. Accordingly, freestanding providers of care components are generally good joint venture partners for the development of an integrated levels of care system.

COMMON PITFALLS

As the saying goes, the best laid plans often go awry. Despite the best planning efforts by the most sophisticated organizations, implementation does not usually proceed smoothly. The box below contains a list and following is a brief explanation of some of the most common pitfalls in the development of an integrated levels of care system.

Common Pitfalls in the Development of an Integrated System of Care

- Thinking too narrowly
- Targeting the wrong patients for each level of care
- Underestimating the importance of admission and discharge criteria
- Discounting the existing hospital culture and reputation
- Excluding physicians from the planning process
- Assuming each level should stand alone financially

The first common pitfall is to think too narrowly. For many acute care hospitals, it has historically been difficult to think of themselves as being in more than just the acute inpatient business because that is where most of the money resides. However, PPS and the growth of managed care have diminished this problem for acute care hospitals.

Another common pitfall is targeting the wrong patients for each level of care. It is important for organizations to understand what resources are available within the integrated system, which are controlled by the organization, and what patient flow works best for each organization and the system as a whole.

Underestimating the importance of admission and discharge criteria can seriously reduce the chances that an integrated system will meet clinical and financial goals. As indicated previously, these criteria are so important for determining patient flow that they must almost be part of the strategic planning for the system.

It is said that structural integration is easy but cultural integration is difficult. Accordingly, discounting the existing hospital culture and reputation can be a devastating mistake in the development of the integrated system. For instance, if interviews conducted as part of the planning process reveal that a majority of physicians on the medical staff do not believe that a particular component of the integrated system will be utilized based on local referral patterns, that input should be used to significantly modify volume projections based on population use rates. In addition, once acute care hospital cultural issues are overcome, it is important to realize that each of the distinct components of the integrated system has a unique culture. If these cultures cannot be melded, it may be necessary to segregate one or more components into a separate division to help them maintain their identity.

Given the impact the development of integrated levels of care can have on physicians and the impact physicians through their referral patterns can have on the success of the integrated system, physicians must be included in the planning and development processes from the beginning.

Finally, a fully functioning, successfully integrated levels of care system is designed to optimize the clinical outcome for the patient and the financial outcome for the entire organization. In order to accomplish these goals, each level of care may not be able to support itself financially. As long as the entire system performs better as a result, the whole is greater than the sum of the parts. In order to appropriately monitor financial performance, the system should be evaluated on a consolidated, integrated basis.

• • •

By transferring patients to postacute care settings, health systems are able to continue the course of patient treatment and tap into new payment streams for that care while avoiding losses incurred for extended inpatient stays under PPS. However, since most postacute care settings are currently reimbursed based on costs, the current incentive for health systems is to develop or have access to and utilize a variety of postacute care settings, but not necessarily to provide integrated care across those settings. While most health care systems speak of providing integrated care, few actually do.

Several market forces are now making health systems once again look at how care is provided across the continuum. The implementation of PPS for postacute settings by HCFA will encourage health systems to coordinate care better among the individual components. However, the development of provider-sponsored networks and the growth of

Medicare managed care create the necessary incentives for health systems to not only have or have access to the entire continuum of care, but also to integrate care across each level.

Developing integrated systems of care takes time. The effort is intuitively sensible and its cost-effectiveness can be supported with empirical data. However, many tough decisions must be made in order to implement an integrated levels of care system. In the face of financial incentives contrary to the purpose of integrated care, these decisions become even more difficult. Not until health systems begin to close underutilized facilities and consolidate services can it be assumed that the financial goals of integrated care are being given more than just lip service.

4

Changing Hospitals in a Changing Environment

Integrating Information Technology with an Outcomes Management Program

Linda Cole and Susan Houston

Health care has changed dramatically over the past few years. These changes have affected not only the delivery of care, but also the technology used to provide that care. Health care delivery has entered the computer age with sophisticated monitoring systems, diagnostic tools, and computerized medical records.

With this computer age comes a demand for data, data management, outcomes measurement and management, and decision support. This has resulted in the emergence of a new field called *health informatics.* This article explores the development of health informatics and information management in health care, the relationship of information management to outcomes measurement and management, and the future of information technology.

IMPACT OF INFORMATICS ON HEALTH CARE

Traditionally, information systems have been viewed as hospital-based systems used for the automation of care processes. Examples of these processes include admission–discharge–transfer (ADT), order entry, results reporting, and billing applications. However, these applications are only a small dimension of what information systems are and will need to be in the future.

Ledley and Lusted[1] characterized an information system as having three essential parts: (1) a system for organizing or recording the data in a file, (2) a process for locating in this file the data on a specific subject, and (3) a process for keeping the data in the current file. Lindberg[1] described a medical information system as a set of orderly arrangements where facts about health and the health care of individual patients were stored and processed in computers. This description leads to the realization that a medical information system is a complex structure encompassing data from multiple sources. This structure is further complicated in integrated delivery systems and managed care organizations where additional data elements are recorded. Additionally, there is a growing desire to support clinical decision making related to interventions and outcomes. The definition of information systems must be refined to keep pace with changing demands. As a result, the science of health informatics continues to evolve.

WHAT IS HEALTH INFORMATICS?

The word "informatics" is derived from the French word "informatique" and in the 1960s was first associated with medical informatics, a broad term for computer use in health care.[2] Since this early association, informatics has grown to include nursing, den-

Critical Care Nursing Quarterly, 1997, 19(4): 71–79
© 1997 Aspen Publishers, Inc.

tistry, pharmacy, and other health science disciplines.

Currently, health informatics is more than computer applications. Health informatics is the study and application of information (ie, data) in the health sciences.[2] Information sciences, biomedical computing, scientific communications, clinical decision making, health care applications, and educational technology are encompassed under the umbrella of health informatics. The concept of health informatics provides the foundation to support the needs and demands of health care providers, administrators, and third-party payers for patient data and outcomes information. Within health informatics there are still some basic issues that must be addressed. These issues include data and its management; access and security; and the impact on outcomes management, quality, and research issues.

TYPES OF DATA

The types of data found in a health-related information system can be categorized based on the uses of that data (see Fig 1). These categories include descriptive data, clinical data, operational data, benchmarking data, and outcomes data. The sources of these data are as varied and complex as the institutions themselves (see Fig 2).

Descriptive data are those elements that are used to describe the patient population in question. Common elements include age, gender, geographical location, length of stay (LOS), admitting physician, payer, and diagnosis. Many of these data elements are housed in the medical records databases and can be extracted using medical records software or decision support software that has been programmed with the medical records data. Descriptive data are needed to define the patient population under

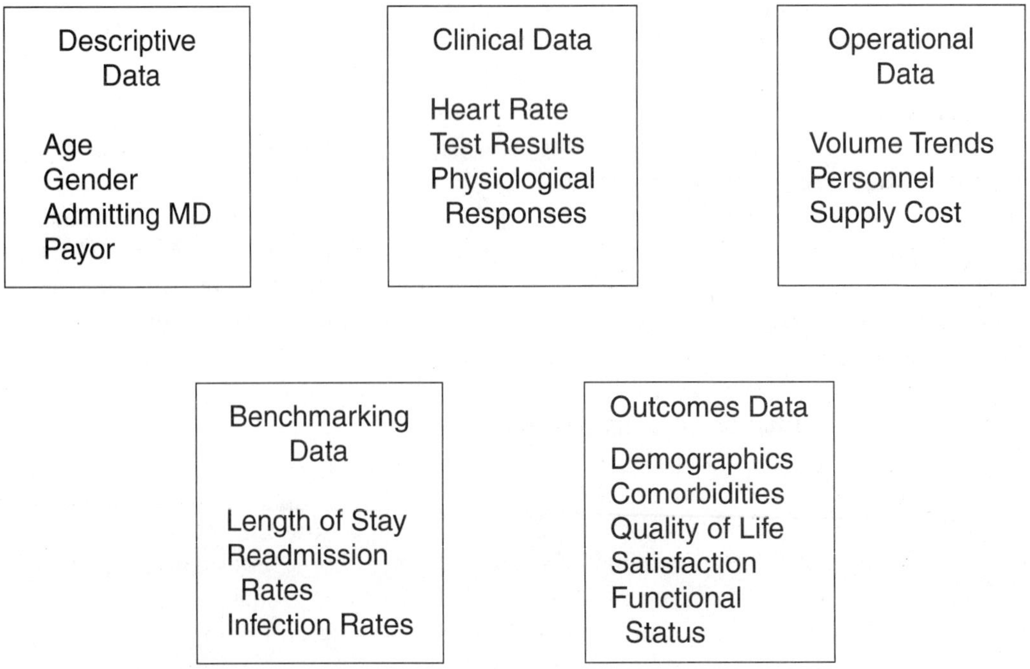

Figure 1. Types of data sets.

Figure 2. Sources of data.

analysis. If restricted to using only descriptive data, no link between interventions and outcomes is obtained.

Clinical data are the physiologic types of data such as vital signs, test results, and physiologic variations and responses to treatment. Although these data elements are often recorded by an automated system, storage or integration in an automated system may not occur. For example, heart rate, blood pressure, and pulmonary artery catheter readings are captured by an automated hemodynamic monitoring system. The nurse then records these readings on a paper document, thus losing the ability to graph and trend these readings in relation to interventions performed.

Administrative decisions require operational data for accurate direction and forecasts. Personnel data, supply use, departmental costs, and volume trends are examples of operational data. Accounting systems, payroll systems, and scheduling systems permit extraction and analysis of these data elements. Operational data are essential for the overall operation and strategic planning of the organization. Viewed in isolation, such data can give an incomplete picture. Descriptive and clinical data are needed to balance the analysis for a more accurate interpretation of operational needs and projections.

Benchmarking data provide a means of comparison for the institution. An institution may choose to compare itself with other institutions on a local, regional, or national basis or within the institution. Many of the existing data sets, such as Medicare data, permit comparison at different provider perspectives including physicians, hospitals, networks, and geographic areas.[3] Examples of benchmarking data are LOS, resource use, readmission rates, and infection rates. A weakness of benchmarking data is the frequent use of claims data. As a result, accurate coding is essential. Because claims data are used for reimbursement, the inclusion of secondary diagnoses that may be important from a clinical standpoint may not occur if reimbursement is not affected.[3] A word of caution about benchmarking data: adjustments in the health status and severity of the patients' illnesses used in the database are needed to ensure a homogeneous population. Without these adjustments, interpretations should be made cautiously to avoid an "apples to oranges" comparison.

The use of information for outcomes measurement, management, and research has moved to the forefront as a valuable mechanism for quantifying the effects of health care on consumers' health status. Information technology is essential to the measurement and management of patient outcomes because of its ability to assist in the collection, storage, aggregation, and segmentation of data. Through informatics, the quality of health care can be evaluated and improved, thus enhancing the processes that drive the resulting outcomes.

Currently many institutions are developing outcomes-related databases to improve the provision of care. These databases generally consist of three components: (1) patient information data used to describe managed patient populations, including demographics, comorbid conditions, health history information, billing events, and cost information (often referred to as administrative data); (2) clinical and quality information used to describe processes and clinical results, including clinical events, conditions, processes, and results; and (3) patient/provider surveys used to measure outcomes, including satisfaction, quality of life, and health care access.[4] These databases are developed for specific patient populations, thus allowing for concurrent and longitudinal mapping of patient outcomes in relation to a particular condition or procedure. Some of these data originate in the types of data and databases previously discussed. An example of how various data are synthesized into an outcomes database can be seen in Figure 3.

QUALITY CONTROL OF DATA

Institutions developing outcomes databases are not without limitations. Inconsistent data definitions and incomplete data hinder the ability to aggregate and draw sound conclusions regarding specific patient outcomes. Most institutions work furiously to develop internal standard definitions that promote data use and reliability.

Outcomes databases are derived from data elements and data sets. Data elements are the smallest pieces of knowledge or information that health care providers have to work with and include blood pressure, the presence of postoperative ileus, lack of discharge plan, or mortality. These data elements then make up data sets such as those displayed in Figure 3. Each data element can be uniquely defined by the following items[5]:

- whether the element is patient related,
- existence of the element,
- value of the element (the presence or absence of a number value),
- time of the observation,
- person who made the observation,
- method used to obtain the element, and
- certainty of the element.

Using these components to define a data element can help ensure the completeness and accuracy of the data, which promotes the use of data for clinical decision making and for answering epidemiologic questions regarding the impact of care.

The collection of data eventually requires a coding or classification system that promotes storage in a standardized and consistent way.

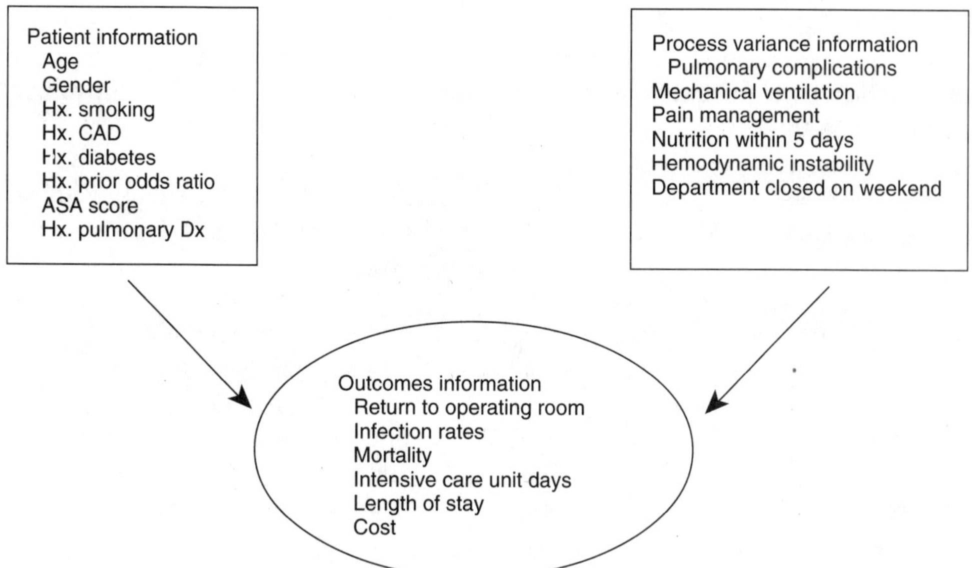

Figure 3. Database for diagnosis-related group (DRG) 149: small and large bowel procedures. Note: Hx=history; Dx=disease; CAD=coronary artery disease; ASA=American Society of Anesthesiologists.

Ideally, the coding or classification system should already conform or be translatable into nationally or internationally accepted codes. This facilitates the comparison of local data to external sources. The consistent use of a coding system also promotes accuracy in data entry and ease in interpreting data. Currently, a variety of natural language processing methods and techniques are being researched.[6,7] These approaches offer simpler user interface and would allow for comparison of data at the local, regional, and national levels.

As with any data collection effort, quantifying the data becomes a necessity. Establishing evidence of reliability and validity is an arduous task but one that pays tenfold when asking health care providers to make decisions based on data collected and analyzed. For categorical data, the use of standard data element definitions promote improved intra- and inter-rater reliability. A panel of experts can assist in determining the appropriateness of the data being collected and help establish content validity. In the use of surveys or questionnaires, quality control measures such as internal constancy and equivalency are necessary to ensure the reliability of the data obtained.

Completeness of data is also an issue that must be addressed. Whether data collectors are health care or informatics personnel, the need to understand the relationship between data collection and use is paramount. The ability of data collection personnel to witness and visualize the use of data to improve patient outcomes promotes support of the data collection effort. The completeness of data ultimately affects the ability to generalize findings within an institution.

A data collection effort can be costly and labor intensive. The products of outcomes databases are numerous and require the ability to provide detailed patient information, outcomes data, hypothesis generation and testing, and potential external benchmarking.[3] An outcomes database can be a rich data source with a commitment from everyone to ensure the reliability and validity of the data comprising the databases.

OUTCOMES MANAGEMENT

An outcomes database is a necessary component of any outcomes management effort. Precluding, as well as simultaneously occurring, outcomes management is the measurement of outcomes that comprise an essential component of an outcomes database. Outcomes management is defined as the use of outcomes assessment information to improve clinical and financial outcomes through exemplary practice. An outcomes database is a necessary component of any outcomes management effort and is developed over time.[8] Thus, outcomes data are essential to the management of patient outcomes.

Outcomes are managed through a variety of vehicles such as structured care methodologies (pathways, guidelines, and so forth), quality enhancement, and research. All of these vehicles allow health care providers to explore and determine best practice for specific patient populations. Therefore, the impact of best practice scenarios is ultimately reflected in patient outcomes. Informatics is crucial in determining the impact of best practice scenarios on patient outcomes through its ability to store and track patient outcomes concurrently and longitudinally.

THE SHAPE OF THINGS TO COME

The information systems of the future must be able to move beyond current conventional applications and incorporate clinical data with process data to assist health care providers in making the best decisions for a specific patient at a particular time. Distribution of hospital clinical databases to physicians' offices and clinics will be the key to management and outcomes analysis across the continuum of care.[9]

According to Mathews et al.,[10] information technology must support efforts such as the following:

- outcomes measurement by enrollees within a managed care contract,
- outcomes measurement across the continuum of care for all types of patients and services,
- coordination of services across the continuum,
- data comparison between providers, and
- data on an enterprise level as well as a community health network level.

To accomplish these efforts, individual health information must be accessed via an electronic health record. Peter Waegemann, executive director of the Medical Records Institute, has defined the electronic health record as "a computer-stored collection of health information about one person linked by a person identifier.[11(pp26–27)] To obtain this type of health record, behavioral and technologic changes must be made. From a behavioral standpoint, health care providers should no longer implement traditional methods of data entry such as handwriting and dictation, but instead interface directly with the computer. In the technologic arena, providers should access control systems that identify and authenticate the user and incorporate an electronic signature. System security features are essential.

How soon will this type of computerized health record be a reality? According to Waegemann,[11] there are five levels of computerization (Fig 4). Currently, only Levels 1 and 2 have been accomplished.

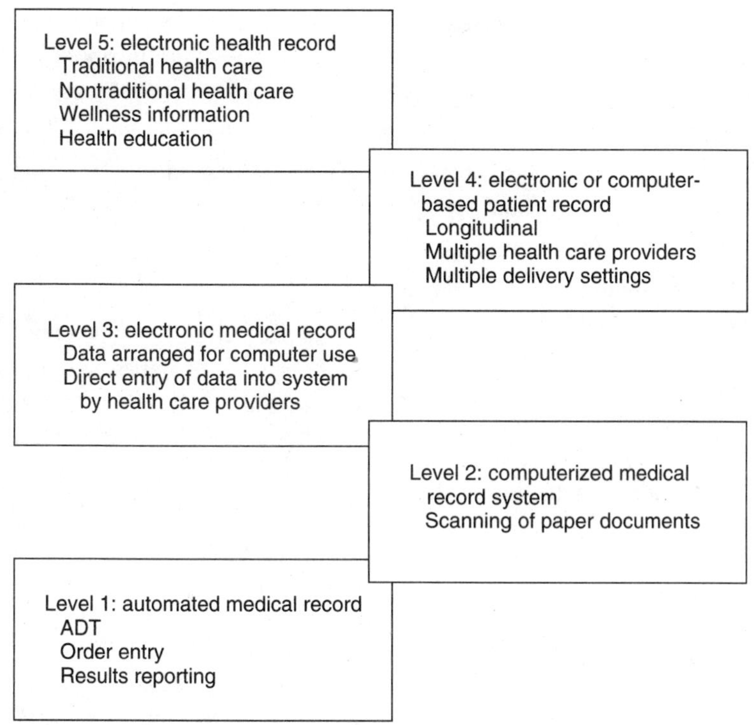

Figure 4. Levels of computerization of patient records. *Source:* P. Waegemann, The five levels of the ultimate electronic health record, *Healthcare Info,* November 1995, pp. 26–35, ©1995.

Level 1: Automated Medical Record

This level involves automating the paper-based medical record. ADT systems, digital dictation systems, patient accounting linked to clinical data, order entry, and results reporting are examples of automated processes in a hospital environment. These processes are parallel to the paper-based system in that the paper-based medical record is unchanged by these systems.

Level 2: Computerized Medical Record System

In Level 2, a system is developed to digitize the medical record, address record storage issues, and create an electronically available medical record. This is done by scanning paper-based documents into a document imaging system. This process offers a method to transfer the medical record to a paperless format using technology currently available.

Level 3: Electronic Medical Record

As an upgraded version of the computerized medical record, the electronic medical record has the same information as the paper-based medical record, but the data are rearranged for computer use. The success or failure of the electronic medical record hinges on two system capabilities: user friendliness and acceptance, and system design and functionality. Electronic medical record systems must fuse these two capabilities if they are to be attractive enough to persuade caregivers to change from traditional modes of handling patient information to computerized systems.

Level 4: Electronic or Computer-Based Patient Record

The patient record contains a broader scope of information than the medical record. The electronic patient record provides information about the patient from a variety of health care providers across the continuum of care. With patient permission, the patient record can become a longitudinal survey of data and outcomes throughout a lifetime. Several prerequisites must exist before movement to Level 4. These include the development of a system to identify patient information available nationwide or worldwide; the incorporation of data from multiple sources and settings into an electronic patient record; the standardization of terminology, data sets, and structures; and the agreement on security issues such as access, control, electronic signature, and data integrity.

Level 5: Electronic Health Record

The word "patient" conjures up images of treatment in a traditional health care setting. However, the electronic health record would also capture nontraditional health care, such as acupuncture, wellness information, and health education. The electronic health record would be maintained by the patient, who controls his or her health information in cooperation with the health care provider.

• • •

As the demand for outcomes data steadily increases, information technology is rapidly growing to keep pace. Health care providers must become knowledgeable in the information technology movement to develop systems that are appropriate for health care and use data to manage outcomes. Health care providers must access, analyze, and develop practice patterns from the outcomes measures and data available in various information systems. The future of health care and information technology is exciting as well as challenging. With information technology linked with outcomes management, best practice patterns can be achieved while meeting the expectations of payers and patients.

REFERENCES

1. Collen, M. A brief historical overview of hospital information system (HIS) evolution in the United States. *International Journal of Biomedical Comp.* 1991;29:169–89.
2. Singarella, T. Health informatics and biocommunications. *Journal of Biocommunication.* 1991;18:12–13.
3. Rosen, A., and Peterson, E. Influence of data sources on outcomes research. *Journal of Outcomes Management.* 1994;1:9–14.
4. Aller, K. Information systems for the outcomes movement. *Journal of Healthcare Information Management Systems Society.* 1996;10:37–52.
5. Mertens, R., and Cuesters, W. Quality assurance, infection surveillance, and hospital information systems: avoiding the Bermuda triangle. *Statistics Hospital Epidemiology.* 1994;15: 203–09.
6. Baud, R., Rassinoux, A., and Scherrer, J. Natural language processing and semantical representation of medical texts. *Methods in Infectious Medicine.* 1992;31:117–25.
7. Dujols, P., Aubas, P., Baylon, C., and Gremy, F. Morphosemantic analysis and translation of medical compound terms. *Methods in Infectious Medicine.* 1991;30:30–35.
8. Houston, S., Cole, L., Wojner, A., and Luquire, R. What is outcomes management? In: S. Houston, L. Cole, A. Wojner, eds. *Outcomes Management: A User's Guide.* 2nd ed. Houston, TX: St. Luke's Episcopal Hospital; 1996:1–20.
9. O'Desky, R., Ball, M., and Ball, E. Computers in health care for the 21st century. *Methods in Infectious Medicine.* 1990;29:158–161.
10. Mathews, P., Carter, N., and Smith, K. Using data to measure outcomes. *Healthcare Information Management Systems Society.* 1996;10:3–16.
11. Waegemann, P. The five levels of the ultimate electronic health record. *Healthcare Information.* November 1995;26–35.

5

Nursing Care Is Managed Care

Essentials for Successful Patient Care Redesign

Diane Schaming Hupp

As managed care continues to penetrate the health care industry, organizations struggle to deliver quality care in a more cost effective manner. Many hospitals have redesigned their patient care delivery systems to include the use of unlicensed assistive personnel (UAP) to reduce costs and allow nurses to focus more of their time on direct patient care. As the use of UAPs increases, nurses must learn the skill of delegation, a skill that will play a key role in the successful implementation of new patient care delivery systems.

A SIGNIFICANT SHIFT IN PRACTICE

At Children's Hospital of Pittsburgh (CHP), the majority of nurses who have worked during the past decade have practiced primary nursing. Working without assistive personnel, they have been responsible for *all* patient care, including nursing assistant-type tasks. Our implementation of a new patient care delivery system includes the introduction of assistive roles named Patient Care Partners (PCPs). Nurses at CHP are learning to partner with and delegate to this new level of caregiver to accomplish their work.

For some of the nurses at CHP, the shift from working solely with Registered Nurses (RNs) to working with a team including PCPs has been challenging for the following reasons:

- Nurses are accustomed to providing individual holistic nursing care.
- At times, nurses have been reluctant to relinquish their traditional tasks.
- It takes time for nurses to feel comfortable that patient care can be delivered in a timely, accurate manner through the use of other caregivers.
- Nurses lack of comfort may stem from fear of having never worked within a partnership.
- Everyone has to recognize that, due to external driving forces, the organization of health care, including nursing, has to change.

THE CHALLENGE OF CHANGE

Prior to the redesign of the new care delivery system, individual nurses were responsible for accomplishing all patient care required during each shift. CHP, like other pediatric organizations, has consistently used a higher ratio of professional staff. In part, this has been due to the special care and attention required by a pediatric population vs. an adult one. Under the new care delivery system, the percent of RN staff now ranges from 65 percent to 90 percent on the different units dependent on the acuity of the patients.

This shift in the skill mix shed a dramatic new light on nursing and care delivery. It

Aspen's Advisor for Nurse Executives, 1997, 13(3): 7–8
© 1997 Aspen Publishers, Inc.

meant changing the way that nurses think and provide care. For many nurses, this has been a positive change. For others it has taken longer to become comfortable delegating tasks they are accustomed to performing themselves.

PRE-IMPLEMENTATION WORK

The planning process for Phase 1 for the new patient care model began just one year ago. Phase 1 included two acute care inpatient units and the Same Day Surgery unit. The first unit implemented the new model in April 1996. The factors that required most nurses' time and commitment were recruiting the PCPs and training all staff.

Hiring

To build initial trust with the new caregivers, it was important to have the RNs involved in the hiring of UAP. A panel of three or four staff nurses interviewed each of the PCP applicants. The nurses were particularly interested in the experience and skills the PCP would bring to the job, as well as their demeanor. Would this candidate fit with the team?

The manager met with the nurses' panel to obtain their input on specific qualities and questions that would assist them in their decision making, as well as to review specific questions to avoid in regards to legal issues. Together they developed an interview tool, which included the specific questions each candidate would be asked to maintain consistency during the interview process. Following the interviews, the staff nurses rated each candidate. Decisions were made by consensus of the panel and ultimately, recommendations were made to the manager.

The outcome of recruitment was excellent—nurses having selected their own partners. The process was lengthy, including five full days of interviewing to hire fifteen PCPs. There was an abundance of quality candidates. RN involvement was essential.

Education

After completing the recruitment process, education was a priority. The nurses attended a class entitled "Leadership in Patient Care Coordination: Delegating to PCPs". The objective of the class was to educate the nurses regarding delegation principles. For many nurses at CHP, this was a new and challenging skill. During the training, appropriate communication methods for effective delegation were addressed, as well as strategies to assist the nurses in coordinating their patient care responsibilities. Nurses were given case scenarios to practice appropriate delegation, decision-making, negotiating, and conflict resolution with their new team members. (See Box.)

Case Scenario for Delegation Training

Mary, an experienced nurse on the surgical unit, has been assigned five busy patients. She is partnered with Tracey, a PCP who was hired four months ago. Mary is having difficulty completing her work before the shift ends. She becomes frustrated when she notices Tracey sitting and chatting at the desk while she is providing care at a constant and busy pace.

Staff nurses were requested to answer and discuss among their peers the following questions:

a. How should Mary address the situation?
b. Can Tracey refuse to take on additional work?
c. What process should Mary use to determine what tasks she could delegate to Tracey?

Several nurses communicated uncertainty with delegating to the new partners. In particular, issues were raised regarding the nurse's legal responsibility for the PCPs' actions. It was helpful to have our legal counsel present for part of the day to assist in addressing these concerns.

Nurses were also required to attend internal educational programs to learn the roles and responsibilities of the different caregivers. A detailed job description and a skill competency list were reviewed with the nurses. The manager of the first unit to implement the new model thoroughly reviewed the scope of the PCP role. It was important for the nurses to understand clearly the organization's policies and procedures regarding the scope of the PCPs, since this may vary from one organization to another.

WHERE ARE WE TODAY?

After one year, nurses are delegating at different levels due to their own abilities and comfort with the skill. Some have learned very well, demonstrating excellent delegation abilities. They have established trust with their PCPs and view them as competent caregivers essential in helping the nurses to complete their daily assignments.

The nurses who delegate well also demonstrate excellent leadership skills. They are able to prioritize, problem solve, and make decisions appropriately to ensure the best possible patient care. They understand the organization's policies and procedures regarding the PCPs' scope of practice. These nurses have made the successful transition to their new role of managing, supervising, and delegating patient care responsibilities.

For other nurses, the transition has not been as easy. Some initial difficulties experienced by nurses who struggled with delegation skills included poor communication, unwillingness to relinquish certain tasks, lack of confidence in the PCPs, inability to confront peers, and a lack of leadership skills. We continually strive to assist nurses who are experiencing difficulty with their new roles. Weekly staff meetings are held to discuss general delegation issues and provide time for staff to encourage and support their peers.

EVALUATION OF PCPS

Evaluations provided a means for the nurses to articulate expectations of their partners, provide constructive feedback, and develop plans for successful care delivery as a partnership. Each PCP was evaluated by his or her staff nurse preceptor mid-orientation (at one month) and at the completion of orientation.

The evaluation consisted of a verbal and written discussion of the PCP's performance during orientation, including clinical competence, behavioral characteristics, initiative, receptiveness to delegated tasks, and teamwork. The staff nurse and PCP in collaboration with the nurse educator were responsible for developing goals to assist in the PCP's development over the next six months.

STRATEGIES FOR SUCCESS

We have found the following factors invaluable in developing the nurse's skill of delegating when redesigning patient care delivery systems:

- Ensure adequate educational training for all staff. Both the RN and UAP staff should attend training that includes clear role definitions, scope of practices, and principles of effective delegation.
- Involve RNs as much as possible from the beginning of the redesign. RNs should be a key in the selection of the UAP as well as in the evaluation process.

- Communicate clearly that the delivery method of nursing care is changing. Nurses must accept the change and be willing to relinquish appropriate tasks to be successful in the new care delivery system.
- Support and reward nurses who are successful delegators. Recognize and encourage those nurses who demonstrate consistent and effective delegation measures with the UAP.
- Realize that some nurses may be unable to function in the new care model due to lack of delegation skills. Although delegation is a skill that takes time and practice, realize that some nurses may be unable to practice successfully in the new model. Each organization will need to address the roles within their organization of those nurses who are not successful with the new patient care delivery system.

It is an organization's responsibility to prepare its nurses for the inevitable changes in patient care delivery systems. However, nurses must be committed and willing to learn the new skills and shift their nursing paradigms for the redesign to be successful. Successful implementation will ensure that health care organizations will continue to provide cost-effective, quality care.

Staff Mix Models: Complementary or Substitution Roles for Nurses

Linda McGillis Hall

Health care reform has had a marked effect on the practice of nursing in hospital environments. This is particularly evident when examining the staff mix models employed for the delivery of patient care. Tremendous shifts in staff mix have occurred in hospitals with the increased use of unlicensed assistive personnel as part of the care delivery team. These shifts represent a significant change in the level of care provider participating in the patient care process. While a number of models exist, it is not clear whether they are intended to complement the nursing role or be a substitute for it. Furthermore, measures of the effectiveness of these staff mix models on outcomes of care are unclear. The overall impact of staff mix models on the patient and the health care system is therefore not known.

EVOLUTION OF STAFF MIX MODELS

Background

Staff mix models are a component of health human resource planning where the overall goal is to achieve the most effective, flexible, and cost-effective use of health personnel. A wide array of staff mixes and models for staff mix are described in the literature, although few are empirically based. Staff mix is the combination or grouping of different categories of workers that is employed for the provision of care to patients. An all-registered nurse (RN) staff is one example of staff mix. Other mixes may include combinations of RNs, registered practical nurses, licensed practical nurses (LPNs), health care aides, nurse aides, and unlicensed assistive personnel or multiskilled workers. The range of possible categories of worker is quite broad, both in the literature and in health care practice environments.

There is no question that the most prevalent influence on staff mix has been financial. Globally, a tremendous shift in the economy toward fiscal restraint has occurred in the past decade. Because of their 24-hour presence with patients, nurses are often considered a large labor source in health care organizations, perceived as costly rather than cost-effective.[1,2] Another factor contributing to the development of these models was a desire by nurse administrators to redesign the way nurses performed their work. The aim of re-

This article is based, in part, on the author's doctoral dissertation for the Graduate Department of Nursing Science at the University of Toronto, in partial fulfillment of the requirements for the Doctor of Philosophy degree. It is part of the author's doctoral research, which was generously funded by the Canadian Nurses' Foundation, the National Health and Development Research Program in Canada, and Sigma Theta Tau International Honour Society for Nurses.

Nurs Admin Q, 1997, 21(2): 31–39
© 1997 Aspen Publishers, Inc.

design was often to increase the time spent by nurses in "direct" patient care activities and relieve them of tasks that could be performed by less skilled workers. And finally, the quality of patient care had been identified as an important aspect of patient care delivery models.

The staff mix models present in the literature can be divided into two groups based on their relationship to the nursing role. "Complementary" models use unlicensed workers as ancillary or support staff for nurses, usually to perform nonnursing tasks. On the other hand, "substitution" models use these unlicensed workers as ancillary support with responsibilities that include some nursing care or care functions traditionally provided by other health care practitioners. In addition, blends or mixes of these two groupings appear to exist.

Staff mix models appear to have evolved in the 1980s in the United States as a result of the nursing shortage. While there is evidence in the literature of an examination of staff mix in countries such as the United Kingdom and Australia, by far the majority of work has been done in the United States. The initial models that resulted from the nursing shortage were "nurse extenders" designed to complement the role of nurse.[3–7] In the 1990s, as the nursing shortage was resolved, health care spending has become an issue. Staff mix models were examined as a potential means for health care administrators to explore more efficient care, since existing models for nurse staffing were not perceived to be cost-effective. What has emerged from these initial models could be called substitution models or hybrid blends of these.

Staff mix models are often linked to reengineered work as the product of a redesign process.[8–14] *Work redesign* is a term broadly used to describe the process an organization uses to examine how work is being carried out, analyze how efficient and effective this is, and alter it to best meet the needs of the organization and the customer. The language associated with redesign has become quite common in health care today, including the concepts of reengineering, retooling, reconceptualizing, restructuring, reworking, and reconfiguring of the work processes. Many of the methods that have emerged as a result of work redesign in health care focus on patient-centered care and several are linked to the concept of "multiskilling."[15–20]

Multiskilling is a phenomenon that is not unique to nursing and health care. Multiskilling evolved in the late 1980s and early 1990s as corporations downsized. The process involves staff developing knowledge and taking on roles beyond those of their specialty area.[15] Examples exist outside of nursing where jobs are merged and one person picks up some of the functions of another role, creating an employee with multiple skills in a variety of functions.

Some confusion stems from the use of the term *multiskilling* in nursing. First, we see nurses multiskilling, developing knowledge beyond that of their original specialty. This may be attributed in part to changes in patterns of hospitalization and shortened lengths of stay for patients. Cross-training between specialties can also be seen, with one of the most prevalent illustrations occurring in labor and delivery and postpartum areas.[21] Examples of cross-training have also been described in critical care and emergency nursing. Donlevy and Pietruch describe a model where acute care nursing staff are cross-trained to provide home care.[22] The paradox for nursing lies not in the fact that nurses are cross-trained, nor that they are multiskilling. The confusion comes from the emergence of a new worker, usually envisioned in a support role for the nurse, that is also labelled as a "multiskilled" worker. In the nursing literature, unlike any other field, multiskilling has taken on two forms.

Complementary Models

Beginning in 1988, complementary models for the nurse using a nurse extender model are described in several publications.[3–6] The intent of each of these models was that the extender, often categorized as a unit assistant, would remain focused on environmental functions, freeing the nurse to spend more time on direct patient care. The role of the extenders often included housekeeping and stocking of supplies. It is of interest to note that even the early models stemming from the nursing shortage identified that some attention was being paid to cost savings.

In the nurse extender model described by Eastaugh and Regan-Donovan, the authors describe a small decrease in RN staffing numbers as nurse extenders are introduced.[3,4] Associated savings in salary costs are also projected with this change. To a lesser extent, a similar pattern can be seen in the model described by Harrison Powers, Dickey, and Ford, where an RN position is converted into two nursing assistant or extender positions on the pilot study unit.[5] One of the interesting points noted by these authors is that the costs associated with the use of overtime, sick time, and on-call increased after the nurse extender role was implemented, particularly within the nursing assistant or extender staff group.[5] At the same time, the actual time nurses spent on direct care and care planning did not increase. This was attributed to an increase in the nurse–patient ratios from 1:4 to 1:7 with a corresponding increase in patient responsibility.

While nurse extenders were integrated as support staff for the nurse, subsequent changes were usually made to the assignment levels. Another nurse extender model developed by Manthey describes "partners-in-practice."[6,7] These practice partners or technical assistants work with an experienced nurse, with the nurse making decisions about the activities the practice partner is able to perform. A partnership agreement was signed and partners work the same shifts as one another. Initial experience with this model indicated that each partner team could handle a workload comparable to that of two nurses, amounting to substantial savings in salary dollars.

The ProACT model was developed by Tonges in 1989.[23,24] ProACT is an acronym for "professionally advanced care team," a model that includes two distinct nursing roles as well as expanded roles for clinical and nonclinical support staff at the unit level. Several articles have been published by this researcher and her associates as they evaluated the model over time.[10,13,23,24] The model was designed to be budget neutral, such that no new costs would be incurred to implement it. In critical care, the original plans to modify RN staffing were not realized.[13] Designed with a mix of acute and semiacute patients intended for patient care assignments, the ProACT model had to be adjusted to accommodate for a shift to heavier patient acuity. This shift left fewer less-acute patients to be assigned, increasing the need for RN care providers. The authors suggest that the model itself may also have contributed to this occurrence. As nursing staff developed enhanced skills they were able to move the less-acute patient through the system faster, creating a confound in the model.

Blended Staff Mix Models

Since the early 1990s there has been tremendous growth in the number and variation of staff mix models described in the literature. A report from the American Hospital

Association in 1991 identified that 97 percent of its member hospitals employed some form of nurse extender.[25] However, as different staff mix models continue to emerge, one might challenge whether the roles created are complementary to that of the RN.

Some staff mix models could be considered as "blends" of complementary and substitution roles. Although designed to create roles to work along with that of the nurse, they often result in a reduction of nursing positions. This contributes to the perception within the nursing profession that unlicensed workers are being substituted for the RN. In fact, data presented in the literature on staff mix models often support this contention.

Abts and associates describe a pilot study where the roles of LPNs and nurse's assistants were expanded in a modular care delivery model in an Iowa hospital.[9] A 17 percent decrease in the number of RNs employed was achieved and an annual savings for the change in staff mix was predicted to be $60,000 for the unit piloting the study. Similarly, Davis describes a three-year summary of a nurse extender model developed in 1990 in an Alabama hospital that used nursing students and nursing assistants as "clinical assistants."[2] Eight RN positions were converted into 24 clinical assistant positions. Work sampling data collected six months following implementation of the model indicate that both RNs and LPNs showed an increase in time spent on direct nursing care activities such as assessments, teaching, and support. The $17,160 reported annual savings realized result from a decrease in education costs as new nursing staff were recruited from the pool of clinical assistants requiring less orientation. Hesterly and Robinson describe the introduction of the patient care assistant role in a California hospital to defer the costs associated with using replacement nurses from outside the hospital.[26] The authors indicate that $1.3 million in savings is projected in the first year.

Mularz and associates also developed a staff mix model using patient care assistants in a New Jersey hospital.[27] Here, the LPN and nurse aide roles were converted into patient care assistants (PCAs) and the number of RN positions was decreased. The authors note that the ratio of nurses to assistant roles went from 2:1 to a single nurse for every 3 PCAs. O'Brien and Stepura describe the development of a staff mix model for a rural hospital in Maryland incorporating a partnership comprising a professional nurse and members of a dyad that includes a nurse technician, supported by a patient care assistant, and auxillary workers.[28] A 12 percent reduction in RN working time is reported, although overall expenses in the start-up year were increased by the implementation of additional nonprofessional workers.

A study conducted by Pearson and Schwartz in 1990 in an Illinois hospital using certified nursing assistants and nurses in the partners-in-practice model reported up to a 50 percent decrease in the percentage of RNs employed in the staff mix on one of the six units described in the study.[29] A decrease in hours per patient day was noted on five of the units, and a total of $832,688 in actual savings realized year-to-date from a target of $1,119,873. Further savings in orientation costs were projected, and limited change in the amount of sick time, overtime, and use of agency staff was noted. These models, although designed to provide complementary roles for the nurse, all demonstrate similar findings in that the registered nurse staff level is decreased.

Rizzo and colleagues describe a redesigned care delivery model developed on an orthopaedic unit in a Connecticut community hospital.[14] Changes to the staff mix included an increase in the number of ancillary staff from 29 to 43 percent and a decrease in professional nursing staff from 71 to 57 percent. Cost savings associated with this staff mix change on one unit amounted to $30,000. Smeltzer and colleagues present findings on a restructuring initiative from a Florida hospital.[11] In an effort to increase nursing time spent on direct patient care and reallocate nonnursing tasks to less skilled workers, a patient care technician role was developed along with a decentralized housekeeping role. The staff mix model resulted in a 20 percent decrease in total RN positions for a cost saving of $1,856,454 to the hospital nursing budget.

A report of role restructuring in another Florida hospital conducted in 1992 is described by Smith and associates.[12] The model, entitled "Patient Care Management Model," includes a move to managed care and case management. Changes to staff mix included a 4 percent decrease in RN positions, a 21 percent decrease in LPN positions, a 1 percent increase in support staff, and the development of a new role—an extender nursing assistant role that comprised 23 percent of the staff mix. Potential savings of $200,000 were projected with this new model.

Substitution Staff Mix Models

More recent models appear to extend the idea of a "blend" into what can be interpreted as "substitution" for the RN. It is important to note that the authors do not describe these as models intended to substitute for the nursing role, although their articulation of the roles calls this into question. Fritz and Cheeseman describe a nurse extender staff mix model employed for an intensive care unit in Texas.[30] In this model, patient care specialty technicians (PCSTs) were employed to perform some of the care requirements for the unit. Their responsibilities included assisting with activities of daily living, maintaining documentation, completing routine vital signs, conducting intakes and outputs, weighing patients, performing phlebotomy, and providing postmortem care. Unit aide positions were eliminated and vacant nursing positions were realigned to create these new roles. Many of the new positions were filled by the unit aides downsized out of their jobs, and the staff mix for this unit moved from 88 to 75 percent RN. PCSTs received on-site training for their new roles. The authors are estimating a $1 million saving along with the elimination of the use of agency nurses, overtime, and premium pay for regular nursing staff.

Similarly, Kostovich, et al. describe the adaptation of a clinical technician role as part of a patient-focused care delivery model on a medical unit in an Illinois hospital.[31] The role outlined for the clinical technicians included performing venous and arterial bloodwork, doing central venous line dressings, performing electrocardiograms and Holter monitoring, performing oxygen monitoring and oxygen rounds, and conducting pulse oximetry, incentive breathing exercises, ambulation of patients, and range of motion and other exercises with patients. Phlebotomists were hired into this role and provided with in-house training in the skills required to perform in the role. A total of 5.5 positions from the nursing unit were converted to 7 clinical technicians while 19 positions were to be transferred in from the labs, respiratory therapy, physiotherapy, cardiology, and nursing to cover the $490,000 cost to make this initiative budget neutral. This model provides an example of multiskilling across specialty areas.

Lengacher and colleagues describe the implementation of a "multiskilled technician" as a partner in patient care.[32] This multiskilled technician functions under the direction of the RN and performs select nursing care activities and services or treatments from other specialties. The role includes performing 12-lead electrocardiograms; applying, recording, and removing telemetry; recognizing abnormal cardiac rhythms; drawing blood specimens; setting up oxygen therapy; assisting patients with incentive spirometry; providing basic mobility for physical therapy activities; stocking supplies; cleaning equipment; and providing basic nursing care such as taking vital signs, assisting with patient hygiene and activities of daily living, changing dressings, and ambulating patients. The authors report that there was a decrease in the number of nurses employed using this model as it is aimed at budget neutrality. It is of interest to note that all of the latter "substitution models" label the new worker as a "technician" and the scope of their practice is multiskilled across a wide array of specialty areas.

EVALUATION OF STAFF MIX MODELS

Many of the staff mix models described in the literature have not been evaluated in an empirical manner. However, some authors have attempted to demonstrate the impact of the staff mix model on outcomes. The two most prevalent outcomes that have been examined are the overall quality of care and patient satisfaction.

Patient Satisfaction

In terms of patient satisfaction, Bostrom and Zimmerman found no significant changes in the level of patient satisfaction when the model of staff care delivery was changed to include certified nursing assistants.[8] These authors reported that patients were overwhelmingly positive about the change. Similarly, Brett and Tonges found that patient satisfaction remained stable when measured at three intervals, before, during, and after implementation of the ProACT model, despite markedly fewer RNs being used in the staff mix model.[10] Fritz and Cheeseman described an increase in patient satisfaction with the implementation of the PCST and attributed this to a better explanation of tasks and procedures to patients.[30] Kostovich and associates reported a 7 percent increase in the patient satisfaction ratings for overall nursing care following the implementation of the clinical technician role.[31] Mularz and colleagues reported a 10 percent decrease in negative responses following the implementation of the patient care assistant model.[27] Neidlinger and others reported a slight improvement in patient satisfaction with nursing care after the introduction of unlicensed workers.[33]

Quality of Care

Bostrom and Zimmerman found no significant change in the frequency of incident reports following the introduction of certified nursing assistants as part of the staff mix model.[8] Similarly, Brett and Tonges reported no change in the number of incidents per patient day or infection rates with the implementation of multiple care provider roles in the ProACT model.[10] Fritz and Cheeseman describe a positive trend in pressure ulcer management and patient teaching following the implementation of the PCST role.[30] Mularz and colleagues described a 10 percent improvement in medication errors, decubitus ulcers, and patient falls following the development of the patient care assistant role.[27] However, Neidlinger and associates identified an unspecified decline in quality indicators with the implementation of unlicensed personnel as part of a new care delivery model.[33] The authors questioned whether this result was real or a measurement artifact.

While these findings suggest some evidence that patient satisfaction and quality of care are not at risk with the implementation of these staff mix models, they need to be interpreted with a degree of caution. Few models have been examined over time using empirical methods. Some provide little evidence that the researchers controlled for other factors that may have contributed to the findings. While we know for certain that a range of staff mix models exists in our practice environments, we know very little of their true impact on the cost and quality of care.

Several concerns with the staff mix models that exist today are important to consider. First, breaking up the work of nursing and parceling it out to a variety of unlicensed support workers takes patient care back to a "task-based" focus. This focus concentrates on skills and tasks rather than the cognitive and conceptual practice of nursing—the knowledge work of nursing. Second, cost constraints in health care are currently driving the implementation of these models, and the realistic result is a decrease in the number of nurses being employed as part of the staff mix. Nurse researchers and administrators do not yet know what that means for the patient or consumer. Often the language being used to describe these models reflects the financial forces that are driving their implementation.[2,3,25,26] Most stem from the nursing shortage of the late 1980s and the financial constraints in health care that emerged thereafter.

• • •

What is most disturbing about the field of study linked to staff mix models is the lack of evaluation of existing models while new models emerge rapidly. Many of the reports in the literature are anecdotal discussions of the models that have been initiated, providing descriptive comments from staff and patients. While the "structure" and "process" analysis of staff mix models does exist in the literature, very few build on previous models or on research from these, or reliably test outcomes. It is important for nurse leaders and administrators to realize that the fact that such models exist in practice and in the literature does not mean they produce what they were actually designed to do. Without solid evaluation of staff mix models one simply cannot know if they are cost-effective, what kind of impact they have on the quality of patient care, and how satisfied consumers and care providers are with them. At this point in the midst of health care reform, we seem to be in the middle of a somewhat rampant development of staff mix models.

REFERENCES

1. P.A. Prescott, "Nursing: An Important Component of Hospital Survival under a Reformed Health Care System," *Nursing Economics* 11, no. 4 (1993): 192–99.
2. B. Davis, "Effective Utilization of a Scarce Resource: RNs," *Nursing Management* 25, no. 2 (1994): 78, 80.
3. S.R. Eastaugh and M. Regan-Donovan, "Nurse Extenders Offer a Way To Trim Staff Expenses," *Healthcare Financial Management* 44 (1990): 58–62.
4. S.R. Eastaugh, "Hospital Nursing Technical Efficiency: Nurse Extenders and Enhanced Productivity," *Hospital and Health Services Administration* 35, no. 4 (1990): 561–73.
5. P. Harrison Powers, et al., "Evaluating an RN/ Co-worker Model," *Journal of Nursing Administration* 20, no. 3 (1990): 11–15.
6. M. Manthey, "Practice Partnerships: The Newest Concept in Care Delivery," *Journal of Nursing Administration* 19, no. 2 (1989): 33–35.
7. M. Manthey, "Primary Practice Partners (A Nurse Extender System)," *Journal of Nursing Administration* 19, no. 3 (1988): 58–59.
8. J. Bostrom and J. Zimmerman, "Restructuring Nursing for a Competitive Health Care Environment," *Nursing Economics* 11, no. 1 (1993): 35–41, 54.

9. D. Abts, et al., "Redefining Care Delivery: A Modular System," *Nursing Management* 25, no. 2 (1994): 40–43, 46.
10. J.L. Brett and M.C. Tonges, "Restructured Patient Care Delivery: Evaluation of the ProACT Model," *Nursing Economics* 8, no. 1 (1990): 308–16.
11. C.H. Smeltzer, et al., "Work Restructuring: The Process of Decision Making," *Nursing Economics* 11, no. 4 (1993): 215–22, 258.
12. G.B. Smith, et al., "Role Restructuring: Nurse, Case Manager, and Educator," *Nursing Administration Quarterly* 19, no. 1 (1994): 21–32.
13. J. Ritter and M.C. Tonges, "Work Redesign in High-Intensity Environments: ProACT for Critical Care," *Journal of Nursing Administration* 21, no. 12 (1991): 26–35.
14. J.A. Rizzo, et al., "Facilitating Care Delivery Redesign Using Measures of Using Culture and Work Characteristics," *Journal of Nursing Administration* 24, no. 5 (1994): 32–37.
15. J.P. Lathrop, *Restructuring Health Care: The Patient-Focused Paradigm* (San Francisco: Jossey-Bass, Publishers, 1993).
16. K. Marshall, "Multiskilling: Re-engineering Work Process," *Healthcare Management Forum* 8, no. 2 (1995): 32–36.
17. E.C. McGuire, et al., "Design and Implementation of a Health Care Technician Program," *Journal of Nursing Care Quality* 9, no. 3 (1995): 20–28.
18. J. O'Malley and D. Serpico-Thompson, "Redesigning Roles for Patient-Centered Care," *Journal of Nursing Administration* 22, no. 7/8 (1992): 30–34.
19. D.G. Vaughan, et al., "Utilization and Management of Multiskilled Health Practitioners in U.S. Hospitals," *Hospitals and Health Services Administration* 36, no. 3 (1991): 397–419.
20. P.M. Watson, et al., "Operational Restructuring: A Patient-Focused Approach," *Nursing Administration Quarterly* 16, no. 1 (1991): 45–52.
21. S. Crissman and N. Jelsma, "Cross-Training: Practicing Effectively on Two Levels," *Nursing Management* 21, no. 3 (1990): 64A, 64D, 64H.
22. J. Donlevy and B. Pietruch, "The Connection Delivery Model: Reengineering Nursing to Provide Care Across the Continuum," *Nursing Administration Quarterly* 20, no. 3 (1996): 73–78.
23. M.C. Tonges, "Redesigning Hospital Nursing Practice: The Professionally Advanced Care Team (ProACT) Model, Part I," *Journal of Nursing Administration* 19, no. 7 (1989): 31–38.
24. M.C. Tonges, "Redesigning Hospital Nursing Practice: The Professionally Advanced Care Team (ProACT) Model, Part 2," *Journal of Nursing Administration* 19, no. 9 (1989): 19–22.
25. L.R. Merker, et al., *1990 Utilization of Nurse Extenders* (Chicago: American Hospital Association, 1991).
26. S.C. Hesterly and M. Robinson, "Alternative Caregivers: Cost-effective Utilization of RNs," *Nursing Administration Quarterly* 14, no. 3 (1990): 18–23.
27. L.A. Mularz, et al., "Theory M. A Restructuring Process," *Nursing Management* 26, no. 1 (1995): 49–52.
28. Y.M. O'Brien and B.A. Stepura, "Designing Roles for Assistive Personnel in a Rural Hospital," *Journal of Nursing Administration* 22, no. 10 (1992): 34–37.
29. M.A. Pearson and P. Schwartz, "Primary Practice Partners: Analysis of Cost and Staff Satisfaction," *Nursing Economics* 9, no. 3 (1991): 201–4.
30. D.J. Fritz and S. Cheeseman, "Blueprint for Integrating Nurse Extenders in Critical Care," *Nursing Economics* 12, no. 6 (1994): 327–31, 326.
31. C.T. Kostovich, et al., "The Clinical Technician as a Member of the Patient-Focused Healthcare Delivery Team," *Journal of Nursing Administration* 24, no. 12 (1994): 32–38.
32. C.A. Lengacher, et al., "Redesigning Nursing Practice. The Partners-in-Patient Care Model," *Journal of Nursing Administration* 23, no. 12 (1993): 31–37.
33. S.H. Neidlinger, et al., "Incorporating Nursing Assistive Personnel into a Nursing Professional Practice Model," *Journal of Nursing Administration* 23, no. 3 (1993): 29–37.

6

Nursing Ethics in a Managed Care System

The Impact of Ethical Climate on Job Satisfaction of Nurses

Jacob Joseph and Satish P. Deshpande

Increased government intervention, pressure from insurance companies, and competition have forced many hospitals to improve services and lower prices.[1,2] Hospitals are also striving to increase their efficiency to buffer themselves against the possible adverse effects of health care reform. Many hospitals are targeting efficiency of nurses since they account for a major proportion of the labor expenses.[3]

The American Hospital Association reports that while the nursing shortage is easing, inadequate staffing problems continue to exist in selected areas.[4] A major study funded by the Robert Wood Johnson Foundation revealed that nursing staffing shortages had negative implications.[5] Nurses were more rushed, suffered low morale, and produced more strain among coworkers. Patients were not medicated or monitored properly. Psychosocial intervention and paperwork of patients were also affected.

Previous research has also indicated that patients in understaffed hospitals have suffered from complications that could have been prevented by good nursing care.[6] This problem could get more severe in the future in areas of shortage. In addition to the current shortage of selected nurses in certain geographic regions, current workforce trends indicate an increasing overall demand for nurses in hospitals. Next to retail sales, registered nurses are the fastest growing occupation in the United States. Compared to 1990, it is expected that 44 percent more registered nurses will be needed in the year 2005.[7]

Previous studies have shown that low job satisfaction is a major cause of turnover among nurses. In addition, job satisfaction may affect quality of service and organizational commitment.[8,9] This has resulted in an increased emphasis in recent years on studying job satisfaction among nurses.[8,10] The purpose of this article is to examine the impact of various ethical climate types on various facets of job satisfaction of nurses. This thesis is consistent with a recent study on the ethical climate of a large charitable organization that suggested that an organization can influence various facets of job satisfaction of its employees by manipulating the ethical climate of the organization.[11]

Specifically, this article will examine: (a) the ethical climate types present in the hospital; (b) the levels of different facets of job satisfaction and overall job satisfaction; and (c) the influence of different ethical climate types on facets of job satisfaction and overall job satisfaction.

Health Care Manage Rev, 1997, 22(1): 76–81
© 1997 Aspen Publishers, Inc.

THE STUDY

Sample Characteristics and Procedure

The sample for this study consisted of nurses who worked for a large 169-bed non-profit private hospital in the northwestern United States. Surveys were distributed to the nurses at the workplace by a hospital administrator. Participation was voluntary and anonymity was guaranteed. Participants were assured that the hospital would not have any access to the completed survey. The nurses were provided stamped, prepaid envelopes so that they could send the completed surveys directly to the authors. Of the 226 nurses employed by the hospital, 114 returned completed surveys (response rate = 50 percent). An average subject was a 40-year-old married female who has worked for the hospital for nearly 9 years. A hospital administrator indicated that the demographics of our sample were consistent with the overall demographics of nurses in the hospital.

Ethical Climate

The ethical climate of an organization is defined by the shared perception of how ethical issues should be addressed and what is ethically correct behavior. Victor and Cullen[12] used previous work done on ethical theory,[13,14] moral development,[15,16] and sociocultural theories of organizations to develop six climate types (professional, caring, rule oriented, instrumental, efficient, and independent). We adapted items based on these climate types to measure the impact of ethical climate on job satisfaction. Each type was measured using a 4-point Likert scale (1 = mostly false and 4 = mostly true). Therefore, a low score shows the absence of a climate and a high score shows the presence of a climate. The respondents were asked to respond to these questions in terms of how the climate of their hospital actually is and not how they would like the climate to be. The items comprising these scales appear in Appendix A.

According to Table 1, most of the respondents identified the presence of a professional climate (mean = 3.88). This was followed by a rules climate (mean = 3.74), caring climate (mean = 2.84), efficiency climate (mean = 2.73), instrumental climate (mean = 2.24), and independence climate (mean = 1.95). In an analysis not shown here, the intercorrelations among various climate types ranged from –.41 to .65. This is consistent with previous research, which has shown that more than one climate type can exist at the workplace.

Job Satisfaction

The second issue we wanted to examine was the different facets of job satisfaction. Satisfaction with pay, satisfaction with promotion, satisfaction with coworkers, satisfaction with supervisors, and satisfaction with work itself were measured using four items for each facet (see Appendix B). Items used to measure these facets were combined to form a measure of overall job satisfaction. This scale, initially developed by Cellucci and DeVries[18] has been used by various researchers in various fields including business

Table 1 Dimensions of Ethical Climate*

Climate	*Mean*	*Standard Deviation*
1. Professionalism	3.88	.41
2. Caring	2.84	.84
3. Rules	3.74	.56
4. Instrumental	2.24	.87
5. Efficiency	2.73	.84
6. Independence	1.95	.95

*A 4-point Likert scale was used (1 = mostly false and 4 = mostly true).

ethics.[11,14] Each item was measured using a 4-point Likert scale (4 = strongly agree and 1 = strongly disagree). Thus, a low score indicates high dissatisfaction and a high score indicates high satisfaction. Table 2 presents the mean, standard deviation, and the coefficient alpha for overall job satisfaction and each facet of job satisfaction.

Among the various facets of job satisfaction, respondents of this study were most satisfied with their work (mean = 3.18). This was followed by satisfaction with coworkers (mean = 3.06), satisfaction with supervisors (mean = 2.90), satisfaction with pay (mean = 2.74), and satisfaction with promotions (mean = 2.44). The coefficient alpha for these measures were satisfactory and ranged from .60 to .86.

Ethical Climate and Job Satisfaction

The third purpose of this article was to examine the influence of different ethical climate types on various facets of job satisfaction. Table 3 presents correlation and regression results. Since many of the predictors are intercorrelated, it would be premature to draw conclusions from the correlations results. Ordinary least square (OLS) regression procedure provides a stronger test of the impact of ethical climate types on facets of job satisfaction.

Regression analysis indicated that professional, instrumental, and independence climate types had no impact on any facet of job satisfaction or overall job satisfaction of nurses. A caring climate significantly influenced overall job satisfaction and satisfaction with pay and supervisors. Those nurses who believed that their hospital had a rules climate were more satisfied with pay, promotion, and supervisor. A rules climate also had a significant positive impact on overall job satisfaction of nurses. An efficiency climate had a significant negative influence on satisfaction with supervisors. None of the climate types significantly affected work or coworker satisfaction.

IMPLICATIONS AND CONCLUSIONS

The study on which this article is based has some important implications. The results of this study indicate that a hospital can have various types of ethical climates. It also provides support to the thesis that managers may be able to enhance job satisfaction by influencing an organization's ethical climate.

In an analysis not shown here, 36 percent of the nurses reported a relatively high level

Table 2 Means, Standard Deviation, and Coefficient Alpha of Different Facets of Job Satisfaction*

Variable	*Mean*	*Standard Deviation*	*Coefficient Alpha*
Pay satisfaction	2.74	.46	.60
Promotion satisfaction	2.44	.49	.76
Coworker satisfaction	3.06	.46	.77
Supervisor satisfaction	2.90	.66	.86
Work satisfaction	3.18	.49	.73
Overall job satisfaction	2.86	.35	.85

*A 4-point Likert scale was used (1 = strongly disagree and 4 = strongly agree).

Table 3 Correlation and Regression for Facets of Job Satisfaction

	Pay Satisfaction		Promotion Satisfaction		Coworker Satisfaction		Supervisor Satisfaction		Work Satisfaction		Overall Job Satisfaction	
	Corr.	*Beta*	*Corr.*	*Beta*	*Corr.*	*Beta*	*Corr.*	*Beta*	*Corr.*	*Beta*	*Corr.*	*Beta*
1. Professionalism	.02	−.18	.00	−.21	.08	.04	.09	−.14	.12	.03	.10	−.14
2. Caring	.18	.20*	.16	.19	.17	.20	.28**	.24*	.06	.03	.26**	.24*
3. Rules	.16	.34**	.20*	.37**	.09	.07	.23*	.25*	.15	.15	.25*	.34**
4. Instrumental	.09	.19	.03	.20	−.03	.05	−.17	−.05	−.09	.00	−.07	.12
5. Efficiency	−.13	−.18	−.02	−.03	−.17	−.12	−.22*	−.18*	−.16	−.14	−.21*	−.19
6. Independence	.05	.04	.06	.08	.12	.17	−.03	.03	.01	.03	.05	.09
F		2.63*		2.25*		1.66		3.51**		0.95*		3.22**
N		110		108		110		110		112		101

*$p < .05$ (2-tailed test)
**$p \leq .01$ (2-tailed)

of dissatisfaction with supervisors (this information was a combination of "disagree" and "strongly disagree" for the four measures of satisfaction with supervisors). Previous research has shown that productivity declines and turnover increases when nurses are not treated fairly or supported by their supervisors. Undesirable work schedules, lack of autonomy, and lack of input into decision making can affect satisfaction with supervisors. One strategy that has been suggested to address this issue is to formalize a mentoring relationship between younger and older nurses.[8] It is suggested that mentors, by focusing on support intervention efforts in difficult situations may improve nurses' satisfaction with supervision. But this may not work in cases of low-quality supervisors. This can be addressed by training the supervisors or making better selection decisions in the hiring process.

The study also indicated that over 62 percent of the respondents were dissatisfied with promotion opportunities in the hospital. As a part of their reorganization efforts, many hospitals have reduced supervisory and administrative nursing positions. This has limited promotion opportunities for nurses. Many businesses have addressed this issue by forming work teams, giving employees control over their jobs, and even involving them in institutional problem solving. This increases their commitment to the firm and often increases the satisfaction they receive from their existing job. It should also be noted that while reducing the levels of supervisors leads to limited promotion opportunities, it also results in increased autonomy (which might be linked to *higher* job satisfaction).

Nurses reported the presence of various climate types. Professionalism was the most reported climate by nurses (99 percent). Hospital administrators reinforce and support this climate by a code of ethics and company policies that ensure that employees comply with legal and professional standards. But professionalism did not impact any facet of job satisfaction of nurses in this study.

This study also implies that those nurses who believe that their hospital has a caring climate are more satisfied with their pay and supervisors. Hospitals can foster a caring environment by ensuring that the major consideration is what is best for everyone in the hospital. A caring environment also exists in organizations where people look out for each other. Training programs that emphasize utilitarian reasoning can ensure a caring environment.

It is not surprising that an efficiency climate has a significant negative influence on satisfaction with supervisors. An efficiency climate assumes that the major responsibility of each person is to control costs. Typically, the most efficient way is considered as the right way of doing things in such an environment. An environment that emphasizes cost control may have negative implications on quality of care and service provided by nurses. This can adversely affect the relationship between a nurse and his or her supervisor.

A rules climate ensures that all employees strictly obey company regulations, procedures, and policies. This climate emphasizes no favoritism. Results of this study imply that hospital administrators can positively influence pay, promotion, supervisor, and overall job satisfaction of nurses by nurturing such a climate. Forty-three percent of the respondents stated that their hospital had an instrumental climate. An instrumental climate is present in those organizations where people protect their own interests above all else. Strategies that organizations may use to control such a climate include ethics audits and the use of moral character as selection and promotion criteria.[14] For example, while Boeing has an ethics committee, consisting of senior managers, that reports directly to the Board of Directors, Pitney Bowes has an ethical ombudsman and offers training seminars on ethics for employees. Many companies use honesty tests in making personnel decisions.

Thirty-one percent of the respondents reported an independent climate. An independent climate is present in those organizations where employees decide for themselves what is right and wrong. One important conclusion of the study is that an instrumental or an independence climate had no impact on any facet of job satisfaction of nurses.

Future research should examine if the results of this study hold true in other types of hospitals (for example, for-profit and private) in geographical regions other than the northwestern United States. Future research can also examine the success of various strategies used by firms to enforce various culture types in hospitals. Researchers can also examine the impact of ethical climate in hospitals on other factors like organizational commitment and intent to leave.

REFERENCES

1. Giffin, R. "PHOs: The Past or the Future of Physician Alliance Strategies?" *Health Care Strategic Management* 11 (1993): 1.
2. Melnick, G.A., et al. "The Effects of Market Structure and Bargaining Position on Hospital Prices." *Journal of Health Economics* 11 (1992): 217–33.
3. Behner, K.G., et al. "Nursing Resource Management: Analyzing the Relationship Between Costs and Quality in Staffing Decisions." *Health Care Management Review* 15 (1990): 63–71.
4. "Labor Letter: A Nurse Shortage." *The Wall Street Journal*, (5 January 1993): A1: 5.
5. Prescott, P.A., et al. "Nursing Shortage in Transition." *Image* 17 (1985): 127–33.
6. Flood, S.D., and Diers, D. "Nurse Staffing, Patient Outcome and Cost." *Nursing Management* 19 (1988): 34–43.
7. Mathis, R., and Jackson, J. *Human Resource Management*, 7th Edition, West Publishing, 1994.
8. Beall, C., et al. "Job Satisfaction of Public Health Nurses: Is There A Predictable Decline?" *Journal of Health and Human Services Administration* (Fall 1994): 243–60.
9. Curry, J.P., et al. "Determinants of Turnover among Nursing Department Employees." *Research In Nursing Health* 8 (1985): 397–411.
10. Alpander, G.G. "Relationship Between Commitment to Hospital Goals and Job Satisfaction: A Case Study of a Nursing Department." *Health Care Management Review* 15 (1990): 51–62.
11. Deshpande, S.P. "The Impact of Ethical Climate Types on Facets of Job Satisfaction: An Empirical Investigation." *Journal of Business Ethics* (1995).
12. Victor, B., and Cullen, J.B. "A Theory and Measure of

Ethical Climate in Organizations." In *Business Ethics: Research Issues and Empirical Studies*, edited by W.C. Frederick and L.E. Preston. Greenwich, CT: JAI Press, 1990.

13. Fritzche, D.J., and Becker, H. "Linking Management Behavior to Ethical Philosophy." *Academy of Management Journal* 27 (1984): 166–75.
14. Williams, B. *Ethics and the Limits of Philosophy*. Cambridge, MA: Harvard University Press, 1985.
15. Kohlberg, L. "Moral and Religious Education and the Public Schools: A Developmental View." In *Religion and Public Education*, edited by T. Sizer. Boston: Houghton Mifflin, 1967.
16. Kohlberg, L. *The Philosophy of Moral Development*. New York: Harper & Row, 1984.
17. Schneider, B. "Work Climates: An Interactionist Perspective." In *Environmental Psychology: Directions and Perspectives*, edited by N.W. Feimer and E.S. Geller. New York: Praeger, 1983.
18. Cellucci, A.J., and DeVries, D.L. *Measuring Managerial Satisfaction: A Manual for the MJSQ, Technical Report II*. Center for Creative Leadership, 1978.

APPENDIX A

Items Used To Measure Ethical Climate Types

Type	*Item*
a. Professionalism	People are expected to comply with the law and professional standards.
b. Caring	Our major consideration is what is best for everyone in the organization.
c. Rules	Everyone is expected to stick by organization rules and procedures.
d. Instrumental	In this organization, people protect their own interest above all else.
e. Efficiency	The most efficient way is the right way in this organization.
f. Independence	Each person in this organization decides for himself or herself what is right and wrong.

Appendix B

List of Satisfaction Items

Type	Item
1. Satisfaction with pay	1. My organization pays better than competitors. 2. My pay is adequate, considering the responsibilities I have. 3. I am underpaid for what I do.* 4. My fringe benefits are generous.
2. Satisfaction with promotions	1. I do not like the basis on which my organization promotes people.* 2. Promotions are infrequent in my organization.* 3. If I do a good job, I am likely to get promoted. 4. I am satisfied with my rate of advancement.
3. Satisfaction with coworkers	1. The people I work with do not give me enough support.* 2. When I ask people to do things, the job gets done. 3. I enjoy working with the people here. 4. I work with responsible people.
4. Satisfaction with supervisors	1. The managers I work for back me up. 2. The managers I work for are "top notch." 3. My superiors don't listen to me.* 4. My management doesn't treat me fairly.*
5. Satisfaction with work itself	1. My job is interesting. 2. I feel good about the amount of responsibility in my job. 3. I would rather be doing another job.* 4. I get little sense of accomplishment from doing my job.*

*These items are reverse coded.

Dirty Hands: The Underside of Marketplace Health Care

Wanda K. Mohr and Margaret M. Mahon

Advocacy has long been recognized as central to the nurse–patient relationship. Indeed, advocacy is a primary motivating factor for the pursuance of a health care profession. The centrality of advocacy as a moral principle suggests that nurses and other professionals recognize that conflict between professionals involved in patient care and the subordination of the good of the patient to an ethic of utility are real possibilities. In the American Nurses' Association code of ethics,[1] the concept of advocacy is clearly stated in principle 3, in which the professional nurse must "safeguard the client and the public when health care and safety are affected by incompetent, unethical, or illegal practice of any person."[1(p3)] The American Nurses' Association has developed standards of nursing that specify the nurse's responsibility to foster environments that are congruent with therapeutic goals.[2] In addition, various Nurse Practice Acts provide for and set a standard in which registered nurses will report any unethical conduct or exposure of patients to risk of harm.

Legal requirements, standards of practice, and ethical directives exemplify cherished professional ideals and represent "ought" statements that constitute guidelines for registered nurses. These documents were formulated by professional leaders and experts with the assumption that these moral "oughts" could indeed be adhered to autonomously by individual practitioners. Thus, evaluations of ethical practice are based on the premise that individual practitioners can follow these guidelines.

This assumption that nurses can indeed fulfill their professional mandate of advocacy and ethical directives underlies nursing education and practice acts. Little formal consideration is given to the consideration of impossible "oughts" or guidelines that place the professional actor in compromising moral situations. Yet given some of the changes that have taken place in the increasingly complex health care "industry," the question of choices, morals, ethical practice, and the specifics of what individual practitioners and professionals can effect must be reevaluated. This article explores the idea of seemingly unattainable moral behavior, specifically challenged with the moral dilemma that is known as "dirty hands."

DIRTY HANDS

One of the most intractable problems in moral philosophy is how to act morally in apparently immoral situations. Problems of this kind have been labeled by some as "dirty hands" situations, because the circumstances are such that the agent is left with a "moral stain" after taking an action.[3] These situations differ from most moral dilemmas in that those

Adv Nurs Sci, 1996, 19(1): 28–37
© 1996 Aspen Publishers, Inc.

commonly encountered are cases in which there is no right act open to an agent; every option is simply wrong. Dirty hands cases are those instances in which one agent is morally forced by someone else's immorality to do what is, or otherwise would be, wrong. A key element of dirty hands situations is not only the choice between two options, but also the role of immorality in creating situations that necessitate and justify acting with dirty hands. The classic case that is frequently invoked is that described in William Styron's[4] novel *Sophie's Choice*, in which the protagonist is forced by a Nazi officer to choose which of her two children is to be condemned to the gas chamber. She must make the choice or both children will be gassed.

Stocker argued that the justifying or necessitating circumstances of this kind of decision making are themselves immoral and that they are immoral in a particular way: "They are violations of moral autonomy and selfhood—and this in a particularly vicious way. The agent is immorally coerced to take part in, perhaps even to help implement an immoral project."[3(p20)] Thus, two essential features of dirty hands exist: There is a moral conflict, and one is morally compromised in doing what is morally justified or perhaps even required. The concept of dirty hands has particular relevance for the profession of nursing today. In health care environments that are increasingly driven by market forces, unwary practitioners can unwittingly find themselves in circumstances where they must commit acts that can be justified, even obligatory, but are nonetheless wrong.

SITUATIONS—UNFETTERED MARKETPLACES

In the 1960s health care was not called an industry.[5] By the mid- to late 1980s, it had become the nation's largest industry.[6] During that time manufacturing was in decline, and major corporations were moving their operations to developing countries. By 1986 other investor-owned corporations had acquired 20% of acute care hospitals, and in 1990 proprietary chains owned 80% of chronic care facilities.[5] Community pharmacy is likewise corporatized, with more than 70% of the U.S. prescription market being controlled by corporate empires such as Wal-Mart or pharmacy benefits management firms.[7]

This transformation of health care into an enormous industry, which Relman[8] called the "medical industrial complex," has diminished the function of health care encounters as therapeutic and has increased their role as a profitable provision of service. This shift has commodified health care provision, made it into a lucrative business, and subjected it to the same performance standards as any other business enterprise. Health care has entered the brand name era. Various organizations compete to attract patients to a logo or image in much the same way that computer and soap companies attract their clients. Health services are now "product lines," administrators seek to "corner markets," and faceless investors look for return on equity based on the profitable manipulation of the interaction between the health care provider and the health care consumer.

In this world of corporate enterprise, where Darwinian rules apply, it is inevitable that the business of health care is subjected to the same pressures that face any other business—survival being the priority issue. In such a competitive environment managers or administrators have no choice but to view health care encounters as business transactions. Forced into mean and competitive markets to make sufficient money to meet payrolls, retire bond debt, or provide acceptable profit margins, they must do so mainly by cutting costs and expanding reimbursable services. To do so in a labor-intensive industry without affecting the quality of care is extremely difficult. Patients are sometimes offered disincentives for seeking care, so that fewer costs are incurred or so that greater monies will accrue from those procedures that still generate substantial profit. Fewer people must be employed to reduce payroll expenses; market shares must be increased to generate more income.

Nothing is inherently evil about the idea of application of marketplace principles to health care delivery, nor is there anything to fault about the idea of cost containment initiatives. Correcting inefficiencies and eliminating unnecessary expenditures are worthy and appropriate enterprises. These goals, however, should not be achieved at the expense of the moral foundation of the health care system itself. When such a situation does exist—when the competitive dynamics of the invisible hand transcend a commitment to operate within socially responsible parameters—the stage is set for the compromise of values and the possibility of being left with dirty hands.

Such a situation did exist during the 1980s when nurses and other professionals were placed in morally compromising positions. One of the authors has researched and written extensively on what has become known as the "for-profit psychiatric hospital scandal."[9–11] Certain large investor-owned chains were investigated by state and federal authorities for illegal and unethical conduct in 1991. Complaints about these institutions included

- excessive medication and therapy;
- questionable and potentially abusive therapies;
- exorbitant charges and charges for services never rendered;
- overly aggressive and deceptive marketing;
- bounties paid to professionals and marketing personnel to deliver paying patients to treatment facilities;
- holding patients against their will without medical justification;
- isolating patients from families, friends, and legal counsel by withholding telephone, mail, and visitation privileges;
- falsifying diagnoses to match insurance benefits;
- "dumping" patients regardless of their condition once insurance benefits were exhausted; and
- unnecessary hospitalization of patients whose conditions could have been treated in a less restrictive environment.[12]

Investigations based on these complaints continue, and hundreds of lawsuits have been filed on behalf of patients who believe they were mistreated, cheated, or damaged by inappropriate incarceration in these facilities.

Some of the material that follows has been reported elsewhere,[10] and it is based on interviews conducted with nurse informants who discussed their struggles to advocate for their patients within deviant work environments. Nurses too often found themselves unable to take appropriate action on behalf of patients because they were frightened that they would lose their jobs. They were also subjected to intimidation tactics that included being threatened with legal action if they spoke out. Several nurses in this study who spoke out against abusive conditions did in fact have suits filed against them for slander by hospitals and professionals associated with hospitals.[10]

DEVIANT DECISIONS, DEVIANT ENVIRONMENTS, OR BOTH?

Alleged psychiatric hospital fraud, abuse, and unethical behavior first came to national attention in 1991. These abuses were at the center of much of the subsequent suits of for-profit psychiatric hospitals by the Texas State Attorney General's office and resulted in both federal and state investigations of major psychiatric hospital chains. The Texas State Senate Interim Committee on Health and Human Services reported, "Many of these problems festered without attracting attention from state agencies responsible for addressing them, and violations of state law and agency rules went unpunished."[12(p6)] If the problems they referred to took place over time and in a systematic manner, it is reasonable to assume that nurses and other professionals within the organization would have some knowledge of them. However, it took a state investigation and complaints of patients and families to bring these abuses to light and for any action to take place.

At issue for the profession is whether nurses who were confronted with these problems were in fact aware of them and whether or not they fulfilled their advocacy responsibilities to the patients in their care. It was not known whether they stayed and struggled with their situations or whether they simply left these environments by quitting. To date there has been scant attention paid in the nursing literature to these events and the resulting problems with respect to the profession or with respect to the effects of any exploitation or abuse of patients.

During the course of the research on which this article is based, nurses were questioned as to what actions they took, if any, when they realized that they were in situations that posed multiple ethical contradictions for them, in particular those that required them to engage in patient advocacy. Nurses reported experiences of pain and suffering that occurred during their employment when they came to realize that they were working in deviant circumstances. This suffering most closely approached the concept of angst, an idea that has been best developed by existentialist philosophers. The existentialists describe angst as an encompassing attitude that entails a range of emotions or moods—sometimes anguish, sometimes anxiety, and sometimes dread.[13] Sometimes angst is used to refer to excruciating distress or suffering, sometimes to an all-embracing extreme fear of everything or a fear of oneself, including one's own emotions or identity. One poignant example of this came from a nurse who reported the following:

> *#019:* So, what did it all mean, it was just an intimidation, it was unbelievable. And in fact when I verbalized it to you, I know it happened, you know? But it sounds so unreal. So, no, we could not [advocate]—there'd be times, getting back to your original question, we could not be advocates of patients [because] we were told immediately that was the way it was. . . . That's what we were given—statistics. Not that this was how we helped individuals, but this was our average daily census, our FTE [full-time equivalent] to patient ratio, our profit margin, always the statistics. There was no room for treatment issues. And we were comparing [how] much money . . . that we have here. . . . That's what we were given, national statistics. . . . There was no room for people. Or human concerns. And that's what it all meant.[10]

Themes of fear and powerlessness in the face of the "corporate embrace"[14] were reported by another:

> *#017:* We went through God knows how many administrators. In fact there were some jokes about

the "administrator du jour." We were taken [over] during the last year and a half I was there. We were bought by a major corporation, which came in with an administrator who was eventually fired. But who was—let me put it kindly—who was a tyrant . . . who didn't know very well how to deal with hospitals or anything about health care but how to be a dictator. It was organized totalitarianism, no, it was totalitarian chaos. . . . We were like doormats getting chewed out on a weekly basis like children. And it was always, you know, that we were not making enough money, that we had to keep down staffing, that we have to look at ways to reduce expenditures, and that there was no way that we could ask at this point in time for anything for our patients. That we needed to put our heads together and if we were not better managers, essentially we would not be there. So the message was conveyed to us so very strongly that we didn't even dare. One time we sat at the conference table, we needed some copies made, the copy machine was broken, so we wouldn't even ask to go make them on the outside. [Laughter] It sounds silly, it sounds, you know, stupid. I look back and I tried to talk to my colleagues and remember if it was really that way. We were, it was, and what we had also amazingly enough, was scare tactics. We were individually asked to report our colleagues if we saw something that they were doing or saying against the hospital. And not promoting the hospital or saying negative things about the hospital. . . . It was a reward system, and sometimes it was a punishment system. If you don't go by, you know, what we are saying, you know, you won't be here—essentially that was the message. And people were fired right and left without going through the guidelines of the policies and procedures. They were there one day, and one day they were told to leave. It happened to several program directors. Of course, we were told that we were working for a good corporation and jobs were hard to come by, which is true.[10]

THE DANGERS OF DIRTY HANDS

Dirty hands, then, is the moral quandary of working within externally imposed parameters that directly counter the provision of high-quality patient care and the principle and value of beneficence. Goffman[15,16] suggested that in situations that present these kinds of threats to integrity or values, people often engage in a form of avoidance as a self-protective strategy. One form of avoidance is to simply stay away from the circumstance. But if people are unable to do so, and must remain in the noxious situation, they must find a way to ensure that their interactions within those circumstances are as structured or predictable as possible to avoid negative encounters. This means restricting the range of activities associated with their positions, and the safest way of doing this is to focus only on one's fragmented job and to ignore its many ramifications. Lifton[17] called this phenomenon "psychological doubling," which he described as a conscious or unconscious division of the self into two functioning wholes in such a way that each part functions as an entire self.[17(p418)] One nurse who engaged in this form of resistance called it "going into my place."[10] Another described the process as "focusing on what you have to get through to do your job and put the rest away. Off somewhere where it won't get in the way."[10]

Two nurses who found that they had to protect themselves from the grief, anxiety, and rage that they said were beginning to overwhelm them related the following:

> *#001:* But I was stuck, so I just went to work and did what they wanted, almost everything they wanted. . . . It was like I was there but I wasn't. I was doing these functions, like passing [medications] and writing on charts and sitting in the treatment team meetings, but I'm sorry to say I wasn't nursing. I stayed away from the patients as much as I could because I thought that I really didn't want to get involved. I guess it was a feeling that if I got to feeling like they had a human relationship with me, then I would start to feel myself, and I didn't want to do that. If I felt something, then I would get angry at the situation, and somehow things would go badly for me. So I just kind of pretended . . . and it kept me from feeling. I just did things, you know—things? It wasn't that hard to do either, because everyone was kept pretty busy doing things. You just did yours for the minute and then on to the next, and before you knew it the day was over and you could go home.[10]

Another nurse reported that she engaged in similar disengagement in her work setting during which she simply attended to what had to be done to get through her shift:

> *#020:* After 4½ years I believe I have just learned to put my frustrations in a box and put them aside and say, okay, now I've got to set up the 9:00 [medications] . . . I've got to take off the orders. You learn to stifle it, the rage. You learn to put aside your feelings and your expectations and your hopes and dreams and get on with the business at hand.[10]

In these two responses, nurses related that when there was no escape, they could avoid or at least attenuate the meaning and emotional impact of remaining at their job. Even as they found themselves in these circumstances, they tried to bring some semblance of structure to their jobs in an attempt to maintain a vestige of order where disorder seemed to be the rule. And (because statistics do not feel and charts do not bleed) these nurses removed themselves to an FTE corporate world. This retreat represented an impersonal defection in which they could relate more to tasks than to people.

Other nurses relating the same phenomenon described "splitting off one part of another," "becoming a different person at work," and "becoming anesthetized."[10] These are interesting phrases because they communicate the kind of "splitting off" that Lifton[17] described in his studies on psychological doubling. He found that most people feel poorly equipped to make a conceptual restructuring of their accustomed picture of the world to make it fit dimensions that are alien to their lifelong learning. In other words, to feel forced to function in a world that is antithetical to one's beliefs is very difficult and can be psychologically damaging. As a means of dealing with their situations, they focus on "little lumps" of reality, engaging in a form of dissociative emotional distancing or "dehumanized behavior."[17(p7)] This emotional distancing involves a bypassing, a suppression, or a stifling of components of full psychic functioning. Certain aspects of psychic functioning, such as empathy, are shunted aside. The person's relationships to others become stereotyped, rigid, and above all inexpressive of interpersonal mutuality. Lifton maintained that certain occupations require a certain amount of selectively "dehumanized" behavior, among which he listed nursing and medicine. Without this mechanism, he maintained that emotional reactions would interfere with "the efficient and responsible performance of what has to be done."[17(p214)]

Nevertheless, the psychologically damaging aspect of this experience emerged when nurses talked about their feelings of guilt. They discussed being caught in the middle, blaming themselves on the one hand and knowing on another level that another choice could have been made, as illustrated in the following:

> *#030:* It makes me sick to think of it now. It's like I was put in the position of the "I was just following orders" defense. Just by virtue of staying, I mean I wouldn't even have had to do anything overt. All I can say is that when my eyes were opened and I saw what was going on it scared me to death, and I was scared the whole 9 months, a constant grating of every nerve in my head being on edge. I was scared of a lot, but most of all I was scared I was going to become sucked in.[10]

The above examples were chosen from nurses' narratives to illustrate the deviant environments that can lead to dirty hands situations. These nurses' experiences foreshadow what may have profound implications for the profession of nursing and its future. As administrators with advanced financial training decide which workers are to carry out what tasks according to predetermined methods, nurses will lose more and more autonomy. Marx[18] observed that workers' loss of autonomous decision making, discretion, and creativity within the work process has the potential to result in a pervasive source of alienation. Deskilling and alienation are the underside of what appears on the surface to be rationalized managerial control over the work process.

TOWARD A 21ST-CENTURY RESEARCH AGENDA

There is little question that health care has undergone substantial structural and qualitative changes and that it has become megabusiness in the mold of Fortune 500 companies.[5,19] An unfortunate aspect of those changes may include deviant or criminal activity that creates an ethos that can compromise professionals and those under their care.[9–11,20] Mills[21] proposed that such deviance is a ubiquitous feature of business culture, being more the rule than the exception. The widespread existence of such deviance was underscored by research reporting that over 65% of Fortune 500 companies were charged with corporate crimes in 1975 and 1976.[22]

Organizational theorists have long believed that huge bureaucracies can lead to "legitimate" abandonment of personal responsibility in the support of organizational goals.[23] Because corporations shape the symbolic field in which employees find themselves situated, they also can shape employees' definitions of situations. Organizational goals (sometimes deviant) become virtually identical to employee goals, leading to dirty hands situations.

• • •

The authors propose that dirty hands is a phenomenon that has been insufficiently examined in the nursing ethics literature and that should be placed on the ethics research and theory development agenda. In rarefied discussions of moral conflicts, too often the focus is more on the dilemma in the abstract, the principles, or the conflict rather than on the complex contextual factors that give rise to and influence those decisions. In addition, the personal and moral toll as well as the effect on the profession and subsequently on health care itself is rarely played out. Ethics has also become the stepchild to "real research," which is outcome and intervention oriented and geared to what can or cannot be funded in a competitive atmosphere. But elegant outcomes studies benefit no one if they cannot be implemented in hostile and unsupportive environments or in environments that are threatening.

We argue that in situations in which one's own position becomes threatened, such as in difficult job markets or during situations of deprivation, the pull of self-preservation becomes strong. In addition, the tug of loyalty to one's group can sometimes result in a temptation to "go along and get along" in order to avoid negative sanctions. Thus, when "doubling" or "ethical numbing"[24] becomes a structurally normative practice as a result of an environment in which individuals are pressured to follow institutional agendas that conflict with personal agendas, the dangers are not to be underestimated. The disturbing aspect of this doubling or numbing for the profession as a whole is that such mental manipulation has the potential of becoming a maintenance behavior. That is, this form of avoidance, if it becomes a systematic practice, has the potential for making anyone who works with people regularly perceive and treat them as nonhuman, as statistics, commodities, or interchangeable pieces in a large and profitable numbers game. It might easily lead to a diminished sense of responsibility for those same people, who are no longer cognitively represented as human.

It might also lead to an attenuation of a sense of responsibility for one's own actions with respect to those who are now nonhumans, which Lifton called a "we're just running the trains" mentality.[17(p400)] What starts out as a protection against feelings of anxiety, frustration, and rage toward the feeling that one has become an insubstantial human widget in a vast bureaucracy actually becomes what it started out to prevent. In a tragic dialectic, the reaction against dehumanization itself becomes dehumanization. Those who would be susceptible to this staining are within our own ranks. They are our own colleagues. Even more vulnerable are the people for whom nurses are pledged to care and advocate. As a profession we owe it to the vulnerable among us to address and study the issue of dirty hands and the contexts that lead to this moral staining and to develop strategies that mitigate morally crippling environments.

REFERENCES

1. American Nurses' Association. *American Nurses' Association Code of Ethics with Interpretive Statements*. Kansas City, Mo: ANA; 1985.
2. American Nurses' Association. *Standards of Psychiatric and Mental Health Practice*. Kansas City, Mo: ANA; 1982.
3. Stocker M. *Plural and Conflicting Values*. Oxford, England: Oxford University Press; 1990.
4. Styron W. *Sophie's Choice*. New York, NY: Random House; 1979.
5. Salmon JW. A perspective on the corporate transformation of health care. *Int J Health Serv*. 1995;25(1):11–42.
6. Wohl S. The medical industrial complex: another view of the influence of business on medical care. In: McCue JD, ed. *The Medical Cost-containment Crisis: Fears, Opin-*

ions and Facts. Ann Arbor, Mich: Health Administration Press Perspectives; 1989.

7. Rodwin MA. *Medicine, Money and Morals*. New York, NY: Oxford University Press; 1993.
8. Relman A. The new medical industrial complex. *N Engl J Med.* 1980;303:963–970.
9. Mohr W. The private psychiatric hospital scandal: a critical social approach. *Arch Psychiatr Nurs*. 1994;8(1):4–8.
10. Mohr W. Multiple ideologies and their proposed roles in the outcomes of nurse practice setting: the for-profit psychiatric hospital scandal as a paradigm case. *Nurs Outlook*. 1995;43(1):35–43.
11. Mohr WK. *The Nature of Nurses' Experiences in For-profit Psychiatric Hospital Settings*. Austin, Tex: University of Texas at Austin; 1995. PhD dissertation.
12. *Texas State Senate Interim Committee Report on Private Psychiatric Substance Abuse and Medical Rehabilitation Services*. Austin, Tex: State of Texas Department of Health and Human Services; 1992.
13. Barnes HE. *An Existentialist Ethics*. New York, NY: Knopf; 1967.
14. Woolhandler S, Himmelstein DU. Extreme risk—the new corporate proposition for physicians. *N Engl J Med*. 1995;333:1706–1707.
15. Goffman E. *The Presentation of Self in Everyday Life*. Garden City, NY: Doubleday-Anchor; 1959.
16. Goffman E. *Asylums*. New York, NY: Doubleday-Anchor; 1961.
17. Lifton R. *The Nazi Doctors: Medical Killing and the Politics of Genocide*. New York, NY: Basic Books; 1986.
18. Elster J. *Making Sense of Marx*. New York, NY: Oxford University Press; 1987.
19. Brown P, Cooksey E. Mental health monopoly: corporate trends in mental health services. *Soc Sci Med*. 1989;28:1129–1138.
20. Luske B, Vandenburgh HW. Heads on beds: toward a critical ethnography of the selling of psychiatric hospitalization. *Per Soc Prob*. 1995;7:203–222.
21. Mills CW. *The Power Elite*. New York, NY: Oxford University Press; 1956.
22. Clinard M. Corporate ethics and crime: a view of middle management. In: Ermann MD, Lundman DJ, eds. *Corporate and Governmental Deviance*. New York, NY: Oxford University Press; 1986.
23. Weber M. *The Protestant Ethic and the Spirit of Capitalism*. New York, NY: Scribner's; 1904 (1958).
24. Drucker PF. Corporate takeovers—what is to be done? *Pub Interest*. 1986;8:23–24.

The Synergistic Relationship between Ethics and Quality Improvement: Thriving in Managed Care

Kathleen Mitchell, Katherine Cardone Uehlinger, and Janet Owen

Health care delivery has become increasingly complex with rapidly changing technology and scientific advances, shrinking financial resources, shifting paradigms in the health care marketplace, and uncertainty over who will eventually be the gatekeeper of this huge and intricate system. As monetary concerns increasingly dominate health care decisions, professionals are asking: How are these decisions being made? Who is making the decisions? What factors influence these decisions? How do we know these are the "right" decisions?

The answers are varied, but what is clear is that some enlightened institutions and organizations are uniting the parallel functions of ethics and quality improvement as a framework for ensuring ethical decision making and quality patient outcomes. This article provides a review of the separate historical evolution of ethics, health care reimbursement, and quality improvement and demonstrates the practical aspects of reflecting ethical integrity in decision making while following quality improvement principles through a case study.

HISTORICAL PERSPECTIVES

Ethics

Ethics and ethical considerations have been identified since the days of Plato and Socrates. Bioethics, the application of ethics to the biological sciences and health care, came into existence as an independent discipline in the early 1970s.[1] Contemporary bioethical principles that are at the heart of any discussion are autonomy, beneficence and nonmaleficence, and justice.

Autonomy

Two essential features of autonomy are the ability to think freely and the ability to act on one's decisions. A truly autonomous patient has a right to self-determination. At times, there is a concern that the patient may not be capable of a full understanding of his or her choices and thus may not be able to make autonomous decisions. With a paternalistic perspective, patient autonomy may be compromised, but the intent frequently is to provide direction to assist the patient, not benefit the caregiver.[2]

Beneficence and Nonmaleficence

Some individuals view these concepts as indistinguishable, but there are distinct differences. Beneficence refers to active intervention to achieve good. Nonmaleficence demands that no harm be actively inflicted. Nonmaleficence by extension includes not killing, not causing pain or offense, not incapacitating, and not depriving of goods.[2] Thus nonmaleficence provides a basis for legal

J Nurs Care Qual, 1996, 11(1): 9–21
© 1996 Aspen Publishers, Inc.

prohibitions, such as a ban on physician-assisted suicide. Standards of care based on nonmaleficence require that decisions be made on clinical rather than economic grounds. This is the heart of the moral dilemma for today's physicians.[3]

Justice

Justice has been defined as follows:

> A situation of justice is present whenever persons are due benefits or burdens because of their particular properties or circumstances, . . . an injustice therefore involves a wrongful act or omission that denies people benefits to which they have a right or fails to distribute burdens fairly. . . . In health care, the term distributive justice most commonly refers to fair, equitable, and appropriate distribution in society determined by justified norms that structure the terms of social cooperation.[2(pp.236–237)]

Ethical issues or dilemmas are increasingly commonplace in health care. An ethical issue is a "concern involving disagreements or opposing views among two or more parties (patients, families, physicians, and nurses) about what is the right or best decision related to patient care."[4(p.88)]

Health care organizations are continually challenged to develop structures and processes that support ethical integrity and responsible decision making. The assumption is made that not only do individual health care professionals have responsibility for moral decisions and actions but health care organizations also have moral obligations and can be held accountable for their decisions and deeds. A study of organizational integrity revealed that "From the perspective of integrity, the task of ethics management is to define and give life to an organization's guiding values, to create an environment that supports ethically sound behavior and to instill a sense of shared accountability among employees."[5(p.108)] Organizations, therefore, through their expectations, authority, and practices, serve to define the decision-making processes of their human representatives.[4]

Many policies in hospitals relate directly and indirectly to ethical decision making. These policies construct a framework that enhances the health care provider's efforts to provide ethical patient care. The Joint Commission on Accreditation of Healthcare Organizations has standards devoted to patient rights and organization ethics. The box on page 92 displays examples of such policies and procedures. Although ethics-related policies and procedures may be in place in an organization, occasionally there is an unawareness or lack of understanding regarding these policies among employees. A frequently overheard remark is: "You mean the hospital has a policy on this?"

An organization is in a strong position to promote structures and processes for ethical decision making when trust and information are provided, appropriate groups are included in decisions, opposing views are permitted, and questioning and debating are encouraged.[6] Hospital ethics committees were established to assist health care providers in decision-making processes, policy development, and education. According to a survey completed by the American Hospital Association in 1993, 60 percent of hospitals reported having an in-house ethics committee.[7] The fact that there is an ethics committee does not automatically create an ethical environment or affect the actions of caregivers, patients, and families. If ethical issues are not brought to the attention of the committee, however, there is little that the committee can do in the way of exploring approaches to ethical dilemmas.

Policies and Procedures on Patient Rights and Organization Ethics

- Patient self-determination
- Patient consents and release
- Patient rights
- Hospital ethics committee
- Consent for postmortem examination
- Guidelines for the management of suspected child/adolescent abuse and neglect
- Hospital computer security
- Decision to withhold cardiopulmonary resuscitation
- Withholding or withdrawing life-sustaining treatment
- Patient rights and responsibilities under the end-stage renal disease program
- Organ and tissue donation and required request
- Institutional review board
- Confidential patient information and patient privacy
- Volunteers and patient relations
- Conflict of interest
- Patient referral to other facilities and agencies
- Management of pain
- Access to protective services
- Management of staff requests not to participate in care

Health Care Reimbursement

Before the advent of insurance, the physician charged directly for care rendered. Although not always guaranteeing reimbursement, this simple transaction between provider and recipient was free of regulatory intervention. As household economies became dependent on wages, however, the fear of sickness interrupting income increased. Workers in Europe began to organize mutual benefit societies, which were soon subsidized by the government. These first programs were meant to preserve income and were not particularly for medical insurance. In 1883, Germany established the first compulsory sickness insurance. Other European countries followed suit, with England being among the last to implement insurance in 1911.[8]

As a result of a strong fear of regulatory interference and a highly decentralized approach to governing, the U.S. government did not champion national insurance.[9] The anti-German fervor of World War II and strong opposition from American medical societies also contributed to the lack of government interest in organizing insurance.[8]

As unions rose to power, support increased for insurance paid by employers. In 1929, a coverage program for school teachers was instituted at Baylor University Hospital, with a charge of $6 per day for 21 days of hospitalization.[8] In 1938, Edgar Kaiser started an insurance program for workers on the Grand Coulee Dam, and in 1942 the Kaiser Permanente Foundation was established.[8] By 1940, only 9 percent of the U.S. population had some type of health insurance.[9] In 1965, Medicare and Medicaid were established as an addition to Social Security and heralded the beginning of higher health care costs and the birth of the technology boom. Medicare actually boosted prices by its rules governing choice of payment.[9] In practice, this system rewarded high-cost institutions with higher payments and penalized low-cost providers with lower payments.[9]

Increased longevity of subsequent generations (when Social Security was enacted, the life expectancy was 62 years of age; today it is 76 and climbing) and greater percentages of the Gross National Product being dedicated to health care (9 percent in 1980 and about 14 percent in 1993) forced an examination nationwide of the allocation of health care dollars.[10] Health care costs in the United States are approaching $1 trillion, constituting 15 percent of the Gross National Product and, until recently, increasing at almost twice the rate of the economy at large. As a result, considerable pressures for cost containment have come from both the private and public sectors.[11] Those who paid the bills naturally began the revolution to control spending, and the federal government was one of the largest payers. Diagnosis-related group–based reimbursement for Medicare was the first salvo from the federal government designed to reel in costs in the 1980s. Private insurers were quick to follow suit.

Employers as payers also began to tackle rising costs by exploring mechanisms to provide low-cost employee benefit programs. Appleby notes that employers are now becoming even more aggressive about costs: "Business leaders are exacting cost and service concessions from providers that would have been unthinkable even 5 years ago. In scores of cities, companies large and small have formed business coalitions to grab the health care industry by the scruff of the neck and shake it till it responds with more efficiency and quality."[12(p.26)]

Managed care markets have evolved to place the payer in the driver's seat. Costs have leveled off as managed care penetration has risen to 60 percent on the west coast and 40 percent in much of the northeast.[13] Capitation of spending reverses the traditional logic of health care institutions. Shortell and colleagues summarize the paradigm shift of capitation:

> In the old world of largely fee-for-service payment, greater volume was associated with more revenue, which resulted in higher earnings and profits at a given level of costs. In the new world of capitated payment, revenue is earned up front when the contract is negotiated on the basis of so much per member per month for a defined population of enrollees. In this case hospitals as well as other provider units become cost centers, not revenue centers. The incentives are to contain costs by providing the needed care within the fixed revenue budget and to keep the population well. As a result, many providers try to streamline operations and reengineer clinical processes so that patients are treated at the most appropriate point in the continuum of care where the greatest value is added. For the most part, this point is in settings outside of the hospital. As a result, some hospitals face excess inpatient bed capacity of up to 50 percent, resulting in significant downsizing of both facilities and staff.[11(p.133)]

The goal of managed care is to get the decision makers (providers, consumers, and payers) to consider carefully the relative efficacy and the importance of various services, procedures, and treatment modalities and to make decisions regarding the allocation of their limited resources accordingly.[11]

Quality Improvement

The quest for quality in health care can be traced back to Florence Nightingale's observation of patient outcomes related to care processes. Her inquiry, done in a systematic fashion during the 1860s, is one of the first documented studies of care provided. In the early 20th century, Boston surgeon Ernest Codmon called for a valid evaluation process to improve care. Subsequently, the American College of Surgeons was founded in 1913 and charged with establishing quality standards.[14] Four years later, the Hospital Standardization Program was created. The purpose was to set minimum standards on organizing medical staff, to limit membership to qualified physicians, to initiate clinical peer review, to maintain medical records, and to establish supervised diagnostic facilities such as laboratories and radiology departments.[15]

In 1952, the American College of Physicians, the American Medical Association, the American Hospital Association, and the Canadian Medical Association joined the American College of Surgeons to form the Joint Commission on Accreditation of Hospitals (JCAH).[15] Standards for accreditation developed slowly through the 1950s and 1960s. In 1966, Donabedian formulated a theoretical framework for the evaluation of patient care. His model features structure (the physical and staffing characteristics of caring for patients), process (the method of delivery), and outcome (the results of care) as key facets.[15]

Initial JCAH accreditation surveys focused on the structure and process aspects of Donabedian's model. Patient outcomes were not directly addressed. In the 1970s, the JCAH began looking at outcomes such as blood use and antibiotic use. In 1987, it changed its name to the Joint Commission on Accreditation of Healthcare Organizations (Joint Commission) to reflect that its surveys included long-term care settings, ambulatory care, and hospices.[15]

Also in 1987, Donald Berwick, M.D., and Paul Batalden, M.D., who had researched the Japanese industrial approach to quality and challenged their peers to question the traditional approach of quality assessment, developed the National Demonstration Project on Quality Improvement in Healthcare. Brent James, M.D., another member of that project, then focused on patient and clinical outcomes in multisystem hospitals.[14]

In 1988, the Joint Commission announced its Agenda for Change as a new way of looking at quality improvement. Suddenly, there was a push to a multidisciplinary approach to improving patient care. "All of the workers—administrators, physicians, nurses, housekeepers, clerks—in an emergency department, for instance, might form a task force that would continually analyze and improve care."[15]

With the growth of managed care, the business aspect of hospitals became as prominent as the traditional aspects of research, practice, and education. Clinical databases that facilitate benchmarking allow organizations to compare similar patient outcomes. Borrowing from industry, quality improvement with emphasis on continual activity, outcomes, and customer satisfaction has successfully found its niche in health care.

The Impact of the Three Evolutions on Professionals

A time line of these three evolutions is summarized in Figure 1. In examining the impact on health care professionals, one should consider the driving forces for each evolution as well as the timing. The fact that there is parallel and distinct growth rather than a melding is noteworthy.

Quality improvement, under one name or another, has been an accepted duty of a profession to the public that it serves. For most professions, such as law or education, the relationship between provider and recipient has been direct in all facets. In health care, however, there have been gradual changes in the relationship between providers and patients to include third party payers as interfaces. Initially, this arrangement was not perceived negatively by health care providers, but with the shift to managed care and the ascendancy of business decisions driving care provision, this aspect has created much concern and discussion. Recent media attention has showcased potential conflicts of interest between business proponents and patient care proponents surrounding topics such as bone mar-

	Ethics	Reimbursement	Quality
1860			Florence Nightingale
1917			Hospital Standardization Program
1929		Blue Cross	
1942		Kaiser Permanente	
1950s			Joint Commission on Accreditation of Hospitals
1960s		Medicaid and Medicare	
1970s	Bioethics		
1980s		Diagnosis-related groups	
1985	Hospital Ethics Committee		
1987			National demonstration project on quality improvement in health care
1990s		Managed care	

Figure 1. Evolution of medical ethics, health care reimbursement, and quality improvement.

row transplants for breast cancer patients and shorter stays for maternity patients.

At times, it would appear that caregivers have no recourse but to accept what is mandated as appropriate by the insurer. The concept of the clinician as the sole decision maker has been challenged. Outcomes data are no longer used just to improve practice clinically but also to justify reductions in service. "Managed care provides financial incentives for patients to use the providers and facilities within the plan and the assumption of some financial risk by doctors, thus fundamentally altering their role from serving as agent for the patient's welfare to balancing the patient's needs against the need for cost control. . . ."[16(p.742)]

According to Pellegrino:

> . . . managed care, by its nature, places the good of the patient in conflict with the self-interest of the physician. . . . Physician decisions are embedded in a matrix of conflicting legal, ethical, economic, and societal obligations. . . . It is essential therefore to establish some order of priority . . . medical ethics puts the vulnerability and genuine needs of the patient at the center.[17(p.316)]

The ethical dilemma to be resolved is that of rationing. Health care professionals are challenged to balance quality care and also to balance the books. As Mariner states, managed care organizations "were created to achieve economic objectives that may be fundamentally incompatible with traditional principles of medical ethics."[18(p.236)] Both physicians and managed care organizations have an obligation to weigh all sides of a question before proceeding to a plan of care. The caregiver who is profligate with supplies or orders unnecessary treatments is no less culpable than the insurer who refuses coverage for certain conditions.

At issue here is the framework upon which allocation decisions are made. If one passively assumes that the payer "has all the cards," the payer may indeed make all the decisions. Moss expresses concern that managed care will cause economic considerations to dominate the health care market and that institutional policies that protect the private provider–patient ethic will falter under the pressure.[19] If the assumption is that all parties to care must follow an ethical framework and act in the best interest of outcomes, however, quality rather than cost can be the determining factor.

SYNERGY

If one accepts the premise that ethical dimensions of health care delivery, particularly decision making, will lead to improved quality of patient care, a mechanism must be developed to link ethics and quality. May, a well-known bioethicist and theologian, writes about the danger of losing sight of the patient and family after the ethical decision has been made. It should always be remembered that the patient and family have to understand the decision and live with its consequences.[20] The focus of any ethical issue should be patient care and sound practice, not the professionals involved in the debate.

According to Wolf:

> . . . health care professionals' duties have been passionately championed in modern bioethics for the last quarter century. Bioethicists have urged a radical reorganization of medical practice so that patients' values govern and medical decision making is patient-centered. But patients and consumers themselves have yet to assert real influence over the ethical practices they encounter. Quality assessment has the potential to become a way of doing so. If quality assessment tools are to be used to assess medical practice and health care organizations, patients have enormous stakes in making sure these tools assess not just technical medical care, but ethical behavior as well.[21(p.111)]

Wolf is quick to concede that ethics has been a "soft" science but holds that "quality assessment can take bioethics the next step—toward a fuller picture of actual practice and its relationship to standards, toward the creation of informational feedback loops allowing concrete efforts to change practice, and toward reporting to the consumer."[21(p.115)] Her argument is based on the observation that ethical decisions are not systematically followed by empirical study to determine to what extent health care providers are aware of their ethical obligations and act accordingly. "Quality of other dimensions of care is routinely assessed. Ethics is not."[21(p.123)] The converse bears comment. Although the implication that quality improvement advocates are unethical is abhorrent, there is little research to date to support the integration of ethical concepts into quality improvement.

Facilitating the Strength of the Synergy

As health care decisions become more driven by financial considerations, we seek to find practical ways of merging ethical frameworks with quality improvement efforts to ensure that care remains patient focused. Quality improvement initiatives brought tools, education, and the power to change patient outcomes with data and research. The switch from quality assessment to quality improvement took the task of assessing and monitoring out of the hands of a few and empowered professionals to work together to improve outcomes. There are many health care journals dedicated to quality improvement that testify to the success of these multidisciplinary teams.

As members of the health care team, nurses have traditionally viewed patient advocacy as a hallmark of their profession, and it is imperative to preserve this aspect of the practice in the current climate. Knowledge of the ethical concepts of autonomy, beneficence and nonmaleficence, and distributive justice should be a core competency for nursing. Nurses need to embrace an ethic of care as we participate in quality improvement and reengineering groups that assume responsibility for the development of critical paths based on research that helps identify appropriate and inappropriate practices. There is hope that this knowledge and advocacy will bring an ethical dimension to the process.

Strategies To Promote Ethical Integration

Ethical decision making still remains in the hands of a few in many organizations. One method of broadening the exposure of all health care providers to ethics is an ethics consult service comprising members of the hospital ethics committee or bioethicists in the organization. An ethics consult can be requested by anyone involved in a case, including the patient, the family, and members of the health care team. A consult involves a meeting where ethicists, health care team members, and the patient and/or family are present. The purpose is to promote discussion among the parties to define the ethical issues to facilitate a decision. When a health care organization provides an ethics consult service, it is important that it communicates the availability of this service to patients, families, and providers.

Many nurses have found themselves faced with an increasing number of ethical dilemmas. Studies have indicated that, when nurses confront ethical issues, they tend to rely on intuition and instinct to settle the issue quickly.[22] Although nurses are able to identify the ethical issues quickly, they believe themselves powerless to initiate a formal ethical discussion as a result of a knowledge deficit in ethical theoretical background.[22] Ironically, nurses had felt powerless or inadequate to institute substantial changes in patient outcomes as a result of a lack of knowledge of quality improvement theory as well. It is imperative that support and education about ethical decision making be provided to nurses and other health care providers.

One method of providing education and support that is proving to be effective at Georgetown University Medical Center is the small group discussion. In this forum, nurses discuss concerns regarding ethical issues that they encounter in the delivery of patient care. Using the format of the ethics consult, nurses write up case studies and present them in the informal atmosphere of the small group. A facilitator guides the discussion and keeps the group focused on the ethical issue(s).

The information for an ethics case presentation can be summarized as follows:

1. *background*—the patient's medical history
2. *social history*—brief background information pertinent to the case
3. *hospital course*—the course of the patient's treatment and prognosis
4. *issues*—the ethical issue(s) to be discussed, appropriately framed
5. *ethical question*—the question(s) to be answered

Methods of determining the effectiveness of the nursing ethics rounds educational process include measuring the interest shown through increased attendance, discussion, questioning, and debate. Another outcome of this process involves nurses examining their own value judgments that are rooted in their clinical practice and decision making.[21] The participation of other disciplines (e.g., social work, occupational therapy, medicine, physical therapy) in this process also indicates greater collaboration that should positively affect patient care. Satisfaction surveys provided to patients and families can also indicate that improved ethical decision making is being provided.

Integrating Ethics and Quality Improvement

There are many acronyms for quality improvement processes. For the purposes of this discussion, FOCUS PDCA is used as the model:

F: Find an opportunity to improve
O: Organize a team
C: Clarify the current situation
U: Understand the variations
S: Select the process(es) to improve
P: Plan
D: Do
C: Check
A: Act to maintain the gain

Health care quality improvement teams are interdisciplinary, short term, and focused. Involvement in teams promotes education of staff and continued awareness of the power that an individual has to make a difference as goals are reached. Consideration of economic savings is integrated into the choices that teams examine. Health care workers who embrace such an approach to continually improving patient care provide a valued dimension to successful clinical outcomes and business outcomes. Tangible results of quality improvement teams that are based on the scientific process of quality improvement form a strong foundation for patient-focused care.

A comparison of a work-up for an ethical consult service to the FOCUS PDCA method yields compatible methodologies that are strengthened when combined. The ethics work-up is a simple format consisting of the following five steps:

1. *What are the facts?* Clarify the facts both medical and social. Who are the persons involved? What are the diagnosis, prognosis, and therapeutic options? What are the time constraints? What was the chronology of events? What is the medical setting? What are the reasons supporting the claims? What are the goals of care? (Find an opportunity for improvement, Organize the team)
2. *What is the issue?* Identify the precise ethical issue in the case. (Clarify the current situation)
3. *Frame the issue.* One or more moral approaches may be used, but the case should be analyzed given the following areas of concern:
   - the decision maker(s)
   - the criteria to be used in reaching clinical decisions
   - specific biomedical good of the patient
   - the broader good to and interests of the patient
   - the good to and interests of other parties
   - the health care professional's moral/professional obligations

   (Understand the variation)
4. *Decide.* Data are analyzed and reflected upon morally, and a conclusion is reached. The decision must have a moral justification. Sources for justification are the nature of the health care professional–patient relationship, approaches (theories) to ethical inquiry, and grounding and source of ethics (philosophical, theological, sociocultural. (Select processes to improve)
5. *Critique.* This can be accomplished by weighing the major actions and responding appropriately or by changing the decision. Some cases may need to be sent to the hospital ethics committee for a deci-

sion. Retrospective analysis may be used to prepare for another time when a similar case is presented. (Plan, Do)

Common issues brought to the ethics consult service include patient capacity for decision making, determining the appropriate decision maker, withholding and withdrawing treatment, disagreement about the appropriate level of care between families and physicians, feeding tubes, and Do Not Resuscitate orders. "Doing the right thing right" is another link between ethics and quality.

Where the similarity ends is the Check aspect. As Wolf states:

> Outcome measures will probably be the most controversial, since a range of case resolutions may all be ethical, and at the same time, people may disagree as to the best ethical resolution of a given case. Yet one can imagine an array of relevant measures, even if they require interpretation. One might ask patients questions to assess whether settled ethical obligations were fulfilled—did the physician explain treatment options including their projected pros and cons? Was there opportunity for discussion? Was the patient's treatment choice respected? and so on.[21(p.124)]

Managed care consumers will use quality assessment measures of outcomes to choose among health care providers and plans. Will ethics and ethical behavior be included in those outcomes?

Wolf asserts that the need for ethical reflection will survive because determining quality standards, measuring conformance, and deciding what to do with information will be constant.[21] As managed care, quality improvement, and ethics enter a common arena, integrating ethics and quality improvement will provide the strongest force for the patient, payer, and provider to grapple with. "Act to maintain the gain" is a clarion call for all health care professionals to work within ethical frameworks while improving patient-centered care.

CASE STUDY: RESTRAINTS

Mechanical and chemical restraints have been studied extensively in recent years. It is now believed that between 7 percent and 22 percent of all patients admitted to a general hospital will be restrained at some time during their hospitalization.[23] Researchers have found that the majority of patients admitted to acute care hospitals who will be restrained at some point during their stay are older and cognitively impaired and have multiple medical problems.[24] This is a change from the once predominant use of restraint among the violent mentally ill.

The original impetus for study of this issue was ethical in nature in that it is an issue of patient autonomy, but it became clear that decreased use of restraints led to improvements in the patients' physical conditions as well. Thus caregivers were at risk for harming the patient even as they attempted to render aid. This was a reversal from the generally accepted belief that it is necessary to restrain patients to prevent harm (e.g., falls, inadvertent removal of tubes, etc.).

Currently there is a considerable amount of data on the harm that comes from restraint use. Recent studies indicate that physical restraints cause problems with elimination and contribute to the development of aspiration pneumonia, circulatory obstruction, cardiac stress, skin breakdown, poor appetite, and dehydration. There are also documented cases of accidental death from strangulation. Comparison studies of fall rates have found no significant increase of falls among the unrestrained.[25] There has been little research demonstrating that the use of restraints has a positive impact on patient safety. The use of physical restraints increases the patient's disorientation, decreases sensory perception, and leads to a loss of self-image.[26] Hospital stays for patients who have been restrained are frequently prolonged as a result of the development of nosocomial infections and pressure ulcers and reduced functional capacity. The ethical principles have grown from paternalism versus autonomy as well as beneficence versus nonmaleficence.

Interjecting these ethical principles into the FOCUS PDCA process forces the examination of traditional use of restraints. For example, when staff at Georgetown University Medical Center are determining whether restraints should be applied, the following guidelines are available to assist them in making the correct decision[27]:

1. Determine whether there is high risk for injury.
2. Modify or eliminate the risk factors using the least restrictive measures, including but not limited to constant companions, geriatric chairs with trays, and the like.
3. If a protective device is used, ensure that the patient will be released from the device at least every 2 hours and that fluid needs, elimination needs, and exercise are addressed.
4. The use of less restrictive devices will be periodically attempted and their effectiveness documented.

After the restraint reduction program was implemented in early 1995, the entire patient population was surveyed. Of 300 patients, 8 (2.6 percent) were restrained. This was a 55 percent decrease from the last monitoring in October 1993. Of the 8 patients with restraints, 5 (62.5 percent) were located in the critical areas; there were no adult medical or surgical patients restrained on acute care units. Data collection methods included patient chart review, direct observation, and verbal discussion with nursing staff. Future plans include continued monitoring of areas where restraint use is high, evaluation of alternative measures, and a cost comparison of measures. Further education will continue to be needed not only in the use of restraints but also in the associated ethical principles.

Ethics- and research-based practice grounded in quality outcomes may indeed justify allocation of additional personnel as an alternative to restraints. Patients must be safely monitored whether they are in or out of restraints. The cost of frequent observation of the unrestrained patient who is at risk for injury may equal or be less than the cost of frequent interventions with the restrained patient. Additionally, collection of data that link restraints to pressure sore development, incontinence, contractures, and other problems prolonging acute care stays is quality driven and ethically motivated.

Improvement models rather than assessment models of quality require examination of practices with no proven efficacy. Research-based practice that compares different approaches and outcomes benefits the patient and all disciplines of the health care team. Research-based practice provides justification, reinforces high standards, and provides statistical evidence to nonclinicians to guide their decisions.

• • •

Those who are ethically obligated by virtue of their professional knowledge must do more to determine the standards on which they base their decisions. Most if not all good practice will result in good outcomes, but this has not been demonstrated adequately to date. By firmly integrating the framework of ethics with the quality improvement process, health care providers will be better positioned to keep care patient focused and to thrive in the managed care environment. With the adoption of an ethical framework to guide practice, quality can continue to be the major factor in treatment decisions. Clinicians are responsible for refocusing the debate away from cost and toward care by holding those who are accountable for financial decisions to ethical principles.

REFERENCES

1. Husted, G.L., and Husted, J.H. *Ethical Decision Making in Nursing*. St. Louis, Mo.: Mosby, 1991.
2. Beauchamp, T.L., and Childress, J.F. *Principles of Biomedical Ethics*. 4th ed. New York, N.Y.: Oxford University Press, 1994.
3. Pellegrino, E. "Rationing Health Care: The Ethics of Medical Gatekeeping." *Journal of Contemporary Health Law and Policy* 2 (1986): 23–45.
4. Olson, L. "Ethical Climate in Health Care Organizations." *International Nursing Review* 42 (1995): 85–90, 95.
5. Paine, L.S. "Managing for Organizational Integrity." *Harvard Business Review* 72 (1994): 106–117.
6. Hoffman, D.E. "Evaluating Ethics Committees: A View from the Outside." *Milbank Quarterly* 71 (1993): 677–699.
7. American Hospital Association. *Hospital Statistics*. Chicago, Ill.: American Hospital Association, 1995.
8. Starr, P. *The Social Transformation of American Medicine*. New York, N.Y.: Basic Books, 1982.
9. Bovbjerg, R., Griffin, C., and Carroll, C. "U.S. Health Care Coverage and Costs: Historical Development and Choices for the 1990s." *Journal of Law, Medicine, and Ethics* 21 (1993): 141–162.
10. Office of the Actuary, Health Care Financing Administration. *Social Security Statistics*. Washington, D.C.: Congressional Research Office, 1994.
11. Shortell, S., Gillies, R., and Devers, K. "Reinventing the American Hospital." *Milbank Quarterly* 73 (1995): 131–160.
12. Appleby, C. "Health Care's New Heavy Weights." *Hospital and Health Networks* 69 (1995): 26–28, 30, 32–34.
13. Clark, B.W. "Negotiating Successful Managed Care Contracts." *Health Care Financial Management* (1995): 27–30.
14. Tackett, S., ed. *Guide to Quality Management*. 4th ed. Skokie, Ill.: National Association for Healthcare Quality, 1994.
15. Luce, J., Bindman, A., and Lee, P. "A Brief History of Health Care Quality Assessment and Improvement in the United States." *Western Journal of Medicine* 160 (1994): 263–268.
16. Iglehart, J. "Managed Care." *New England Journal of Medicine* 327 (1992): 742–747.
17. Pellegrino, E. "Allocation of Resources at the Bedside: The Intersection of Economics, Law and Ethics." *Kennedy Institute of Ethics Journal* 4 (1994): 309–317.
18. Mariner, W. "Business vs. Medical Ethics: Conflicting Standards for Managed Care." *Journal of Law, Medicine, and Ethics* 23 (1995): 236–246.
19. Moss, M. "Principles, Values, and Ethics Set the Stage for Managed Care Nursing." *Nursing Economics* 13 (1995): 276–284, 294.
20. Melia, K.M. "The Task of Nursing Ethics." *Journal of Medical Ethics* 20 (1994): 7–11.
21. Wolf, S. "Quality Assessment of Ethics in Health Care: The Accountability Revolution." *American Journal of Law and Medicine* 20 (1994): 105–128.
22. Sofaer, B. "Enhancing Humanistic Skills: An Experiential Approach to Learning about Ethical Issues in Health Care." *Journal of Medical Ethics* 21 (1995): 31–34.
23. Janelli, L.M. "Physical Restraint Use in Acute Care Settings." *Journal of Nursing Care Quality* 9 (1995): 86–92.
24. MacPherson, D.S., et al. "Deciding To Restrain Medical Patients." *Journal of the American Geriatric Society* 38 (1990): 516–520.
25. Evans, L.K., and Stumpf, N.E. "Tying Down the Elderly: A Review of the Literature on Physical Restraint." *Journal of the American Geriatric Society* 37 (1989): 65–74.
26. Stolley, J.M., et al. "Developing a Restraint Use Policy for Acute Care." *Journal of Nursing Administration* 23 (1993): 49–54.
27. Department of Nursing Quality Improvement Council, Georgetown University Medical Center. *Summary Report: Restraint Usage*. Washington, D.C.: Georgetown University Medical Center, 1995.

Strength of Character through the Ethics of Nursing

Gladys L. Husted and James H. Husted

Acres of Diamonds is the title of a famous book written by Russell Conwell (1959). The book tells the story of a young man who early in life left home to travel around the world in order to make his fortune. After the passing of many years he returned home broke and discouraged. Several years later, by accident, he discovered a diamond mine in the field behind his home.

Nursing, if approached from a certain perspective, offers a benefit more valuable than any other profession on earth. This benefit is a diamond mine for a nurse's personal development—and it lies in every nurse's backyard.

PURPOSE

Every person has a constant need to be concerned with her life, health, and well-being. A nurse is a person. A nurse's patient is a person whose life, health, and well-being are immediately pressing concerns. A patient's purposes—his vision of life and what his life means to him, the potentialities his life offers him, and his survival to realize these potentialities—are virtually his only concern. They are the concerns that his nurse shares.

His nurse, as his agent, needs to make it the determining factor of her actions as a professional. A nurse who holds a clear view of her patient's purposes and actions in the health care setting has, at the very least, the necessary perspective for competent professional interaction and a unique resource for professional development.

LIFE IN THE HEALTH CARE SETTING

A patient's first, most important need is to be faithful to himself and the reality of his life. A nurse can teach her patient how to be faithful. And she, herself, on a less stressful level, can learn fidelity to herself by teaching it to her patient.

A nurse can never know too much of the meaning and realities of human life. The need for fidelity to one's life is a reality that, ethically and existentially, begins with life itself. Nothing can teach her this reality, nor how to engage it, better than interaction with her patient. Because he is disabled, he needs to struggle to maintain his perspective, his well-being, and his future. And, in different ways, so does she in her situation—whatever that situation might be.

A patient needs to regard himself as a beneficiary worthy of his own actions. A nurse—in fact every human being—also needs this perspective on her actions. A patient needs

Note: The pronoun *she* is used to designate the nurse and the pronoun *he* is used to designate the patient. This device is employed to facilitate understanding.

Adv Prac Nurs Q, 1998, 3(4): 23–25
© 1998 Aspen Publishers, Inc.

the courage to accept his situation and, at the same time, to work and to change it. A nurse needs courage too.

A patient needs to hold the desire to direct his own life and a vision as to its direction. A nurse also needs such direction. If she can help her patient to maintain his understanding of this need, she can maintain her own.

They learn from each other. Under ideal circumstances, their interactions will be characterized by reciprocity—each doing justice to the other. And this process begins from their first action in acquiring knowledge of, and from, each other.

For a successful result to come from the nurse–patient interaction, both nurse and patient must grow as a result of their relationship. A nurse's patient has a need to become more confident, more assertive, and more courageous. A nurse needs to become more competent, more knowledgeable, and more dedicated.

CHARACTER AND THE EMOTIONS

In the ethical aspect of a nurse's development, that which is to be developed is a somewhat nebulous aspect of what it is to be a human. It is called "character." It can stop at the development of mere interpersonal relationships, which is a caricature of development, or it can include the development of her personal, professional, and human excellence.

According to Aristotle in his Nichomachean Ethics (McKeon, 1941), a person's character is structured by three aspects:

1. The knowledge of an agent—practical wisdom—that produces a propensity to perceive, in a way appropriate to an ethical agent, the conditions necessary to bring about happiness.
2. The psychological makeup of a person through which she feels the right emotion, at the right time, toward the right situation, to an appropriate extent, and upon the right occasions, establishing within herself an attitude of high-mindedness and generosity.
3. The habit of making the right choices, at the right time, toward the right objects, and for the right reasons—choices conducive to the actualizing of an agent's flourishing.

Knowledge provides an agent with a direction toward success. A set habit of character enables her to establish an appropriate relationship to her circumstances. Appropriate emotions provide the energy necessary to a successful outcome.

CHARACTER AND CHOICES

Some degree of knowledge is necessary to character because some degree of knowledge is necessary to effective ethical action. The idea that effective ethical action is a necessary component of good character is not currently fashionable. But it is an idea that a nurse cannot reject without producing, within herself, an attitude of disappointment, cynicism, and burnout. These components can be aspects of a person's character, but not ethical aspects.

A nurse's character develops along with knowledge and choices (Husted & Husted, 1995). The appropriateness and intelligibility of her emotions develop along with her character. Her emotions do not develop by themselves. They are produced by, and develop with, her knowledge and choices, and the results of her choices. An agent's emotions are the completion of her character.

It is a tragic mistake, however, for a nurse to assume that her emotions are her character, or that her patient's emotions are his character. One's emotions are no more the same as one's character than one's temperature is the same as the processes that produce one's temperature. An agent's emotions, by themselves, can produce her character. They will produce a weak character. The forming of her character will occur when she is passive where there is a need and opportunity to make active choices.

The choices that lead to the personal development of a nurse are choices that will bring about results most in line with the purposes of nursing. That is to say, they will bring about the best results in the life and well-being of her patient.

In her nursing interactions her ethical choices and her ethical character are of primary importance. At the same time, the ethical choices and character of her patient are of central importance. She acts from the first point and directs her actions onto the second.

Her empathy with her patient is her instructor. The experience of an intimate and, at the same time, an objective empathy with a patient's expenditure of time and effort in the pursuit of his life, health, and well-being is a learning process.

It is not necessary, and not reasonable, to objectify a patient to the extent that a nurse looks at him only as an example of virtue and vice. Yet, she either makes herself aware of the virtues that guide and produce his effort or she keeps herself from seeing the dynamics of his life situation. If she withdraws, she learns nothing. But if she connects with her patient she will learn about his life and her own. And, as she learns, she actualizes the conditions of her flourishing. This learning is the richest possible source of a nurse's professional—and personal—development. It is the diamond mine of her character.

How it will apply in the life of any nurse depends on the present, external circumstances of her life and her inner character and motivations. One of an ocean of possible examples follows.

George is Margaret's patient. George is dying. He has end-stage liver disease because of chronic hepatitis. He is in no acute discomfort. His main complaints are weakness and some shortness of breath.

After a stormy 20-year marriage and divorce, and from coping with a delinquent son, Margaret is slipping into alcoholism.

Margaret supports George's efforts to bring the loose ends of his life together. In her evenings she deliberates on the broken strands of her life with a view of how she can bring them together. Every value George can seek is a tragically short-term value but, to George, a value nonetheless. In her sober moments Margaret envisions the values she can pursue that will give her life meaning.

Margaret sees the value of every moment of his life to George. It brings to her an awareness of the value that her life might be—and a desire for this value. She feels shame at the way she is betraying her life.

George demonstrates to Margaret the value of living the life of a unique human being. It makes her aware that, in an alcoholic oblivion, no one is unique, and one is not really living. But she can reclaim who she is and create what she can be.

Margaret observes that while George is not lonely, he is alone. Life is a journey we must all make one by one. Where we pause, where we stop, and when we begin again, only we can decide.

Through her interactions with George, Margaret gains wisdom—wisdom being the ability to look outside of herself and to see herself—outside of herself and in relation to other things.

Margaret looks at her bottle. But she remembers a place she wants to visit. And, she decides, as soon as the time comes to say goodbye to George, she will call the airline.

If George, her friend, had not called her attention to her life she might not have seen it so clearly. And maybe she would not have seen it at all.

REFERENCES

Conwell, R. (1959). *Acres of diamonds.* Philadelphia, PA: Temple University.

Husted, G.L., & Husted, J.H. (1995). *Ethical decision making in nursing.* St. Louis, MO: Mosby.

McKeon, R. (Ed.). (1941). *The basic works of Aristotle.* New York: Random House.

7

Reengineering Nursing

Consumer-Focused Preadmission Testing: A Paradigm Shift

Mary Ellen Clyne and Mary Forlenza

As we face these turbulent times in the health care arena, health care organizations must effectively manage resources to conserve increasingly limited financial and human resource reserves. Paradigms must shift from a system that is hospital and staff convenient to one that is customer focused. An examination of who our customers are and what their needs are is of paramount importance to providing a customer-focused product line. Anticipating, meeting, and then exceeding customers' expectations about a health care experience create positive feelings about the organization.

The New Jersey Orthopaedic Unit of the Hospital Center at Orange is striving to achieve customer satisfaction, economic growth through a decrease in length of stay, an increase in the number of same-day surgery (SDS) cases, an increase in the number of third party payers, and a focus on cost-effective services. The bottom line in this managed care environment is to provide quality health care while producing revenue. To achieve our goals, we needed to develop a seamless, patient-focused product line to serve our orthopedic SDS population.

LITERATURE REVIEW

The underlying theme in a patient-focused model of care is that services are brought to the patient instead of the patient going to the point of service. According to Farris, the goals of patient-focused care are to move patient care activities to the bedside, increase staff members' care-related time, reduce coordination of activities, and provide greater continuity of care.[1] The quality of the hospital stay is enhanced through increased customer satisfaction through improved services as well as a decrease in the patient's length of stay.

Clouten and Weber state that a patient-focused care model reduces personnel costs by as much as 40 percent.[2] Because idle time for staff contributes to increased costs of procedures (60% percent of the cost of a procedure is related to idle time[2]), cost can be drastically reduced by using a patient-focused care model, and the bottom line can be improved.

Tasks such as admission/registration, specimen collection, and radiological studies, when moved closer to the patient, require fewer people and fewer steps. Strasen reported reduced expenses through redesign of the daily operations of one institution by reintegration of respiratory therapy responsibilities into nursing's domain.[3] The result was downsizing of the respiratory therapy department by almost one third and elimination of duplicated services.

The concept of a multicompetent employee is considered an advantage by health professions alumni and hospital administra-

J Nurs Care Qual, 1997, 11(3): 9–15
© 1997 Aspen Publishers, Inc.

tors because it provides greater versatility as well as coverage for absences and improves staffing patterns.[4] Potential combinations with the greatest potential for benefit include nursing and respiratory therapy, physical therapy and occupational therapy, and technology and radiology.

Registered professional nurses are one of the most valued resources a hospital has for achieving a competitive advantage because they contribute to cost savings and deliver high-quality patient care. As Prescott writes, "What will be new for some hospitals under managed competition is that cost savings and system efficiency alone will not be sufficient for survival. . . . Hospitals will have to convince consumers that the quality of provided services equals or exceeds that offered by competing healthcare institutions."[5(p.193)] It will be the personal touches that a hospital provides to its customers that will make the facility successful.

As competition for patients increases, we must create a culture that values patient perceptions. Organizing work around patient values and expectations is a transformation that middle managers must make to be successful and truly patient focused.[6] This is one of the truly positive aspects of the managed care arena.

The results of adapting a patient-focused care model have included higher-quality care, increased customer satisfaction, improved services, and a decrease in the length of stay.[1] These outcomes will have an enormous impact on organizations that embrace the concept of patient-focused care redesign.

PROGRAM DEVELOPMENT

Our orthopedic SDS patients were selected for this quality improvement effort for several reasons. First, this population is essentially healthy and requires only the basic laboratory and radiological studies. Also, this population utilizes several health-related disciplines that, in some organizations, can be streamlined into a true team approach. In addition, specific outcomes for discharge can be identified for this group, allowing for easier evaluation. An analysis of the daily patient census for the SDS unit revealed that 45 percent of the population represented orthopedic patients. It was believed that ambulatory services as a whole would benefit from the reengineering of this busy product line.

The goals for this program redefinition were to increase productivity, decrease idle time for staff and patients, increase patient care time, and create a program that has a solid customer focus. Accomplishment of this task would put in place a system that would increase customer satisfaction, attract third party payers, and decrease length of stay.

To begin this paradigm shift, it was decided that the care delivery model would be redesigned into a patient-focused care framework that would create a seamless preadmission testing (PAT) process for orthopedic patients. This "one-stop shopping" concept would bring the points of service to the patient in one central area and be provided by a single, cross-trained registered professional nurse. The next step was to elicit comments from the users of this system, namely the physicians, former patients, and SDS staff. Being truly customer focused requires an institution to adjust the present hospital-convenient systems to be more user friendly. Through informal studies with the main users it was determined that the following areas needed to be improved:

- patient preoperative and postoperative teaching
- parking
- waiting areas for family members
- hours of PAT availability

- social service, discharge planning, and rehabilitation assessments
- waiting times for each step of the PAT process

The methodology for reengineering our care delivery system utilized the philosophy of continuous quality improvement. The FADE process is a 4-step process involving *f*ocusing, *a*nalyzing, *d*eveloping, and *e*xecuting; it is a systematic approach to problem identification and problem resolution within a quality improvement framework.

Focusing

The focusing phase identifies and zeros in on the problem and the factors that contribute to inefficiency. It also defines the impact of the problem on the institution and articulates the desired state of operation after the changes.

An analysis of our current PAT process revealed that SDS patients had to go through multiple steps and interact with more than 12 employees to complete PAT. Patients were required to get from place to place on their own, and there was no accessible waiting area for significant others. The hours of operation of the PAT departments were not convenient for patients. In addition, orthopedic patients had surgery in a different building from where PAT took place. Patients were then required to orient themselves to a different environment and hospital staff on the day of surgery, which increased their anxiety level. Also, preoperative and postoperative teaching was not completed until the day of surgery.

The present system caused customers to be frustrated and dissatisfied, which in turn resulted in negative word of mouth regarding the hospital. Third party payers are more likely to assign contracts to hospitals that have cost-effective systems and require physicians to admit patients only to those facilities. Also, as mentioned earlier, staff idle time can equal a financial loss for the organization.

The desired state after the enhancement of the orthopedic product line was to have significant quality improvement in the PAT process that would be cost effective and customer driven. The nurses from the SDS were to be cross-trained to provide a unique service for this client base that would have a positive impact on job satisfaction through role enhancement.

Analyzing

The analyzing phase involves determining whether the stated problem is the actual problem and outlining contributing factors. Flowcharts are used to provide clarity during this process. In addition, benchmarking studies are conducted with other facilities offering a similar service to determine how they solve their problems.

One issue echoed repeatedly by physicians was the current parking situation. The lack of adequate parking space reserved for orthopedic patients and significant others was a source of dissatisfaction for the customer.

The existence of a traditional PAT process (see the box titled "Current PAT Process") resulted in significant idle time for patients and staff. Inconvenient hours of operation and long waits for services made this system confusing and inefficient. Patients were also expected to be ready for the operating room in a timely manner on the day of surgery. Nursing histories and assessments as well as preoperative and postoperative teaching were currently initiated on the day of surgery, which could be anxiety producing and time consuming.

Another factor was the need for discharge planning. There was no initiation of a risk or needs assessment from social services for the

Current PAT Process

1. Patient is scheduled for surgery.
2. Patient schedules appointment for PAT.
3. Patient arrives at facility, parks car, walks across street.
4. Patient is greeted by security officer, given directions.
5. Patient takes escalator up to admitting.
6. Patient registers for PAT in admitting.
7. Security officer directs patient to appropriate location.
8. Patient is sent to laboratory, checks in for blood work, waits.
9. Laboratory technician draws blood.
10. Patient is sent to bathroom to obtain urine specimen.
11. Patient returns urine specimen to laboratory receptionist.
12. Patient is sent to radiology, checks in with receptionist, waits.
13. Radiology technician takes radiograph(s).
14. Patient is sent to cardiology, takes elevator to 7th floor.
15. Patient is given electrocardiogram test.
16. Patient takes elevator to admitting to verify completion of all PAT requirements.
17. Patient exits down escalator.
18. Patient walks to parking lot.
19. Patient pays parking fee.
20. Patient leaves facility.

patient before the surgery. It was imperative to be able to anticipate the discharge planning needs of orthopedic patients in collaboration with the physician and family before admission to the hospital. Our problem was that we had a tendency to react in a crisis mode when the discharge plan changed during the postoperative period before discharge. This limited our ability to move patients efficiently toward their discharge plan and thus increased the length of stay, which affected the financial status of the institution.

Benchmarking studies against other hospitals in New York revealed that orthopedic patients benefit from rehabilitative services twice a day. Currently we were only providing physical therapy once a day. Providing therapy twice a day not only would result in better patient outcomes but also would have a positive impact on the length of stay.

It is the responsibility of the orthopedic nursing staff to ensure that patients are meeting expectations for maintaining quality outcomes each day. Informal benchmarking studies conducted with four area hospitals revealed that no other facility offers a program other than the conventional system for PAT. This information fueled our desire to change our present system into one that is truly customer focused.

Developing

The developing phase involves formulating solutions for the identified areas of concern. All issues are reviewed for their quality improvement potential. Adjustments to the plan are made as needed based on the monitoring plan.

Quality improvements that were made from our paradigm shift included the following innovations (see the box titled "Customer-Focused PAT Process"):

- redesign of our PAT process to a patient-focused model
- cross-training of SDS nurses to perform electrocardiography, phlebotomy, and urine pregnancy testing
- expanded hours of operation for PAT

Customer-Focused PAT Process

1. Patient is scheduled for surgery.
2. PAT appointment is scheduled.
3. Patient arrives at facility; car parked by valet.
4. Patient is directed to orthopedic PAT suite.
5. One registered nurse completes entire PAT process.
6. Patient goes to radiology on the way out and has radiographs taken.
7. Valet brings patient's car to facility exit.
8. Patient leaves facility (no parking fee).

- complimentary valet parking
- complimentary newspapers
- completion of physical therapy preoperative teaching
- provision of physical therapy to inpatients twice a day instead of once a day
- completion of social services assessment before admission and development of a discharge plan

In addition, patients no longer have to go to the admitting department to register for PAT or for admission to the hospital. Patient televisions and telephones are turned on immediately at the patient's request.

Executing

The final step in the FADE process involves the development of an action plan to execute the quality improvements outlined in the developing phase. At our organization, all changes were implemented over a 3-week period. This was accomplished through exceptional multidisciplinary cooperation and upper management support for the changes.

The SDS nurses were educated in admission/registration functions, phlebotomy, specimen collection, urine pregnancy testing, and electrocardiography. Costs associated with this program were kept to a minimum because all needed supplies were collected from the general SDS area and cooperating departments. Registration and admission computers required only printer changes to go live. The cardiology department stored the electrocardiogram machine in the PAT suite. PAT hours were expanded from normal business hours to coincide with the SDS hours; PAT is now available from 6:30 A.M. until 7:00 P.M. 5 days a week. The SDS nurses are now responsible for completing preoperative and postoperative teaching during PAT. The nurses have said that in the current, less stressful environment it appears that the educational process is enhanced and that more information is retained by the patients. The only department to which patients must travel is radiology for necessary studies; here, they are entitled to express radiographic services. Orthopedic PAT patients get first priority, which decreases idle time. Once the radiographs are obtained, the patient can return home.

Complimentary valet parking services were contracted for with an outside agency for patient convenience. This service operates 7 days a week and is open to patients utilizing services within the New Jersey Orthopaedic Unit, including outpatient physical therapy patients. An adjustment in the plan occurred just 1 week before the opening day of our new orthopedic product line. Because of a scheduling error, the parking attendants could not begin the program for at least 3 weeks. The New Jersey Orthopaedic Unit called upon its volunteers and retired employees to pitch in and assist with our parking needs. The response to the call for help was outstanding, and a parking crisis was averted. The entire 3 weeks were covered, and there was no interruption in valet service.

Social workers are available and can be reached via pager to speak in person with the patients about their discharge needs. A physical therapist is present to provide exercise instructions for the postoperative period. The waiting area for the orthopedic patients has been updated to provide reading materials, daily newspapers, coffee, tea, telephone, and television at no additional cost.

The new express delivery system for orthopedic SDS was marketed through direct advertising to physicians' offices by literature outlining the program. Follow-up telephone calls were made to the office managers for clarifications; this call was well received by both the physicians and the office managers. Physician luncheons were held for a 4-week period to promote the new program.

PAT time has been reduced from at least 2.5 hours to 30 to 45 minutes. Evaluation is currently in progress to monitor waiting times, patient satisfaction, cost savings for the organization, and the impact that the program will have on length of stay.

AREAS FOR FUTURE DEVELOPMENT

This program turned out to be quite successful for the New Jersey Orthopaedic Unit. There has been an overall positive feeling about the new program from patients, physicians, and hospital staff. Because of the apparent success, the hospital plans to expand services to all SDS patients, regardless of their admission procedure. Some patients may require other services (e.g., respiratory therapy) involving other members of the health care team. Although the nursing staff believe that the patient retains more preoperative and postoperative teaching when it is completed during PAT, additional studies need to be conducted to determine whether this is true. Finally, we will be expanding our PAT hours further to include Saturdays from 8:00 A.M. until 11:00 A.M.

• • •

The New Jersey Orthopaedic Unit of the Hospital Center at Orange is confident that it has accomplished its goal of providing a customer-focused PAT system within a primary care framework. By offering a service that is unique among other area hospitals, we hope to achieve our primary goal: satisfied customers who are receiving cost-efficient, quality health care services and outcomes.

REFERENCES

1. Farris, B.J. "Converting a Unit to Patient Focused Care: An Innovative Approach Can Reduce the Cost and Complexity of Delivering Care." *Health Progress* 74 (1993): 22–25.
2. Clouten, K., and Weber, R. "Patient-Focused Care . . . Playing to Win." *Nursing Management* 25 (1994): 34–36.
3. Strasen, L. "Redesigning Patient Focused Care To Empower Nurses and Increase Productivity." *Nursing Economics* 7 (1989): 32–35.
4. Beechey, W. "Multicompetent Health Professionals: Needs, Combinations, and Curriculum Development." *Journal of Allied Health* 17 (1988): 319–329.
5. Prescott, P.A. "Nursing: An Important Component of Hospital Survival under a Reformed Health Care System." *Nursing Economics* 11 (1993): 192–199.
6. Kerfoot, K.M., and LeClair, C. "Building a Patient-Focused Unit: The Nurse Manager's Challenge." *Nursing Economics* 9 (1994): 441–443.

The Connection Delivery Model: Reengineering Nursing To Provide Care across the Continuum

Jeanne Donlevy and Bonnie Pietruch

Health care of the 1990s has given us a whole set of new challenges in an already challenging environment. Buzzwords like reengineering, work redesign, downsizing, and right sizing have carried with them fears of job loss, dilution of professional practice, and the uncertainty that accompanies change. There was a time when hospitals and health care organizations were looked upon as stable employment environments. Payers have tightened reimbursements and have increased their emphasis on providing quality patient care in a cost-effective and efficient manner while maintaining positive patient outcomes. In response to shrinking operating budgets, many institutions have instituted staffing reductions and the addition of nurse extenders to meet these challenges. This has resulted in an environment of uncertainty both for employees and employers. The Good Samaritan Hospital in Lebanon, Pennsylvania, has approached restructuring from a positive framework, creating a model of care delivery that has promoted professional growth, not diffusion of the professional nurse's role. This model has promoted professional collaboration in a team management approach to patient care across the continuum.

This organization's model is consumer oriented, flexible in its approach to delivering care to specific patient populations, and places a primary focus on education and prevention of complications. As inpatient acuity continues to rise and patients are being discharged earlier, the readmission rates are continuing to rise for many patients with chronic diseases. Recognizing this trend, The Good Samaritan Hospital has developed a team management approach that assists patients and their families to develop self-care practices that prevent or minimize complications. Through active participation in planning and delivering care, patients become increasingly involved in their care and are then more prepared to comply with treatment goals.

In order to manage patients effectively across the continuum of care, the traditional walls and approaches to providing care must come down. Nurses can no longer consider themselves inpatient nurses or home care nurses. We must be prepared to deliver care to our patients regardless of the setting. Accomplishing this will require developing a model that cross-trains nurses to provide care to patients efficiently and cost-effectively in any delivery setting. Discharge planning must begin prior to admission or as early in the admission process as possible. We have come full circle in health care; with the addition of nurse extender roles in many institutions, team nursing concepts have returned as a method of delivering care. With decreasing inpatient stays, patients are discharged earlier, yet with more complex care needs.

Nurs Admin Q, 1996, 20(3): 73–78
© 1996 Aspen Publishers, Inc.

Home care agencies are growing while inpatient facilities often downsize staffing to remain competitive and provide cost-effective care. The model designed at The Good Samaritan Hospital has allowed us to meet the demands of the industry while avoiding staffing reductions. We have cross-trained our acute care nurses to provide care to patients in the home care setting where the demand for staffing is growing on a consistent basis.

EVOLUTION OF THE PROGRAM

In October of 1992, this program was initiated in response to the changes in the health care environment as well as an internal reorganization that resulted in our home care agency reporting to the nursing executive. The home care agency was experiencing an increase in consultations and was not able to maximize patient visits due to staffing levels. At the same time, the inpatient census was experiencing a decrease in patient days as a result of payer pressures to discharge patients earlier. We were asking inpatient nurses to take time off without pay or to use benefit time during low census periods.

In response to the need for additional staffing in the home care agency, our senior vice president for patient services envisioned the opportunity to meet the increased demand for home care services by using inpatient nurses to supplement the need in home care. As a result of discharging patients earlier, the patient acuity within the home care population was increasing and the patient care needs were becoming more specialized; inpatient nurses were available with the acute care expertise necessary to meet these patient needs. The decision was made to supplement the staffing in the home care agency with cross-trained inpatient nurses. The opportunity was viewed as a way of promoting professional growth for those staff nurses interested in expanding their expertise by applying it in a setting that would allow increased autonomy and creative problem solving in their daily nursing practice.

When the nurse managers asked for volunteers from their staff willing to cross-train to home care, the response was overwhelming, with the largest initial response coming from our obstetrics department. Due to industry trends these nurses were experiencing decreased patient days and decreased lengths of stay. Nursing staff was also identifying decreased opportunities for the education and support many postpartum patients require prior to discharge. Furthermore, the pediatricians identified increased difficulties for mothers discharged early who had chosen to breastfeed. The obstetrics program was the first organized team approach to managing patients in the home care environment. Patients with specialty needs were matched to nurses from the acute care setting with the expertise and comfort level to meet those specialized needs. This program was very successful and resulted in the home care agency receiving referrals from local obstetricians to fulfill the needs of the Healthy Beginnings Program, which concentrates on prenatal as well as postpartum visits for high-risk patients.

The remainder of the inpatient nurses who chose to be cross-trained were oriented to provide visits to patients within the home care population. The orientation provided at that time prepared nurses to complete visits, not to assume case manager responsibilities. This met the initial goals of the program in providing the additional staff to supplement the increased demand for home care services. Initially, the medical–surgical nurses were not matched to patients within their specialty, but rather visited patients with a wide range of medical and surgical care needs.

CHALLENGES EXPERIENCED AS THE PROGRAM GREW

The implementation of this new program was not without its share of challenges. As with any process involving change, there were concerns that became apparent as the program evolved, especially the need to redesign the orientation process. Venipuncture experiences were added to the orientation as well as an introduction to the variety of ambulatory infusion pumps a nurse may be required to use in the home.

Inpatient nurses needed to consider their nurse–patient relationships from a different perspective. Though they were still providing care to patients, they were doing so in a new environment. Viewing their role as caregiver but also as a guest in a patient's home was emphasized in the orientation process.

Scheduling was a challenge in the early phases of the program. Inpatient areas would float nursing staff as the availability was identified by the nurse managers. The scheduling process in the hospital was centralized and coordinated, using an automated program. The scheduling process for home care, an off-site department, was not automated, but rather coordinated by nursing supervisors at the agency. Since the processes were not coordinated at a central location, miscommunications sometimes occurred that resulted in frustrations for both the inpatient staff and the home care agency. The home care schedule is now automated on the same system as the hospital's, allowing the nursing supervisors to coordinate staffing across the system. Staff sick calls are directed to the nursing supervisors, who can then evaluate needs in all nursing units. Home care is viewed as another nursing unit, and staff preassigned to that area are not pulled back to their home unit to meet staffing needs created by sick calls.

Continuity became a concern early in the program as nurses were scheduled to provide home care visits. The home care agency might have received four or five different nurses during any given week of a schedule to supplement their staffing. Concern was voiced by both the inpatient and cross-trained staff that continuity of care would be compromised. In response to this concern, the nurse managers began scheduling their cross-trained staff for week-long blocks of time in the home care agency. The nursing staff satisfaction with this scheduling format was realized soon after it was implemented. Acute care nurses visited the same patients for an extended period and began to feel like integrated members of the home care staff. Acute care nurses became integrated into the routines of the agency and could anticipate their assignments on a daily basis. As a result of the cross-trained staff's desire to promote continuity of care, the team approaches to managing patient populations with similar needs and diagnoses were developed. Those staff nurses who had volunteered to be cross-trained did so because it provided them with a variety of professional experiences. They could enjoy the challenges of home care as well as the acute care nursing experiences they enjoyed without giving up one setting for the other.

TEAM MANAGEMENT OF HIGH RISK POPULATIONS

This model has assisted our institution in meeting the challenges of an environment that is experiencing increased market penetration by managed care. The program permits flexibility in meeting demands of specific populations within our service area. No two components of the program are designed the same. This approach makes sense, given the fact that patient needs differ for each population. The model places heavy emphasis on education and ancillary support services. Many of the programs within this model are prevention based, developed with the specific intent of educating patients and primary caregivers to recognize signs and symptoms that might indicate exacerbation of illness. Providing patients with the tools they need to manage their care has made them willing participants in their own treatment planning.

Patients with congestive heart failure (CHF) have been managed across the continuum of care since April of 1994. Through a nursing quality improvement effort directed at discharge planning in high-risk patients, the CHF population were found to be a population that required a different and more intense approach to discharge planning. This specific population of patients was a high-volume diagnosis with an 11 percent readmission rate. The committee conducted a chart audit of CHF patients to identify the reasons for the high readmission rate within this particular group of patients. Only 13 percent of this high-risk group of patients was referred to home care for follow-up. Referrals to social services for coordination of discharge planning occurred with only 36 percent of these patients. Dietary consultations were noted in only 12 percent of the inpatient stays. Four percent of these patients were instructed on weight monitoring and energy conservation. Since all of these interventions and consultations were deemed necessary to successfully manage this group of patients in an attempt to prevent exacerbation of illness and inpatient admissions, the group considered mechanisms to improve their discharge planning.

In April of 1994, the CHF team was developed to manage these patients in the home care setting. It was felt that if the patients were followed after discharge and were provided education in the areas identified as deficiencies in the initial chart audit, we could positively impact readmission rates. A team approach was used to meet scheduling challenges and the patients with diagnoses of CHF were managed as a separate caseload within the home care agency. The team consisted of a mix of home care staff and inpatient cross-trained staff from our intermediate cardiac care unit, a discharge planner, a dietician, a cardiac rehabilitation personnel representative, and the primary physicians involved with each patient.

Educational materials were developed for use with this population. The team members felt that patients were often receiving educational materials from a variety of sources, the materials were not clearly organized, and many CHF patients were overwhelmed with the volume of materials. A CHF clinical pathway was developed that provided a plan of care for each visit and outlined a concise teaching program. The pathway offered structure to the visits but still allowed for flexibility in meeting the individualized needs of patients.

The team members defined admission criteria as well as goals for the program. The development of the team interventions was handled by the staff nurses responsible for managing this patient population. The process allowed collaboration with interdisciplinary team members and became a challenge for the nurses involved.

After one year of operations, the team has admitted 150 patients and has experienced only a 2 percent readmission rate among this patient population. Those patients who have opted not to be followed in the home care setting have demonstrated a readmission rate that remains at 11 percent. Of the patients readmitted, the average length of stay was three and a half days, while the average length of stay for nonteam patients was 10 days. It seems evident that providing follow-up care for these patients can positively affect readmissions as well as decrease the length of stay when readmissions occur by providing patients and primary caregivers with the information necessary to play an active role in their care.

A follow-up chart audit of CHF inpatient stays in March 1995 was conducted. One hundred percent of the patients reviewed had appropriate referrals for home care services, 83 percent of those patients were referred to cardiac rehabilitation for education on the inpatient side, 90 percent had documented social services referrals, 87 percent had received dietary instruction, and 80 percent had received instruction on weight monitoring and energy conservation. The success of this approach prompted the nursing department to look at other high-risk populations.

FOCUS ON PRIMARY CARE AND PREVENTION

We are currently developing models to manage high-risk patients within our pediatric population. The primary focus of this program will be to intervene in high-risk family units to encourage activities that will promote wellness among the pediatric population within our community. In cooperation with our family practice residency program we will provide home visits to patients identified as at-risk patients. Many of these patients have been identified as "no-shows" for office appointments. Others within this population may be followed when environmental or social issues are identified. Many have had little or no prenatal care and require parenting classes. We currently have a number of nurses interested in following this group of patients in the primary care site.

Diabetic patients will also be managed in the primary care setting with emphasis placed on self-care promotion. We currently have 15 nurses from both the home care agency and the acute care setting orienting with our certified diabetic educator to provide education to diabetics in the ambulatory setting. Our goal with this group of patients is to target educational needs and focus on individualized educational and support plans. This program will add an exercise component as well as support group activities for patients with similar needs. Again, by supplying this group with the tools they require to manage their disease process, we would expect to see a decrease in complication rates among these individuals.

These programs will target prevention and self-care activities. Lack of time to educate patients in the inpatient setting seems to be a frustration for nursing staff. As inpatient stays shorten, there is less available time to provide patients with the education they need to participate actively in their care. Nurses employed in acute care settings and home care settings have not always had the opportunity to involve themselves in preventive education as part of their routine. This will provide the nursing staff another opportunity for professional growth and increased autonomy.

This program continues to evolve. Many of the programs in place and in the planning phases have originated from the staff nurses in our organization, providing opportunities for all staff to become involved. By maintaining voluntary involvement, we have a staff committed to the success of the program and also committed to providing quality care regardless of the setting in which they practice. By maintaining flexibility within the model, we have not excluded nursing staff who have opted not to cross-train to home care but have provided them with the opportunity to participate in other delivery settings. Downsizing has not been necessary, and our nursing staff has viewed this model as an opportunity to expand their practice while maintaining job security when other institutions have found it necessary to eliminate positions. Reengineering the role of nurses does not have to create an atmosphere of fear. When reengineering is approached in a positive manner and is designed to use the full expertise of the staff, organizations can meet the challenges of remaining competitive, while providing cost-effective care without compromising quality.

8

Change: The New Constant

Stress Resulting from Change and Restructuring: A Cognitive Approach

Steven B. Dowd and Norman E. Bolus

People fear the stress associated with change, and stress has been linked to heart conditions and high blood pressure.[1] Traditionally, stress management has focused on affective means of alleviating stress in employees. Is this the best method, or do we need to reframe employees' thinking processes to make them better at handling, and perhaps implementing, change? Are some employees thinking simplistically and not considering necessary alternatives? Simplistic modes of thinking tend to make individuals believe that there is only "one right way" to do things; this leads to resistance to change. Of course, there are situations in which one right answer exists, but there are many more situations in which there are multiple alternatives and there is a need to think along contradictory lines of reasoning, called "critical thinking."[2] The need for critical thinking in health care and health care administration is well established,[3] as well as its relationship to bringing about positive change.[4]

Yet many health care workers are working in perceived stressful managed care environments while believing that the old fee-for-service system was the best. The old system is seen as one in which jobs and other resources were plentiful; therefore, that system must be "good" and any one in which resources must be conserved must be "bad." These people work in one system while clinging to another. Often, they must espouse or at least work under managed care ideals without really believing in them. They see managed care as "bad" or "the enemy," which leads to stress, instead of perhaps seeing that one imperfect system is in the process of replacing another imperfect system. Health care administrators are seen as another enemy who supposedly only care about profit, not patients. This leads to the perception that health care providers are also the enemy because they are involved in the change of the health care system as it was. This perception leads to stress resulting from the change or restructuring because individuals are resisting change due to dichotomous thinking or "simplistic thinking."

Certainly managers—who are looking for individuals able to do many things (multiskilling) as well as adapt to a new health care environment with a new focus on the client and profitability—want to hire practitioners able to engage in thinking that extends beyond simplistic "one right way" of doing things. And employees with the ability to think critically will be able to respond to changes in the health care environment more quickly and survive restructuring better than those who merely have learned a compartment of technical skills. This should lead to reduced stress for health care providers implementing that change.

Fam Community Health, 1998, 21(2): 70–78
© 1998 Aspen Publishers, Inc.

A general overview of dichotomous and simplistic thinking, the relationship of simplistic thinking to (a lack of) change, and some examples of simplistic thinking are presented next.

WHAT IS DICHOTOMOUS THINKING?

The tendency to view things as polarized is sometimes called "dichotomous thinking." According to Kohl,[5] a dichotomy often refers to the division of a group into two parts that are mutually exclusive. Dichotomies, he states, can be neutral (eg, male and female) or have positive and negative charges (eg, good and bad). Unfortunately, often dichotomies that should be neutral, such as male and female, often take on positive and negative charges when constituent groups try to assert the supposed superiority of either males or females. Thus, there is a lack of recognition that differences are not nccessarily good or bad. A male or female trait can be good or bad, depending on circumstances, and certainly, as human beings, males and females can appropriately adapt to circumstances.

Another dichotomy mentioned by Kohl is that of manufactured vs natural goods. Some individuals believe that anything natural must be good and anything manufactured bad. Thus, solar power is good; nuclear power, bad; and natural foods such as honey are good, whereas white sugar is bad. When questioned "why?," proponents of such views rarely have sufficient information to formulate such a value judgment. What is bad is bad simply because it is bad; a tautological fallacy that in order to be disconnected from the cycle of its own illogic requires direct and persistent confrontation.

Politicians seem especially adept at recognizing the natural dichotomies of life and how individuals identify with them; this is perhaps reflected in our two-party system of government and our stands on gun control, abortion, and the legalization of drugs. This process is also seen in television talk shows, which try to polarize the audience "for" or "against" a guest for maximum impact. Sometimes politicians are so adept at these maneuvers that they line up on both sides of a debate, as seen in the "If by Whiskey" speech attributed to a Prohibition-era politician:

> If by whiskey, you mean the Devil's brew, the Poison scourge, the bloody monster that defies innocence, dethrones reason, creates misery and poverty, yea, literally takes the bread out of the mouths of babes; if you mean the evil drink that topples men and women from pinnacles of righteous, gracious living into the bottomless pit of despair, degradation, shame, helplessness and hopelessness—then I am against it with all my power.
>
> But if by whiskey, you mean the oil of conversation, the philosophic wine and ale that is consumed when good fellows get together, that puts a song in their hearts, laughter on their lips and the warm glow of contentment in their eyes; if you mean that sterling drink that puts the spring in an old man's step on a frosty morning; if you mean that drink, the sale of which pours into our treasury millions of dollars which are used to provide tender care for our little crippled children, our pitifully aged and infirm and to build our highways and schools, then Brother, I am for it.[6(p64)]

Another type of dichotomy that is not value-laden (positive and negative) is that of "Buridian's ass," originally posed by the

French philosopher Jean Buridian (c.1295–1358). Buridian used as his example an ass that, finding itself between two equally attractive bales of hay and unable to decide which to eat, starved to death. Thus, the question posed by Buridian was, given two equally desirable alternatives, how is one to choose between them? Such questions often arise in medical ethics, where two equally plausible situations arise, and a difficult decision must be made between two of them. The opposite situation is the double bind, which are apparently no-win situations (both sides equally bad).

Consider, for example, the nurse asked to "float" from her normal unit.[7] Floating is often used during times of restructuring to compensate for short-term personnel shortages. Whether the nurse says no or yes, patient care may suffer; in the first case because of a lack of personnel, and in the second case, due to her lack of skills on that specialized unit. Such decisions require a careful balancing of alternatives. This is not natural to the human mind, which wants to find such situations either "good" or "bad," not sometimes good, sometimes bad, and sometimes lacking a clear delineation. For the nurse who typically values taking care of patients, yes is the typical, but not always best, answer.

IS DICHOTOMOUS THINKING NATURAL?

The neurophysiology of learning and human development indicates that categorization into dichotomies is natural. Bower's[8] experiments with the cognitive development of infants indicated that initial development is dichotomous. An infant given a piece of food to eat will reach for the food. However, if the food is put under a napkin, the infant will not realize the food is there. Later, infants develop the cognitive ability to recognize food in the abstract, realizing the food has not disappeared but is only hidden. The infant learns through experience that out of sight or a changed perception does not necessarily mean something is not there. The initial thought patterns are dichotomous in nature and only through experience does that change. One interesting question is the extent to which this is a constant. Does this also explain the dichotomous thought processes adult humans exhibit?

WHAT IS BAD ABOUT SIMPLISTIC AND DICHOTOMOUS THINKING?

Resistance to Change

A number of research studies have looked at dichotomous thinking, especially in students and young people. Perry[9] studied male students who had a dualistic world view of we-right-good vs other-wrong-bad. Thus, ideas and beliefs they held were thought to be "good" and correct, whereas the views of others were "wrong" and incorrect. The unwillingness to view change as something other than "bad" or "wrong" results in a tendency to resist change, thus causing stress in the implementers of change. Piaget and Inhelder's[10] description of heteronomy, in which children valued conforming to the commands of an authority figure, expands on this premise. Perry's college students tolerated no gray areas, and found also comfort in agreeing with authority.

Piaget's theory of human development stopped in the formal operation stage, in which individuals were able to find fundamental fixed realities such as laws. Many psychologists have proposed extensions to Piaget's theory, usually termed "dialectical thinking," which provides adults the ability to accept alternative truths, other ways of thinking, and a tolerance for ambiguities.[11,12]

Opportunity for Stress

As stated above, implementers of change often end up dealing with the resistance to change due to dichotomous or simplistic thinking. This leads to stress because individuals are unwilling to change from "status quo." The old ways are seen as the best ways; new ways are seen as wrong ways or even as evil.

In the critical thinking literature, Paul[13] has noted the existence of monological or one-dimensional thinking, similar to dichotomous thinking, in that only one point of view is seen as valid. Monological thinking limits alternatives by allowing only those beliefs, thoughts, and actions that conform to "the right way" to be considered.

Paul[13] also postulates the existence of "weak-sense critical thinkers." Such individuals have mastered some of the processes of critical thinking but not the underlying philosophic assumption, and are unwilling to use critical thinking to challenge their own views. They use critical thinking to "shore up their own beliefs." Anyone who has taken college courses has seen students or even professors, who, when confronted with a contrary idea or view, rapidly mobilize their "thinking armaments" to fight this idea, instead of considering whether the idea has merit. One also sees this in scholarly and some other forms of writing, in which certain passages are cited to the extent of excluding the broader ideas of the author, which may include exclusions or the tentativeness of the notion.

Of course, most ideas have some merit, and a function of maturity and experience is the ability to recognize what is good about—and what should be discarded from—any idea. A major theme in the adult education literature is the degree to which one becomes more relativistic in one's thought processes.[14] Unfortunately, this relativism is often misinterpreted by critics as an overintellectualized "anything goes" (or "situational ethics") approach—which it is not.

Klauser[15] notes one type of dichotomous thinking, which she calls "bifurcation," in the case of the teenager who tells her parents, "If you don't buy me a car, I won't be able to get to work on time!" Of course, such a view does not take into consideration the fact that the teenager could simply take the bus to work, get up earlier and walk, or share a ride with a coworker. According to Klauser, advertisers in the United States make a lot of use of bifurcation in order to convince us that we simply must have some sort of item or our lives will be incomplete. Thus, the binary distinction is that our life will be good if we have a certain item, and bad if we do not. Again, this can be seen as a function of maturity, which is one reason why advertisements directed at younger consumers are viewed with skepticism—they are seen to lack the discrimination necessary to know that their lives are not over simply because they do not possess a certain item.

An example of how bifurcation is used in health care lies in the constant debates on whether a fee-for-service or a "socialized medicine" approach would be best for the US health care system. Of course, our inability to resolve this debate resulted in a managed care system that is somewhat imperfect but probably the only workable method—for now.

IS DICHOTOMOUS THINKING ALWAYS BAD?

Berlin[16] indicates that dichotomous thinking highlights extremes, superimposes a value hierarchy (typically prematurely), neglects nuances of meaning, and leaves us with limited possibilities for understanding and action. She argues, however, that using dichotomies as contrasting truths can broaden what we know and what we can do. This would expand upon a dichotomy that is a narrow set of either–or options into a dialectical method of problem solving, or as our mothers used to tell us, "There are two sides to every story."

In fact, as a first step, it is often useful to dichotomize a thought or argument. Ballar[17] notes the functional utility of polarization in circumstances that are too complex for a fuller integration. For example, in discussing ethical issues such as the death penalty or a mandatory national health care insurance, there are the obvious polar extremes of "for" and "against." With additional reasoning, it is easy to see that there are circumstances in which being either for or against in all instances would be overly limiting, as in the death penalty when unjustly convicted prisoners are put to death, or in a mandatory national health care insurance when individuals abuse the system by smoking or being grossly overweight. Thus, a useful definition might be that dichotomous thinking recognizes two alternatives and quickly assigns a value to them (eg, good–bad), whereas dialectical thinking recognizes at least two alternatives but develops an internal "balance sheet" that collects evidence before assigning a permanent value to each choice. Dichotomous thinking leads to rapid polarization while use of the dialectic implies logical, reasoned approaches to dualities, and the search for middle ground between them. This approach leads to less stress because one is able to adapt to change with an open mind seeing all the alternatives that the change can bring about.

Are people able to make some simple abstractions but not more complex ones? Kramer[18] theorized that rudimentary dialectical thinking began in childhood, but probably was not fully developed until perhaps late in middle age, if at all.

Humans have limited "on-line memory" and naturally reduce complexities and categorize information in a way that emphasizes consistency rather than differences; this makes the external environment familiar and (ostensibly) under their control.[15] Popper has argued that humans have an inborn disposition to search for environmental regularities.[19] Certainly, historically, this has fostered the survival of the human race—the ability to recognize what happens and to adapt behavior to these regularities. However, in a system with few regularities and great change, this natural method of adaptation may be more of a hindrance than a help.

Finally, what is a dichotomy to individuals in one culture may not be to individuals in another, another reason why dichotomies cannot always be considered good or bad. For example, Karno[20] found that competition and collectivism, traditionally considered dichotomous in scope in Western culture, were not considered as such by Chinese entrepreneurs. Thus, Chinese entrepreneurs find it easier to integrate the conflicting notions of both systems into one workable system, something that might stymie the average, yet successful American entrepreneur forced to work in such a situation.

CHANGE AND SIMPLISTIC MODES OF THINKING

John Dewey,[21,22] the dialectical philosopher and main proponent of progressive education in the United States, noted the relationship between humanity's predilection for thinking in terms of extreme opposites (known as "either–ors"), the corollary predilection to not recognize intermediate possibilities, and trying to bring about change through education. Dialectical philosophy is based on the principle that an idea or event, known as the thesis, generates an opposite known as its antithesis, which can then lead to a reconciliation of opposites (synthesis).

In the United States, the notion of Hegel's dialectic (thesis-antithesis-synthesis) was expanded on by pragmatists such as Charles S. Pierce, William James, and, as previously mentioned, John Dewey. Recently, health care has begun to reexamine the need for pragmatic problem-solving approaches, and their use by managers and employees to bring about practical workplace change.[23] One of the advantages of pragmatism is that it is based on "what works," rather than some abstract notion of truth or goodness. This helps alleviate the stress involved in dealing with change. Many employees in health care are laboring under what psychologists call "cognitive dissonance," in which individuals hold incompatible and competing ideas simultaneously.

The old fee-for-service and practitioner-centered system often led to dichotomous ways of thinking. The practitioner was often oriented on an illness only and solving the problem of the illness. Decisions were rarely data-driven (at least in terms of epidemiologic data and outcomes studies) except in terms of the immediate quest to cure an illness. The needs of the patient or client were secondary to the illness. Today the practitioner is more and more relied upon to explain what treatments are available to the patient and execute these options based on a dialogue between practitioner and patient, a dialectical decision-making process. However, such a large scale change may be frightening to the practitioner as it eliminates the assurances of the old system—that is, "I treat and you comply."

Practitioners need to look at what was good and bad about the old fee-for-service system (thesis), then analyze objectively what is good and bad about managed care (antithesis), and come to some synthesized view of how they can both work as employees and providers while functioning as change agents to make the current system better. Unfortunately, too many individuals, especially well-educated employees and providers, know precisely how to operate as "weak-sense critical thinkers"—finding all the bad points in restructuring strategies without trying to find their good points. While the old systems of care may have seemed good, as resources were apparently plentiful, in actuality resources were being expended without regard to their most effective distribution. Current systems of managed care and health care restructuring may be imperfect, but the goal should not be to fight this system but to find one that works.

However, currently many health care workers are also operating as received knowers, expecting some authority to tell them how to "combat" these notions. This became clear to one of the authors of this article when he gave a lecture on patient-focused care to a group of well-educated health care workers. The lecture was designed to show workers how this trend may affect their workplace in the future. The group grew increasingly discomfited as the lecture went on until one participant blurted out, "What are you doing to stop all of this? After all, you are a leader in our professional society!" The answer—that one cannot "fight" such trends but must learn how to integrate them into effective patient care, perhaps developing entirely new systems—was not well received.

Although this may seem somewhat incongruous, Riegel's original work with dialectical thinking indicated that individuals might be very advanced in one aspect of thinking (eg, in the technical aspects of their profession) but lack the ability to think in more complex ways outside of that frame of reference (as in the popular saying, "out of the box").[10] Studies such as Maynard's[24] have confirmed that there is often no relationship between the entity known as "professional competence" (ie, nursing skills) and critical thinking ability.

• • •

In order to help health care practitioners adapt to and bring about change and reduce stress, they must be properly armed with both facts and the thinking skills needed for effective change agentry. By recognizing dichotomies and people's natural tendency to dichotomize and perhaps oversimplify arguments, health care providers and others responsible for bringing about change and helping employees adapt to change, can respond appropriately. The key is to realize the human nature of dichotomous thinking and the stress that it can lead to when change is introduced.

REFERENCES

1. Madden K, Savard GK. Effects of mental state on heart rate and blood pressure variability in men and women. *Clin Physiol.* 1995;15(6):557–569.
2. Giurgevich PL. Perspectives on dichotomous thinking. *Nurse Educ.* 1996;21:41–44.
3. McKenzie L. Critical thinking in health care supervision. *Health Care Superv.* 1992;10(4):1–11.
4. Cassidy J. Systems thinking helps leaders handle change. *Health Prog.* 1996;77(1):44–45.
5. Kohl H. *From Archetype to Zeitgeist: Powerful Ideas for Powerful Thinking.* Boston: Little, Brown & Co; 1992.
6. Regan G, Regan MH. *The Book of Bourbon.* Shelburne, VT: Chapters Publishing; 1995.
7. Brownson K, Dowd SB. Floating: a nurse's nightmare? *Health Care Superv.* 1997;15(3):10–15.
8. Bower TGR. *Development in Infancy*, 2nd ed. San Francisco: W.H. Freeman and Co; 1982.
9. Perry WG. *Forms of Intellectual and Ethical Development in the College Years.* New York: Holt, Rinehart, & Winston; 1970.
10. Piaget J, Inhelder B. *The Psychology of the Child.* New York: Basic Books; 1969.
11. Riegel KF. The dialectics of human development. *Am Psychol.* 1976;31:689–700.
12. Basseches M. *Dialectical Thinking and Adult Development.* Norwood, NJ: Ablex; 1984.
13. Paul R. *Critical Thinking*, 3rd ed. Sonoma, CA: Foundation for Critical Thinking; 1993.
14. Merriam SB, Caffarella RS. *Learning in Adulthood.* San Francisco: Jossey-Bass; 1991.
15. Klauser HA. *Writing on Both Sides of the Brain.* San Francisco: Harper; 1987.
16. Berlin SB. Dichotomous and complex thinking. *Soc Serv Rev.* 1990;64:46–59.
17. Ballar D. *The Duality of Human Existence.* Boston: Beacon Press; 1966.
18. Kramer DA. Development of an awareness of contradiction across the life span and the question of postformal operations. In: Commons ML, Sinnot JD, Richards FA, et al, eds. *Adult Development: Comparisons and Applications of Developmental Models*; New York: Prager; 1989.
19. Popper K. *Conjectures and Refutations.* London: Routledge and Kegan Paul; 1963.
20. Karno SR. Chinese Entrepreneurship: An Integrative Method of Measurement and Evaluation (Nationalism, Globalism, Individualism, Collectivism). Minneapolis, MN: Walden University; 1995. Dissertation.
21. Dewey J. *How We Think.* Chicago: University of Chicago; 1910.
22. Jones D. Murrayesque expressivism: a Deweyan reconsideration of contemporary composition's dangerous dichotomies. (ERIC doc no. ED 369 076), 1994.
23. Pryjmachuk S. Pragmatism and change: some implications for nurses, nurse managers and nursing. *J Nurs Manage.* 1996;4:201–205.
24. Maynard CA. Relationship of critical thinking ability to professional nursing competence. *J Nurs Educ.* 1996;35:12–18.

Nurse Executives in the 1990s: Empowered or Oppressed?

Susan Jo Roberts

As the 1990s began, many had high hopes for nursing. Nursing was included at high levels of discussion about health care policy, advanced practice nurses were considered vital to health care delivery, and nursing was being viewed as a powerful force. More recently, the emphasis on cost control, management of care by insurers, and a change in political climate has created differences for nursing: restructuring of care facilities has led to fewer RNs in hospitals; new systems of care have called for new roles; and structures and providers of care have less control over decision making.

Nursing executives have been at the center of these changes. They have been profoundly involved in the reengineering of the workplace and have often had to implement new mixes of personnel, new systems and "downsizing" of their staff. This article explores oppressed group behavior and its implications for nursing executives at this time of great flux and opportunity in the health care system. The purpose of this exploration is to encourage a dialogue about its relevance in order to enhance empowerment and to break the cycle of oppression where it exists.

OPPRESSED GROUP BEHAVIOR

The oppressed group model is developed from writings about colonized Africans[1–4] and South Americans,[5] African Americans,[6] Jews,[7] and American women.[8] Freire[5] developed his model of oppression based on his observations of native Brazilians who had been taken over and dominated by Europeans. He noted that the oppressed have certain characteristics (see the box titled "Characteristics of Oppressed Groups"). He explained that these characteristics come about because the powerful, dominant group determines in a society what attributes (i.e., skin color, clothing, gender, language) are valued and rewarded. These attributes are, of course, the attributes of the powerful group.

Miller, in observing American women, found a similar process. She noted that the oppressed group feel "defective" or substandard in various ways"[8(p.6)] because they cannot look like the dominant group. This makes the group members devalue their own worth and develop poor self-esteem. She also notes that the dominant group "define one or more acceptable roles for the subordinant... which typically involve providing services that no dominant group wants to perform."[8(p.6)]

Members of the less powerful, or oppressed, group who wish to succeed, are therefore forced to attempt to look and act as much like the oppressor as possible. This is often impossible (i.e., the person would have to change his or her skin color, gender, or racial background). Lewin[7] called these people

Nurs Admin Q, 1997, 22(1): 64–71
© 1997 Aspen Publishers, Inc.

Characteristics of Oppressed Groups

Has low self esteem
Possesses self-hatred
Tries to hide evidence of belonging to own culture
Takes on characteristics of dominant group
Becomes passive-aggressive
Develops horizontal violence

"marginal" because they try to look like the oppressor by attempting to deny their own characteristics and by taking on as many characteristics of the oppressor as possible. They end up being unable to identify with either group.

This marginal status leads to feelings of low self-esteem and self-hatred because of the need to devalue and reject their own attributes. The oppressed attempt to "pass" by hiding their own identity, but at the same time they develop a feeling of shame about themselves and their own group.[4] These feelings of self-hatred, as well as frustrated aggression against the oppressor, lead to lack of trust and fighting within the group.[5] The oppressed do not fight against the oppressor for fear that direct confrontation will be punished, but rather take a passive-aggressive attitude that is rarely successful in gaining any power. Having lost their cultural identity, they have little faith in their own ability and become dependent on the oppressor for self-definition and support. This dependence and fear leads to a reluctance to revolt even if the force were available to accomplish it. A cycle develops in which low self-esteem leads to further dependence and passive-aggressiveness and further dominance.

The oppression is therefore maintained. There are other ways in which it is maintained that are more subtle.

1. The educational system in the society perpetuates the validity of the system of values and beliefs that were developed to support the attributes of the oppressor. Over time, the groups internalize these beliefs and forget that they developed in a situation where the dominant group had more force and power. Both groups begin to believe that the oppressed and their attributes have always been *inherently inferior.*
2. Rewards in the form of jobs and privileges are given to those in the oppressed group who proclaim that the dominant values are correct and devalue those of their own group.[6] Often the leadership of oppressed groups are made up of these most marginal members who are interested in pleasing the oppressor and are forced to degrade their own group in order to do so.
3. There are often token rewards given to the group if it appears that a revolt may be possible. These changes halt the momentum and often further entrench the powerless.

Freire[5] outlined a strategy for liberation of oppressed groups (see the box entitled "Steps in Liberation"). Understanding of the oppression cycle is the first step in this liberation process. The second step is to dispel the myth that the dominant group is inherently superior. Liberation therefore involves rejecting the negative images of the oppressed culture and replacing them with pride. Consciousness-raising groups

Steps in Liberation

Understands the dynamics of oppression
Expels the myths of the old order
Develops pride in their own characteristics
Actively seeks autonomy

were used by feminists to discover the myths that they had been taught. An example of a strategy to make just such a change is "Black is beautiful"—a slogan from the Black power movement in this country.

Oppressed groups also often need to realize that many of their "best and brightest," who are often their leadership, have become coopted and "marginal." A leadership needs to be developed by those who are interested in change and who can develop a broad base of support among their own group. Often this change involves grass roots organizing and the development of a less hierarchical system in which leadership is shared.

NURSING AS AN OPPRESSED GROUP

Other articles have discussed in detail the argument that nursing is an oppressed group[9–13] and so it will be dealt with only briefly here. The argument is based on the assumption that nurses have internalized the values of physicians and the medical model to the extent that they can be said to be "marginal." Allan and Hall[14] have argued that the values of nursing are rarely recognizable, let alone operationalized in patient care. This assertion is supported by the observation that, until recently, what is "nursing" has been and, is still for some nurses, difficult to define because all of health care has been subsumed by medicine. Lack of self-esteem[15,16] and passive-aggressiveness[17,18] are characteristics noted to be found in nurses. Leaders in nursing have often been an elite and marginal group that have maintained the status quo in return for rewards from physicians in power.[19] Nurses have been subtly and directly encouraged to think and act like physicians and to organize care arenas to convenience physicians rather than patients.

In view of this, it is particularly interesting to think about nursing executives. Increasingly, nurse managers and executives have become a part of the management team. Nurses have won a victory by being included in the decision-making arena. Often, however, the vice-president of nursing is the only nurse included at this level and in the meetings where other administrators, lawyers, fiscal personnel, and physicians make important decisions about the day-to-day operations and the future planning. The peer group of the nursing executive has increasingly become non-nurses. The nursing executive is expected to develop and increasingly refine knowledge and skills in complex financial and budgetary issues, computer systems, and management theory. The nurse executive has become responsible not only for nursing, but for the success of the entire organization. Nursing executives are chosen based on their abilities to take on such a role. Some nursing executives have been so successful in their organizations that they have been selected to be administrators of parts of the organization of which nurses are only a part and the nursing executive reports to an administrator outside the nursing arena.

One of the ongoing realities of nursing executives is the lack of a nursing peer group. They become isolated in their own organizations by the emphasis on administrative and fiscal responsibilities. The competitiveness between health care facilities does not allow for nursing directors of other organizations as supports and confidants. The nature of their hierarchical authority often makes it difficult for nursing executives to use their staff for support and input. Increasingly, the mid-level nursing administration has been reduced or eliminated so that administrative colleagues within nursing are becoming rare.

Nursing executives may therefore develop their identity as a manager separate from nursing. They may pride themselves on being part of the management team and are pleased about being "not just a nurse." They feel that they were chosen from the other nurses because of their ability to be a managerial person. They may feel that their employees do not understand the business or administrative needs of the organization. They may feel negatively about nurses and their inability to take on and support management policy. They may be rewarded by their superiors for thinking about the global needs of the organization and discouraged from advocating for nurses and nursing care. They may like to have more nurses involved in the decision making, but feel that speaking up for more nursing input could jeopardize their position in the organization. They feel that they are more successful if they focus on the needs of the organization rather than nursing, and that benefits for nursing will follow if they are successful. Nurses who have left nursing for administrative positions may be hesitant to mention that they are nurses because the identification would diminish their power and respect.

NURSING EXECUTIVES AS A "MARGINAL" GROUP

This situation in which the nurse executives find themselves can be analyzed as being "marginal." "Marginality" means that, in order to "get ahead" in a system dominated by medicine and increasingly business and insurance personnel, nurse executives have learned and taken on a different set of values. Many nurse executives and managers feel that their association with nursing weakens their power and prestige and their association with power brokers is useful to nursing.

Cleland has noted that nursing leaders have been compared to Black "Uncle Toms":

> Administrative positions in nursing generally are available only with the approval of the male system in medicine, hospital administration and higher education. The top nurse communicates to the male system with authority and finality on all questions relating to the nursing community.[19(p.1544)]

Cleland called these nurses "Aunt Janes" because they are aligned with medicine and administration, and often act against the best interests of nursing. Nursing leaders have often represented an elite and marginal group who have been promoted because of their allegiance to maintenance of the status quo. Even though nurses often control the search committees for nurse executives and administrators, they have so internalized the needs of the powerful others, that they automatically eliminate candidates that they think are too "nursing oriented" to be approved by medicine or administrators.

Grissum and Spengler[20] have said that nurse leaders, like other women leaders, can easily become "Queen Bees." They noted that these nurse leaders are removed from other nurses who they view as a potential threat to their hard-won position. "Because of the rewards they receive, they do not feel animosity toward the system or the men in the system. They reject the ideas of current feminist thinking and blame women themselves for their status as second class citizens."[20(p.103)] These leaders represent nurses but vote against the best interests of nursing in order to keep their power in the organization. This kind of leadership leads to divisiveness and competition among nurses and does not foster united efforts to change the system.

STRATEGIES FOR LIBERATION FOR NURSING EXECUTIVES

The first step in liberation from oppression is to understand the dynamics of oppression.

This realization can be freeing for nurses who previously had no model by which to understand their situation in society and their own behavior. This includes the realization that nurses are not inherently inferior but instead have been placed in a culture that devalues their attributes.

This awareness should not be a depressing one, but rather an informed call to action based on a strategy for change. Lynaugh and Fagin have suggested that this realization calls for celebration:

> This confluence of paradoxes, problems and characteristics of nursing development can be responded to in two ways. One is to bewail our failures and accept the inevitability in the face of an historically hostile environment. The other is to wonder at and celebrate the extraordinary accomplishments of nurses, mostly of the wrong sex and class, who have the wrong history and education, who persist and achieve in spite of being held back by some of the most powerful forces in our society.[21(p.184)]

This analysis of nursing's situation begins the process of establishing an air of celebration and pride in the history and development that has taken place. The acknowledgment of pride both personally and collectively begins to reverse the cycle of low self-esteem and internalized hostility that has led to much of the negativity and divisiveness. This process may involve the unleashing of pent-up hostility, as was the case in the feminist movement of the 1970s. The idea of having "consciousness-raising" or support groups for nurse executives to explore and express their feelings in a safe environment may be very helpful.

Another lesson of the oppression model is that the process of liberation has to come from the grassroots. An elitist leadership cannot give power nor set the agenda for change. Nursing leaders can benefit from discussions with themselves and their colleagues about the subtle ways in which they may be "Aunt Janes" or "Queen Bees." Nursing must have leaders that value nursing if the nurses and nursing leaders are to be empowered. Similarly, the process of decision making needs to become more non-hierarchical and the priorities should reflect the needs of the nurses and their view of patient care.

The power of the executive, which truly emanates from the staff, is empowering to both and sets up a cooperative system of governance. Rather than a shared governance, the executive can view herself as working for the nurses in a way that encourages communication and support. This non-hierarchical model allows for grassroots support and cooperation.

Chandler[22] has discussed the need for relationship as the major empowering force for nurses. Similarly for the nurse executive, the development of a broad range of relationships allows for varied input and a broad base of support, and avoids the isolation from other nurses. This broad base allows the nursing leader to truly represent nursing on the management teams rather than being an authority figure who is primarily related to others on the management team and dependent on them for a power base.

Schmieding[23] has also argued that a "shared vision" and "process of inquiry" are vital to empowerment in the organization. Particularly in this time of change, a discussion of the vision of nursing and the basic values of the work become vitally important to the reengineering work that is pervasive in our workplaces. She calls for the nursing executive to have a "process of inquiry," which uses appropriate personnel in discussion of the vision, the priorities, and the ongoing administration rather than making decisions in isolation. She notes that, although the structure and context may change, the need for shared vision and ongoing dialogue are vital to the empowered organization.

The oppression model suggests that an ongoing vision quest is useful to nursing in understanding its roots, its values, and its beliefs in view of the overpowering influence of medicine. As Torres has noted

> Consistent with the theory of oppression, nurses have been led to believe that it is right or natural for medicine to maintain control of the entire health care enterprise. The freedom to develop nursing's own destiny can only come from nursing's own initiative and will not be freely given."[13(p.10)]

The challenge is to look at the current system and to imagine a vision of the importance of nursing care in the system that can be articulated as a critical element of caring. Discussions of changes in the system are suggesting that if nursing is clear about its vision, its place in the system will be crucial.[24]

The nursing executive of the 1990s has a particularly difficult task in organizing and implementing this type of system. The changes that have occurred have brought reduction in midlevel nursing managers, reduction in hospital staff, and more arenas in which nurses work in ambulatory and community-based positions.[24] Nurse leaders are facing a more decentralized system in which their peers are other administrators. Each professional group is trying to maintain a segment of shrinking financial resources for their group. Nursing leaders can benefit from an awareness of their status as an oppressed group leader and of the need to identify with nursing and its concerns. Although this is a difficult task, the theory tells us that alignment with other groups does not in the long run empower nursing. Although there may be some short-term gain for the leader herself, empowerment and control by nursing only comes when nursing itself is valued and supported.

• • •

The oppressed group model suggests that empowerment in subordinate groups comes from the development of a unified group who have clarified their own values as separate from the dominant group and who actively challenge the disparity of power in the system. Leadership in oppressed groups are often marginalized because, in an attempt to get ahead and gain control and power, they champion the values of the dominant and powerful groups. At this time of change and opportunity in the health care system, it is particularly vital that nursing be focused and united. Nursing executives are at high risk to become marginalized and look for support and esteem outside of nursing.

Nursing executives can benefit from an analysis of their own nursing group with regard to oppressed group behavior in order to enhance unity and empowerment. An effort to develop a shared set of values and goals, as well as a broad-based power structure within nursing, can empower both the staff nurses and the nursing executives. The oppression model suggests that until all are empowered then none are really so.

REFERENCES

1. F. Fanon, *The Wretched of the Earth*. (New York: Grove Press, 1963).
2. F. Fanon, *Black Skins, White Masks*. (New York: Grove Press, 1967).
3. A. Memmi, *The Colonizer and the Colonized*. (New York: Orion Press, 1965).
4. A. Memmi, *Dominated Man*. (New York: Orion Press, 1968).

5. P. Freire, *Pedagory of the Oppressed*. (New York: Herder & Herder 1971).

6. S. Carmichael, and C. Hamilton, *Black Power*. (New York: Random House, 1967).

7. K. Lewin, *Resolving Social Conflicts*. (New York: Harper & Row, 1948).

8. J.B. Miller, *Toward a New Psychology of Women*, 2d ed. (Boston: Beacon Press, 1986).

9. K.N. Bent, "Perspectives on Critical and Feminist Theory in Developing Nursing Praxis." *Journal of Professional Nursing* 9, no. 5 (1993): 296–303.

10. P.G. Clifford, "The Myth of Empowerment," *Nursing Administration Quarterly* 16, no. 3 (1992): 1–5.

11. B. Hedin, "A Case Study of Oppressed Group Behavior in Nursing," *Image* 18, no. 2 (1992): 53–57.

12. S.J. Roberts, "Oppressed Group Behavior: Implications for Nursing," *Advances in Nursing Science* 5, no. 3 (1983): 21–30.

13. G. Torres, "The Nursing Education Administrator: Accountable, Vulnerable and Oppressed," *Advances in Nursing Science* 3 (1981): 1–16.

14. J. Allen and B. Hall, "Challenging the Focus on Technology: A Critique of the Medical Model in a Changing Health Care System," *Advances in Nursing Science* 10, no. 3 (1988): 22–34.

15. N. Greenleaf, "The Politics of Self-Esteem," *Nursing Digest* 6, no. 3 (1978): 1–7.

16. M. Bush and D. Kjervik, "The Nurse's Self-Image," in *Women in Stress: A Nursing Perspective*, eds. D. Kjervik and I. Martinson, (New York: Appleton-Century Crofts, 1978).

17. P. Munhall, "Methodological Issues in Nursing Research: Beyond the wax apple," *Advances in Nursing Science* 8, no. 3 (1986):1–5.

18. L. Stein, "The Nurse-Doctor Game," *Archives of General Psychiatry* 16 (1967): 699–703.

19. V. Cleland, "Sex Discrimination: Nursing's Most Pervasive Problem," *American Journal of Nursing* 71 (1971): 1542–1547.

20. M. Grissum and C. Spengler, *Women Power and Health Care*. (Boston: Little Brown & Co, 1979).

21. J. Lynaugh and C. Fagin, "Nursing Comes of Age," *Image* 20, no. 4 (1988): 184–189.

22. G. Chandler, "The Source and Process of Empowerment," *Nursing Administration Quarterly* 16, no. 3 (1992):65–71.

23. J. Schmieding, "Nurse Empowerment through Context, Structure and Process," *Journal of Professional Nursing* 9, no. 4 (1993): 239–245.

24. M. Barker et al., "The Changing Health Care Delivery Structure: Opportunities for Nursing Practice and Administration," *Nursing Administration Quarterly* 19, no. 3 (1995): 74–80.

Understanding and Managing Change in Health Care Organizations

Kyoko Nagaike

Health care expenditure represented about 14 percent of the gross domestic product (GDP) in 1992 as opposed to 9 percent in 1980. It will rise to 19 percent of the GDP by the year 2000[1] and cost $1.7 trillion unless cost-effective strategies are implemented.[2] Rising personnel and operational costs associated with technological advances, regulations such as the introduction of prospective payment, and the Joint Commission on Accreditation of Healthcare Organizations (Joint Commission) all demand that health care organizations change and deal with rising costs and decreasing revenue. In addition, continued decrease in reimbursements and shifts from inpatient to outpatient care will require further changes. Other factors including changes in nursing personnel numbers, increased demand by patients for quality services, and political focus on health care have also affected health care organizations.[2,3]

CONCEPTUAL FRAMEWORK OF CHANGE

Robbins defines change as "an alteration in structure, technology, or people."[4(p.381)] Changing structure refers to any alteration in structural variables such as authority relations, coordination mechanisms, degree of centralization, and job designs. Changing technology includes the methods and equipment used or modifications in the way to work. The last category of change, people, refers to alteration in staff attitudes, expectations, perceptions, or behavior.

Change in Structure

Restructuring results in change in an organizational structure. An organizational structure is defined in terms of its degree of complexity (the amount of differentiation in an organization), formalization (the degree to which an organization relies on rules and procedures to direct the behavior of employees), and centralization (the concentration of decision-making authority in upper management).[4] Presently, the health care industry is managed more in a business context to be cost-effective without giving up comprehensive and high-quality care.

Organizations become multilevel and multilateral corporate systems (i.e., they are not stand-alone entities). For example, health care organizations provide health care plans for comprehensive health care services. Such organizations will accommodate new customer demands while ensuring appropriate services in the marketplace to survive economically.[5]

Another example of structural change is an introduction of the flatter or horizontal corporation, cutting off several management levels,

Nurs Admin Q, 1997, 21(1): 65–73
© 1997 Aspen Publishers, Inc.

whereas traditional organizations have a pyramid-shaped hierarchy. For instance, AT&T and General Electric are managed by the horizontal or flat structure. This has resulted in a business-process redesign and nonbureaucratic decision making. It also requires goal-oriented team concepts with reengineering, multiskills rather than specialized skills, customer-driven performance, and a reward system.[6]

Another change is a shift from a functional structure to a matrix and product structures. A matrix structure is defined as a structural design that assigns specialists from functional departments to work on one or more projects led by a project manager.[4] This could be useful for functional specializations to increase accountability although it can result in redundancy of activities and resources. Thus, it may create a dual chain confusion about who reports to whom.

Another structural change in health care is managed care, in which the delivery of care is arranged for or approved by someone who is not the primary care provider.[7] Managed care was introduced by the New England Medical Center in 1985.[8] Many health care administrators have recognized the need for managed care and have introduced it in health care organizations. At least 35% of health care organizations in the U.S. mainland have adapted managed care (K. Hanold, personal communication, 4 April 1996).

Product-line management (PLM), originally introduced by Proctor & Gamble in 1928, has also been introduced into the health care system.[9] Its management approach aims at marketing, planning, implementing (organizing, directing, controlling), and evaluating the product line while providing quality and cost-effective care.[9–11] PLM can be developed by specialty programs, procedures, or clinical service areas such as cardiovascular, laboratory, orthopaedic, and emergency services.[11] Moye states that "related products are grouped in an effort to provide a comprehensive, coordinated response to identified patient needs."[11(p.56)] This change may require actual structural redesign as well as redesigning nursing methods, job descriptions, and so forth. Porter-O'Grady states that PLM will not be effective to provide quality care in a cost-effective manner unless health organizations remain autocratic and control employees such as nurses who provide direct care.[12]

Nursing management is shifting from controlling to mentoring, coaching, or facilitating. Professional practice models such as shared or professional governance are models in which staff are more autonomous and accountable to care. Nursing case management is another option. Sioux Valley Hospital in South Dakota[13] reported successfully developing a professional practice model during the restructuring of the patient care delivery system. The model was based on differentiating nursing roles of associate degrees, baccalaureate, and master-prepared (clinical nurse specialists) nurses using case management with shared governance. It is uncertain how professional practice models will fit into PLM systems. On the other hand, Capuano[8] states that total quality management (TQM) helps make case management feasible. TQM has become popular in the health care system and has been considered as a means to improve quality care and reduce costs while meeting patients' needs. TQM is embraced by the Joint Commission and the American Hospital Association.[14]

Technology

In addition to structural changes, technological changes are affecting health care organizations in various ways. Technology is a powerful tool to change organizations. Computerization is probably the most visible change in recent years.[4] Hospital information systems (HIS) are run by sophisticated computers. HIS allow organizations to handle large amounts of information, manipulate and store the information, and make it possible to supply necessary information to patient care areas and administrators as needed.[15] Other information systems such as electronic-mail and patient information have also been used to improve communication. Systems assist clinical areas such as laboratory and radiology and financial and material management. However, nursing informatics is still being developed and has yet to make a major impact on care. The quality of nursing informatics will depend on interactions between nurses and computer experts.[16]

With more sick patients and personnel budget cuts, the need for automated computers with bedside terminals is apparent.[17] There are unique tools that meet this need, although there may be some disadvantages such as "high-tech but not necessarily high-touch solution."[17(p.140)] One study measured the use of computers and found positive and negative results.[18] For instance, there was more readable and complete documentation, as well as timely documentation and less time spent to document. On the other hand, employees felt some resistance toward computers, frustration with vendors who did not respond quickly to problems, and an increased volume of documentation with no time to sit down.

In addition to information systems related to management and delivery of patient care, computers have been integrated into education.[15] Computer Assisted Instruction (CAI) is used to provide orientation and practice to both staff and patients. CAI allows an individual to work at his or her own pace and also works in a small group that collaborates. Such a system can improve quality of care and practice and enhance morale of those providing the services.[19]

People

Finally, changes have occurred to people in health care organizations. Historically speaking, nurses worked within a medical practice model in which hospitals and physicians maintained a "symbiotic relationship."[20(p.1)] In this relationship there were unlimited resources and growth of expenditure and revenues.[20] Nurses are recognized as quality and cost-effective providers in the current environment.[21] Health care administrators view physicians as customers of the hospitals rather than providers. Hospitals are an organizational entity to provide care for physicians who are key to bringing original customers, patients, into hospitals.[7]

Decentralized decision making has resulted in nurses' role change. More team work, interdisciplinary and multidisciplinary, is required in the decision-making process. Decentralized decision making occurs in case management, which monitors, plans, and coordinates treatment provided to patients with costly conditions. Training, education, and empowerment of employees are part of the process of change when teams have decision-making authority.[22] Empowering first-line managers is one of the keys to success in restructuring in addition to empowering staff who directly provide care. First-line managers can ensure open and direct communication in the team and provide feedback, which helps move the change process forward. They can observe problems and success and offer suggestions to address problems and provide recognition and rewards for successes.[23]

Nurses are educated and empowered by self-study, orientation, continuing education, and clinical practice. Education and training are costly. Hospitals prefer to provide continuing education and cross-training to existing staff rather than orientation to newly hired nurses. Cross-training will prepare nurses to function effectively in more than one area. When nurses are more specialized, nurse replacement becomes harder. Cross-training will increase the organization's ability to deal with change in census and acuity. Staff nurses have more professional satisfaction with increased stimulation in more than one unit.[24] An educational consortium is formed within the health care system for cross-training. This will achieve cost-effective and high quality education/orientation and increase productivity.[25]

Nurses who are reorganized in a resource team, defined as "a group of employees who have no specific long term unit assignment,"[26(p.1)] may experience a change in role. Hospitals may experience some dissatisfaction, such as poor employee performance and lack of incentive, for employees who work in the resource team. However, dissatisfaction will be resolved by creating a good design for the team and a commitment to manage for success. Resource teams immediately provide flexibility to respond to demands.[26]

Although recognition and rewards or incentives are new concepts in the health care environment, they are important. A study done by the Council of Communication Management showed that "recognition for a job well done is the top motivator of employee performance."[27(p.xv)] Although the study did not include health care organizations, Nelson[27] listed reasons it is important. Some are relevant in the current health care environment. Administrators must work as coaches rather than controlling or coercing the desired behavior. Administrators need to provide a positive and reinforcing working environment as employees are asked to become more autonomous. Finally, administrators need to have employees work in a cost-effective manner and encourage higher levels of performance. More studies need to be conducted on the use of incentives in health care organizations.

Patients are now customers in health care who have expectations to be cared for properly. As part of health care organizations' cost containment measures, patients and their caregivers' roles have changed. Patients and their family members take a more participative role in their own health care decisions.[4,21] Collaborative care within multidisciplinary teams includes traditional professionals, volunteers, and trained nonprofessional employees to satisfy patients' needs at a lower cost. For example, the University of California Los Angeles (UCLA) Medical Center introduced a model using patient care partners for professional nurses. There were resistance and negative responses among the nursing profession in the beginning. However, this model resulted in successful outcomes of high quality care using employees hired and trained by autonomous nurse councils.[28] On the other hand, Barter and colleagues suggested that while this study demonstrated significant cost-effectiveness to use unlicensed assistive personnel who assisted RNs, it did not reveal conclusive measurements about the quality of care.[29]

Adaptation

Jean Piaget, one of the theorists of human development, believes that adaptation results from interaction with the environment via two activities. As people adapt, they are using the first type of activity, called assimilation, which is already in the child's repertoire. In the second type of activity, called accommodation, people change their activities to conform to environmental demands.[30]

Employees who are able to adapt are pivotal to successful change in structure, technology, or people within health care organizations. Nurse administrators are able to help employees positively adapt to changes by facilitating the two activities of assimilation and accommodation in a planned change. Thus, preparation must include creating learning opportunities from the environment and knowing and accepting the demands in the environment.

Discussion

Change has occurred in health care organizations that allows them to survive in an environment that demands cost-effective quality care. Employees who understand the various types of change and the rationale for these changes will be better prepared to accept and proceed with the changes. However, in many cases change occurred suddenly without enough information given. Uncertainty and unpreparedness create chaotic circumstances and cause many negative feelings such as anger, helplessness, confusion, and loss of trust among employees.

One of the areas for additional research should be change in technology to provide services in a cost-effective manner. Technology should be used wisely. For example, use of advanced medical technology costs more or increases costs while it helps health care services become more sophisticated and makes procedures easy and patients comfortable. Thus, it could be necessary to measure how to use medical technology with optimum effects on costs and quality of care and patients' needs. Several major local health care organizations have undergone restructuring in the past two years. One health care organization, which downsized about two years ago, still has employees who are reacting negatively to the changes. An administrator has expressed that the employees' reactions are necessary stages similar to human reactions that occur as people grow up (i.e., going through the developmental stages). The role of the administrators, like parents, is to assist the employees to adapt to the changes. Overall, this organization works objectively toward their goals of "Better Care and Better Cost."

Another large medical center has restructured recently. This organization is a good example of one that has introduced a flatter organizational structure. Prior to this change, it introduced reengineering to its employees. Patient services had also been working with its nursing units on a care delivery model of shared governance. Shared governance was developed on the inpatient floors' nursing staff for several years. However, employees still felt the organizational changes happened suddenly. They were impacted and were confused (B. Mathews, personal communication, 30 April 1996). Thus, nurse administrators must assist employees through changes and minimize the employees' negative reactions and impact. Nurse administrators should remember that employees at any level must be satisfied and happy before they can contribute to the organizational change and provide quality of care.

Points to examine for successful change in a health care organization include the following.

Defining Change

Before restructuring, a health care organization must clearly define its value of services and determine its principles and conceptual framework to provide the services after carefully examining the ability of the organization and its staff to adapt to the environment. Value is also derived from the organizational mission and philosophy. The organizational structure, which is a measure of the degree of complexity, formalization, and centralization, is reviewed and redesigned if necessary. For example, the organization must consider what is the unity of command, authority, and responsibility, such as the line and its authority and the methodology of care delivery. It must also determine the degree to which employees are involved in decision making and have employees who are ready to make decisions in the new structure. Clear job descriptions and reporting relationships will support behavior change. These actions will assist employees to work within the structural changes in the organization.

Meaning of Change

All employees need to understand the context of the why, what, and how to change as well as the desired outcomes throughout the change. This information must be given to employees in a timely manner. Employees must have a clear and positive image of the outcomes and perform as part of the organization. Then, they will understand the link between the vision and change activities (i.e., they will be able to answer the question why and what they are doing). Those activities will further assist employees to understand their roles, attitudes and expectations.

Clear and Consistent Communication

Clear and consistent communication is critical since every employee is a stakeholder in the change. Health care professionals as rational problem solvers will be ready to change and become part of change by having constant information and communication. They will be able to identify problems and give feedback with resolutions with more information. Therefore, communication routes and methods should be clearly defined at the time of change. Communication is important to facilitate all areas of change—structure, technology, and people.

Accurate Information

Information consists of data. Goal-oriented outcomes must be measured by data. To achieve optimal goals, consultation by experts on information systems and other areas may be necessary. However, the role of consultants should be well established and understood by all parties involved. For instance, an automated and computerized system can make the work relatively easy and provide quality. Data will indicate what is wrong and corrective steps can be taken. Accurate information will assist changes in structure, technology, and people.

Adaptable Plan and Flexibility

Administrators and councils/committees should determine a process of change for improving performance and cost-effectiveness. Knowing what matters most and the difficulties to change and making adaptable plans with a clear process are important in facilitating effective changes. Flexibility helps discover and convey the best outcomes. Administrators can learn different approaches to facilitate the change by observing patients' and employees' reactions. For example, surveys can determine how to proceed with the changes, such as going slowly or taking different actions. An adaptable and flexible plan assists change in all three areas.

Administrative Support

When preparing for change, creating a flexible system for its recipients is a major administrative responsibility. Executives and administrators should identify what councils or committees will take responsibility for what issues or problems and must act as role models. Each council works internally and externally considering employees' opinions and reactions. Then, the outcomes must be periodically evaluated and all employees informed, to continue toward effective change. Inviting employees to participate on the councils may provide opportunities for employees to change. Participation will further clarify changes in peoples' roles, attitudes, and expectations.

Education and Empowerment

Employees who have more clinical knowledge and skills and are patient advocates can successfully provide patient care. Employees who understand interpersonal and organizational skills can be prepared to function more effectively in new organizations. Employees must have professional and personal growth. For example, educational programs include personalized training by clinical nurse specialists and in-service programs to develop knowledge and skills and empower employees. In addition, organizations should be designed to promote better use of their employees' skills. To achieve the goals, administrators need cost-effective strategies such as cross-training to build their own self-confidence and credibility. Finally, the staff become a new resource for finding and resolving problems. Education and empowerment are especially important in changes involving employee attitudes, behaviors, and roles.

Teamwork

Patient care must be carried out collaboratively among health care professions. Employees function independently, interdependently, or dependently, varying with the problems or situations. Organizations must define types of caregivers who can take on a variety of responsibilities and roles in the practice models. This will minimize the number of caregiver categories, which will decrease costs and increase staff use. For example, trained staff or volunteers help nurses, who are coached and mentored by a case manager/clinical nurse specialist. Another example is cross-trained nurses who can help nurses in other similar settings. Teamwork is essential to successful change in structure and people.

Needs and Satisfaction

Patients perceive care as good or bad every single moment. Employees as direct providers take responsibility for quality of care at the front line. They must know their patients' needs. In return, quality care that satisfies patients produces positive responses from the patients, which then satisfies employees. Administrators must communicate what their needs are and how satisfied they are with the care given. In this way, administrators provide satisfaction to their employees. In this circle, each participant has an important part in reinforcing changing roles.

Rewards

Effective use of rewards/incentives will facilitate positive working attitudes and environment. Administrators must create clear and fair formal reward systems to teams rather than individuals. Informal rewards from the immediate supervisor should also be used on a timely basis. Rewards assist employees toward positive attitudes, behaviors, and role changes.

• • •

Nurse administrators must play an active and essential part as dynamic leaders and role models in health care organizations as health care organizations are challenged to become more effective and efficient in an ever-changing health care environment.

Robbins's categories of change, which include changes in structure, technology, and people, were used to describe the multitude of changes occurring in health care organizations.[4] Nurse administrators can use this framework to better understand the changes. Once they have an understanding of the changes, nurse administrators must consider areas that assist employees to adapt to the changes. These include a clear definition and meaning of changes, clear and consistent communication with accurate information, adaptable plans and flexibility, administrative support, opportunities for education and empowerment and teamwork, patients' and employees' needs and satisfaction, and rewards for quality care. This process will help health care organizations achieve successful change.

REFERENCES

1. "Why We Need Reform," in *The President's Health Security Plan* (New York: Times Books, 1993), 1–20.
2. S.T. Burner, D.R. Waldo, and D.R. McKusick, "National Health Expenditures Projections through 2030," *Health Care Financing Review* 14, no. 1 (1992): 1–29.
3. L.H. Bender and P. Christensen, "Models of Nursing Care in a Changing Environment: Current Challenges and Future Directions," *Orthopaedic Nursing* 13, no. 2 (March/April 1994): 64–70.
4. S.P. Robbins, "Managing Change and Innovation," in *Management*. 4th ed. (Englewood Cliffs, NJ: Prentice Hall, 1994), 379–408.
5. T. Porter-O'Grady, "Restructuring the Nursing Organization for a Consumer-Driven Marketplace," *Nursing Administration Quarterly* 12, no. 3 (1988): 60–65.
6. J.A. Byrne, "The Horizontal Corporation: It's Managing Across, not Up and Down," *Business Week* (20 December 1993): 76–81.
7. S.A. Finkler and C.T. Kovner, "The Health Care Environment," in *Financial Management for Nurse Managers and Executives* (Philadelphia: W.B. Saunders Company, 1993).
8. T.A. Capuano, "Clinical Pathways: Practical Approaches, Positive Outcomes," *Nursing Management* 26, no. 1 (1995): 34–37.
9. S.A. Price, "Marketing Nurse and Nursing Services," in *The Professional Practice of Nursing Administration*, 2d ed., ed. N.E. Ervin, et al. (Albany, NY: Delmar Publishers, 1994), 434–48.
10. D. Yano-Fong, "Advantages and Disadvantages of Product-Line Management," in *Issues in Nursing Administration, Selected Readings*, eds. S.A. Price and M.J. Ward (St. Louis, MO: Mosby-Year Book, 1991), 360–66.
11. C.E. Moye, "Product Line Management," *Orthopaedic Nursing* 10, no. 1 (1991): 56–61.
12. T. Porter-O'Grady, "Shared Governance and New Organizational Models," in *Issues in Nursing Administration, Selected Readings*, eds. S.A. Price and M.J. Ward (St. Louis, MO: Mosby-Year Book, 1991), 315–21.
13. S.S. Bunkers, et al., "Change: A Professional Challenge," *Nursing Administration Quarterly* 16, no. 1 (1991): 15–21.
14. M.L. Masters and R.J. Masters, "Building TQM into Nursing Management," *Nursing Economics* 11, no. 5 (1993): 274–78, 291.
15. U.G. Jelger and H. Peterson, "Hospital Information Systems," in *Nursing Informatics: Where Caring and Technology Meet,* ed. M.J. Ball, et al. (New York: Springer-Verlag, 1988), 179–89.
16. M.F. Hendrickson, "The Nurse Engineer: A Way to Better Nursing Information System," *Computer in Nursing* 9, no. 12 (1993): 67–71.
17. S. Hughes, "Bedside Information Systems: State of the Art," in *Nursing Informatics: Where Caring and Technology Meet*, ed. M.J. Ball, et al. (New York: Springer-Verlag, 1988), 138–145.
18. S.A. Finkler, et al. "Changing the Delivery of Nursing Care: Implementation Issues and Qualitative Findings," *Journal of Nursing Administration* 23, no. 11 (1993): 24–34.
19. C.T. Barry and L.K. Gibbons, "Information Systems Technology: Barriers and Challenges to Implementation," *Journal of Nursing Administration* 20, no. 2 (1990): 40–42.
20. T. Porter-O'Grady, "Changing Realities for Nursing New Models, New Roles for Nursing Care Delivery, *Nursing Administration Quarterly* 12, no. 1 (1991): 1–6.
21. V. Deback and R. Waite, "Consumer Response: A Reflection on Change," *Nursing Administration Quarterly* 12, no. 3 (1988): 57–59.
22. L. McHenry, "Implementing Self-Directed Teams," *Nursing Management* 25, no. 3 (March 1994): 80I–80L.
23. D. Boynton and L. Rothman, "Charge Nurses: Critical Change Agents for Successful Restructuring," *Recruitment, Retention and Restructuring Report* 9, no. 2 (1996): 1–4.
24. B.L. Rowland and H.S. Rowland, "Adjustment Techniques for Staffing," in *Nursing Administration Handbook*, 3d ed., eds. B.L. Rowland and H.S. Rowland (Gaithersburg, MD: Aspen Publishers, 1992), 325–36.
25. K.W. Blanchard, et al., "Development and Implementation of a Perinatal Education Consortium," *Journal of Obstetric Gynecology and Neonatal Nurse* 24, no. 8 (1995): 707–12.
26. Lawrenz and Associates, Inc., "Resource Team: More Relevant than Ever, Part 1," *Perspectives on Staffing and Scheduling* 15, no. 1 (January 1996): 1–4.
27. B. Nelson, *1001 Ways to Reward Employees* (New York: Workman Publishing, 1994).
28. P.P. Hines, "An Interview with Moira Kally," *Nursing Economics* 12, no. 3 (1994): 113–19.
29. M. Barter, et al., "Use of Unlicensed Assistive Personnel by Hospitals," *Nursing Economics* 12, no. 12 (1994): 82–87.
30. G.R. Lefrancois, "Theories of Human Development," in *The Lifespan*, ed. G.R. Lefrancois (Belmont, CA: Wadsworth Publishing Company, 1987), 30–63.

9

Staff Transition

Nurse Leaders: Roles Driving Organizational Transition

Debra Bumsted Hernandez, Linda Berger Spivack, and Cheryl Zwingman-Bagley

The demands of managed care and our many customers have changed the health care environment significantly. For nurse executives, traditional practices at managing organizational change do not work in today's environment. Individuals and their organizations are now in constant transformation and demand change initiatives that respond rapidly, consolidate energies, and define structure. This sense of urgency in today's chaotic settings inspire individuals who are motivated by challenge, commitment, and autonomy to assume unique roles. These transition leaders are introducing extraordinary, eclectic methodologies in order to manage change. Transition leaders combine theories, innovation, and even magic to create the methodologies that guide the change process.

WHY NURSES?

Our Customers

Nurses have the knowledge and experience of the system of care and of our organization's culture, processes, values, strengths, and weaknesses. Transition leader roles have three primary sets of customers: patients; employees, staff, and physicians; and administrators. Nurses with management and administrative experience are ideal transition leaders because of their customer knowledge and commitment. Transition leaders keep patients at the center of decision making by maintaining direct interaction with them, individually and in focus groups; listening; and integrating their feedback.

A transition leader's knowledge of employees, staff, and physicians originates from the unique role of internal consultant. Since transition leaders are not in a "line" position, they are viewed as having influence but no line authority. Therefore, transition leaders are often told "the way things really are" from the customer's perspective. The customers see us as missionaries of the vision; someone who has no investment, stake, or potential loss from having it reach fruition in their work area.

Administration authorizes the transition leader to initiate movement of the vision to reality, provide administration with feedback, and challenge administration on its assumptions in order to promote the organization's transformation.

The Art of Nursing

Nurses learn a unique set of skills, such as creativity, patient centeredness, coordination, multiple priority management, problem solving and critical thinking, and (health care) system navigation experience. But, the most important thing transition leaders, who are

Nurs Admin Q, 1997, 22(1): 38–46
© 1997 Aspen Publishers, Inc.

nurses, bring from their nursing background is caring. Jean Watson proposed the goal of nursing:

> to help persons gain a higher degree of harmony with the mind, body, and soul which generates self-knowledge, self-reverence, self-healing, and self-care processes while allowing increasing diversity. This goal is pursued through the human-to-human caring process and caring transactions that respond to the subjective inner world of the person in such a way that the nurse helps individuals find meaning in their existence, disharmony, suffering, and turmoil and promotes self-control, choice, and self-determination.[1(p.49)]

Transition leaders help constituents during the crisis of change and reorganization. Such threats as loss of identity, own job, and coworkers can create the same kind of pain as that experienced by a patient who is ill. According to Watson, nurses apply the values learned early in their education:

> Human care requires high regard and reverence for a person and human life, nonpaternalistic values that are related to human autonomy, and freedom of choice. There is a high value on the subjective-internal world of the experiencing person and how the person (both patient and nurse) is perceiving and experiencing health-illness conditions. An emphasis is placed upon helping a person gain more self-knowledge, self-control, and readiness for self-healing, regardless of the external health condition. The nurse is viewed as a coparticipant in the human care process. Therefore, a high value is placed on the relationship between the nurse and the person.[2(p.34)]

These values are a perfect fit when considering the transformations many transition leaders are trying to achieve in organizations. Some of these changes include enabling empowerment and autonomy for staff; recreating a community within our workplace (such as with self-managed work teams); and emphasizing a learning organization with employees taking responsibility for their own learning.

The combination of the caring values from nursing with the knowledge of our customers is explained by Mayerhoff,

> We sometimes speak as if caring did not require knowledge, as if caring for someone, for example, were simply a matter of good intentions or warm regard. . . . To care for someone, I must know many things. I must know for example, who the other is, what his powers and limitations are, what his needs are, and what is conducive to his growth; I must know how to respond to his needs and what my own powers and limitations are. Such knowledge is both general and specific.[3(p.13)]

Watson supports the complexity of caring with concepts that are essential to functioning as a transition leader:

> As such human care is an epistemic endeavor that defines both nurse and person and a level of space and time, it requires serious study, reflection,

> action, and a search for new knowledge and new insights that will help to discover new meanings and understanding of the person and human care process during health-illness experiences.[4(p.30)]

Transformation

Transition leaders bring some new attributes that are not necessarily typical of nurses, but may be found more frequently among transformational nurse leaders. We find the following attributes indispensable in our roles:

- seeks windows of opportunity within the chaos and capitalizes upon them;
- is results driven with no fear of failure;
- works outside the "line" hierarchy, not using positional authority to accomplish change and hold others accountable;
- is value driven and principle focused in a constantly changing environment without clear boundaries; and
- takes risks by using bold and revolutionary processes.

Transition leaders are entrepreneurs, willing to take risks, always pushing the envelope. As transition leaders, we pull out of our hats surprise techniques that no one expects, and transform quickly failing health care environments into viable, flexible health care systems behind the scenes.

THEORIES/CONCEPTUAL FRAMEWORKS

Transition leaders are familiar with several change-related theories. The value of using a theory rests in reframing beliefs, creating a structure; determining process, as well as delivering results. The chosen theory will assist in setting boundaries and scopes that a scattered, transforming organization cannot do. The transition leader integrates knowledge of the organization and the strategic outcomes it desires when deciding on a theoretical framework in order to create some semblance of order "to get the work done." The following are examples of how transition leaders applied theories and conceptual frameworks to reach organizational outcomes.

Transition Management

According to William Bridges, "*Change* is situational: the new site, the new boss, the new team roles, the new policy. *Transition* is the psychological process people go through to come to terms with the new situation. Change is external, transition is internal."[5(p.3)] Transitions begin with experiencing a loss and the letting go of old behaviors, processes, identities, or systems. Change, on the other hand, is the beginning of something new (the creation). However, according to Bridges "unless transition occurs the change will not work."[6(p.4)]

Bridges has identified three phases of transition: ending, neutral zone, and new beginning (Figure 1). The transition process begins with the ending phase. The role of the transition leader is to identify the loss, assist in expressing the loss, and control negative behaviors. A symbolic event finalizes the losses. During the neutral zone phase, the transition leader taps into creativity and encourages the origination of ideas. The transition leader guides the individual and organization into realizing that the old ways do not work and new beginnings are essential. Establishing temporary, productive systems that will evolve into the anticipated environment occurs. Finally, according to Bridges, in the new beginning phase, "People need The Four P's: the purpose, a picture, the plan, and a part

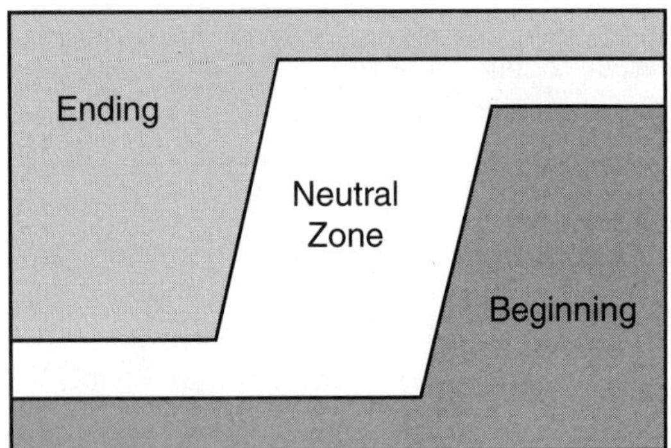

Figure 1. Phases of transition. *Source:* W. Bridges, TRANSITIONS, (figure 1 - page 70). © 1980 Addison-Wesley Publishing Company Inc. Reprinted by permission of Addison-Wesley Longman.

to play"[6(p.52)] to reach stability. Also, the transition leader is responsible for ensuring that communication is consistent, success is public, outcomes are rewarded, and achievements are celebrated.

The following is an example from our practice. An interdisciplinary team from a variety of organizations and settings within the Connecticut Alliance for Integrated Care (CAIC), a newly formed local integrated delivery system, had the charge to create a case management practice. An experienced consultant (Kathleen A. Bower, RN, DNSc, Principal and Co-Owner, The Center for Case Management, Inc., South Natick, Massachusetts) and an internal transition leader facilitated the completion of the design process within four months.

Initially (ending phase), the participants discussed concerns and implications related to loss of autonomy from the organization's and professional discipline's perspective. Both the new entity of the CAIC and Case Management had the potential to create this threat. Losses and threats were reframed as team members focused on customer needs, agreed to preserve their own internal organizational activities, and concentrated on the collaborative role of the case manager. Three team members attended a national conference on case management igniting the team with possibilities, marking the final good-bye to the old ways and welcome to the future.

During the neutral zone phase the members of the team investigated present models, determined how the practice would operate, proposed a budget, and drafted a multitude of practice standards. The transition leader facilitated the team to create a framework for the delivery of care within CAIC and to identify lacking services. The team was cautious when decision making; calling upon the consultant and CAIC board members. The neutral zone phase was a time when the team had more of an opportunity to get to know each other since the sessions were day long and held at the participating organizations. As the team evolved and the case management practice began to have structure, the members tested some of the proposed ideas and processes, when interacting, to manage patients.

The team's struggle with the case manager role requirements marked the new beginning phase. The team *pictured* the desired outcome by finalizing written practice standards. The team created two *plans*: a logistics plan outlining immediate CAIC board decisions needed and the design document. The board sanctioned the CAIC's new beginning phase by approving the proposal, rewarding the team with a celebration dinner, resolving the logistics issues, and hiring one case manager.

Renaissance Process

McWhinney[7] describes change opportunities through a "renaissance process or path." His renaissance path is an ideal methodology for an organization when the situation seems hopeless. If there is limited ability to resolve conflict, nonexistent morale and leadership, perceived lack of value, and apathy, the renaissance path may lead to rebirth. According to McWhinney and associates "Rebirthing an organization creates a new foundation of meaning for the organization or one of its elements. It lets go of established principles, with the accompanying policies, boundaries, purposes, in search of a new identity."[7(p.57)] The various phases or modes evolve the organization from close to death to rebirth, and into implementation (Figure 2). As a change methodology, the renaissance path defines the conflict, guides the use of multiple methodologies, and can achieve a dramatic change.

Rebirthing begins with the organization being dissatisfied with the present system, and the employees refusing to hold it together (*sensory mode*). The structure is meaningless and they allow it to consciously dissolve. This lack of structure leads to system death, eliminates the need to resolve problems, and creates an open scope. Next, the process of deframing, mourning, and reframing occurs (*social mode*). The values from reframing activities become the shared values of the new entity. The rebirth originates from the new vision and purpose; the creation of a new identity (*mythic mode*). This is a time of high innovation and unpredictability. The new organization has an infrastructure, one that will support continued rebirth. The organization begins to acquire the tools and processes necessary to generate a product, such as policies and standards, roles and associated activities, and supplies and resources (*unitary mode*). The participants of the renaissance path set behavior rules and work ethics in order to compose the culture. The organization begins to produce and all of the activity is striving to achieve the goals previously designed (*sensory mode*). As the vision evolves into reality it will be the reality of everyone; conflict will be much less, and the high level of value and goal-driven activity will regenerate rebirths.

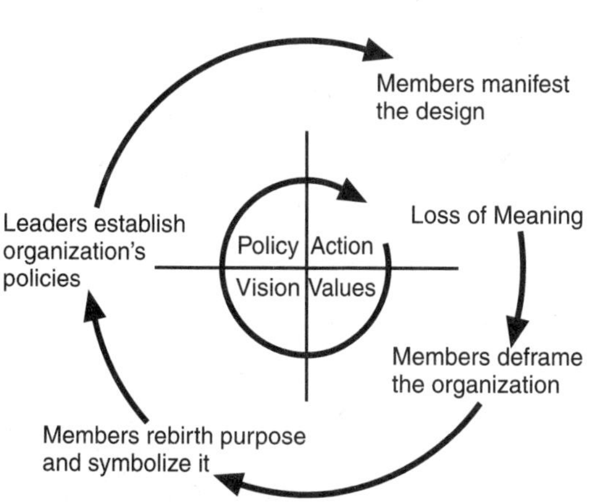

Figure 2. Renaissance path. Source: Reprinted with permission from W. McWhinney, et al. "The Paths of Change," in Creating Paths of Change (Venice, CA: Enthusion, Inc, 1993). ©1993, Enthusion, Inc.

The following experience describes how this path was used as the framework to rebirth the nursing coordinator team (NCT) as a self-managed work team. The outcomes achieved were NCT and management satisfaction, NCT cohesiveness, and increased NCT autonomy. At the time the NCT began to accept the responsibilities, self-managed work teams did not exist in the organization; now there are two! The director in this example is also a transition leader and, as the team evolved, the director became the team's coach.

The team had hit an all time low (*sensory mode*); half of the positions were unfilled, overworked staff were unable to meet staffing needs, and the members felt disconnected from each other and the organization. The team was very close to death. The director contemplated various models for accomplishing the NCT functions; a self-managed work team was chosen.

During the *social mode*, as part of deframing, the director disregarded previous structures that fostered dependence and handed scheduling over to the team. The director expected the NCT to communicate directly with other individuals rather than informing the director of issues. During the mourning phase a few staff members continued to "check in" and make sure that the director was in agreement with the actions taken. There were few staff members left who were part of the old ways, so the team quickly moved into reframing. The NCT agreed to three values or principles for team decision making: the NCT is in control and responsible for the team, the NCT is a professional team and expected to follow professional standards, and the director is the coach of the team.

As the NCT evolved into a more cohesive, self-managed team, the director facilitated the exciting *mythic mode*. The team and the director had lively discussions of the responsibilities and operation norms of self-managed work teams. The vision constructed included self-scheduling and covering each other, communicating directly with the organization, complying with education and regulatory requirements, hiring new staff, and accepting responsibility for projects. The team outlined a phase two development plan that included evaluating peers, resolving disciplinary problems, and integrating into the organizational communication structure. Shortly after the first meeting, a staff member resigned.

The team moved rather rapidly into the *unitary mode*, primarily due to the need to recruit and hire into the open position. Members of the team participated in the panel interview, with the director, and recommended a candidate. This individual was hired. The team created and completed the orientation.

The last mode of the renaissance path, *sensory mode*, continues as the NCT strives to achieve the vision. The team achieved the initial outcomes identified. Most recently, the team participated in a disciplinary action of a team member and decided on a new staffing model. The team is planning a retreat to learn more about and create a plan to implement peer review. The three original values still hold true and provide a framework for team rebirth.

ADDING THE MAGIC

Transition leaders combine the knowledge of the customer, the art of nursing, and the attributes derived from chaos, with today's trendy change theories. With these, there is still plenty of room for the imagination. Abracadabra! "Change-magic!"

Position

Periodically moving and repositioning the transition leader through the organization encourages influential interaction with a great number of staff and widespread, result-driven implementation of strategic initiatives. Also, new positions may appear during management restructuring; these positions may be broad in scope and collaborative in nature, which allow transition leaders to capitalize on "change-magic" opportunities. As a member of many teams, including some at the senior administration level, the transition leader listens for and communicates the pulse of the organization, previews the staff's potential response to decisions, and represents the patient to senior management.

During a recent management restructuring a new position emerged (Director, Care Management/Delivery). By virtue of this position, this transition leader continues to monitor, influence, and guide the implementation of care delivery redesign; coordinate the development and organize the services of care management; and integrate cost and quality of care outcomes. This transition leader is also responsible for implementing the new Service Access Center, one of the organization's strategic initiatives. The organization is relying on this transition leader to implement and achieve outcomes, test new structures and methods of management, and advance the integrated delivery system. The sorceress is performing her "change-magic."

Networking

The "knowing who to go to" and "for what" are the intricate underground alliances that are the backbone of the transition leader. Many senior administrators will not or cannot take the risk of challenging the status quo, yet will use authority inherent in their position to sustain the transition leader. The senior administrator provides the most current information, identifies potential obstructions, or resolves a barrier for the transition leader. With regard to this occult networking, it is essential to maintain confidentiality, report the facts, show appreciation, and achieve results. By providing this service, the senior administrator expects payment in the form of organizational change. Similarly, with staff and physicians, secret desires for change are able to come to light with the transition leader as the beacon.

Change Agent

The role of change agent is not new; it is the addition of the magic that makes the transition leader mysterious. The transition leader, as a consultant, casts the spell, convinces others by appealing to their needs and wants, influences the assignment of committee structure and membership, inspires new position appointments, predicts success of a change effort, and performs backroom negotiations.

In another transition leader role, the Director of Transition Planning integrates organizational initiatives into the strategic imperative transitions operations, and moves a new hospital to a new site. As staff support to the Chief Executive Officer, the transition leader utilizes the art of skillful, direct, honest communication, and motivates the organization to focus on patient centeredness, staff ownership of their future, and integration opportunities. The glue (i.e., transition leader), invisible and strong, integrates the transition activities into a master planning and action process. By spreading the magical sparkle seeds, the transition leader supportively influences the creation of the organization's new operations.

Teams

A transition leader succeeds only when involving other people. The magic of teams is the interplay between the members and the charge. They expand the participation and commitment to a cause; have the power to enchant a supernatural, synergistic relationship; organize a formal channel of change-effort-based authority; and are the medium for the completion of work. Transition leaders need to compare the cost and results of traditional, frequent, ongoing, short, often unproductive meetings against meetings with dedicated time in full days per week, for a period of a few months. Initially the dedicated days appear too highly resource consumptive; however, the structure prevents disruption or distraction from operational issues and promotes team cohesiveness.

Retreats

A powerful team event for mass communication and commitment is a retreat. As an example, the Redesign Team struggled with determining a process for care delivery redesign implementation. The Redesign Team mobilized all of the involved individuals and teams together at two, day-long retreats. A small team crafted the retreat agendas and chose an internal facilitator to lead both retreats. The transition leader participated in the retreats. In those two days, the team agreed upon the sequencing and dates of redesign role education, clinical validation, and model implementation. Also, the patient care area and central departments collaborated to create staffing and scheduling plans during classroom and clinical education.

• • •

The transition leader uses many tools from the discipline of nursing, from other disciplines' theories and frameworks, and from transformational leadership concepts, but the magic is from the exquisite interplay of them all. We plant our seeds all over the organization. Some are magical and grow like Jack's beanstalk, leading us to places we never anticipated going when we began. We find partners and allies to fertilize and water the seedlings and wave our wand to bring in bees for cross pollination. We perform our magic by bringing different species together to create new, more effective, resilient products. We appear and disappear throughout the organization. While our crops are growing, we read voraciously to learn from others' experiences and we seek out communities of other transition leaders to share our experiences, successes, failures, and magic potions. And most of all, at harvest finale, we give thanks and credit to our teams and we honor our sponsors.

REFERENCES

1. J. Watson, "Nature of Human Life as Subject Matter of Nursing," in *Nursing: Human Science and Human Care* (New York: National League for Nursing, 1988).
2. J. Watson, "Nature of Human Care and Caring Values in Nursing," in *Nursing: Human Science and Human Care* (New York: National League for Nursing, 1988).
3. M. Mayerhoff, *On Caring*. (New York: Harper & Row, 1971).
4. J. Watson, "Human Care in Nursing," in *Nursing: Human Science and Human Care* (New York: National League for Nursing, 1988).
5. W. Bridges, "It Isn't the Changes That Do You In," in *Managing Transitions* (Reading, MA: Addison-Wesley Publishing Co., 1991).
6. W. Bridges, "Launching a New Beginning," in *Managing Transitions* (Reading, MA: Addison-Wesley Publishing Co., 1991).
7. W. McWhinney et al., "The Paths of Change," in *Creating Paths of Change* (Venice, CA: Enthusion, Inc., 1993).

10

The Nursing Studies: Implications for Nursing

The Challenge for Education in a Transformed Health Care System

Marjorie M. Heinzer, Terry McGoldrick, and Sharon McLane

A trauma center registered nurse (RN) was enrolled in the first clinical nursing course in pursuit of a baccalaureate degree. As she read the syllabus, she realized all her clinical experiences would take place in a local high school setting. She was to visit the school, talk with the health teacher, assess the needs of the students, and plan a program of health promotion teaching for a semester. The equipment she would bring with her were her own talents in communicating, her insight into developmental stages, and her knowledge of the needs of adolescents. She returned to class after the first week and stated that clinical time in a high school was not a good use of her abilities, wasted her precious time, and was unnecessary for her learning, as "this experience is too basic."

A senior student in the generic baccalaureate program was assigned to spend a day in a local day care center during a clinical experience in pediatric nursing. His objectives were to assess the health education needs of the preschoolers in the center, plan a brief health teaching session, and implement that informal session during the course of the day. He had been directed to assess developmental patterns and identify any health concerns of the children. Upon return to the acute care clinical setting, the student submitted a written summary of the experience that stated that "there is no reason to spend time with healthy children" when what he needed was experience in pediatric nursing in the acute care setting.

The scenarios are real and the individuals portray the all too common thinking that the only real nursing care is acute care nursing in the hospital setting. The paradigm shift to a health promotion, disease prevention, and wellness focus in addition to complex acute care is in progress. Targeting care for vulnerable populations, enhancing primary health care services, and providing access to health care are issues included by the Pew Health Professions Commission in its focus on competencies in the emerging health care system.[1]

Nursing administrators face significant challenges in managing health care delivery and nursing within the multidisciplinary team in this time of rapid change. Change in the health care system will happen with or without the input of nursing. If the profession is committed to shaping the future of nursing practice and ensuring optimal health care outcomes, then education must be directed to meet these challenges. The purpose of this article is to identify the changes in the scope of nursing and make recommendations for nursing education in response to the changing needs of a different health care environment.

Nurs Admin Q, 1996, 20(4): 80–88
© 1996 Aspen Publishers, Inc.

THE CHALLENGE TO PROFESSIONAL NURSING EDUCATION

The winds of change have arrived with force and have altered the health care system and the delivery of nursing care in the 1990s. The trend toward the inclusion of health promotion and disease prevention content was anticipated within nursing academic communities and was the focus of intense curricular modifications over the past decade.[2,3] Courses encompassing holistic health appraisal were designed and replaced the basic physical assessment content. Health promotion strategies were included in initial clinical courses for beginning nursing students as well as for RNs who were returning for degree completion. Health education teaching became a focus of clinical nursing practice in community settings of schools, day care agencies, senior citizens' centers, residential facilities for the homeless or the older person, and neighborhood nursing centers. Nursing practice in primary health care environments was less high technology and more critical thinking in nature, while anticipatory health guidance and risk behavior interventions were added to the curriculum. The baccalaureate nursing programs were proactive and well positioned to address the change that Nola Pender discussed in the preface of her book *Health Promotion in Nursing Practice*: "Nursing as the largest health profession needs to evaluate carefully its education programs for current and future social relevancy. Education for professional nurses should be based on a health-wellness model rather than an illness-disease model."[4(p.x)]

With this model of nursing care, the high technology focus on acute care needs of the critically ill patient in the hospital would involve a smaller cadre of professional nurses. Certainly, nursing programs continue to educate and prepare practitioners to manage the intense nursing needs of patients with complex medical and surgical problems. However, the appearance of human immunodeficiency virus (HIV)/acquired immune deficiency syndrome (AIDS), resistant strains of tuberculosis, emerging potent viruses, antibiotic-resistant bacterial infections, burgeoning homeless populations, and the sophisticated care of persons having bypass and transplant surgeries stress the need for improved assessment, planning, intervention, and evaluation skills of nurses. Higher levels of acuity within the patient population in all health care agencies mandate clinical expertise and greater accuracy in decision-making abilities of even novice nurses. The advent of interactional computer programs, computer assisted instruction (CAI) programs, and video simulations bring the patient reality into the practice laboratory settings. The students can access programs to enhance anatomy and physiology knowledge and understanding; refine skills in assessment techniques, recognition of the normal and abnormal, and the interpretation of those data; and practice standardized test performance. Teaching strategies are taught and role-played to give both groups of students experience in newer and more effective modes of health care teaching across the life span as well as across cultures.

Attention must continue to be directed to both major practice areas within the academic setting, primary health care and high acuity nursing, if nursing students and professional nurses who are returning to the educational setting are to comprehensively practice professional nursing. The measures of the value of nursing care are treatment and patient outcomes, the benefits to the consumers of health care. Whether this is truly a new model of care, an evolving model, or a redefining of an "old" model may be debatable at this time. Historically, settings for nursing care were homes and community sites; hospitals as primary sites for nursing care were developed within the 20th century.

Coupled with the focus on wellness, health care reform issues have defined the economic need for the earlier return to the home setting for illness and recuperative care. A major proponent of this recent acceleration of the changed health care environment has been the redesign of health care provider reimbursement. American business and political sectors have targeted spiraling health care costs as a principal component to maintaining competitiveness in the emerging world market. Third party payers have responded to these pressures, reducing reimbursement to hospital and other health care providers. Consequently, hospitals are implementing budget pruning initiatives, including reduced length of stay, reduced work forces, skill mix changes, job redesign, and organizational flattening. These budget reduction efforts have highlighted opportunities to improve patient care and patient satisfaction while reducing expenses.

In addition to fiscal trimming in health care institutions, the placement of health promotion and disease prevention interventions has been moved outside the traditional health care delivery systems. These challenges for implementing the redesigned education and health care practice were explicated in the objectives of the *Healthy People 2000* document released in 1991 by the federal government's Department of Health and Human Services.[5]

Societal needs for wellness promotion in the community, chronic illness management in the home, and posthospitalization acute care in the home demand attention in this changed model of health care delivery. Thorne and Robinson have discussed similar adaptations in Canada and have stated, "Not only is the nature of health care delivery changing, but the nature of illness is also changing."[6(p.294)]

The shift from acute illness to chronicity for the majority of health care services signals a move to the care orientation from the cure orientation. Just as leaders in a changing management role must unbundle old skills,[7] so must nurses in the changed practice environment. Education is again the connection to meeting the needs of the client in the nontraditional setting and the needs of the nurse in the changed role. Using newly adapted skills or learning new skills becomes the challenge for the professional in the role of the caregiver in the changed setting. The lack of structure within these noninpatient settings along with the flexibility in the planning and implementation of care may be uncomfortable for some nurses, yet the autonomy, independence, and accountability provide increased professional growth and satisfaction. Positive personal benefits are the potential unplanned and welcomed rewards for nurses as they step into these new professional roles.

Within the baccalaureate nursing educational program, RNs as well as basic students learn the dimensions of the wellness focus, a focus that identifies the value of health care beyond the disease management and treatment scope. Courses and clinical content address the changing environments, the basic needs of the person within the family, aspects of decision making for nursing care, the release of high-technology output to a practice of high cognitive output (using the brain rather than manipulating equipment), and the unlimited scope of a health care practice within the professional nursing role. The critical care nurse, the public health nurse, or the primary health care practitioner is transformed to the critical thinking nurse. The nursing student, likewise, learns and develops the role of the critical thinker. The profound impact of this transformation lies in the change agency potential of the professional nurse to decrease volume, intensity, and complications of inpatient acute care needs in the future.

THE CHALLENGE TO CONTINUING EDUCATION

Ongoing development and educational support for the professional nurse requires recognition of the learning needs in the transformed workplace. Professional role development initially implies an ongoing personal commitment to education. Nurses are expected and accountable to participate as active learners. To enable this, resources for learning such as professional journals and continuing education programs must be available and affordable with minimal financial and time constraints.

Accessibility necessitates varying educational formats. In addition to lecture and demonstration, the use of self-learning modules, video, and CAI tools will allow nurses to learn on their own time and at their own pace. Awarding continuing education credits with each offering will support recertification and licensure requirements while providing for ongoing instruction and information.

The workplace now requires nurses to function as expert specialists in certain areas, yet maintain the skills of a competent generalist. The flexibility and diversity required to meet this challenge implies continuous educational support and competency validation. Program content requires emphasis on demonstrated proficiency in establishing priorities for care grounded in outcome-oriented, research-based standards of care. According to Benner,[8] a competent practitioner demonstrates technical skill, adherence to policy and procedure, and the ability to manage the environment. Expert practice, however, includes the components of caring, clinical knowledge, and judgment. Emphasis in continuing education programs must move from focusing strictly on what the nurse "does" into the wider arena of "what patient needs are met." The ability of the nurse to relate patient need to outcome and thus to plan, prioritize, and delegate effectively defines all content needs.

Computer support of expert practice has been attempted through both decision making (expert system) and decision support software. Expert systems are programmed to actually make decisions and order or implement actions without requiring any human intervention. Decision support systems work with the nurse to supplement knowledge; recommend alternatives; and augment, thus improve, clinical judgments. Brennan and McHugh[9] describe the types of decisions that are appropriate for computer decision making. Included as requirements are clearly defined, objective data elements that point to a single diagnosis. This diagnosis should then logically determine a specific set of interventions. Clinical decisions are also influenced by the size or complexity of the nursing process and the need for individualization of the care plan indicates the need for a "human" component to the expert decision process. To date, the most efficient use of computer accessible expertise is in the area of decision support. The interface or integration of clinical data with an appropriate knowledge-based decision support system is ideally suited to enhance the novice nurse's diagnostic capabilities to a more expert level.

The major challenge facing continuing education is to prepare staff to maneuver and ultimately conquer the paradigm shift from an independent, acute care focus of care delivery to an interdisciplinary team-continuum of care approach. The nurse is uniquely positioned to be care manager in the collaborative endeavor of patient case management. Added to the nurse's known abilities to assess, plan, implement, and evaluate patient needs are the many skills necessary to enable delegation and collaboration. To effectively achieve patient outcomes, the nurse must now be proficient in assignment and supervision of care delivery. To accomplish this, a firm understanding of licensure, accountability, and the roles and responsibilities of each team member is required. Nurses are expected to use their expert clinical knowledge to prioritize care needs to delegate appropriately. Competence, therefore, goes beyond clinical skill and implies teamwork, relationships, and trust. Additionally, assertiveness, conflict management, and time management skills are presumed.

In assessing need for and planning continuing education, the effects of change and the emotional overlay for the nurse in the redesigned workplace cannot be ignored. Knowles' concepts of adult education advocate a syllabus based on experience, readiness to learn, and performance-centered criteria.[10] This readiness is further described by Rogers as the perception by the learners of information relevant to their own purposes.[11] Rogers further recommends reducing external threats when learning material is perceived to be threatening to the self.[11] Setting the stage for learning must therefore include strategies for educators to tune in to the organizational climate and develop learning experiences designed to help nurses become more open minded and less defensive about their past ways of thinking and doing.[10] The role of a preceptor or mentor is invaluable to the learner and facilitates the progression from novice to competence and on to the expert role.

Curricula must be designed to foster the baseline tools of professional practice and to support the activities of the professional nurse. Continuing education classes must be performance centered, organized to promote problem-solving skills, analytic thinking, and critical decision making. Case scenarios and role play situations that teach conceptual content and provide multiple practical examples to demonstrate application of skills are necessary. Well-designed courses will use the nurse's expert clinical knowledge base as a foundational support and baseline for building principles of practice. For example, the nursing care needs of the ventilated patient are similar in the critical care unit and in the home; the application and implementation of the care plan, however, will vary and requires the use of the expanded skill set of the professional nurse.

The requirements of a practical, realistic continuing education program must include

1. recognition of the skill set required for the nurse in the transformed work environment,
2. acknowledgment of the effects of change on the learning environment,
3. content necessary to build competence in standard care concepts,
4. practical application and examples in multiple settings and situations,
5. opportunities to role play or model the skill,
6. mentoring or preceptorship when appropriate,
7. sensitivity to the nurse's time constraints,
8. accessibility and affordability, and
9. availability on all days and shifts.

Continuing education is an integral component of the professional development of nurses in every diverse setting. Community and home care agencies, as well as acute care facilities, have invested in the development of their nursing staff and have acknowledged the need for such programs.

CHALLENGES TO THE ROLE OF THE NURSE ADMINISTRATOR

Throughout their nursing educational programs, students learned to discern and fulfill the role of the professional nurse—to assess the individual needs of the patient, develop a plan of care designed to meet those needs, implement the care plan, evaluate the results of care delivery, and modify the care plan based on the response of the patient, incorporating critical thinking skills throughout the process. Nonetheless, the nucleus of professional identity for many practitioners has become the psychomotor skills associated with the tasks and technology specific to care delivery.

It is worthwhile to reflect for a moment on why the technical and psychomotor skills of practice evolved as a major focus of bedside clinicians. Certainly, dexterity and skill in administering complex care interventions are valuable and justifiably respected. Technical skills are also more easily observed and measured than other aspects of the professional role; it is often difficult to quantify and measure the critical thinking skills of the expert practitioner. But at some point along the path of professional maturation, psychomotor skills and their appropriate and skillful application became the essence of professional practice for many clinical practitioners. As health care systems embark on work redesign, crosstraining, and changes in skill mix in response to the demands of the multiple consumers of services, professional nurses are threatened by the disruption of their professional identity, concerned about the quality of patient care outcomes related to these changes, questioning job security, and uncertain regarding professional expectations in this new framework. In many cases these nurses are acting without many of the skills, such as delegation, supervision, coaching, evaluation, and counseling of the nonprofessional care team members, necessary to successfully provide care in this new paradigm.

The challenge to nursing managers and administrators is to communicate and dialogue with staff about the changes and causes of the evolution of health care. Administrators need to ensure that staff clearly understand the "whys" of the health care revolution, the consequent implications for reimbursement, and the types of responses that health care organizations are implementing. Staff who clearly understand the forces at play are in a better position to begin to formulate effective responses.

To successfully lead staff into the future, today's nurse leader needs to master the skills of navigation, communication, and partnering. Navigation begins with careful articulation and communication of a compelling vision of the changes and outcomes of care delivery within the organization, one that incorporates the mission and values of the health care organization and nursing department and describes how that vision will look, sound, and feel. This vision is critical, as it will serve as a "lighthouse" or "cornerstone" for leaders and staff during difficult times when complex and seemingly conflicting issues and concerns create confusion and uncertainty. With this vision serving as a guidepost, the nurse leader must guide, support, and coach staff in rediscovering, valuing, and embracing their fundamental role in care delivery.

Effective communication skills are essential to effective leadership. Key elements of effective communication in our rapidly changing environments are embracing and conveying to nurses the inevitability of continuous change and the value of change to the future. Nurses need to understand that change *will* happen and that maintaining the status quo is a death knell. We must inspire staff with the conviction that change is not a threat, but rather an opportunity for continual improvement—in patient care and enhancement of personal career development. This inspiration needs to include the understanding that change will happen with or without professional nursing input, and that failure to participate in defining the outcomes of change effectively surrenders our ability to influence and shape our future.

Development of partnerships is the third determinant of tomorrow's successful leader. This expectation demands significant changes in interaction with all nursing staff in and out of the acute care setting. The leadership role will need to be transformed from managing and controlling to collaborating with interdisciplinary team members as equals at the conference table in order to restructure the nursing care delivery system. The partnership skill set includes mentoring, empowering others, risk taking, negotiating, challenging the status quo and assumptions, team building, and mastering group process and conflict management. Managers, executives, and nursing staff are embarking on a process of mutual exploration and learning, and the nurse leader must be willing to serve as the primary helmsperson as, collectively and individually, the department launches on the voyage of change.

Central to the evolution of care delivery redesign is ensuring that clinical decision making is transferred to the level of the practitioner. For many, the skills necessary to collaborate and negotiate with peers and others in decision making will be unfamiliar and uncomfortable. Nursing leaders must step into the chasm between vision and reality. Governance and decision-making structures, such as shared governance, will need to be defined and implemented to support the development of decision-making skills. Empowering nurses to assume these responsibilities will require expert navigation skills by the leader, including guidance, mentoring, facilitation, coaching, nurturing, and nourishment.

Partnering is not limited to relationships within the nursing department. Nurses need guidance to develop collaborative and collegial partnerships with the members of other departments, agencies, and networks, as well as to provide support and direction to ensure the needs of the patient/client are central to discussions and negotiations. Maintaining a focus on what is in the best interest of the patient during these dialogues will provide a key guidepost should professional and departmental "turf" issues arise, as nursing staff is assisted to recognize that insular and narrow professional or departmental protective behaviors will defeat realization of the goal of continually improving patient care and outcomes.

The paradigm described defines a leadership role transformation for all managers. Nursing administrators need to become adept with these skills to carefully evaluate staff proficiency and guide the development of the individual's competency and expert practice.

THE CHALLENGE FOR EDUCATION

The composition of skills required and the paradigm shift demanded by the changes inherent in the transformed health care system force all nurses to accept the personal challenge to define and adopt the transformed role of the professional nurse. The concept of professional practice characterized by the nurse partnering with the patient in the promotion of wellness and managing care during periods of illness, regardless of the setting, becomes a hallmark of successful transformation. All nurses must confront this change, get over it, and get on with it, and thus become active participants in the transformation process. Professional practice must be anchored in research-based theory, directed by nursing leadership, and nurtured by ongoing education and professional development. The challenge for education today, therefore, is to support the transformation of the nurse in the transformed workplace. Are we able to meet the challenge?

REFERENCES

1. Pew Health Professions Commission. *Critical Challenges: Revitalizing the Health Care Professions for the Twenty-First Century.* San Francisco, CA: UCSF Center for the Health Professions, 1995.
2. Hegge, M. "Restructuring Registered Nurse Curricula." *Nurse Educator* 20, no 6 (1995): 39–44.
3. Faller, H.S., Dowell, M.A., and Jackson, M.A. "Bridge to the Future: Nontraditional Clinical Settings, Concepts and Issues." *Journal of Nursing Education* 34, no. 8 (1995): 344–49.
4. Pender, N.J. *Health Promotion in Nursing Practice.* 2nd ed. Norwalk, Conn.: Appleton & Lange, 1987.
5. *Healthy People 2000: National Health Promotion and Disease Prevention Objectives.* Washington, D.C.: U.S. Department of Health and Human Services, 1991.
6. Thorne, S.E., and Robinson, C.A. "Health Care Relationships: The Chronic Illness Perspective." *Research in Nursing and Health* 11 (1988): 293–300.
7. Porter-O'Grady, T. "Transformational Leadership in an Age of Chaos." *Nursing Administration Quarterly* 17, no. 1 (1992): 17–24.
8. Benner, P. *From Novice to Expert: Excellence and Power in Clinical Nursing Practice.* Menlo Park, Calif.: Addison-Wesley, 1984.
9. Brennan, P., and McHugh, M. "Clinical Decision Making and Computer Support." *Applied Nursing Research* 1, no. 2 (August 1988): 89–93.
10. Knowles, M. *The Modern Practice of Adult Education.* New York, N.Y.: Association Press, 1980. 44–45.
11. Rogers, C. *Freedom to Learn.* Columbus, Ohio: Charles E. Merrill, 1969.

Building Healthier Communities in a Managed Care Environment: Opportunities for Advanced Practice Nurses

Sara E. Barger

It is almost impossible to pick up a newspaper or magazine, much less a professional journal, without reading something about managed care and its impact on the health care that providers render and consumers receive. Simultaneously there is growing interest by health care providers, governments, and foundations in partnering with communities to design, implement, and evaluate health care services. It is clear that these two paradigm shifts—managed care and community partnerships—are potentially in conflict. Moreover, it is certain that both will influence the practice of growing numbers of advanced practice nurses (APNs). A less obvious, but critically important, question is how APNs will affect both of these major paradigm shifts.

MANAGED CARE

While it is generally recognized that managed care represents an integration of the financing of health care with the provision of that care (Packard, 1993), a more complete definition forms the basis for this discussion. Hart (1995) defines managed care as:

> A system of managing and financing health care delivery to ensure that services provided to managed care plan members are necessary, efficiently provided, and appropriately priced. Through a variety of techniques such as preadmission certification, concurrent review, financial incentives or penalties, managed care attempts to control access to provider sites where services are received, contain costs, manage utilization of services and resources, and ensure favorable patient outcomes. The term covers a broad spectrum of arrangements for health care delivery and financing, including managed indemnity plans (MIP), health maintenance organizations (HMO), preferred provider organizations (PPO), point-of-service plans (POS), as well as direct contracting arrangements between employers and providers (p. 31).

Principles

It is clear that the rationale for this model is cost containment. Thus, a functional principle of managed care is that when health care choices are made by clients, clinicians, and administrators, there is a cost associated with each choice. Another principle of managed care is that the more one exercises freedom of choice

Adv Prac Nurs Q, 1997, 2(4): 9–14
© 1997 Aspen Publishers, Inc.

in selecting health services, the greater the personal cost. Therefore, the approach used by managed care is that of changing the incentives that drive behaviors of both patients and care providers within the health care system (Packard, 1993).

In managed care systems, the focal point shifts from hospitals to primary care with the emphasis changing from treatment to keeping people healthy. As Sovie (1995) relates, "The objective is to treat members or enrollees in the lowest cost setting where the greatest value can be obtained" (p. 72).

Trends

Managed care systems are expected to be the prevailing form of care delivery in America's future. The Pew Health Professions Commission (1995) predicts that within another decade 80% to 90% of the insured population of the United States will receive their care through one of these systems. Because of the anticipated broad-sweeping effects managed care will have on health care systems, the managed care trend may fuel the most dramatic changes ever observed in our country's history of health care delivery (Packard, 1993).

Those studying the evolution of managed care describe four stages: unstructured, loose framework, consolidation, and managed competition. In stage one there is no structure to care delivery. In stage two, loose framework, local HMOs and PPOs emerge, there is excess inpatient capacity, and hospital discounts widen. In the next stage, consolidation occurs when dominant HMOs emerge, there is 31% to 50% coverage by HMOs, hospital systems form, physician hospital organizations (PHOs) develop, primary care providers become central players, capitation becomes prominent, and there is risk-based reimbursement and bundled pricing. The fourth and final stage, managed competition, occurs when integrated health systems compete for covered lives, there is greater than 50% penetration by HMOs, there is payment up front per covered life, all system components are cost centers, the focus is on health care, priorities are health promotion and illness prevention, patient satisfaction is important, and there are health insurers and HMO report cards (Iglehart, 1992; Iglehart, 1993).

The progression through these stages is occurring at an uneven rate throughout the country. California has been at the forefront. The greatest growth has been seen on the coasts and in the Midwest (Packard, 1993).

Strategies

Managed care plans use specific strategies in pursuit of their goal of controlling cost. The most controversial strategy is limiting the patient's freedom of choice of providers. Patients have been reluctant to accept limitations on their personal choice of providers claiming it compromises the patient–provider relationship. Similarly, physicians are also reluctant because they value patients' freedom of choice of providers and their own clinical autonomy (Moran & Wolfe, 1991).

Related to the strategy of limiting choice of providers is the concept of "gatekeeping." The gatekeeper—typically a primary care provider—becomes the entry point to the health care delivery system. This individual conducts the initial assessment of the patient and determines what, if any, specialist services are needed. Patients are no longer able to make an appointment directly with a specialist without first being seen by a gatekeeper. The gatekeeper decides whether such services are indicated.

Another strategy is the selection of only the most effective and efficient care providers. Unfortunately, because clinical guidelines or standards and criteria for evaluation have generally been lacking in managed care until recently, determining success of this strategy has been difficult (Spitz, 1987). Information systems are needed to evaluate the use of patient care resources and, to date, these systems have been lacking as well (Berenson, 1991).

Conclusions

The first paradigm shift toward managed care focuses on controlling health care costs by integrating health care financing and care provisions. This system places the financial burden of choice of resource use on providers and patients (Packard, 1993). While the specific stages of managed care will determine current risks and opportunities for APNs, it is clear that APNs in all areas of the country will feel the impact sooner or later. Specifically, the emphasis on primary care and the role of gatekeeper fits well with the preparation of family nurse practitioners. Determining judicious use of health care resources throughout covered lives, particularly for those with chronic illness, is the appropriate role of the nurse case manager.

In other ways, however, APNs could fall short in managed care delivery systems. For example, preparation of APNs has not focused on the efficient provision of care, although this area will be a major emphasis in managed care. At the same time, APNs are just beginning to use the information systems necessary to manage efficient use of patient care resources. APNs within a managed care environment will require sophisticated skills in the area of assessment of effectiveness and efficiency of services (Packard, 1993). Information systems will be necessary survival tools.

COMMUNITY PARTNERSHIPS

At the same time that the American health care system is experiencing the most dramatic transformation in its history (Pew Health Professions Commission, 1995), community empowerment and coalition building are capturing the attention of governments, foundations, health professions, and academic institutions (Eng, 1993). Eng describes a model or theory of community partnerships that includes three stages of network formation that fall along a continuum. At the most "embryonic" end of the continuum is a loose grouping of organizations called an exchange network. Information is traded within the network, and communication among boundary spanners is on a personal and an as-needed basis. At this elementary level, the players' actions serve to meet each organization's respective needs. "As an exchange network, the organizations have not yet established a common goal. This coalition has yet to determine what its common project will be" (Eng, 1993, p. 29).

Eng defines the second stage of coalition building as an action network. In this stage, organizations adopt a common goal and work together toward its achievement. However, these actions "are project-specific in that they are limited in time and in the amount of resources involved" (Eng, 1993, p. 29). Because the common goal is usually tangential to the major mission of each organization, organizations are willing to pool resources, but have not yet "adjusted or restructured their operations to accommodate the overall scheme of the action network" (Eng, 1993, p. 30). Little autonomy is lost.

In the third stage of network formation, a systemic network goes beyond meeting the needs that are shared among the members to functioning as a fully developed system. Organizations collaborate on activities that are enduring and essential for meeting the needs of society. Decision makers from each of these organizations have made joint policies to integrate their missions and divide the tasks required.

Critical to the functioning of this model is the role of the boundary spanner. These individuals engage in networking, coordinating, and integrating tasks. Eng believes that nurses have a history and a tradition of service and advocacy for populations that have fallen between the cracks that make them ideal in the role. "Nursing practice models have roots in social and behavioral sciences content about social change and community organizing" (Eng, 1993, p. 33). Eng's model of community partnerships clearly delineates nurses as the boundary spanners who empower organizations and communities and facilitate change.

Trends

Nursing's involvement in community partnerships has been stressed by the National Institute of Nursing Research's (NINR) Priority Expert Panel on Community-Based Health Care: Nursing Strategies, one of a series of expert panels constituted by the National Center for Nursing Research (NCNR) in conjunction with the development of the National Nursing Research Agenda. According to the panel, community-based care is founded on partnerships between consumers and providers of care. Through these partnerships, services are developed and promoted that are "both sensitive and relevant to the cultures and mores of the individuals, families, populations and communities to which care is directed" (NINR, 1995, p. 2).

Most experts agree that interdisciplinary approaches combining the expertise of a wide variety of providers are needed to provide effective community-based health care. Nurses generally are well positioned to play a critical role in facilitating these cooperative efforts. Currently they link formal and informal systems of care and facilitate transition care. APNs are particularly well prepared to serve as brokers between community members and multidisciplinary health care teams (American Nurses Association, 1993).

Strategies

NINR (1995) reports various community-based strategies for both rural and urban areas that emphasize community involvement, cultural sensitivity, and relevance. Included are several assessment models that have been used successfully for community interventions. It was noted that "community-based health care strategies are often initiated in response to a single problem or the health needs of a particular age group or population" (NINR, 1995, p. 6). Thus outcomes traditionally have been measured across only one dimension. Other strategies have engaged institutions within and peripheral to the community. Likewise, interventions have involved people indigenous to the community. Nevertheless, more comprehensive community-based strategies addressing multiple health care problems and the continuum of care are needed along with evaluations of their effectiveness (NINR, 1995).

Examples

Examples of community partnerships are provided by the W.K. Kellogg Foundation (1995). In order to improve the health of older individuals, these projects establish linkages among providers and build on the support of traditional institutional partners (hospitals, universities, clinics, and social service agencies) and community stakeholders (businesses, churches, schools, local volunteers, and service organizations).

The block nurse program is a well-known example. Located in urban and rural communities in Minnesota, the program trains and coordinates neighborhood nurses and companion volunteers to provide health and social services that enable older persons to remain in their home communities. The program is supported by a national foundation, local voluntary organizations, business donations, the Veterans Administration, state-level grants, and fees for services. The program began with six informal community leaders who developed a plan slowly and worked through linkages with local government to lay the groundwork for support.

Less well known, but equally successful, is the Rural Elderly Enhancement Program run by Auburn University at Montgomery School of Nursing. Beginning with the provision and coordination of health services and a plan for local volunteers, the community's efforts expanded to address water, housing, and transportation issues. Funding sources include state and federal agencies and private funders in addition to the W.K. Kellogg Foundation (1995).

This second paradigm shift where communities are empowered to assess and address their own health issues has a rich heritage of nursing involvement. Nevertheless, the impact on APNs, when combined with the shift toward managed care, needs to be defined.

IMPACT OF MANAGED CARE AND COMMUNITY PARTNERSHIPS ON APNs

For the purpose of this discussion, APNs are defined as "all registered nurses with a master's degree in nursing" (NINR, 1995, p. 2). Thus, the term APN includes nurse practitioners, clinical specialists, nurse midwives, certified nurse anesthetists, and even nurse case managers when these individuals are prepared at the master's level. A broad definition was intentionally selected due to the likelihood that the effects of managed care and community partnerships will be felt by all nurses who practice at an advanced level. Moreover, APNs will feel these effects in at least three areas: resource management, clinical decision making, and time management.

Skillful resource management by APNs will be important in maintaining patient satisfaction and organizational viability. Regardless of specialization or area of practice, APNs who work in emerging, large, integrated delivery systems will survive solely on their ability to provide low-cost, high-quality care.

In order to do so, the APN will need to exercise a high degree of discrimination in determining how and when resources are used. As the costs of resource use are absorbed by both the health care organization and the client/consumer, both will expect the front-line APN to use resources effectively. This expectation will take many forms. For example, nurses who routinely make a large number of referrals for what is considered routine care may find no market for their services. APNs must be able to select the lowest level of care that can produce a satisfactory outcome based on the client's presenting health status.

At the same time, a growing number of managed care plans are making use of practice guidelines to assist practitioners in making decisions about appropriate health care for specific clinical conditions. A recent study by the U.S. General Accounting Office (GAO, 1996) found that health plans adopted guidelines due to pressure to moderate expenditures, show a high performance level across key quality indicators when compared with other plans, and comply with accreditation and regulatory requirements. Guidelines were used for services or conditions that are high cost, high liability risk, and high incidence for the plan's patient population. Typically, plans adapted national guidelines through physician consensus and a review of outcomes of clinical studies.

APNs must look for opportunities to participate in local modification of national standards and guidelines because they uniquely understand the front-line concerns of patients and providers. Given that practice under these guidelines must still result in satisfied customers, it is important that issues of patient acceptability be given consideration as local guidelines are developed. (As discussed earlier under stage four of managed care, managed competition, patient satisfaction is an important indicator of success.) APNs are well positioned to know client concerns and ensure they are considered in guideline development. Moreover, APNs have a vested interest in this process because after local adoption, these guidelines will become the framework for their own practice.

A third area of impact felt by APNs is time management. While most APNs have been educated in a system that encourages more time spent with patients than the traditional medical system, this approach may require modification. For example, one director of a primary care network related that she hired both physician assistants (PAs) and nurse practitioners. While she was very satisfied with the quality of care provided by nurse practitioners, she simply could not afford the time spent per patient, an average of 45 minutes. Although she had hired nurse practitioner graduates from four or more programs, all had the same problem of efficient use of time. In contrast, she had found PAs to be very efficient in moving patients through the system. Obviously, it will be necessary for APNs to be more efficient in their use of time while remaining wellness oriented and quality conscious. This effort may require a reassessment of the tasks of APNs to determine those that can be assigned to less costly personnel.

IMPACT OF APNs ON MANAGED CARE AND COMMUNITY PARTNERSHIPS

The impact of APNs in the development of practice guidelines has already been discussed. However, there are several related areas where APNs can be expected to have an impact. These areas include individual and community education and decision making; cultural sensitivity; and cost, quality, and outcomes (cost-effectiveness).

Nurses have a long-standing tradition of educating individuals, families, and communities about factors affecting their health. With these new integrated delivery systems, APNs will have a major role as boundary spanners as they help communities understand how these systems work. Their knowledge of community agencies and organizations can be critical in bringing disparate parts of the system together. Now the education provided will not only address health but also the health system and where, when, and how to access it.

In order for this education to be effective, APNs will need to call upon their knowledge of and sensitivity to cultural differences. Their expertise will enable delivery systems to design and deliver important information about system access and cost-effective health promotion programs.

Last, APNs will have many opportunities to impact the cost, quality, and outcomes of care, which collectively translate to the cost-effectiveness of health care. As primary care providers, APNs are well positioned and well prepared to provide quality primary care at a reasonable cost. As case managers, they are able to link people to the level of services they need, ensuring that patients get the care they need when they need it, but only as much care as they need.

In systems where both the consumer and the managed care organization demand accountability, it will be even more important to document outcomes. The report by NINR (1995) noted that information on the effectiveness of nurse case management models was not evident. Although there is certainly more evidence on the effectiveness of nurse practitioners, even here, documentation of outcomes must be expanded.

While more focus on outcomes is needed, APNs are probably in the best position of any health care provider to merge the paradigms of managed care and community partnerships. However, to be successful APNs must focus more intently on the foundations of both paradigms. These paradigms will not always be in concert. Nevertheless, APNs have exciting opportunities to enhance their own value by linking their roles as boundary spanners with their commitment to the provision of accessible, high-quality, cost-effective health care.

REFERENCES

American Nurses Association. (1993). Advanced practice nursing: A new age in health care. In *Nursing facts.* Washington, DC: American Nurses Association.

Berenson, R. (1991). A physician's view of managed care. *Health Affairs, 10,* 37–47.

Eng, E. (1993). Partnership theory. In *Nurse leadership caring for the emerging majority: Empowering nurses through partnerships & coalitions* (pp. 27–34). Washington, DC: U.S. Dept. of Health and Human Services, Public Health Service.

Hart, S. (1995). *Managed care curriculum for baccalaureate nursing programs.* Washington, DC: American Nurses Association.

Iglehart, J.K. (1992). The American health care system—managed care. *New England Journal of Medicine, 327,* 742–747.

Iglehart, J.K. (1993). The American health care system. *Teaching Hospitals, 329*(14), 1052–1056.

W.K. Kellogg Foundation. (1995). *Timely opportunities: What works in community care for the elderly.* Battle Creek, MI: W.K. Kellogg Foundation.

Moran, D.W., & Wolfe, P.R. (1991). Can managed care control costs? *Health Affairs, 10,* 120–128.

National Institute of Nursing Research. (1995). *Community based health care: Nursing strategies* (NIH Publication No. 95-3917). Bethesda, MD: National Institutes of Health.

Packard, N.J. (1993). The price of choice: Managed care in America. *Nursing Administration Quarterly, 17*(3), 8–15.

Pew Health Professions Commission. (1995). *Critical challenges: Revitalizing the health professions for the twenty-first century.* San Francisco, CA: UCSF Center for the Health Professions.

Sovie, M. (1995). Tailoring hospitals for managed care and integrated health systems. *Nursing Economics, 13*(2), 72–83.

Spitz, B. (1987). A survey of Medicaid case-management programs. *Health Affairs, 6,* 61–70.

U.S. General Accounting Office. (1996). *Practice guidelines: Managed care plans customize guidelines to meet local interests.* (Report No. B-265993). Washington, DC: U.S. General Accounting Office.

11

Differentiated Professional Practice: What Is It?

Differentiated Primary Care and Evidence-Based Practice: The Columbia Nursing Experiment

Annette M. Totten, Elizabeth R. Lenz, and Mary O. Mundinger

More than 30 years ago the first program for pediatric nurse practitioners (PNPs) was established at the University of Colorado. Citing a rate of population growth that was exceeding the increase in health resources, the founders predicted that segments of the population, particularly lower socioeconomic groups, would suffer from inadequate care unless changes were made in the patterns of health services delivery (Silver, Ford, & Stearly, 1967). In this context they presented their innovative program as a means to increase provider efficiency and respond to a pressing need for health care for an increasing population of children (Silver, Ford, & Day, 1968).

Throughout the 1970s and 1980s, federal and state government initiatives and demonstration projects funded the growth and development of nurse practitioner (NP) programs. By 1992 there were more than 100,000 advanced practice nurses in the United States, almost equally split between primary care (NPs and nurse midwives) and clinical nurse specialists (American Nurses Association, 1993).

Today, there is once again debate about the appropriate numbers, types, and roles of health providers. An aging population and the transformation of acute conditions into chronic illnesses have shifted the emphasis from hospital care to prevention, long-term maintenance, and a comprehensive approach to the medical, psychological, and social determinants of health. Furthermore, the rapid growth of managed care has created a demand for primary care providers that exceeds the current supply. Planning for future health care needs is difficult because the task is not only to produce the right number of providers but also to prepare them to function in a radically transformed health care system. The Pew Health Professions Commission's third report concluded that the health care professions must make fundamental changes in the organization of their work, in the regulations that govern practice, in the size of the health care work force, and in the skills of the providers (O'Neil, 1995).

Reflecting on their experience over a decade after the beginning of the first PNP program, one of the founders noted that while the soundest rationale for the expansion of nurses' roles is based on patient needs, it was the scarcity of medical resources at the time that provided the "opportunity to test out the potential of nurses" (Ford, 1979, p. 517). Now, the need for more appropriately trained primary care providers, the increasing emphasis on prevention and chronic illness management, and the organizational changes in health care again present opportunities for NPs. Education programs for primary care NPs tend to build on the baccalaureate nurs-

Adv Prac Nurs Q, 1997, 3(3): 9–16
© 1997 Aspen Publishers, Inc.

ing skills of prevention, health education, and management of care in community settings. Morever, the core curriculum in NP programs is similar to primary care training for medical residents. Therefore, the graduate NP has core competency in generic primary care and can use these new skills in the context of nursing care that emphasizes family and community resources and the paradigm of health and individual empowerment.

While primary care is in great demand, NPs face several challenges in order to take full advantage of the present opportunity. The four principal challenges involve removing the obstacles that limit NP roles and scope of practice thereby preventing NPs from working to the full extent of their abilities. In some cases the challenges involve changing laws, regulations, and reimbursement procedures. Other challenges involve informing and changing the opinions and perceptions of colleagues, patients, and the general public.

For NPs the first challenge is to reform the scope of practice regulations. These regulations continue to vary from state to state (Sekscenski, Sansom, Bazell, Salmon, & Mullan, 1994) with some states applying broad definitions that include full prescriptive authority and the ability to practice independently. The second related challenge is to secure direct reimbursement. The most recent survey of legal authority, reimbursement, and prescriptive authority documented the wide variety of situations under which NPs practice (Pearson, 1997). In states where NPs do not have title protection, independent prescriptive authority, or mechanisms to be paid for their services, they are not as viable as primary care providers. However, the variation among states affects all NPs. As health systems and managed care organizations become national corporations, these differences become burdensome and may discourage the appropriate use of NPs. A legal review of regulations makes an even stronger case for reform and concludes that "at a historical moment when public policy should promote the widest possible utilization of these cost-effective providers of high-quality care, the restrictions embedded in many state laws are not only limiting effective solutions, but exacerbating the problems" (Safriet, 1992, p. 456).

Inseparable from reforming laws and regulations is changing public opinion and furthering general understanding of NPs. The third challenge is to communicate to the general public and other health professionals the capacities and competencies of nurse practitioners. After 30 years, advanced practice nurses should not be a mystery to patients and colleagues. The fourth, and perhaps most important, challenge is to educate the public about the differentiated primary care practiced by NPs. The constellation of value-added skills and the paradigm of health and empowerment distinguish primary care provided by NPs, but this distinction has yet to be sufficiently documented and effectively disseminated.

Addressing these challenges is made even more difficult by the recent competitive tensions between physicians and NPs. These tensions have given rise to hostility and attempts to slow regulatory reform that would expand patient access to advanced nursing practice (Heimoff, 1997) and serve as the motivation for public statements that raise unfounded concerns about NPs as primary care providers.

Advancing NPs as primary care providers will require organized activism and advocacy. However, this activism needs to be based on empirical evidence. To be successful, the public, government, insurers, and other health professionals must be informed about NP primary care practice and convinced of its value. For this reason, it is essential that NPs increase demonstration projects, research, and dissemination activities related to primary care practice. This article describes one such effort, a model primary care practice, its evaluation, and related dissemination activities undertaken by the Columbia University School of Nursing (CUSN).

CENTER FOR ADVANCED PRACTICE

In 1994, CUSN opened an NP-managed comprehensive primary care clinic as one of a network of off-site ambulatory care practices of the Columbia Presbyterian Medical Center (CPMC). The Center for Advanced Practice (CAP) builds on the tradition of NP practice in underserved areas by caring for a primarily Hispanic, Medicaid-eligible population in the Washington Heights–Inwood section of Manhattan. However, a new component was added to NP practice when the medical board of Presbyterian Hospital granted admitting privileges to faculty NPs as one of several initiatives to increase access to primary care.

CAP was possible due to a nexus of national, state, and local health care trends and the changing needs of CPMC and its community. While the federal government was revising formulae for support of health professions education and research to increase the focus on primary care, states were requiring Medicaid recipients to enroll in managed care. In this way both the federal and state governments were increasing the demand for primary care providers.

Locally, between 1975 and 1983, seven hospitals with a total of 1,100 beds closed in northern Manhattan and the Bronx. State districting policies were implemented that limited some patients to specific catchment areas, restricting their ability to utilize other hospitals. The Kellogg Foundation funded researchers at CUSN to conduct household surveys in 1989 and 1990, which were repeated in 1992, to learn about residents' self-perceived health status and access to care. The analysis of these surveys demonstrated decreased access to health care. More respondents failed to get needed services in the previous 12 months (increase from 7% to 24%); fewer respondents had a usual source of care (decrease from 80% to 71%); and fewer had seen a physician in the past 6 months (decrease from 90% to 73%) (Garfield, Broe, & Albano, 1995).

These changes in the health care environment placed the responsibility for the care of the local population on Presbyterian Hospital. This predominantly immigrant community has a population of over 200,000 people (67% Hispanic, 18% White, 12% African American), and nearly half of all residents are at or below 200% of poverty. Between 1980 and 1990 one third of all immigrants to Manhattan settled in this neighborhood. Almost 30% of the residents speak little or no English, and according to the 1990 census about 40% of the adult population have less than a high school education (Garfield & Abramson, 1994).

Presbyterian Hospital responded to the needs of its community by opening a 200-bed community hospital 2 miles north of its main hospital of 800 specialty beds and expanding its network of primary care practices. However, this plan was hampered by the lack of primary care providers in a teaching hospital dominated by specialists and subspecialists.

It was this disparity between needs and resources that led to the partnership between the CUSN and Presbyterian Hospital. In 1986 CUSN had developed a faculty practice model wherein clinical faculty maintained a clinical practice. Therefore, faculty NPs were already functioning as primary care providers in community and institutional settings. In spring 1993, the president of Presbyterian Hospital proposed to the dean of CUSN that faculty NPs should fully manage one of the hospital's new clinics. A group of faculty were given responsibility for administration of the facility and providing patient care at CAP, an independent primary care clinic. This situation presented an unusual opportunity to carefully evaluate NP practice in comparison with physician practice. In order to equalize as many extraneous variables as possible, the dean proposed that NPs be given admitting privileges so that the evaluation and comparison of NP and physician practice would be on the same basis. In June 1994 the Presbyterian Hospital medical board granted admitting privileges to faculty NPs on a 2-year trial basis.

CAP TODAY

CAP has now been operational for 3 years. In fact, in January 1997 it ceased to be a pilot project and became a permanent part of the Ambulatory Care Network Corporation (ACNC) of CPMC on par with traditional physician clinics. Moreover, when the 2-year trial period for admitting privileges expired, the medical board created admitting privileges for faculty NPs as formal policy, subjecting them to the same ongoing credentialing processes as physicians.

THE PROVIDERS

CAP is currently staffed by seven NPs, including four adult NPs and three PNPs who each see patients for four to five sessions (16 to 20 hours) per week. All have national and state certifications and hold faculty appointments at the assistant professor level. Three hold doctorate degrees and the providers include the directors of the geriatric nurse practitioner (GNP), adult nurse practitioner (ANP), and PNP programs. All faculty NPs are full voting members of the Columbia Presbyterian physician network and CAP's current director and the dean of CUSN currently serve on the board of this organization, which negotiates contracts with third-party payers. The Cornell-Columbia physician joint contracting group also accepts CUSN NPs as full voting members.

THE PATIENTS

CAP is similar to other ACNC clinics in that the population it serves is primarily Hispanic and Medicaid-eligible patients. Clients are referred to the CAP clinic by the emergency departments (EDs) at Presbyterian Hospital and its community hospital site, the Allen Pavilion; by other providers including specialists and physicians responsible for inpatient care; and by family members or neighbors. From 1995 through 1997, CAP carried a panel of over 4,000 patients (2,844 adults and 1,458 pediatric patients). Visits have steadily increased from 4,775 in 1995 to 7,197 in 1996. The most common reasons for adult visits are routine examinations (17%), hypertension (10%), and female reproductive symptoms (7%). For pediatric patients most visits are for routine child health examinations (45%) and adolescent health (21%).

FUTURE PLANS

A growing patient panel and increasing visits are indications that CAP provides a needed service and has been well received by the community. CAP has outgrown its current location and moved to a larger site in the summer of 1997 and additional NPs will be added as the panel increases. This success has made CAP a central component in the education and research activities of CUSN. All levels of students (baccalaureate, master's and doctoral) have the opportunity to gain clinical experience or participate in evaluation research at CAP, and students also volunteer as translators or patient liaisons. Several clinical and research projects will be conducted at the CAP site by the faculty. Pending projects include an evaluation of Weed's problem-knowledge couplers system and a program to reduce obesity in diabetic women. These new treatment and research initiatives will complement the large evaluation study currently in progress.

THE EVALUATION OF PRIMARY CARE IN WASHINGTON HEIGHTS PROJECT

When planning for CAP, the CUSN and the College of Physicians and Surgeons recognized that such a clinic presented a unique opportunity to study different models of primary care and specifically to evaluate roles for advanced practice nurses in primary care settings. The Evaluation of Ambulatory Care in Washington Heights Project began in April 1995 and, after 4 months of pilot work, patient recruitment started in August 1995.

The project is particularly important because it is a large, randomized study comparing physicians and NPs in primary care practice. A literature review conducted as part of the planning process for the evaluation of the CAP clinic found that while previous studies have examined primary NP practice, many have been small-scale, nonexperimental, or conducted as short demonstration projects (Carrino & Garfield, 1995). A randomized approach is possible at CPMC because both types of providers are responsible for comprehensive primary care (including outpatient and inpatient) in the same neighborhood and both are subject to the same administrative and reimbursement system.

Evaluation Rationale and Methodology

The study was developed to document similarities and differences in the practices of physicians and advanced practice nurses in several domains with an emphasis on patient outcomes. The domains included patient satisfaction, functional health status, behaviors and knowledge related to three chronic conditions (hypertension, asthma, and diabetes), quality of care, and cost and utilization of health services. Data for these domains are being collected from patient interviews, clinic charts, CPMC computer records, and the New York State Medicaid files.

Patients who do not have a primary care provider are recruited into the study from two EDs and an urgent care center. Recruitment focuses on patients with chronic conditions (asthma, hypertension, and diabetes) that are often described as "ambulatory care sensitive." This designation comes from earlier research that demonstrated that access to primary care is associated with reduced morbidity, hospitalizations, and ED use for patients with these conditions (Billings et al., 1993).

After patients receive the urgent care they need, they are sent to a recruiter who explains the study and requests their consent. If a patient agrees to participate, demographic and baseline functional health status information are collected, the patient is randomized into the physician or NP group, an appointment is scheduled at one of the clinics, and the patient becomes a part of the assigned provider's patient panel. The patient is called the day before the appointment and reminded of its time and location. Interviewers call patients as soon as possible after the appointment date and administer a satisfaction questionnaire over the telephone. Six months after this initial appointment the patient is contacted again and a longer interview is conducted either in the patient's home or at the project's office. The 6-month interview includes a follow-up functional health status instrument, a second satisfaction questionnaire, questions on health services utilization outside the CPMC system, and items on medications prescribed in the last 6 months. In addition, patients with one of the selected chronic conditions are asked several disease-specific questions and are asked to submit to a physiological test.

In addition to this interview, information needed to assess the quality of care and to document health services utilization and costs will be obtained from charts, computer records, and Medicaid. Information will be abstracted from the CPMC patient information systems on primary care and specialty visits as well as hospitalization, ED use, and procedures. A chart review will be used to collect information on quality of care, severity of illness, and additional utilization. Last, Medicaid data will be used to provide information on other paid utilization outside of the Columbia Presbyterian network.

Patient Recruitment and Enrollment

Between August 1995 and May 1997, 1,831 patients were recruited and randomized to either the NP or physician practices. Sixty-six percent kept their first appointment for a total of 1,208 enrolled patients with 790 selected chronic conditions (diabetes, asthma, and hypertension). At 6 months, 77% of enrolled patients completed the follow-up interview.

Patient recruitment and enrollment are scheduled to continue until 900 chronic conditions have been enrolled in the study, thereby ensuring that 700 follow-up interviews can be completed for patients with chronic conditions. At the current rates of patient recruitment and enrollment, this goal will be met by September 1997. Patient interviews will be completed 6 months later in spring 1998, and the data from these interviews, as well as the chart review and health services utilization information, will be synthesized into a final report by late summer 1998.

Preliminary Information

Data collected from August 1995 through December 1996 were used for an interim analysis conducted in March 1997. This analysis was undertaken as a step in the preparations for the final analysis. It provided some limited, but interesting, preliminary results.

Baseline Information

Examinations of demographic characteristics and the information collected at the time of recruitment were used to compare patients assigned to the two groups (NP practice and physician practice) and to compare patients that kept their first appointments with those who did not. As the patient participants are randomized to either the NP or physician group, it is expected that the two groups will be similar and that any differences will be due to chance rather than selection. For patients recruited through December 1996, demographic and baseline health status scores were similar, with only small differences in the number of chronic illnesses and some subscales of the functional health measure.

However, as the recruitment and enrollment numbers illustrate, 34% of the patients recruited and randomized missed their first primary care appointment and were not enrolled in the study. This rate is comparable to no-show rates that have been reported in studies of similar populations (Morse et al., 1984; Pinsker et al., 1995; Vikander et al., 1986), and it is slightly lower than the no-show rate for the primary care clinics of Presbyterian Hospital before the study began (R. Weinstein, personal communication, October, 1996). Although the no-show rate is not unusual for patients new to an ambulatory care practice, the characteristics of the patients who showed and those who did not were examined in order to ensure that the comparability of the NP and physician groups created by random assignment at recruitment is not then compromised at enrollment.

Overall, patients who showed for their first appointment and those who did not differed in this study, similar to the findings of other studies on health behavior and broken appointments (Deyo & Inui, 1980; Vikander et al., 1986). The patients who kept their appointments were more likely to be older, female, and Hispanic. They had to wait fewer days for their appointment, and they appeared to be sicker (they were more likely to have a chronic condition and they had lower scores on the functional health assessment). A difference in the no-show rates for the NP and physician group (33% versus 36%) appears to be related to the availability of appointments in the early months of the study. As more new appointments were available at the newly established NP clinic, patients assigned to the NP group had to wait fewer days for their appointments. Once this difference was recognized, adjustments were made to ensure that the wait times were similar and consistent. To further examine this difference, a regression analysis was conducted using the available information on patients who showed and did not show for the first appointment, and in this analysis patient assignment to NP or physician was not significantly related to whether or not a patient kept the first appointment.

Both the characteristics of the groups as randomized and of the patients who show and do not show for their appointments will be examined again when the entire sample has been recruited. This information will be included in the final reports on this project and will be factored into the final analysis.

Satisfaction Interviews

By the end of December 1996, satisfaction interviews had been completed for over 90% of the study participants who had kept their first appointment. This first satisfaction interview is conducted primarily by telephone with a few conducted in person in order to include patients without telephones. The interview consists of 15 questions on the clinic itself, the interaction with the provider, and the patient's impression of quality. The results of these initial satisfaction surveys will be the first final data completed on this project, and they will be available immediately after patient recruitment is completed in the fail of 1997.

DISSEMINATION ACTIVITIES

At the CUSN both the CAP and the evaluation study have proven to be important means of promoting advanced practice nursing. CAP has become a laboratory where primary care nursing can be developed and refined, a classroom for the next generation of health care providers, and a site for faculty research. The evaluation study has given faculty and students the opportunity to work on a large health services research project, strengthened connections with medical center administration and researchers, and allowed the school to develop the research infrastructure to handle future projects. Planning and implementing the evaluation also have led to relationships with leading health services researchers and health policy experts. A technical advisory board (TAB) of leading physicians and researchers was established at the beginning of the project to advise CUSN on study methodology and to provide impartial oversight. This group, which has expertise in outcomes research, patient satisfaction, regulation, public policy, health economics, and administration, has remained active in the project and will be instrumental in the final analysis and presentation of the results.

However, if the NP clinic and its evaluation are to have an impact beyond CPMC and contribute to future decisions regarding scope of practice and reimbursement for NPs, then it is important to discuss these findings in a larger forum. For this reason, the CUSN will be sharing its experience through articles, presentations, and conferences. These dissemination efforts will be incorporated into other CUSN activities and undertaken by faculty and the project's TAB.

INTERDISCIPLINARY CONFERENCE ON ACCESS TO PRIMARY CARE

In April 1997 the CUSN and the Washington Square Foundation sponsored the first National Interdisciplinary Conference on Access to Primary Care in Chicago, Illinois. This conference brought more that 200 nurses, physicians, administrators, researchers, and students together to discuss current issues surrounding access to health care and possible solutions. In addition to the presentation about CAP and its evaluation (on which this article is based), clinicians and policy analysts addressed several aspects of access to care.

EVIDENCE-BASED PRACTICE

The experience the CUSN has had with CAP demonstrates that it is possible to expand the scope of NP practice in primary care successfully. By responding to a local need for primary care, it set a national precedent for NP practice with the addition of hospital admitting privileges. The recognition by medical center colleagues, including administration and physicians, of NPs' expertise and potential contributions was key to the establishment of CAP. Now that the practice is old enough to stand on its own merits, its strength come from its demonstrated effectiveness and public acceptance.

Research projects such as the Evaluation of Primary Care in Washington Heights help document NP effectiveness in a way that can help sustain these advances and allow NPs to practice to their full capacity. Rigorous research and empirical data will allow NPs to counter attempts to slow or reverse regulatory and reimbursement reforms. By providing data about NPs in primary care practice it will answer many questions, but it will also raise new questions that other researchers must participate in answering. Most important, as both producers and consumers of research, NPs can raise the level of discussion from perceptions and opinions to empirical evidence.

As innovative practices and research contribute to the body of evidence about advanced practice nurses in primary care, replicating successes and the development of new initiatives becomes possible. Conferences, presentations, and papers are the traditional ways to disseminate information, and these vehicles will be used. However, the results and experience need to be shared with a wider audience, and this requirement will necessitate public education, interdisciplinary discussions, and individual advocacy.

The lesson from the CAP to date is that if NPs are to realize their potential as primary care providers they must be much more than simply providers. They must also be researchers, educators, and activists.

REFERENCES

American Nurses Association. (1993). *Nursing facts: Advanced practice nursing: A new age in health care.* Washington, DC: Author.

Billings, J., Zeitel, L., Lukomnik, J., Carey, T.S., Blank, A.E., & Newman, L. (1993). Impact of socio-economic status on hospital use in New York City. *Health Affairs, 1,* 162–173.

Carrino, G.E., & Garfield, R. (1995). The substitutability of nurse practitioners for physicians: A literature review. *Nursing Leadership Forum, 3,* 76–83.

Deyo, R.A., & Inui, T.S. (1980). Dropouts and broken appointments: A literature review and agenda for future research. *Medical Care, 11,* 1146–1157.

Ford, L.C. (1979, August). A nurse for all settings: The nurse practitioner. *Nursing Outlook,* pp. 516–521.

Garfield, R., & Abramson, D. (Eds.). (1994). *Washington Heights/Inwood: The health of a community.* New York: The Health of the Public Program at Columbia University.

Garfield, R., Broe, D., & Albano, B. (1995). The role of academic medical centers in delivery of primary care: An urban study. *Academic Medicine, 5,* 405–409.

Heimoff, S. (1997, May). The mother of all turf wars. *California Medicine,* pp. 20–27.

Morse, D.L., Coulter, M.P., Napodano, R.J., Hwang, H., & Lawrence, C. (1984). Broken appointments at a neighborhood health center. *Medical Care, 9,* 813–817.

Mundinger, M.O. (1994). Advanced-practice nursing—Good medicine for physicians? *New England Journal of Medicine, 330,* 211–214.

O'Neil, E.H. (1995). *Critical challenges: Revitalizing the health professions for the twenty-first century.* San Francisco: The Pew Health Professions Commission.

Pearson, L.J. (1997). Annual update of how each state stands on legislative issues affecting advanced nursing practice. *The Nurse Practitioner, 1,* 18–85.

Pinsker, J., Phillips, R.S., Davis, R.B., & Iezzoni, L.I. (1995). Use of follow-up services by patients referred from a walk-in unit. *American Journal of Medical Quality, 2,* 81–87.

Safriet, B.J. (1992). Health care dollars and regulatory sense: The role of advanced practice nursing. *Yale Journal on Regulation, 9,* 417–487.

Sekscenski, E.S., Sansom, S., Bazell, C., Salmon, M., & Mullan, F. (1994). State practice environments and the supply of physician assistants, nurse practitioners, and certified nurse-midwives. *New England Journal of Medicine, 19,* 1266–1271.

Silver, H.K., Ford, L.C., & Day, L.R. (1968). The pediatric nurse-practitioner program. *JAMA, 4,* 88–92.

Silver, H.K., Ford, L.C., & Stearly, S.G. (1967). A program to increase health care for children: The pediatric nurse practitioner program. *Pediatrics, 5,* 756–760.

Vikander, T., Parnicky, K., Demers, R., Frisof, K., Demers, P., & Chase, N. (1986). New-patient no-shows in an urban family practice center: Analysis and intervention. *Journal of Family Practice, 3,* 263–268.

Assessing, Developing, and Maintaining Staff's Competency in Times of Restructuring

Elvira Miller, Joan Marie Flynn, and Juliet Umadac

Health care organizations have experienced various forms of reorganizations in recent years.[1–5] As hospitals are restructured and downsized, nursing staff are realigned to different areas, thus posing a challenge to nurse educators to provide effective assessment and development of staff competency. Between 1996 and 1997, nurse educators at the Department of Veterans Affairs Medical Center (VAMC) in Manhattan, New York, experienced similar challenges as organizational changes were implemented to focus the facility's resources to its mission as a tertiary care, surgical referral center for a network of VA hospitals in the northeast area of the country. Long-term inpatient programs had to be abandoned, and specialties such as neurosurgery had to be relocated to other units to consolidate all surgical specialties on the same floor. These ward closures and program realignments resulted in a number of staff being displaced. To avoid involuntary separation of staff, management carefully managed their attrition within the two-year period, offered early retirement incentives, and directed multiple initiatives to prepare staff to assume other duties. This article will describe two competency development programs conducted in the hospital, the assessment processes used to measure the effectiveness of the programs, and implications for patient care.

BACKGROUND

The VAMC is located in midtown Manhattan and is affiliated with New York University Medical School and graduate schools in allied health. It provides training for an annual total of approximately 1,200 health professionals, including medical, dental, and nursing students. The VAMC is part of a Veterans Integrated Service Network (VISN), which is composed of seven facilities within an approximately 100-mile radius of New York City and New Jersey. The VISNs attempt to concentrate services in particular VAMCs within the network, thereby avoiding duplication of services and providing each facility with the opportunity to become a referral center for a particular specialty area. There are 22 VISNs and 144 medical centers throughout the country. The VAMC is the network's referral center for cardiovascular and neurosurgery.

The authors thank Marjorie Meyer, MA, RN, former associate chief nurse for education (retired), for contributing concepts used in the courses; Marion Conti-O'Hare, PhD, RN, patient services IOP/research facilitator, for advice in organizing data elements used in the medical-surgical assessment tool; Edna Arquiza, MA, RN, patient services computer applications coordinator, for her advice and work on illustrations; and Milagros Andino, AAS, patient services computer assistant, for her assistance and work on illustration.

J Nurs Care Qual, 1998, 12(6): 9–17
© 1998 Aspen Publishers, Inc.

LITERATURE REVIEW

The literature reports various efforts to implement competency-based education and performance. For instance, Sterling and Allen discussed the differences of competency-based education compared with traditional staff development activities in the perioperative setting.[6] Robins and colleagues described how the Brigham and Women's Hospital's nursing education department quickly devised a simple and cost-effective mechanism to promote the competency of nursing staff in acute cardiac surgical and neurosurgical care when the hospital expanded its capacity to care for these types of patients.[7]

The literature likewise reports various applications of assessment and evaluation of competency in health care facilities. Robinson and Barberris-Ryan wrote about an established clinical development plan that was expanded to form a framework for a competency assessment model.[8] The authors describe a framework to illustrate the technical, interpersonal, and critical thinking component of nursing competency and the relevant behaviors associated with each component as the nurse moves from novice to expert. Summers also proposed the use of novice-to-expert framework to describe and explain the development of clinical research skill acquisition in nursing students and practicing nurses.[9] Glotz and colleagues discussed a competency-based patient care program using evaluative tools designed on site-to-structure clinical privileging, scheduling educational programs, and strengthening career ladder.[10] Inman and Haugen wrote about a set of criteria they developed to use in the evaluation of a competency documentation system.[11] Finally, Quaal described a "skills pass-off" and written assessment, both of which document and validate the nurses' potential and eventual competency to care for the intra-aortic balloon pump patient.[12]

THE COMPETENCY PROCESS

The Joint Commission on Accreditation of Healthcare Organizations (Joint Commission) defines competency as a determination of an individual's capability to perform.[13] For the purpose of this article, the word competency is used to describe an individual's knowledge and skills to perform one or more tasks. The process of assessing, developing, and maintaining competency considers the scope of services the facility offers and the specific area and position of the individual staff member. The nurse educator's major role is developing staff competency by providing educational programs, and the supervisor's is maintaining competency by overseeing and guiding performance. The staff member is actively involved throughout the process and has accountability to participate with the educator and preceptor to ensure his or her own competence.

The competency process is a team effort and a collaborative one in which the nurse educator, the supervisor, preceptor, and the staff member participate to ensure competent staff members (Figure 1). An equation can then be viewed where one's knowledge and skills are combined with accountability for practice to ensure competency (Figure 2). Competency is an ongoing process of initial development, maintenance of knowledge and skills, educational consultation, remediation, and redevelopment (Figure 3). Competency verification methods take on many forms within the overall competency process and include self-assessments, observations, and post-tests.

EDUCATIONAL PROGRAMS

The VAMC's nurse executive and the nursing education manager directed the implementation of two initiatives to ensure

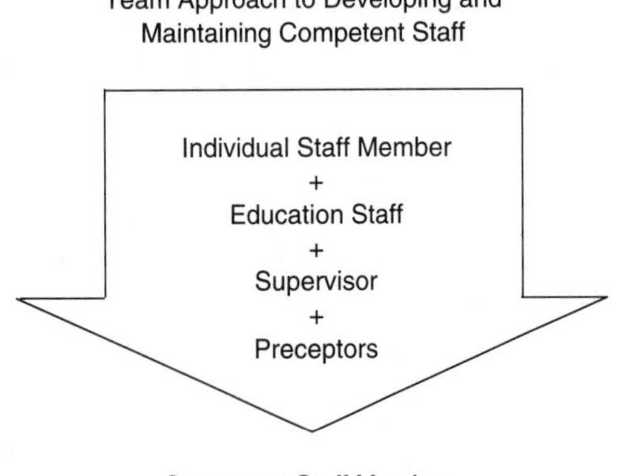

Figure 1. Team approach to developing and maintaining competent staff.

adequate preparation for one group of staff who were reassigned from long-term to medical-surgical areas, and another group working in a surgical ward where the neurosurgical specialty would be transferred. The two initiatives were to be implemented within a short time frame to allow for staff to develop the skills required in new areas of assignments. The nurse executive, the nursing education manager, and nurse educators who assumed the responsibility for the programs discussed systematic plans for conducting and measuring the effectiveness of the programs.

The medical-surgical course was made available not only to displaced staff, but also to staff who needed to upgrade their skills. A total of 33 RNs (registered nurses) and 9 LPNs (licensed practical nurses) participated in this first course. The nurse educator for the course had a graduate degree in nursing and eight years of medical-surgical nursing experience. She developed the assessment tool using a 5-point Likert scale to score 19 elements of competency for the RNs and 17 for the LPNs (see Appendix A for an example of assessment). The tools, reviewed by another graduate-prepared RN for reliability, were completed by the RNs and LPNs for self-assessment before and after the course. The staff's supervisor or patient care team coordinator (PCTC) likewise completed the tool using the same content for the same students before and after the course. The course was offered on two occasions, and the assessments were administered using the same tools and similar methods.

A neuro-assessment educational program was offered for the RNs in the inpatient surgical unit where neurosurgical patients would be transferred, and for RNs who needed to upgrade their skills. A total of 36 RNs participated in this course. The nurse educator for this course had 15 years of experience in surgical nursing as well as a graduate nursing degree, and developed the tool using 10 elements designed as a multiple choice test (Appendix B). The course was offered on two different occasions. The tool was pre-tested for reliability using two surgical nursing professionals and later administered to the students both before, immediately after, and three months after completion of the course.

The nurse executive, nursing education manager, and a research facilitator provided additional consultations in the format and

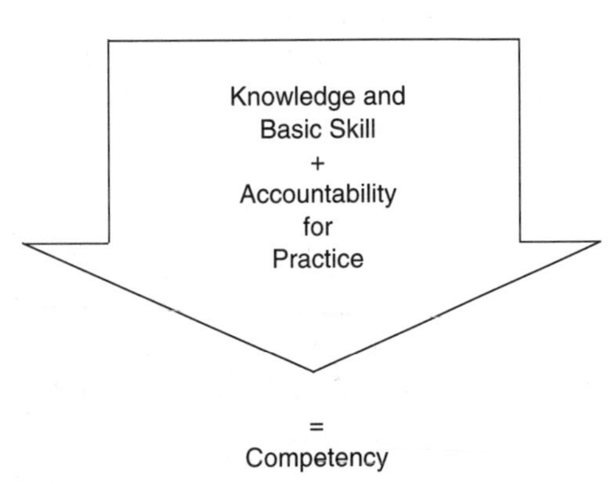

Figure 2. Competency equation.

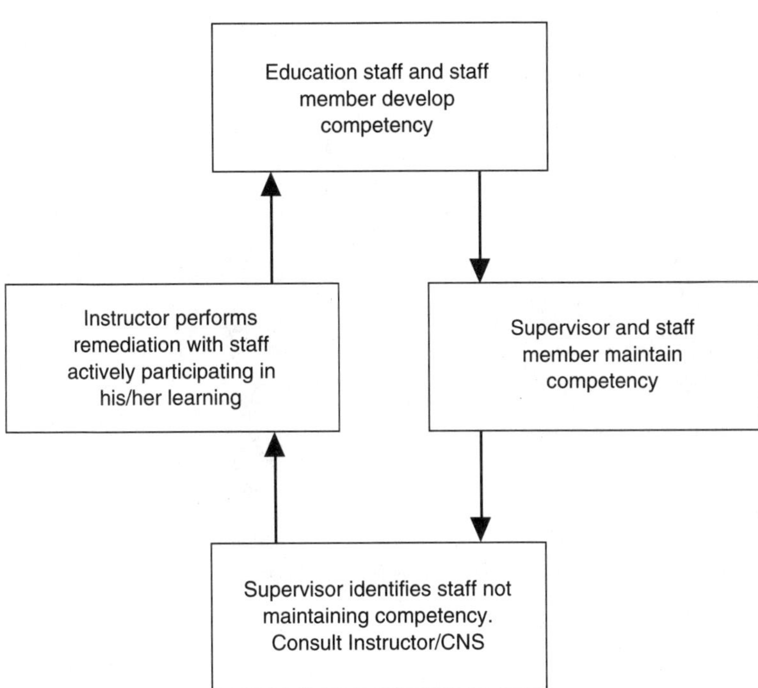

Figure 3. The process of maintaining staff competency.

plans for analysis of data. The teaching strategies used for the two programs included classroom instruction, case studies, and opportunities for staff to practice their skills.

FINDINGS AND DISCUSSION

Results showed that in both instances, competency improved after the courses were provided (Figures 4 and 5). In the medical-surgical course, both the self-assessment and supervisory scores for RNs and LPNs improved after the course. The supervisor's participation in competency assessments for the medical-surgical course further validated the staff's improved competency. A similar improvement was shown in the post-assessment and three-month post-assessment scores for the neuro-assessment course. The systematic assessment of competency demonstrated the value of pre-planned measurements to assure learning by staff who needed specific skills for new assignments.

It is a continual challenge to demonstrate the effectiveness of educational programs; however, it is worth the investment of time and effort to design tools to assess the results of competency development processes. Strategies such as a three-month follow-up of the staff's competency in neuro-assessments and post-assessments by supervisors after the medical-surgical course are equally useful in validating the improvement and continued maintenance of staff knowledge and skills.

MEDICAL SURGICAL COURSE

Mean Scores %

	LPN	RN	PCTC/LPN	PCTC/RN
Pre	56.4	57.6	44.1	47.6
Post	63.4	65.1	46.9	52.9

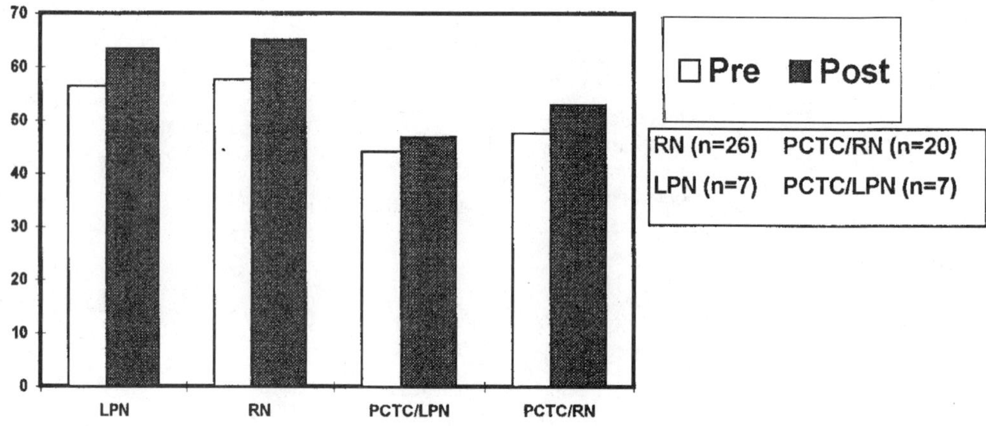

Figure 4. Improvement of competency assessment mean scores for RNs and LPNs.

The assessment tools developed and used by the nurse educators for the two programs benefited not only the staff but, most importantly, the patients who receive care from competent staff.

There are examples of patient-related outcomes associated with the educational programs. Approximately five months prior to the neuro-assessment course, the surgical intensive care unit (SICU) had frequent shortage of beds and extended lengths-of-stay, especially among neurosurgical patients. Since the course was completed, the SICU had shown a 16 percent decrease in its cumulative average length-of-stay and improved timeliness of patients' discharge to the surgical wards. This indicated the surgeons' increasing confidence placed on ward staff competency in the care of acute surgical patients. The medical-surgical units showed a 47 percent decrease in cumulative average length-of-stay between 1996 and 1997, suggesting overall increase in efficiency and quality of patient care processes. Facilitywide monitoring activities showed decreases in patient falls in 50 percent of the inpatient units and no infection control issues or significant decreases in other quality indicators.

CONCLUSION

Restructuring does not have to foreshadow a decrease in the quality of services provided to patients in any health care facility. Systematic assessment, development, and maintenance of staff competency can be a successful

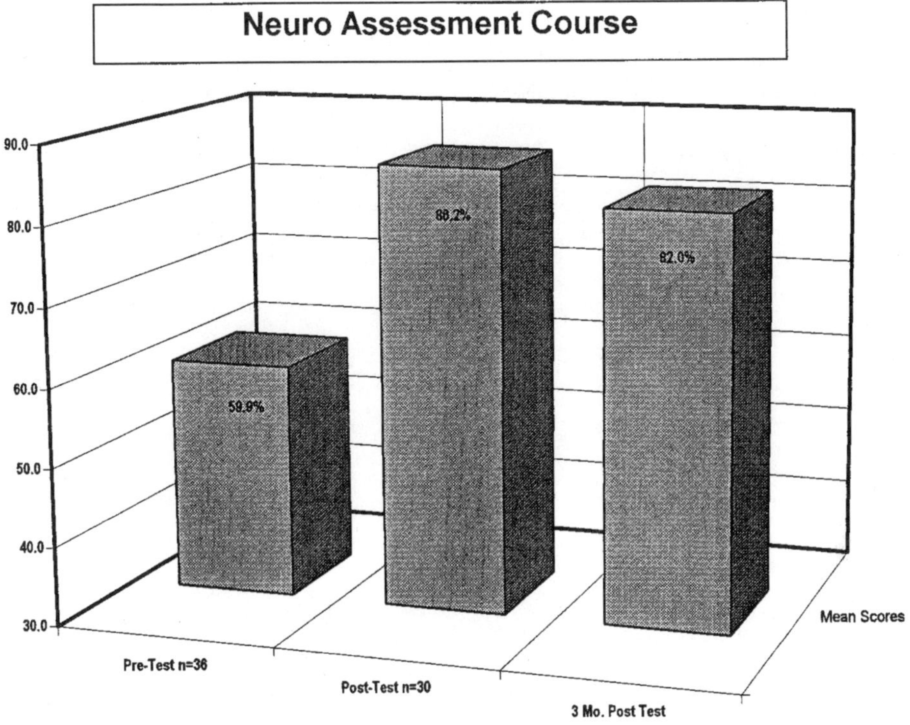

Figure 5. Improvement of competency assessment mean scores for RNs.

and rewarding process for both nurse educators and the staff who need to develop or upgrade their skills during hospital reorganizations. Carefully designed assessment tools and simplified methods of data collection and analysis can lead to effective educational programs and validate the nurse educators' efforts in improving staff competency.

REFERENCES

1. Blancett, S.S., and Flarey, D.L. *Reengineering Nursing and Health Care*. Gaithersburg, MD: Aspen Publishers, 1995.
2. Dienemann, J., and Gessner, T. "Restructuring Nursing Care Delivery Systems." *Nursing Economics* 10, no. 4 (1992): 253–58.
3. Fisher, M.L. *A Quick Reference to Redesigning the Nursing Organization*. Albany, NY: Delmar, 1996.
4. Parsons, M.L., and Murdaugh, C.L. *Patient-Centered Care: A Model for Restructuring*. Gaithersburg, MD: Aspen Publishers, 1994.
5. Shaw, S.M. "Restructuring: An Integrated Approach to Patient Care." *Nursing Clinics of North America* 30, no. 2 (1995): 171–81.
6. Sterling, M.A.A., and Allen, D. "Competency-Based Education: Implications and Application in Perioperative Education." *Seminars in Perioperative Nursing* 4, no. 1 (1995): 57–62.
7. Robins, E.V. et al. "A Strategy for Responding to Training Needs of Nursing Staff in a New Cardiac/Neurosurgical ICU and Telemetry Unit." *Journal of Continuing Education in Nursing* 26, no. 3 (1995): 123–28.

8. Robinson, S.M., and Barberris-Ryan, C. "Competency Assessment: A Systematic Approach." *Nursing Management* 26, no. 2 (1995): 40–44.

9. Summers, S. "Research Preceptors: Assisting the Postanesthesia Nurse to Advance from Novice to Expert Researcher." *Journal of Post-anesthesia Nursing* 9, no. 3 (1994): 164–68.

10. Glotz, N. et al. "Advancing Clinical Excellence: Competency- Based Patient Care." *Nursing Management* 25, no. 1 (1994): 42–44.

11. Inman, L., and Haugen, C. "Six Criteria to Evaluate Skill Competency Documentation." *Dimensions of Critical Care Nursing* 10, no. 4 (1991): 238–45.

12. Quaal, S.J. "Maintaining Competence and Competency in the Care of the Intra-Aortic Balloon Pump Patient." *Critical Care Nursing Clinics of North America* 8, no. 4 (1996): 441–50.

13. Joint Commission on Accreditation of Healthcare Organizations. *1997 Comprehensive Accreditation Manual for Hospitals*. Oakbrook Terrace, IL: Joint Commission, 1997.

APPENDIX A

Department of Veterans Affairs Medical Center
New York, New York 10010

Name: ______________________ Date: ______________________
Title: ______________________ Unit: ______________________

Pre-Program Self-Assessment for RNs:

Directions: Please evaluate the following items by circling the most appropriate response indicated below. This questionnaire will serve to help evaluate the effectiveness of the program. Please be as honest as possible. Thank you.

	Excellent	**Good**	**Fair**	**Poor**	**N/A**
1. My ability to perform thorough admission data collection on my patient is...	4	3	2	1	0
2. My ability to detect early indications of patient distress and take appropriate action is...	4	3	2	1	0
3. My ability to prioritize care when given an assignment on a med-surg floor is...	4	3	2	1	0
4. My understanding of the nursing admission physical that must be performed on a ward is...	4	3	2	1	0
5. My ability to perform an admission physical assessment on a patient is...	4	3	2	1	0
6. My ability to formulate a plan of care for a med-surg patient based on data collection and the physical assessment is...	4	3	2	1	0
7. My understanding of the nursing process and its implications to my practice is...	4	3	2	1	0
8. My ability to care for patients with IDDM employing all aspects of the nursing process is...	4	3	2	1	0
9. My ability to care for patients with CHF employing all aspects of the nursing process is...	4	3	2	1	0

Source: Department of Veterans Affairs Medical Center, New York, New York 10010

	Excellent	Good	Fair	Poor	N/A
10. My ability to care for patients with COPD employing all aspects of the nursing process is...	4	3	2	1	0
11. My ability to care for patients pre and post TURP employing all aspects of the nursing process is...	4	3	2	1	0
12. My ability to care for patients pre and post CABG employing all aspects of the nursing process is...	4	3	2	1	0
13. My ability to care for patients with subdural hematomas employing all aspects of the nursing process is...	4	3	2	1	0
14. My ability to identify significant neurological findings and intervene in neurological emergencies on a ward is...	4	3	2	1	0
15. My ability to discuss and take appropriate nursing interventions before, during, and after a seizure is...	4	3	2	1	0
16. My ability to recognize early signs and symptoms of respiratory distress and take appropriate nursing interventions is...	4	3	2	1	0
17. My ability to recognize signs and symptoms of shock and take appropriate nursing interventions is...	4	3	2	1	0
18. My ability to recognize signs and symptoms of chest pain and take appropriate nursing interventions is...	4	3	2	1	0
19. My ability to prepare appropriately and perform effectively in a CODE 4000 (cardiac arrest) is...	4	3	2	1	0

Please feel free to make comments below: ______________________________

____

____

____

Appendix B

Department of Veterans Affairs Medical Center
New York, New York 10010

NEUROLOGICAL ASSESSMENT

Directions: Circle the letter that represents the best answer to each question.

1. The brain stem consists of the following structures:
   A. Midbrain, pons, medulla oblongata
   B. Hypothalamus, thalamus, medulla oblongata
   C. Cerebellum, medulla oblongata, thalamus
   D. Pons, hypothalamus, and medulla oblongata
2. The arterial cerebral circulation consists of the following *except*:
   A. Arterial circulation (supplied by two internal carotid arteries)
   B. Circle of Willis
   C. Venous sinuses
   D. Posterior circulation (supplied by two vertebral arteries)
3. A patient with intracranial tumor suddenly develops loss of consciousness. This may be attributed to several possible mechanisms:
   A. The tumor has enlarged and caused swelling and displacement of the brain, producing herniation
   B. The tumor situated in the lateral ventricle has suddenly obstructed the flow of cerebrospinal fluid (CSF), producing increased pressure in the ventricles and a sudden downward compression of the brain stem
   C. The tumor has directly destroyed the reticular activating structures in the brain stem, producing deepened obtundation
   D. All of the above
4. Stroke involves the following events *except*:
   A. A blockage or occlusion of the major vessels feeding the brain
   B. Tearing of a superficial vein
   C. A partial or complete obstruction of the major intracranial vessels
   D. Hemorrhage that arises from an intracranial aneurysm

Source: Department of Veterans Affairs Medical Center, New York, New York 10010

5. Intracranial aneurysms may be caused by:
   A. Congenital/developmental defects
   B. Traumatic injuries
   C. Septic events
   D. All of the above
6. A 45-year-old head injury patient suddenly develops fever. Cultures are sent that reveal no infectious processes involved. The rationale for the development of fever in this patient may be a damage to this intracranial structure:
   A. Thalamus
   B. Hypothalamus
   C. Pons
   D. Cerebellum
7. In a complete spinal cord injury, there is total loss of motor and sensory function *below* the level of injury.
   A. True
   B. False
8. The *most* sensitive indicator of early increased intracranial pressure (IICP) is a change in:
   A. Motor response
   B. Level of consciousness
   C. Pupillary size and reaction
   D. Vital signs (Cushing's reflex)
9. The *most* important source of information necessary in assessing a neurologic patient is:
   A. Laboratory data
   B. Clinical history
   C. CAT scan
   D. None of the above
10. Which cranial nerve is responsible for pupillary reaction?
   A. Cranial Nerve II - Optic
   B. Cranial Nerve III - Oculomotor
   C. Cranial Nerve IV - Trochlear
   D. Cranial Nerve IV - Abducens

12

Managed Care Strategies for the Future

Case Management as a Tool for Clinical Integration

Marianne E. Weiss

As health care delivery systems become increasingly complex and diverse, old systems of care must be revised to meet current and future challenges. Hallmarks of the current wave of change include: (a) consolidation of health care delivery organizations into integrated delivery systems, (b) development and application of strategies to manage care and services for populations served by the organization, (c) clinical integration to eliminate duplication and provide a customer friendly, seamless system of care across multiple venues within the delivery system, and (d) partnerships among providers to provide a full range of high-quality services. Integration of the structures and processes of health care delivery is critical to the success of health care organizations. Organized or integrated delivery systems are networks that provide a full and coordinated range of services to a defined population for whom they are held accountable for clinical and fiscal outcomes (Shortell, Gillies, Anderson, Mitchell, & Morgan, 1993). Health outcomes and cost of care are the benchmarks against which the public and purchasers of health care evaluate these organizations.

Quality outcomes achieved through overuse of expensive technology and clinical resources were the hallmarks of the past health care generation. We have moved beyond the notion that expenditures drive quality and now recognize that quality outcomes cost less, in human and economic terms, than poor outcomes. Our challenge is to identify which clinical activities result in quality outcomes so that we can reduce the use of unnecessary and costly tests, procedures, and interventions and focus on those care processes that make a difference in patient outcomes. The role of case management systems and the case manager is to integrate clinical systems to achieve optimal patient outcomes through coordinated utilization of the most appropriate clinical resources. In effect, case management creates the interface between clinical and financial systems that supports achievement of health outcomes as the core business of the health care organization.

CASE MANAGEMENT MODELS IN AN INTEGRATED DELIVERY SYSTEM

Integration is the coordination of work across the organization (Stichler, 1994). Clinical integration refers to the coordination of clinical activities across providers and venues where services are offered. In integrated delivery systems, multiple hospitals, offices, and community centers may offer similar services. Within the system, decisions will be made about which services should be duplicated at each local entity and which should be centralized. The customer may access the system at

Adv Prac Nurs Q, 1998, 4(1): 9–15
© 1998 Aspen Publishers, Inc.

multiple points and may require services from multiple venues within the system. The goal of clinical integration is to provide a cost-effective continuum of services that is easily accessible and that results in improved client outcomes through better coordination of services.

Clinical integration requires strategic and operational planning. Clinical system development must center on the needs of the patient population being served. The system must provide all the elements of care required by the patient population; be accessible; offer options for location of care services; and be user friendly in terms of personnel, appearance of the physical facilities, and scheduling and information services.

Case management has evolved to meet the challenges of contemporary health care. The case manager is concerned with the individual patient as well as the entire system of care. The episode of care is no longer the acute hospitalization. Patients are managed across the continuum of health needs. Planning for patient care in an integrated delivery system requires consideration of quality, standardization, necessity, and access across multiple venues of care. Bushy (1997) described the dual goals of case management as system focused and client focused. System-focused goals include facilitating development of a broad array of care services, ensuring quality and efficiency, coordinating delivery of appropriate services, targeting the at-risk population, controlling costs by preventing admission to institution-based or high-cost specialized services, and improving client outcomes and quality of life. Client-focused goals include ensuring access to an appropriate, acceptable, and seamless continuum of services; reducing and avoiding unnecessary care; bridging the transitions between community, home, and institution-based care; and involving the patient and support systems in the care. Care systems designed to meet the needs of patient populations must meet individual patient needs. The role of the case manager is to manage the interface between the patient and the system of care, meeting the needs of both. The case manager provides expertise for development of care delivery services across the multiple venues of care, manages patient populations using the most appropriate services and service locations to achieve desired patient outcomes, and refines care delivery processes to maximize quality and cost outcomes.

HISTORICAL DEVELOPMENT OF CASE MANAGEMENT

Care Coordination

Early models of case management focused on care coordination. The first descriptions of case management were in the settlement houses for the poor in the 1860s (Kersbergen, 1996). It has been redeveloped and redefined as frequently as our health care systems have changed. Case management, since its inception, has focused on assisting clients in working with complex health care systems, securing services, and managing resources. Case management roles were initially developed to coordinate the care of complex patients in the community, with case managers serving as advocates and procurers of services for the needy, the underserved, and those with complicated needs. Care coordination continues to be an important aspect of the case manager role. Case managers in community-, payer-, and hospital-based settings often serve as the interface between the health care system and the social services system, linking patients with services and funding to support management of their health needs.

Resource Management

Hospital-based case management roles have been developed to manage care and resource utilization for episodic care. Case management was described as second generation primary nursing (Zander, 1985) and focused on facilitating movement of uncomplicated patients through the hospital system toward discharge. Early clinical pathways directed clinicians in the appropriate use and timing of tests, procedures, medications, and treatments. Managing resources provided to the individual client preceded the development of systems of resource management. System approaches to resource management led to the development of multidisciplinary service teams that integrated medical, nursing, pharmacy, laboratory, and other clinical and support services in patient-focused care programs (Parsons, Murdaugh, Purdon, & Jarrell, 1997). Resource management was aimed primarily at reducing cost of care through reductions in use of resources by eliminating excessive utilization and improving quality of care to reduce the use of resources to manage avoidable complications.

Outcome Management

While resource management systems focused on controlling processes of care to achieve financial and clinical results, outcomes management systems use an outcome-driven approach to achieving clinical and cost outcomes. Outcomes management has been defined as the utilization of outcomes assessment information to enhance clinical, quality, and financial outcomes through integration of exemplar practices and services (Houston, Luquire, & Wojner, 1992). Outcomes management is based on a belief that achieving positive health status outcomes will result in improvements in the quality and cost of care. The desired outcomes of care for specific patient populations are defined, processes and systems for delivering the best care to achieve these outcomes are identified through systematic review of the literature and data, outcomes of care are measured, and quality improvement initiatives are implemented. Targeting specific health outcomes results in implementation of appropriate care processes, minimization of complications, and timely discharge, all of which affect the cost of care. Defining appropriate processes to achieve selected outcomes builds on the care coordination and resource management strategies used in earlier case management models.

Tools such as clinical pathways and evidence-based practice guidelines form the basis for the outcomes management plan. Clinical pathways provide direction for achieving outcomes for the episode of care. These pathways include expected patient health outcomes and related multidisciplinary care processes at key time intervals across the continuum of care. Extension of the definition of episode of care to include all elements of care regardless of location results in the development of an outcomes management plan that facilitates transitions to appropriate care and services. Development of these plans requires cooperation and coordination between all providers. Outcomes management across the continuum of care ensures use of the appropriate level and location of care to achieve the desired patient outcomes and best use of health care dollars.

Houston and Luquire (1997) described the role of the outcomes manager in an acute care environment. This role requires the skills of the advanced practice nurse to implement the role components of clinical expert and consultant, quality measurement and research, administrative support and financial analysis, and patient and staff education. While these skills are similar to previous role components of the clinical nurse specialist role, the outcomes manager is responsible to the organization for achieving clinical and financial outcomes for an identified patient population. Outcomes managers manage the application of outcomes management tools (pathways and guidelines), measure outcomes, and refine systems in response to outcome analysis.

Unlike prior case management roles, the role of outcomes manager is part systems manager, part individual case manager. The outcomes manager is responsible for development of systems to facilitate management of an identified population of patients. These populations may be defined by diagnosis-related groups (DRGs), procedure type, service line, provider group, or payer. The outcomes manager monitors outcomes of all cases in the assigned population, implements systems to assist primary direct care providers in providing defined care elements, and assists with care coordination of selected complex cases within the population. In implementing systems of care, the outcomes manager brings together inpatient, outpatient, community-based, and contracted services to create an optimal package of care for the population. The outcomes manager often serves as liaison between patients, families, clinicians, administrators, vendors, and payers.

Outcomes managers may be hospital based, community based, or payer based. Because outcomes managers have a dual responsibility for patient health outcomes and financial outcomes for the health care organization, outcomes managers must be strategically located within the organizational structure to be able to implement system changes across clinical units, inpatient and outpatient facilities, and community-based sites.

Disease Management

Disease management extends the concepts of outcomes management to management of larger populations of patients across an extended continuum of care. Disease management has been described as proactive case management (Ward & Rieve, 1997). In this model, cases for disease management are selected through risk appraisal. Client management occurs from the time of risk identification, through the many clinical interfaces necessary for risk reduction, early detection of disease, disease treatment, and prevention of recidivism. The focus is on managing the client to reduce disease incidence and to manage the demand for illness-related services through education about risk reduction and self-management of symptoms. Most disease management programs exist within health maintenance organizations (HMOs), health plans, and integrated delivery systems with capitated patient populations and target high-cost chronic disease populations (e.g., asthma, congestive heart failure, acquired immune deficiency syndrome, and diabetes).

Case managers within the disease management model are responsible for managing systems for risk appraisal to identify at-risk clients for disease management. Intake assessments conducted by the case manager identify specific factors that will affect the client's ability to work within the disease management plan. The case manager is often responsible for coordinating insurance benefits and seeking additional resources as needed. The disease management plan is developed by the multidisciplinary team involved in the care. The case manager may lead the team effort to develop clinical pathways and evidence-based guidelines that form the structure of the disease management plan. The clinical pathway includes the timing of targeted treatment and prevention services and the plan for ongoing health and risk surveillance. The evidence-based guidelines provide decision support for clinicians in managing prevention and treatment services. In addition, the guidelines serve as a plan for moving patients to different levels and types of services and providers as needed to manage the patient's condition. Evidence-based guidelines can also be provided to patients to guide them in self-management of their symptom pattern. These guidelines help patients respond to early symptom warnings and implement interventions prior to exacerbation. The guidelines also guide patients to appropriate direct access to health services when their condition warrants.

The case manager is frequently responsible for implementation of the disease management plan. Concurrent monitoring of compliance with prescribed surveillance intervals, medication protocols, and other interventions is necessary to ensure penetration of the plan in its totality to all at-risk patients. Initial training and ongoing education of providers and patients are requisites for success. Patient education about self-management is a key aspect of demand management. Demand management is an initiative to reduce the need to access more expensive medical interventions through education in self-care and appropriate use of health care resources. Most important, disease management includes prevention and wellness services to reduce general health risk factors and promote healthy lifestyle behaviors that will support the targeted disease-specific risk reduction efforts.

As in outcomes management, outcome tracking and cost analysis are used to assess results and plan for improvements. Disease management systems are information driven. After implementation of evidence-based practice guidelines, utilization, compliance with program plan, and health outcomes provide data on which to base evaluation of cost and benefit and to recommend refinements. Continuous quality improvement is integral to disease management, as new information becomes available from internal and external sources.

HEALTH MANAGEMENT: A MODEL FOR INTEGRATING CARE ACROSS THE CONTINUUM

The emerging era in care delivery systems is population-based care. Three levels of prevention in public health practice were first described by Leavell and colleagues (1965). Primary prevention includes health promotion efforts targeted at the healthy population, with the focus on prevention of illness and support for improved wellness. Secondary prevention includes efforts targeted toward management of the at-risk population to avert or delay disease onset and promote early identification of disease, and early treatment intervention. Tertiary prevention targets those with identified disease, promoting appropriate treatment, rehabilitation, and prevention of recidivism.

In many hospital and insurance-based case management models, the emphasis has been on tertiary level prevention, where resource management and coordination of transfer to community-based care result in substantial financial savings for the patient and payer. The focus is on management to achieve the best clinical and cost outcomes for individual patients. In the emerging era of managed care, the focus is on population-based care. While effective and efficient use of resources and application of best practices for managing ill clients are key strategies for quality and cost reduction initiatives, the ultimate goal of managed care is to reduce health care expenditures through disease prevention. Managed care requires both population-based and individual approaches to managing care. Population-based approaches are needed for primary and secondary prevention-focused services.

Tertiary prevention requires individual case management.

The three-level prevention model (see Figure 1) can be used as a framework for integrating care and services within a health care organization. Three levels of care can be developed based on the three levels of prevention.

Level 1: Wellness Management

Wellness management is the system of care to provide access to health surveillance, preventive education, and self-management of minor episodic illness. Systems of care are initiated for ongoing health screening and risk appraisal as recommended by the U.S. Preventive Services Task Force (1989) and other relevant sources. Health promotion activities include a broad array of services that might include educational seminars, public service announcements, mailings, and lifestyle modification programs. Self-management of health, as well as minor episodic illness, promotes personal responsibility for health and appropriate use of health and illness-focused services.

The case manager at this level is a system manager, developing the systems of care and evaluating the effectiveness of care systems. The system of care is built to encourage appropriate use of resources, often using demand management strategies (Geary & Smeltzer, 1997). Demand management typically uses self-management education and telephone triage to reduce unnecessary use of health resources. However, case managers can also develop proactive systems to encourage use of health surveillance contacts and wellness education to support health maintenance.

Level 2: Disease Management

Two types of disease management systems are necessary in a clinically integrated system. Those patients that demonstrate health risks need targeted risk reduction services and increased surveillance services to identify the onset of disease at an early stage. For example, individuals with hypercholesterolemia need targeted diet and lifestyle modification education and monitoring to prevent progression toward heart disease. Women

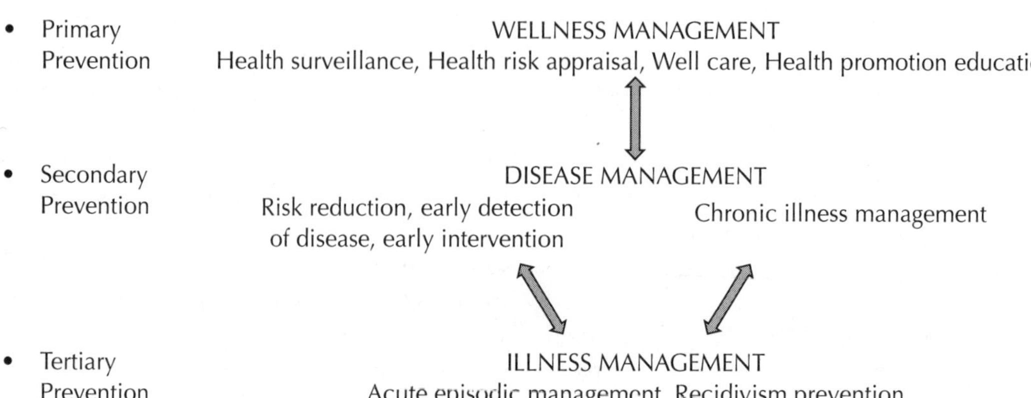

Figure 1. Prevention-focused model for health management across the continuum of care.

with a family history of ovarian cancer need targeted surveillance services to support early detection and intervention. Both of these examples of disease management services focus on the patient at risk for disease development. The role of the case manager is coordination of the systems of care for the at-risk patient. The case manager ensures that appropriate screening services are included in the health management level to identify at-risk patients and that mechanisms are in place to transition patients to disease management programs. Further, the case manager works with providers to develop coordinated systems of care that provide consistent, state-of-the-art procedures and treatments. Clinical pathways and guidelines provide evidence-based approaches to patient care that require multidisciplinary team development. The case manager takes a leadership role in development of these care tools and monitoring of their utilization. The case manager may also provide group or one-to-one direct care to clients in the form of education, testing, and risk surveillance activities. Outcome measurement and analysis provide input for quality improvement efforts.

A second form of disease management involves patients with chronic, long-term, postacute or catastrophic illness. This form of disease management requires both care system development and individual case management to maintain the patient in home- or community-based care. In these cases, patients need ongoing surveillance, care, and risk reduction measures to promote optimal health within the patient's existing health condition and to prevent exacerbation of acute manifestations or deterioration. This form of case management requires substantial coordination of care providers and financial resources. In catastrophic cases, life care planning and coordination of the life care plan may require intensive individual care management. With chronic illnesses such as asthma, the case manager identifies the combination of services that helps patients remain stable and the timing and mechanisms for access to care when the early symptoms of exacerbation develop. With the chronic illness population, the case manager develops evidence-based care systems with the multidisciplinary team and provides individualized care and counseling as needed to help clients manage their condition. Most important, the case manager helps patients manage the transitions between levels of care. These patients need general health maintenance services from the health management level in order to promote general health behaviors. In addition, when acute exacerbations occur, illness management services will be required. The appropriate use of services at all levels will promote optimal health and reduce excessive costs for illness-related services.

Level 3: Illness Management

Illness management is management of acute episodic illness and recurrence of acute illness in those with identified chronic diseases. The goal of case management is to prevent the need for illness management through the combination of population and individual case management at the health management and disease management levels. When acute illness occurs, the case manager coordinates care and services to move the patient toward transition to less acute home-based or community-based care. Illness management is not limited to hospital-based care. With early discharge, management of acute illness extends to home or subacute care sites. Individual case management models need to develop mechanisms for bridging across extended illness episodes.

MANAGING THE TRANSITIONS IN LEVEL OF CARE

Case managers function in multiple settings within and outside organized health systems. They may be based in the hospital, health plan, outpatient clinic, medical office, community center, or social service agency, or in independent practice. Integrating case management across the care delivery system requires attention to the transition points. As patients move from wellness management in level 1 into a risk management program in level 2, there is the possibility of failure to recognize risk status, problems with access to care, and failure to follow up on transfers. Likewise, following acute illness, patients need to be reconnected to follow-up or ongoing management programs in less acute levels of care.

The role of the case manager as a clinical system manager and as an individual case manager is to coordinate the movement of patients within each level of care and between levels of care. A population-based approach to assignment of case managers to clients provides a system whereby the case manager can manage the individual client and participate in the development an effective system of care. System-focused case managers can direct the health management level with coordinated hand-offs of at-risk patients to population-focused case managers for management. Illness management may require the specialized skills of an acute care–based case manager or clinical nurse specialist, with the population (disease-based) case manager coordinating appropriate admission for hospitalization and reintegration to home- and community-based disease management care once the acute illness is over. Within each level of care, and in transitions between levels, the case manager serves as an advocate for the patient.

• • •

The advent of managed care has led to fundamental changes in patient care delivery systems. New systems of care focus on managing populations of clients across the continuum of health care needs. The skills of the case manager are needed to manage the systems of care as well as individual patients. Population-based and individual-focused case management strategies provide mechanisms for integrating clinical care across the health care system. This integration supports system efforts to achieve patient health status and cost of care outcomes. A three-level, coordinated program of care, including health management, disease management, and illness management, facilitates integration of services across the continuum of health care needs and across the varied venues of care in an organized health care system. The case manager assumes the leadership role in achieving outcomes and making the health system work for the patient.

REFERENCES

Bushy, A. (1997). Case management: Considerations for coordinating quality services in rural communities. *Journal of Nursing Care Quality, 12*(1), 26–35.

Geary, C.R., & Smeltzer, C.H. (1997). Case management: Past, present, and future—The drivers of change. *Journal of Nursing Care Quality, 12*(1), 9–19.

Houston, S., & Luquire, R. (1997). Advanced practice nurse as outcomes manager. *Advanced Practice Nursing Quarterly, 3*(2), 1–9.

Houston, S., Luquire, R., & Wojner, A. (1992). *Outcomes management: A user's guide.* (1st ed.). Houston, TX: St. Luke's Episcopal Hospital.

Kersbergen, A.L. (1996). Case management: A rich history of coordinating care to control costs. *Nursing Outlook, 44*(4), 169–172.

Leavell, H., Clark, E.G., Gurney, B., et al. (1965). *Preventive medicine for the doctor in the community: An epidemiologic approach* (3rd ed.). New York: McGraw-Hill.

Parsons, M.L., Murdaugh, C.L., Purdon, T.F., & Jarrell, B.E. (1997). *Guide to clinical resource management.* Gaithersburg, MD: Aspen Publishers, Inc.

Shortell, S.M., Gillies, R.R., Anderson, D.A., Mitchell, J.B., & Morgan, K.L. (1993). Creating organized delivery systems: The barriers and facilitators. *Hospital and Health Services Administration, 38*(4), 447–466.

Stichler, J. (1994). System development and integration in healthcare. *Journal of Nursing Administration, 24*(10), 48–53.

U.S. Preventive Services Task Force. (1989). *Guide to clinical preventive services: An assessment of the effectiveness of 169 interventions.* Baltimore, MD: Williams & Wilkins.

Ward, M.D., & Rieve, J.A. (1997). The role of case management in disease management. In W.E. Todd & D. Nash (Eds.), *Disease management: A systems approach to improving patient outcomes.* Chicago, IL: American Hospital Association Publishing.

Zander, K. (1985). Second generation primary nursing. *Journal of Nursing Administration, 15*(3), 18–24.

Disease State Management in Diabetes Care

Catherine E. Cooke

Over 16 million people in the United States currently suffer from diabetes. The consequences of diabetes can be financially and emotionally debilitating. From a health-system perspective, caring for these patients requires an enormous amount of resources. Managed care organizations are designed to provide quality health care in a cost-effective manner while meeting industry standards. Although several ways exist to help achieve the managed care organization's goal, disease management programs may be a cost-effective method to care for patients with diabetes. A successful disease state management program in diabetes care should achieve optimal therapeutic, economic, and humanistic outcomes. This article focuses on the value and use of disease management programs in diabetes care.

MANAGED CARE

Managed care is a term that describes the way care is offered, delivered, and paid for. Managed care organizations can be defined as integrated health systems offering health care services for a pre-paid fee. Several different types of managed care organizations exist, e.g., health maintenance organizations (HMOs), and preferred provider organizations (PPOs).[1] HMOs can be one of several types as well: staff, group, independent practice association (IPA), and network. The type of managed care organization determines the way care is delivered. In a staff model HMO, the health care providers are salaried by the managed care organization and provide direct patient care to covered members. In an IPA, either a group of physicians within an office or solo practitioners can contract with the managed care organization to provide care for patients with health care coverage from that managed care organization. However, these practitioners, unlike those salaried by the managed care organization, are able to care for patients with other insurance coverage. Increasingly, health care practitioners in various health care fields such as medicine, pharmacy, physical therapy, and nursing are involved with managed care. The penetration of managed care organizations differs by geographic region. Although penetration is greatest in the western United States, over 20% of the population in the continental United States has managed care as their health insurance.[2]

The overall goal of managed care organizations is to achieve quality health care in a cost-effective manner while meeting industry standards. Pharmacy has been important in helping managed care organizations achieve this goal. Traditionally, the pharmacy budget has been carved out and pharmacists have been effective at reducing drug expenditures.

Pharm Pract Manage Q, 1998, 17(4): 1–7
© 1998 Aspen Publishers, Inc.

However, the industry is shifting away from looking solely at the cost of pharmaceutical products. From a health system perspective, it may be cost-effective to use a more expensive medication which reduces hospitalizations or emergency department visits. Using a less costly medication that is less effective in reducing other, more expensive health care expenditures would be short-sighted. However, for this approach to succeed, the pharmacy budget must be integrated into total budget costs. Disease state management is a concept that embraces a comprehensive approach to caring for patients with a particular disease while considering the total costs of care for that disease.

DISEASE STATE MANAGEMENT

Disease state management is a comprehensive integrated approach to patient care and reimbursement.[3] There are two goals of disease state management programs. The first is to improve patient care. Therapeutic and humanistic outcomes are measured to ensure that this first goal is achieved. The second goal is to utilize resources efficiently while caring for patients with a particular disease. Economic parameters (e.g., cost of outpatient visits, hospitalizations, emergency department visits, drug therapy) are used to determine the use of resources for that disease.

Typically, diseases which are targeted in disease state management programs have several common characteristics (see the box titled "Common Characteristics of Diseases Suitable for Disease State Management Programs").[4] Diabetes is a chronic disease which can result in serious sequelae with significant costs if not treated appropriately. There is enough medical literature to support consensus on how best to manage patients with diabetes from a therapeutic outcomes perspective.[5,6] Pharmacoeconomics can determine which treatment regimens are more cost-effective than others, and patient quality-of-life can be measured with various instruments such as the validated Medical Outcomes Study Short Form 36 (MOS SF-36).[7] Currently over 45 percent of HMOs in the United States have implemented disease management initiatives in diabetes care.[8]

Common Characteristics of Diseases Suitable for Disease State Management Programs

1. Chronic disease with high prevalence
2. Significant costs associated with treatment of the disease or its complications
3. Treatment usually involves choices of therapy (lifestyle modifications, pharmacological, surgical)
4. Consensus of appropriate treatment protocols
5. Defined clinical outcomes of efficacy and toxicity

The elements of disease state management programs include clinical practice guidelines, formulary modifications, educational interventions, and outcomes assessment.[9]

Clinical Practice Guidelines

The first element of a disease state management program is developing clinical practice guidelines. Algorithms, care plans, care maps, and critical pathways are synonyms for clinical practice guidelines. Clinical practice guidelines have been developed by government organizations (e.g., the Agency for Health Care Policy and Research [AHCPR]) and professional pharmacy organizations (e.g., American Pharmaceutical Association). Clinical practice guidelines are developed to standardize decision-making for the majority of patients who fit certain specified criteria. Clinical practice guidelines for appropriate screening, prevention, and treatment for patients with diabetes have been developed by the American Diabetes Association.[5] Guidelines incorporate all aspects of patient care from a patient walking into the office, screening for diabetes, and diagnosing a patient with diabetes to chronic care of that patient. Specific information on the history, physical exam, patient education, and therapy should be detailed. Care during hospitalizations, emergency department visits, and pancreas transplants may also be included when developing clinical practice guidelines.

Pharmacists are integral in the design, implementation, and success of disease management programs. Pharmacists, especially community pharmacists who have access to large numbers of patients, can help screen for diabetes. The clinical practice guidelines may help determine who to screen. High-risk patients should be screened. These include the following patients:

- American Indian, Hispanic, or African American races
- those with a positive family history
- age ≥45 years
- obesity (greater than 20% over ideal body weight)
- patients with hypertension or hyperlipidemia (cholesterol ≥240 mg/dL or triglycerides ≥250 mg/dL)
- symptomatic patients (polyuria, polydipsia, polyphagia)
- women with a history of gestational diabetes or babies weighing greater than 9 lbs at birth[5]

For patients with any of these criteria, a fasting plasma glucose test can be performed in the pharmacy. If the patient's glucose level is elevated (for non-pregnant adults, >115 mg/dL fasting), the pharmacist can refer the patient to the physician for a glucose tolerance test.

Following the diagnosis of diabetes, the pharmacist can help determine appropriate therapy for the patient. Pharmacists can educate patients about lifestyle modifications and reinforce healthy lifestyle practices at each visit. Once a patient has failed lifestyle modifications, pharmacotherapy may be required. There are several choices for initial therapy. Although insulin is considered an option for initial therapy, sulfonylureas, metformin, and acarbose are preferred due to patient acceptability, compliance and potential risks associated with insulin therapy. Comparative reductions in HbA_{1c} (glycosylated hemoglobin) are about 1.5 percent–2 percent for sulfonylureas and metformin and 0.5 percent–1 percent for acarbose.[5] To determine the most cost-effective initial therapy, four aspects need to be considered: 1) cost of the agent, 2) efficacy, 3) toxicity, and 4) patient acceptance.

Currently there is no consensus as to which class of agents is preferable for initial monotherapy. Patient variables will dictate the choice of one agent over another. Pharmacists must use clinical judgment to recommend the appropriate therapy for the individual patient. While clinical practice guidelines are intended to provide guidance for the care of the majority of patients with the disease, individual patient characteristics should be considered when determining optimal therapy.

Formulary Modifications

Managed care organizations usually have drug formularies—a list of the drug products that are approved for use by their members. In other words, a formulary is a list of medications for which the managed care organization subsidizes the cost. Typically, patients have to pay only a co-pay, which may be determined by the status of the drug product. For example, generic medications are usually associated with lower co-pays than their trade name counterpart.

In disease state management, the formulary recommendations for the particular disease will be based on the clinical practice guidelines. The clinical practice guidelines may determine that therapy with sulfonylureas is appropriate initial therapy for the patient with Type II diabetes. However, allowing all sulfonylureas on the formulary would not be economically advantageous. If one or two sulfonylureas were chosen for formulary inclusion, the managed care organization could either purchase these agents at a discount or receive a manufacturer's rebate secondary to increased volume. The four factors as mentioned in the *Clinical Practice Guidelines* section above apply to determining the most cost-effective agent within a class. If glipizide, glyburide, and tolbutamide are determined to be the only sulfonylureas that are appropriate for patients with Type II diabetes, then these will be the only approved sulfonylureas on the formulary. Patients are able to receive other sulfonylureas, however, they will incur a greater expense for these products. The same principles hold true for deciding which insulin product should be on the formulary. Metformin and acarbose are the only acceptable agents in their respective classes, and do not compete for formulary inclusion. When other safe and effective biguanides are available, metformin will compete for a place on the formulary.

Educational Interventions

In order for disease state management program goals to be met, physicians and other prescribers must be educated about these goals, clinical practice guidelines, and formulary products available to them. If health care providers are unaware of this information, they may not be treating patients with diabetes in a manner that will achieve optimal therapeutic, economic, and humanistic outcomes. Suggestions for successful education are to involve health care providers in clinical practice guideline development, distribute draft guidelines for feedback, provide one-on-one educational sessions, and continuously re-evaluate the guidelines and the disease state management process. Reporting individual assessment back to the provider has been shown to encourage adherence to the guidelines.[10]

Outcomes Assessment

Outcomes assessment is necessary to determine whether the disease management program is making a difference. Three outcomes used to evaluate care for the patient with diabetes are: therapeutic, economic, and humanistic outcomes (see Table 1). Therapeutic parameters include HbA_{1c}. Based on the Diabetes Control and Complications Trial (DCCT) and the Diabetes Care consensus statement, a desirable HbA_{1c} would be <7 mg/dL.[5,6] Measuring HbA_{1c} would enable the managed care organization to determine how many patients have their diabetes under adequate control. Although the goal in treating diabetes is to decrease morbidity and mortality, using surrogate measures may be more practical. Blood glucose and HbA_{1c} have correlated with microvascular complications such as retinopathy, nephropathy, and neuropathy. Therefore, achieving goal HbA_{1c} levels may lead us to believe that we are decreasing morbidity associated with diabetes. However, HbA_{1c} has not been shown to correlate with macrovascular complications (e.g., atherosclerotic heart disease).[6] That is why a disease state management program for patients with diabetes would include cardiovascular risk reduction practices (e.g., lifestyle modifications, controlling hypertension and hyperlipidemia). As reduction in HbA_{1c} does not correlate with reduction in macrovascular

Table 1. Therapeutic, economic, and humanistic parameters used to evaluate outcomes

Therapeutic	*Economic ($$)*	*Humanistic*
HbA_{1c}	Hospitalizations	Quality-of-life
Blood glucose	Surgeries/procedures: amputations	MOS SF-36
Fasting	Emergency department visits	TyPE specific
Post-prandial	Pharmacotherapy/diabetic supplies	Patient satisfaction
Retinopathy	Physician/provider visits	
Nephropathy	Laboratory/X-ray/ECG tests	
Scr/BUN		
Neuropathy		
Cardiovascular disease		

Note: ECG, electrocardiogram.

complications from diabetes, cardiovascular morbidity and mortality must be measured. Economic parameters evaluate the use of resources and costs associated with their use. Typically, the costs of hospitalizations, emergency department visits, and surgeries/procedures will determine the cost of caring for patients with diabetes. Although these occurrences may be infrequent, the costs associated with one hospitalization or surgery are tremendous. However, all parameters need to be included to determine cost-effective diabetes care. Humanistic parameters include measuring patient quality-of-life and satisfaction. Often times, patient satisfaction surveys are developed internally (e.g., within the managed care organization). Several instruments are available to measure quality-of-life. The SF-36 is intended to measure overall health status and is not disease specific. Quality-of-life questionnaires which have been designed for particular disease states may be more useful in disease state management.

"REGULATORY" AGENCIES

The National Committee for Quality Assurance (NCQA) is an organization which evaluates managed care organizations.[11–13] The two main functions of NCQA are to accredit managed care organizations and to measure and report on their performance according to standardized measures. The NCQA uses a set of standardized performance measures called Health Employer Data Information Set (HEDIS) to evaluate managed care organizations. A helpful analogy is NCQA is to managed care organizations what the Joint Commission on Accreditation of Healthcare Organizations is to hospitals.

The requirements for meeting NCQA standards are driving some managed care organizations to incorporate disease state management programs. Patient satisfaction surveys and quality-of-life issues need to be addressed for NCQA to grant accreditation status.[14] The survival of managed care organizations is probably going to be dependent partly on successful disease state management programs.

Currently, over half of the managed care organizations in the United States have gone through accreditation. Of those, 80% have received accreditation for at least one year. This information is reported publicly to help patients determine the quality of different managed care organizations.

CONCLUSION

Disease state management is one way in which managed health care plans can demonstrate to NCQA and the population that they are providing better diabetes care. The four components that need to be considered for successful disease management programs are the practice guidelines, formulary modifications, educational interventions, and outcomes assessment. Diabetes disease state management may be one way of improving the care of patients who have diabetes in a cost effective manner.

REFERENCES

1. C. Cooke, and M. Wilson, "Managed Care Organizations: Today and Tomorrow," *American Druggist* 211, no. 1 (1994): 67–74.
2. "Trend of the Month: Managed Care in the United States." *Drug Benefit Trends* 7, no. 7 (1995): 6.
3. R.S. Hadsall, and L.J. Sargent, "Disease State Management," in *A Pharmacist's Guide to Principles and Practices of Managed Care Pharmacy*, ed. S.M. Ito and S. Blackburn (Alexandria, Virginia: Foundation for Managed Care Pharmacy, 1995), 163–68.
4. G. Muirhead, "Disease Management: Threat or opportunity for pharmacy?" *Drug Topics* 139, no. 15 (August 7, 1995): 50, 52, 54, 56, 59.
5. American Diabetes Association: Clinical Practice Recommendations 1996, *Diabetes Care* 19, supplement 1 (1996): S1–S118.
6. The Diabetes Control and Complications Trial Research Group, "The Effect of Intensive Treatment of Diabetes on the Development and Progression of Long-term Complications in Insulin-dependent Diabetes Mellitus," *New England Journal of Medicine* 329 (1993): 977–986.
7. C. Jenkinson, L. Wright, and A. Coulter, "Criterion Validity and Reliability of the SF-36 in a Population Sample," *Quality of Life Research* 3, no. 1 (1994): 7–12.
8. Trend of the Month: Disease Management Initiatives Succeeding in HMOs, *Drug Benefit Trends,* 8, no. 12, 1996, 8.
9. E.P. Armstrong, "Disease State Management and its Influence on Health Systems Today," *Drug Benefit Trends* 7 (1996): 18–29.
10. J.M. Schectman, N.K. Kanwal, W.S. Schroth, and E.G. Elinsky, "The Effect of an Education and Feedback Intervention on Group-model and Network-model Health Maintenance Organization Physician Prescribing Behavior," *Medical Care* 33, no. 2 (1995): 139–144.
11. J.K. Iglehart, "The National Committee for Quality Assurance." *New England Journal of Medicine* 335, no. 13 (1996): 995–999.
12. R.H. Brook, E.A. McGlynn, and P.D. Cleary, "Part 2: Measuring Quality of Care," *New England Journal of Medicine* 335, no. 13 (1996): 966–970.
13. M.A. Bloomberg et al., "Development of Clinical Indicators for Performance Measurement and Improvement: An HMO/purchaser Collaborative Effort." *Joint Commission Journal on Quality Improvement* 19 (1993): 586–595.
14. The National Committee for Quality Assurance. 1996. *1996 Reviewer Guidelines for Accreditation of Managed Care Organizations* (effective April 1996 through March 1997).

13

Nursing for the Future

Delivery-of-Care Systems Using Clinical Nursing Assistants: Making It Work

Susan Warner Salmond

A review of the literature reveals conflicting opinions as to the effectiveness of models of care using clinical nursing assistants (CNAs). Opponents of the role speak of poor preparation, inability to trust and delegate to the nursing assistant (NA), clinical expectations beyond the scope and training of the assistant, and excessive downtime for the assistant and lack of downtime for the professional. Advocates for the role maintain that clinical assistants are a cost-effective alternative for implementing nonnursing tasks or routine technical tasks, allowing professional nurses to concentrate on care that requires high-level clinical assessment, planning, decision making, and teaching and counseling. Whatever position you may take, the reality is that fiscal concerns are driving health care, and within this paradigm, the role of the CNA is here to stay. It is imperative, therefore, that nurses invest their energy, not in resisting the change, but in taking charge of the change and developing effective systems of care that support both the professional role of the RN and the role of the CNA. It is this comprehensive emphasis on systems that is the determining factor of success for models of care using CNAs.

As a consultant and researcher focusing on models of care using CNAs,[1–3] I have found it increasingly evident that the biggest mistake made by institutions is underestimating the complexity of implementing this model of care. Although much emphasis is given to developing an overall redesign plan at the upper administrative level, little attention is given to the operational end of this redesign. An effective transition to a delivery system using CNAs requires an administrative commitment to invest the resources needed to confront the multiple areas of concern that frequently present a barrier to effective implementation. This article discusses these areas of concern and proposes essential components of a system designed to support professional-level care with the assistance of CNAs.

WHO IS IN CHARGE?

Administrative commitment is paramount to successful implementation. Minimization of the complexity of the system must be avoided. The administrative strategy group should thoroughly examine the probable barriers to implementation (or the existing barriers once implemented) and develop a formal change plan to address these key issues. Special attention should be given to the consequences of the plan for existing personnel—their roles, sense of competency, sense of trust, and sense of satisfaction. Attention to these human factors associated with change and communication of an empathic under-

Nurs Admin Q, 1997, 21(2): 74–84
© 1997 Aspen Publishers, Inc.

standing is an indispensable part of the success process as it is associated with greater staff commitment and willingness to work with the change.

As the challenges are many and ongoing, appointing one person to be in charge of the process is imperative. It can be anticipated that initially 50 percent of the person's time will be committed to accomplishing these objectives. Once the system is implemented, this time commitment is reduced to 25 to 33 percent of the person's time.

In addition to a top administrative group, action groups comprising staff nurses and NAs should be formed to serve as the vehicles for implementation, ongoing problem solving, and quality review. Formation of these groups should be an outcome of unit-based education and development to ensure that action group members are adequately prepared to take on these roles. Effective action group procedures place much of the accountability for success at the unit level. The key issue is that the action group has administrative support and the resources that accompany the support.

ROLE CHANGES AND HEALTH CARE TRENDS CHALLENGE NURSING VALUES

With administrative commitment present, the first task is to tackle the barriers to success. One very significant barrier that frequently goes unnoticed is the values conflict that nurses have as they are pulled away from the bedside and expected to function in more of a supervisory capacity. The model of primary nursing emphasized collaborative yet independent care of the patient by the RN. Within this system, the nurse relied upon himself or herself to plan, implement, and evaluate care. Nurses were accountable for their own practice, their own knowledge, and their own skills; therefore, the demands for supervision were lessened. The primary nurse was expected to develop close relationships with patients and be present to meet their needs. This was typically facilitated by administering direct patient care, which established the foundation of basic trust and rapport necessary for interviewing, teaching, and counseling, as well as afforded the opportunity for thorough, comprehensive assessments of the patient. Thus, direct care provided the vehicle through which higher-level nursing interventions were implemented or facilitated. In essence, this role was consistent with the primary set of values that many nurses hold regarding the profession—the belief that caring and nurturing form the foundation of nursing care. Being close to the patients, meeting their comfort needs, following through on patients' questions and requests brought both intrinsic and extrinsic rewards that fostered the nurses' motivation and productivity.

For many nurses, reengineering and shifting the role of the nurse away from direct care provider to supervisor of ancillary personnel and coordinator of care challenges the foundation upon which these nurses formed their definition of nursing and removes them from the immediate intrinsic and extrinsic rewards received when good patient care is delivered. Once valued for their expertise in caring for the patient, these nurses now find themselves being criticized for their lack of expertise in guiding other care providers in how to give care. Once valued for their total commitment to the patient and the quality of care administered, these nurses now find that quality has been redefined and that the personnel now caring for the patient lack the skills that were once the cornerstone of quality. It is no wonder that there is resentment and resistance to this change.

Causing further aggravation to the situation is the fact that many administrators' perception of the situation is that this change is simply a return to team nursing as was practiced in the 1960s and 1970s. Models of care change because the context of care and the environment change. The move from team nursing to primary nursing was driven in part by the changing context of care requirements—patients were becoming more acutely ill with higher-level needs and demands. Chronic diseases were on the rise with the accompanying demands for professional care to help patients learn about and manage their illness. An outcome of technological advances was that patients were cared for with more complex diagnostic and treatment protocols than ever before. The environment supported the move toward an all-professional staff to implement this complex care: resources were not rationed; reimbursement was not prospective. Quality was defined as more of the best.

A shift toward models of care using unlicensed and multiskilled workers requires that staff understand the change in the conditions of care of the 1990s. Providing quality care at an effective cost is the quintessence of the new context. These requisites are superimposed on the reality that patients continue to be sicker with more complex needs. The expectation is that care provided to these complex patients be done efficiently and effectively so that patients are promptly moved through the system and discharged within the allocated length of stay. The mandate is to provide quality within this "sicker but quicker" framework.

Staff must be actively involved in the process of accepting the new context and redefining the approach to care. As most administrators are immersed in changing trends, they often assume that staff are also familiar with existing threats and opportunities. This is a misassumption that must be corrected. Many staff, although aware of the forces impacting health care, have chosen to deny the possible consequences to their own role. Although managers may have discussed what might eventually happen, few staff have taken a proactive stance in preparing themselves for these changes.

Small group sessions are a beneficial strategy to facilitate staff's discussion of the changing context of patient care delivery. In these sessions, information must be provided to assist staff in comprehending the magnitude and scope of the impinging competitive and fiscal issues as well as the consequences to the staff and institution if change is not made. The positive in the past can be discussed and grieved, but the overall objective is to expedite discussion of how the good of the past can be incorporated into the changes of the future. This process is critical to letting go of past models and accepting new ones, and failure to address it leaves a significant barrier that will work to undermine change and new delivery models.

Once the old and the new have been discussed, the focus advances to the more challenging issue of defining quality care, not as more of the best, but as the best providing the appropriate level of care. Role definition and role clarity emerge from this discussion. Thus, a new model, reinforcing the values of quality and the values forming the foundation of nursing practice but defining it in a new way, emerges. Unfortunately, few institutions have truly involved the staff in this process but have defined the change for them with more or less token involvement. This clash in values continues to remain a barrier to effective utilization of the new models of care.

ROLE CONFLICT AND ROLE CLARITY

Role confusion remains a major impediment to success of this delivery model, as role confusion results in ineffective delegation. Nurse managers report that failure to delegate is a major barrier to successful role implementation. NAs identify that their role expectations vary from unit to unit and from nurse to nurse. Staff nurses report both misunderstanding and disagreement with the scope of the NA's job description. Contributing to this problem is the fact that many nurses and NAs can remember the job responsibilities from rote memory but do not comprehend the scope of these competencies. For each expected role item, the staff nurse and CNA must be aware of the boundaries of that role responsibility, the skill involved in performing the task, and the communication necessary to facilitate quality patient care following performance of that task. Comprehension of these factors for each role item requires extensive communication and coaching.

Several approaches can be taken to improve role clarity and thereby facilitate more effective delegation. Although most institutions already have job descriptions in place preventing staff input into role responsibilities, ongoing RN sessions that analyze portions of the job description for how this task "gets done on this unit" are productive. This allows for the reinforcing of new expectations (what the RN needs to delegate and where the focus of the professional time should be) while at the same time discussing variations in patient presentation and how professional decision making forms the basis for delegation. For example, in the roles that use CNAs to perform more advanced technical tasks such as suctioning, the question must be asked "suctioning under what conditions?" Perhaps it is acceptable to delegate suctioning when the patient is stable and in a long-term coma state, but it would certainly be unacceptable to delegate the task of suctioning when the patient has a closed head injury with an increase in intracranial pressure. It must be emphasized that this level of clinical decision making is what the institution wants from the nurses. With this reinforced, there is less hesitancy to delegate under the specified conditions. Furthermore, these conferences often surface many other possible barriers to effective delegation such as identified areas of inadequate skills, attitudinal resistance, and excessive role demands. These areas can then be discussed and problem solved.

What is common to this delivery model is a general lack of awareness on the part of both professional nurses and CNAs as to the demands placed on each role when all of the job tasks are combined in the daily assignment and expectations. Each group sees themselves as busier and identifies the other group as "the problem." In implementing role clarity sessions as part of team building, it is inevitable that a group of NAs will discuss the shortcomings of the unit staff nurses and a group of staff nurses will discuss the shortcomings of the unit NAs. An "us versus them" attitude emerges and tremendous amounts of energy are expended in negativity and game playing. It is critical to transform this unempowered group into a more cohesive team so that the concept of "we" emerges and each group can look at the interaction of each of the roles and therefore can negotiate the work that must get done on the unit.

"Spend a day as a nurse or nursing assistant" is an approach to initiate action in this direction. Nurses are assigned to work with an RN and perform as an NA for the day. The nurse is instructed that he or she can make no professional-level decisions, must contact an RN for validation of any observation, and must generally approach the assignment as is the norm for NAs on the unit. NAs are assigned to shadow an RN for the day. They are instructed that they must go wherever the RN goes—to answer a telephone, to assess a patient, to confer with a physician, or to take off orders. The point of the experience is that each group gains insight into the "world" of the other role. They feel first-hand the pressures, the demands, the conflicts, and the confusion. The individuals who were part of this role swap then present back to the staff about the experience and discussion ensues regarding both the role and the need for coordination between the two roles. This activity has proved very successful in improving team relations, team communication, and team coordination. Instead of complaining that the CNA did not come immediately to the patient as requested, the RN has greater insight that in order to come, the NA must first complete some activities with the patient already being cared for (i.e., protection and safety), and the NA has greater insight into the fact that saying "I'm busy" when called is not at all effective for the RN. The outcome is negotiation. Each person learns to provide the appropriate information as to what tasks must be done, what is currently being done, and what can be reasonably expected to occur in this new request.

ESTABLISHING COMPETENCY: NURSING ASSISTANT SKILLS AND KNOWLEDGE

It is impossible to separate the matter of delegation from the issue of competency. The foundation of delegation is trust, and trust cannot be established without competence. A system that maximizes competency must be established to ensure that four key processes are in place. First, there must be a mechanism by which the core and unit-specific competencies expected of the CNA are identified and updated periodically. Core competencies refer to the general set of knowledge and skills that CNAs throughout the institution must possess. Unit-based competencies target the knowledge and skills necessary to care for the types of patients commonly found on a specific unit.

Using the identified competencies as the basic guiding framework, the second requirement is to establish a clear mechanism for training the CNAs. Horror stories exist of employees with no previous experience being given two days of training and then being responsible for performing invasive laboratory and monitoring procedures.[4] Criteria for safe and effective training must be established and decisions made as to how this education will be implemented. Most institutions expect the majority of learning to be on-the-job training done by staff nurses. This is not effective. Staff nurses generally do not have the skills and certainly do not have the time to teach CNAs the scope of their role responsibilities. A follow-up of institutions where the delivery model using CNAs was found to be working[3] all had one individual assigned to develop, implement, and oversee the preparation of the CNA. The critical piece of this was the time spent in "implementing and overseeing." These institutions were committed to providing an educator to work clinically on the units with the NAs to prepare them in the core and unit-specific competencies. The educator collaborates with staff nurses and nurse managers so that these personnel can serve as supportive coaches, but the staff is not assigned the prime responsibility of developing and ensuring initial competence. Within this system, the RN has more confidence in the preparation, communicates directly with the educator providing feedback on performance, and cooperates jointly in further developing the CNA.

The third component to the competency process is to establish a mechanism for ongoing validation of competency. This system should be organized with the nurse manager and staff nurses and allow for both data collection and time to discuss individual specific problems as well as common problems found. If CNAs draw blood, are they doing so without repetitive patient sticks? Are appropriate infection control procedures being followed? If deficiencies are identified in this process, plans can be instituted to remedy the problem. With this mechanism in place, high levels of trust and quality can be maintained.

The final segment of this competency process, which overlaps somewhat with the previous step, is to establish mechanisms to identify areas where ongoing or new education must be given. New trends, changing role expectations, identified deficiencies, and new technologies all create the need for ongoing preparation and training. In the study on effectiveness[3] staff nurses identified that NAs did not have the basic knowledge of the underlying conditions of the patient and therefore did not understand the importance of reporting certain information or complying with certain preventative protocols. For example, nurses from one unit identified that CNAs did not routinely change the anti-embolic (AE) hose despite its being a part of the routine assignment. Further exploration of this deviation showed that when the NAs got busy this is one of the tasks that they chose to eliminate in order to save time. These NAs did not understand the purpose of the AE hose and the reason changing it was important. Once this was identified, a unit-based educator and two staff nurses prepared a program for the NAs and the problem was eliminated.

ESTABLISHING COMPETENCY: STAFF NURSE SKILLS AND KNOWLEDGE

Use of delivery models using CNAs requires a change in knowledge and skill on the part of the staff nurse. Specifically, the RN is expected to assume the role of supervisor, delegator, and coach and these are functions that most staff nurses have had minimal training in. Consequently, leadership development programs are needed to prepare the staff nurses to perform effectively in these roles.

The RN maintains the professional responsibility and accountability for the provision of care, and consequently, effective delegation and assignment making is the key to this responsibility. Assuming that the institution has already addressed the issues surrounding value conflicts and competency of the NA, the RN can be assisted by providing him or her with a model for decision making. Use of the American Association of Critical Care Nurses (AACN) model for delegation[5] provides a concrete set of steps as well as a quantifiable score to guide delegation. This model provides an algorithm for delegation that analyzes task, potential for harm, complexity of task, required problem solving and innovation, unpredictability of the outcome, and extent of patient interaction. The nurse is instructed to consider both the task at hand and the patient involved and to score the factors using a 0–3 scale with 0 indicating no risk and 3 indicating high risk. Institutions using this model indicate that a 3 score on any single factor may indicate a need for an RN either to assist or to supervise more closely a component of the task, and a total score of 9 or 10 suggests the need for total RN responsibility for the task. Using this as a framework, the nurse can be guided in what is safe to delegate but must also remember to look at the total assignment for the time to accomplish the delegated tasks.

Delegating or assigning is not the end of the staff nurse responsibility; rather, ongoing supervision of CNAs is required. It is typical for the staff nurse to expect the nurse manager to assume responsibility for assisting with monitoring and for intervening with the NA if problems are found. This is not a productive interaction style in delivery models using CNAs. The staff nurse is the immediate supervisor to the CNA and as such must assume the responsibilities of guiding, monitoring, and providing feedback. Leadership development targeting communication, reporting, monitoring, and giving feedback must be given as these are role skills that most staff nurses are not proficient in. After initial development, continuing sessions that address ongoing problems with supervision will not only advance the RN skill levels but identify early specific problems so that they can be dealt with before they become major barriers to effective model implementation.

Perhaps the most common error in implementing this staff nurse supervisory role is failure to communicate effectively. What is the specific expectation regarding what should be done? Is there a time expectation as to when the work will be accomplished? What variations should be reported back to the RN? What help is needed throughout the course of the day to effectively provide care to the total group of patients? This communication process is facilitated by examining the rituals established to provide information on the unit. How is the report given? Is it formal or informal? Is it assumed that someone will know what to do or is it specified? Is everyone included in the process? Examination of communication rituals has shown that many institutions have very loosely defined expectations that are open to differences in interpretation. Discuss this with the staff. Find out the type of information nursing assistants want and what information the staff nurses want reported back to them. Organize the report such that the necessary information and coordination of care is ensured. Establish routine times during the day when the RN and CNA confer. This can assist both the RN and assistant in ensuring that expectations are clear and that appropriate information is provided.

Finally, staff nurses must be developed to serve as effective preceptors and coaches. Although often given this responsibility, lack of understanding of both the role and strategies to implement the role, along with limited time, frequently results in either inadequate support to the NA or in the RN simply assuming the duties of the NA. Neither of these options is productive. Training sessions must be planned and follow-up sessions scheduled to ensure mastery of these development skills.

BUILDING RESPONSIBILITY, RECOGNITION, AND RESPECT

Responsibility, recognition, and respect form the basis for effective team work but are often surprisingly overlooked, especially as systems become dysfunctional. Responsibility refers to using personnel at their full capacity and involving them in the planning of care and suggesting of interventions for optimal patient care. It is surprising how few RNs seek input and information from the CNA even though this individual is providing direct hands-on care.

Recognition refers to the amount of feedback an individual receives for effort, competence, and willingness to be flexible. Additionally, it includes an awareness of who the staff are as individuals and what makes them special or unique. It is easy to forget to acknowledge others, especially in systems where superiors do not recognize the work of the staff. Although NAs can certainly give credit to staff nurses as leaders of the CNAs, it is essential that staff nurses give this recognition to the assistants. Receipt of appreciation is inspiring and motivating, as it lets others know that their work is significant and their efforts appreciated. Unfortunately, too many people wait to give recognition until a job is done to perfection, and unfortunately this is often too late. Staff must be encouraged as progress is made and whenever days are extremely stressful and people have bonded together to give care. A sincere thank you or other rewards for a job well done provide a currency that can be deposited in an emotional reserve so that when conditions are stressful or when mistakes are made, there is not a negative reaction.

Respect refers to communication and interaction patterns that reflect basic human caring and sincerity. How people talk to one another, how they give assignments, and how they handle their stress are all reflections of the respect that each holds for the other. Teams that lack respect for one another are inefficient and unproductive. It is important to evaluate the interaction of personnel on the team. Periodic observation can provide the data needed to assess the level of respect and determine whether intervention is needed.

Invariably, in units where the delivery model is not working there exists a lack of responsibility, recognition, and respect. Focus group sessions of homogeneous role groups help to define the extent of this problem, as does periodic participant-observation on the unit. Once gathered, the data can be presented back to the unit in a mixed role session, and clarification and validation is received from all. This process is to continue with group meetings seeking to gain consensus on how the unit would like to set the norms for behavior in these areas. Participants are encouraged not to speak in general, theoretical terms but to describe how it would sound, feel, and look like when the level of responsibility, recognition, and respect that they desire had been reached. This technique is very effective because it provides them a multisensory vision of how they would like individuals on the team to interact, and this in itself exerts some influence on changing behavior. Concurrently, providing all staff with communication workshops or seminars that give them the knowledge and skills of their interaction style and how it may conflict with others assists in readying them for communication flexibility.

Working in an urban, multicultural area, I have found that a factor contributing to the staff nurse's ability to show responsibility, recognition, and respect is the person's cultural background. In hierarchical cultures (Middle Eastern countries, Asian countries), respect to one's superiors is the norm, and an authority or person at a higher level of responsibility giving orders as commands is the accepted way of being. Nurses from these backgrounds are less likely to speak up and disagree with their superior. Additionally, they may give out assignments to NAs in a commanding way without seeking input or perhaps interaction. This behavior is perceived to be authoritative and bossy and appears curt and uncaring to the NA who comes from a United States cultural background that supports equality and individualism and where people speak their own minds. Staff must be mentored on their communication style with a focus on helping them to become bicultural in their interaction approach when in the leader role. They must be helped to understand the expectation for interactions on the unit and given the guidance and support necessary to accomplish this.

TEAM BUILDING STRATEGIES: MOVING TOWARD STAFF EMPOWERMENT

Although staff may have been prepared in competency skills, role clarity sessions, and communication seminars, leaving it at this point does not move the staff to the desired level of individual and group accountability. To achieve this goal, formation and development of unit-based action councils or governance groups is an effective strategy. The group can be formed from general elections, or by seeking nominations from the group as well as by selecting key people that would be influencers of the total team. The action council should consist of members from all role groups represented on the unit and ultimately should rotate the chair for a shared approach to responsibility.

The action council is given additional development in areas of cross-cultural communication, leadership theories, conflict resolution and negotiation strategies, standard setting, and ritual building. Throughout this period the staff continues to meet with an emphasis on discussing unit-based visions, goals, and standards. The emphasis is to get the entire staff focused on quality and what needs to happen on the unit, while at the same time preparing a group from the unit to lead the way. At the completion of the action council development period, the council is given a project or task to accomplish and supported in the process as they learn to interact and influence other staff members.

ESTABLISHING RITUALS FOR PERFORMANCE

Rituals are established to build routines and practices that reinforce the new norms. Reporting practices as described previously, habits for dealing with individuals who deviate from the newly established norms, council meetings, staff meetings, and staff celebrations should all be planned for and ritualized. Formalizing part of the staff celebrations into a monthly forum where progress toward standards and exemplary performance of both individuals and teams is highlighted and rewarded is very effective in building social bonds, motivation and commitment to the team. Failure to establish these rituals will likely result in a return to previous levels of performance. Rituals are the cement needed to firmly establish new ways of being. The unit manager along with select staff, administrative personnel, and educators should all give high priority to these new expectations and evidence commitment to them, especially during high stress times where there are competing demands.

ESTABLISHING EVALUATION SYSTEMS

The last component of the total system for supporting this delivery model is establishing evaluation systems for ongoing feedback and assurance of quality. Set times for evaluation should be established so that it is not overlooked. Information can be gathered qualitatively through focus groups or observation. Quantitative instruments can be used to measure team synergy, or an instrument designed specifically to measure effectiveness of delivery models using CNAs can be used.[3]

In addition to unit-based evaluation, system evaluation should be done to determine whether the proper mechanisms are in place for ensuring a system of quality. The reality is that most practice problems are system problems and failure to periodically review the system can have devastating effects. This can be accomplished with a task force representing staff, education, and administration.

The AACN Certifying Board is in the final stages of developing a standards and evaluation system that if used by hospitals would result in certification. This certification would validate that the institution had in place a total system of quality for ensuring that unlicensed support workers are adequately trained and supervised, and that the systems established support at the appropriate level of differentiated practice. This may provide a vehicle by which quality is enhanced.

An additional component to evaluation that must be emphasized if quality is to be assured is the need to evaluate whether there is an appropriate skill mix of providers to protect optimal outcomes as well as cost-effectiveness. Reports of "speed-ups" to boost productivity, of single RNs being responsible for caring for 40 acutely ill patients, and of increases in negative outcomes such as medication errors, readmissions, and nosocomial infections[4] all signal the urgent need to have in place a real evaluation system that examines quality in relation to staffing patterns. Although fiscal pressures call for redesign, nurse administrators *must* be the advocates for this evaluation system. It is the nurse administrator, guided with a vision for cost-effective, quality care and true to the precious values of nursing and quality patient care, that will make a difference and will succeed in establishing quality delivery models of care using professionals and unlicensed support personnel together.

• • •

The scope of this article illustrates that successful implementation of models of care using CNAs is a complex process that requires investment of commitment as well as resources. The delivery model can be effective in providing quality, cost-effective care if attention is given to the systems nature of the process. There is a unique need for more communication, team conferencing, and team development and support than in other delivery models. Failure to plan for the total system needs will surely result in team negentropy, which draws away from productivity and satisfaction.

REFERENCES

1. S. Salmond, "Clinical Support Workers: A Help or a Hindrance to the Nursing Shortage?" *Orthopaedic Nursing* 9, no. 5 (1990):39–46.
2. S. Salmond, "Models of Care Using Unlicensed Assistive Personnel: Job Scope, Preparation and Utilization Patterns," *Orthopaedic Nursing* 14, no. 5 (1995):20–30.
3. S. Salmond, "Models of Care Using Unlicensed Assistive Personnel: Perceived Effectiveness," *Orthopaedic Nursing* 14, no. 6 (1995):47–58.
4. "Eroding Care, Cuts in RN Staff Anger AJN Readers." 1996. In AJN Newsline [electronic bulletin board]. [cited 20 July 1996]. Available from http://www.ajn.org; Internet.
5. American Association of Critical Care Nurses, *Delegation of Nursing and Nonnursing Activities in Critical Care.* (Aliso Viejo, CA: AACN Publications, 1991).

Crystal Ball Gazing: Back to the Future

Diana Taylor

Advanced practice nurses (APNs), like all health care professionals, will be facing a rapidly emerging health care system. This article presents a few of the future changes, challenges, competencies, and opportunities facing APNs, along with a perspective on a preferred future for APNs.

PRESENT AND FUTURE CHALLENGES

Throughout nursing history, practice has evolved in response to the needs of the public. In the United States, nurses have been providing community-based primary care and medical coordination services since Lillian Wald began the Visiting Nurses Association clinic in the early 1800s in New York City and the first midwifery service began serving the rural poor in Kentucky. Current estimates indicate that nurses constitute an important national resource for providing public and personal health services and primary health care in an era of managed care (American Academy of Nursing, 1996). In order for nurses with basic and advanced practice preparation to provide significant service within the emerging integrated system of health care, nursing practice must be based on a strong foundation of primary care and preventive care services. This foundation must be carefully coordinated with specialty services, and all must be delivered in a context of strong public health services (Pepperdine & Taylor, 1993).

National health needs and priorities have been clearly set forth in *Healthy People 2000: National Health Promotion and Disease Prevention Objectives* (U.S. Public Health Service, 1991). These national goals direct the health care system and health care professionals to reduce and prevent disease from a biopsychosocial perspective and to increase health care access for all Americans. With a focus on health promotion and health protection, primary health care providers must assume significant responsibility for addressing national health priorities including those of encouraging proper nutrition, family planning, mental health, physical activity, reproductive health, and occupational health and safety. They must also prevent smoking, alcohol and drug use, violent and abusive behavior, and unintentional injuries.

For health professionals to implement these national health goals there is a need for both a conceptual and a systemic change in the knowledgebase that informs health care providers about individuals, health, and illness. First, an "individual" client or patient should not be defined as a monolithic category, but as a heterogeneous group that in-

Adv Prac Nurs Q, 1998, 3(4): 44–51
© 1998 Aspen Publishers, Inc.

cludes people of color, people with disabilities, girls, boys, adolescents, middle-aged adults, the homeless, and immigrants. The knowledgebase must focus on the psychosocial issues that contextualize health problems such as racism, sexism, violence against women and children, gender roles, poverty, and health belief systems. This focus presumes an expansion of existing research methodologies and multidisciplinary research to examine the interaction of biology, psychology, and society across different cultures.

The knowledgebase for individual health must progress beyond the current model of health care (aggressive cure of disease) to an expanded model of health care that includes assertive prevention of illness and promotion of health and wellness. Multiple forms of healing must be considered in a model that embraces a holistic approach to the individual throughout all stages of life. The knowledgebase must also include a focus on the environment relevant to personal health such as health care delivery and health care providers. Examination of the barriers to health care that men, women, and their families face is necessary so that appropriate mechanisms for service delivery can be created and utilized. New knowledge is needed on health service delivery in other cultures and the use of noninstitutional settings.

A new knowledgebase will provide the basis for APN clinical competency, the most critical component of future advanced nursing practice. While clinical roles and competencies comprise the core of APN future practice, additional professional attributes will be necessary for the APN in the preferred future health care delivery system. The following section poses a practice model for the future APN along with professional competencies and attributes.

THE APN ROLE IN CREATING A PREFERRED FUTURE

Based on an ecological view of personal health, health care includes a range of personal and public services provided across a person's life span by a range of health care providers in a variety of settings to enhance access to the services (American Academy of Nursing, 1996). While nursing has a long tradition of providing and advocating for individual and community health, the emerging health care system will require nursing's participation in the transformation of the health care delivery system to benefit individuals and their families (see the box entitled, "The APN Role in Creating a Preferred Future in Health Care Delivery").

INVESTING IN A PREFERRED FUTURE HEALTH CARE DELIVERY SYSTEM

A person-centered health care delivery system is more than acute care or disease-related services based on a broad definition of personal and community health. Fundamental features include comprehensive primary health care that comprises primary care (personal health services), mental health services, reproductive health services, long-term care,

The APN Role in Creating a Preferred Future in Health Care Delivery

- What are the problems and opportunities for APNs?
- What are the competencies necessary for APNs to practice in this emerging system?
- What are the skills APNs need to be ethical and successful health care providers?

home care, care coordination, and care management services. APNs must continue their investment in ethical health care practices in spite of the system focus on cost controls. Ethical practice will address issues of health service rationing based on culture, race, class, or age, in addition to sociopolitical issues of access and reproductive choice. Nursing must continue the tradition of being at the forefront of health advocacy, health protection, health promotion, and community empowerment as vehicles for improving the health care delivery system (see the box entitled "The Preferred Future in Health Care Delivery").

The Preferred Future in Health Care Delivery

Comprehensive Primary Health Care across Life Stages—Primary medical care and personal health services for individuals and families across their life stages.

Nursing "Care" Management—An integrated system of primary health care services administered in a caring, coordinated fashion that recognizes the importance of culture, family, and community.

Beyond Disease . . . Moving to Health—Disease prevention, health maintenance, and health promotion are integrated into a seamless primary health care system.

Diversities in Health Care Delivery—Diversities in age, geography, employment, occupation, educational level, social class, degree of acculturation, sexual preference, and religious belief must be understood and integrated into health care delivery.

Social Change and Activism—Health professionals must participate in advocating for healthy environments and the broader circumstances of people's lives that impact health.

Primary Health Care across Life Stages

In the preferred future, a comprehensive package of services will be needed. It must be a real system based on primary care and prevention. (Primary care has been defined as provision of integrated, accessible services by clinicians accountable for addressing the majority of personal health care needs, developing partnerships with patients, and practicing in the context of family and community [Institute of Medicine, 1996]. Nursing's perspective of primary care is defined more broadly and envisions primary care as a subset of primary health care as defined by the World Health Organization [1978]: collaboration among individuals, community, and professionals to determine what health problems to address and how to address them; every individual's right to essential health care and responsibility for self-care as well as promotion of the community's health; and emphasis on health promotion and prevention of problems rather than cure of illness. Primary health care is oriented to a community and the culture of the community.) It provides services ranging from health promotion, education, and counseling to acute and long-term care, with coordination of specialty services, all in the context of a strong public health system (Taylor & Dower, 1997). Gender-specific health care services will identify unique physical and emotional factors of men and women that impact health and illness. Primary care needs will be considered from a life span perspective that will be integrated within a broader framework of public health emphasizing needs of diverse populations. Unique health care requirements based on gender, race, class, and culture will be best served by collaboration among a wide range of health care providers, including nutritionists, social workers, and health educators.

Traditional medical practice has divided treatment of the body among medical specialties (e.g., obstetrics, gynecology, endocrinology, and psychiatry). Graduate nursing education has expanded the medical model to develop curricula that combine biopsychosocial, multicultural, life span, political, and gender-centric frameworks (Cohen, Mitchell, Olesen, Olshansky, & Taylor, 1994). While the curriculum for health practice must incorporate disease management, it must expand far beyond the biomedical framework to include primary prevention and health promotion, create links among medical specialties that fragment the individual, and facilitate health across the life span to diverse populations.

Nursing "Care" Management

A preferred future health delivery system provides an integrated system of primary health services administered in a caring, coordinated fashion that recognizes the importance of culture, family, and community. Care coordination is based on the premise that person-centered care must be carefully coordinated across the continuum of care settings. Care coordination services should include supportive services that help the individual overcome barriers to health care (outreach activities, education about health systems, transportation, translation services), health service planning and evaluation (cultural proficiency training, reducing institutional barriers, changing policies and procedures), and providing specialized services that address specific access barriers of underserved groups (persons with disabilities, low literacy skills, or who are homeless or abusing substances).

Nursing has been at the forefront of surveillance of vulnerable populations and the provision of care management services. A care management model incorporates direct care, prevention, health promotion, and case management principles into a health delivery structure (Taylor, 1992). Nursing care management is based on the premise that client care must be carefully coordinated across the continuum of care settings and must include a broad vision of client care needs, especially as they relate to desired outcomes. The role of the nursing care manager can be combined with multiple nursing roles and specialties. In a community health setting, the nursing case manager may be the public health nurse or the school nurse. In the community or ambulatory clinic setting, the nursing case manager may be the advanced practice nurse (nurse practitioner, nurse midwife, clinical nurse specialist). In the acute care or rehabilitation setting, the nursing case manager may include all of these nursing groups (public health and advanced practice nurses). Nursing care management is an approach to alleviating the effects of fragmentation in the health care system and to individualizing client services.

Beyond Disease . . . Moving to Health

Focusing on diseases is only one part of a preferred future health care delivery system. The 10 leading causes of death of Americans are related to behavior and lifestyle, such as diet, exercise, failure to wear seat belts, guns in the home, environmental exposures, smoking, family violence, and substance abuse. More than any other invention or miracle drug that we could discover, changing our behavior could decrease premature deaths in this country by 1 million, decrease chronic disability by two thirds, and decrease acute disability by one third (U.S. Public Health Service, 1985).

The health care system should deliver services with a focus on first preventing disease and disability, then on intervening early to keep health problems that do occur from becoming worse, and last on providing acute care. Preventive services must include, but not be limited to, regular checkups, screening for cancer, immunizations, and health maintenance services. By taking this approach, traditional illness services are balanced with provisions for health maintenance services that prevent illness, reduce cost, and avoid needless institutionalization.

Diversities in Health Care Delivery

The intersections of social status and roles critically influence personal health and health care providers. While the predominant focus has been on the biomedical basis for health and illness, nursing researchers and social scientists have demonstrated how health and illness are socially and economically produced for and experienced in different ways by diverse groups (Olesen, Taylor, Ruzek, & Clarke, 1996). The ways in which people make a living in the paid or unpaid labor force and their racial or ethnic identity, age, sexual orientation, living conditions, and social and cultural heritage and involvements interact in very complex ways. APNs must accept that there is no "generic" client, and nursing practice must recognize the important differences among and between groups of people. In particular, diversities in age, geography (rural or urban residence), employment, occupation, educational level, social class, degree of acculturation, sexual preferences, and religious beliefs must be understood and integrated into health care delivery.

More diverse health providers, researchers, and policy makers will need to create new ways of interacting and setting priorities to address both the particular and common needs of clients. Health care systems must shape clinical services to fit particular sociocultural needs. Nurses and nursing organizations should be involved with ethnic organizations, disability rights groups, senior health advocacy groups, and other identity movement groups in setting local and national research and service policies. The preferred future health care delivery system must empower individuals in a self-governance system.

An expanding volume of literature is available to assist health professionals in understanding cultures different from the white, middle-class American culture, as well as the impact of culture in health and illness (Olesen et al., 1996). Although population research is lacking, sexual preference must also be considered part of cultural diversity as it relates to health. With approximately 10% to 15% of the American people considering themselves gay or lesbian, health care providers must expect that a substantial number of their clients will be in this cultural group (Stevens & Hall, 1988). Gay men and lesbian women describe negative encounters with the health care system including ostracism, invasive questioning, derogatory comments, breaches of confidentiality, shock, embarrassment, unfriendliness, pity, condescension, and fear (Stevens & Hall, 1988; Taylor & Robertson, 1994). As a result of these negative experiences in health care encounters, many gay men and lesbian women report hesitation in using health care systems and delay seeking necessary care and treatment.

Community approaches that enable change can often effect significant environmental changes and provide the opportunity for healthier lifestyles (Pender, 1987). Working with a diverse community also extends to the community of health care workers. APNs will be expected to collaborate with a variety of health care providers and workers that represent the diversity of patient populations. Necessary skills will include cultural sensitivity along with teamwork and negotiation toward a common goal of humane and effective treatment.

Social Change and Activism

The preferred future health care delivery demands that health professionals participate in advocating for healthy environments. Without attention to the material conditions in which clients live, including their income disparity, poor housing conditions, and threats to their personal safety, personal health services can have only limited effects. Public health activism should address the broader circumstances of people's lives, encompassing sanitation, environmental health, housing, infectious disease surveillance and control, and programs for community-based health systems, such as child care facilities, violence prevention, and protection of reproductive freedoms (American Academy of Nursing, 1996).

Inherent in nursing activism is the formation of community partnerships and empowerment, which enable the opportunity for healthier lifestyles. An empowering health promotion practice holds that certain community processes (organization, mobilization, education) are necessary to enhance personal health and to create environments that are simultaneously more protective of health and more supporting of healthy personal behaviors (Labonte, 1993). Community empowerment does not mean professional power over individuals within a community. However, professionals have not been educated as "citizen practitioners" and may inadvertently continue disempowering behaviors with regard to individuals or communities. Because professionals generally do have more power than their clients, it is the role of the professional to ensure a relationship such that power can be taken. The empowering act exists only as a relational act of power taken and given in the same instance. Empowerment in professional practice exists in balance between "power over" and "power with" (Labonte, 1989). *Power over* relies on the reality of observed entities such as diseases, health behaviors, and risk factors. *Power with* relies on people's voices and their unique reality of lived experiences through language, images, and symbols.

Health delivery systems and programs must stem from a dialogue with and among people in the community. First, at the grassroots level, programs must ground health services in *ongoing* relationships with the individuals they seek to serve through empowerment action. At the level of health professional education, training in qualitative and participatory techniques in health must be encouraged. At a policy level, participants and planners must respond to the diversity of voices that represent the community of interest (Eng, Salmon, & Mullan, 1992).

Because community empowerment and development have not been an inherent part of the health care system, some questions and issues must be considered. For example, the question arises as to how "communities" are defined and who decides. The notion of "social engineering" and the manipulation of external environments for some "right" choice as determined by persons in positions of technocratic power must be avoided. Another potential problem is the extension of control that professionals and institutions have over individuals to whole populations and their environments. Clear distinctions must be made between "community control" and "control of communities."

APN COMPETENCIES IN A PREFERRED FUTURE HEALTH CARE DELIVERY SYSTEM

As the health care delivery system changes along with the roles of nurses, a new set of skills will be needed to make the necessary changes in health care delivery. The Pew Commission for the Health Professions proposed 17 competencies necessary for all future health professionals (Pew Commission for the Health Professions, 1991). While some of these competencies have been mentioned previously, a few of the most important will be highlighted here, especially as they relate to a preferred health care system.

In a preferred health care system, there is a critical need for leadership. This definition of leadership assumes multiple dimensions of leadership. The nurse can be a leader in a clinical setting where she or he models day-to-day behaviors of creativity, collaboration, ethical and humane communication, and cultural competency. Successful leadership behaviors include challenging others in respectful ways; developing trust with multiple and diverse groups; learning to give and receive feedback; working with others to create new futures; and developing new partnerships with health care workers, patients, family members, and the community.

In a preferred system, teams and interdisciplinary groups that include patients and families will be important. Participatory governance will require skills of team designing, team building, and team leading. Required behaviors include advanced communication skills, coordination, and shared responsibility. Patient care and not team cohesion will be the outcome in this system, which will depend on clear communication and decision-making rules with the caveat that teams must be composed of truly equal partners. Unfortunately, the same power inequities that exist in the present health care delivery system also exist among health professionals. Therefore, effective team collaboration must include the application of conflict resolution procedures and skill development (O'Neill, 1995).

The future for advanced nursing practice in a delivery system with emphasis on cost-effectiveness, cost-efficiency, and productivity has the potential for dehumanization. APNs will be challenged to create supportive environments for clients and colleagues as well as for themselves. An important challenge will be to demonstrate and evaluate the APN *process* of care, especially interpersonal and caring interventions (Hamric, Spross, & Hanson, 1996). APNs, as individuals and as groups, will be challenged to address structures that have made APNs shadow providers. Development of standards of care, documentation systems, and critical pathways should capture processes of care as well as outcomes of APN practice (see the box entitled "APN Competencies in a Preferred Future Health Care System").

THE PREFERRED FUTURE FOR APNs THROUGH NURSING EDUCATION, RESEARCH, AND POLICY

The focus of this article has been on the preferred future role and competencies for APNs in clinical practice. In order for APNs to contribute to advancing the preferred future health care delivery over the next decades, nursing education, research, and policy activities will need to be expanded.

APN Competencies in a Preferred Future Health Care System

Developing

- A leadership role at any level of practice
- Creativity and collaboration
- Ethical and humane communication
- Cultural competency

Skill-building

- Challenging others in respectful ways
- Developing trust with multiple and diverse groups
- Learning to give and receive feedback
- Working with others to create new futures
- Developing partnerships with health care workers, patients, family members, and communities
- Employing team design, team building, and team leading for improved patient care

APN education will be challenged to develop credible and stable educational programs using a standardized core curriculum with role-specific preparation. Consistency and quality across educational programs will be essential for the APN role to obtain legitimacy among health care professionals (Harper, 1996). APN education in the preferred future must emphasize diversity across gender, race, and class differences in health, including diagnosis and treatment, and must strengthen public health nursing programs that are gender specific and reflect the diversity within populations. Nursing education must devote increased resources to preparation of nurses for advanced practice, with particular emphasis on primary health care. All educational programs, including those preparing clinical nurse specialists with an acute care emphasis, should prepare nurses for delivery of services to diverse populations within the context of family and communities.

In a preferred future, APN education will identify practice models for better delivery of health services to underserved populations of women in a variety of sites (e.g., schools, workplaces, churches, senior centers, housing sites) and use these sites for education of students. Nursing educators, researchers, and APNs will be challenged to amend practice acts and regulations governing the practice of nursing to reflect the services APNs are certified and prepared to provide. Legislative changes will be necessary to overturn reimbursement schemes restricting the practice of APNs, particularly nurse practitioners and clinical nurse specialists. APNs must influence policy and policy makers by seeking representation by nurses, including APNs, on all provider boards (e.g., hospitals, health departments, managed care organizations) and provider panels.

Continuing the biomedical research on diseases specific to women, men, and children will be important to the preferred future health care delivery system. However, a research agenda must be more than a laundry list of diseases and conditions. Rather, a preferred future health research agenda should encompass a commitment to all research aimed at improving health, with a focus on the individual and his or her environment. Thus research must be aimed not only at reducing disease or studying the biopsychosocial factors of illness, but also at improving the health care delivery system and health care reimbursement systems. Research on the systemic and conceptual changes that influence individual health must also incorporate ethnic and socioeconomic diversity (Woods, 1995).

Seven of the existing research needs include

1. immigration and family separation, culture shock, and under- or unemployment as unique life stresses that contribute to psychological distress or disorders;
2. the relation of poverty to alcoholism and substance abuse among people of color;
3. the links between immune system disorders, the effects of radiation, environmental changes, genetic factors, and the increase of chemical exposure to the increase in cancers and chronic illness;
4. the sociocultural barriers that prevent women in particular from adopting safer sex practices;
5. the barriers to changing teen behavior and reducing rates of teen pregnancy;
6. a wider selection of safe and effective contraceptives; and
7. the effectiveness of alternative models of service delivery.

In addition to the focus on the individual and his or her health problems, a preferred future health research agenda must broaden traditional conceptual categories and look toward institutional change. The preferred APN future will document the impact of APN care on patient outcomes. New partnerships and new technologies will assist in the development of clinical databases so that policy makers, consumers, and others can better understand the dimensions and impact of the care APNs provide (Hamric, Spross, & Hanson, 1996).

CONCLUSION

Vision alone will not be enough if a preferred future is to be realized. Attention must be paid to shaping a vision for the preferred APN future. It is imperative that we in nursing practice, education, and research be knowledgeable about, prepared for, able to advocate for, and participate in the creation of a preferred future in health care policy and practice. Nursing has a clear tradition of creative and concerned leadership in developing and promoting innovation in health care delivery. Advancing our educational programs and orienting our research and activism endeavors in the direction of personal and community health will allow advanced nursing practice and knowledge to continue to have a significant influence on the transformation of health care and delivery systems.

REFERENCES

American Academy of Nursing Expert Panel on Women's Health Writing Group. (1996). *Women's health and women's health care: Recommendations for transformative changes in health care services, nursing education, and practice.* Washington, DC: American Academy of Nursing.

Cohen, S., Mitchell, E., Olesen, V., Olshansky, E., & Taylor, D. (1994). From female disease to women's health: New educational paradigms. In A. Dan (Ed.), *Reframing women's health: Multidisciplinary research and practice.* Thousand Oaks, CA: Sage Publications.

Eng, E., Salmon, M.E., & Mullan, F. (1992). Community empowerment: The critical basis for primary health care. *Family and Community Health, 15*(1), 1–12.

Hamric, A., Spross, J., & Hanson, C. (1996). Surviving the system and professional turbulence. In A. Hamric, J. Spross, & C. Hanson (Eds.), *Advanced nursing practice.* Philadelphia: W.B. Saunders.

Harper, D. (1996). Education for advanced nursing practice. In A. Hamric, J. Spross, & C. Hanson (Eds.), *Advanced nursing practice.* Philadelphia: W.B. Saunders Company.

Institute of Medicine. (1996). *Primary care.* Washington, DC: National Academy Press.

Labonte, R. (1989). Community health promotion strategies. In C.J. Martin & D.V. McQueen (Eds.), *Readings for a new public health.* Edinburgh, Scotland: Edinburgh University Press.

Labonte, R. (1993). *Community health responses to health inequalities.* New York: NY Community Health Promotion Research Unit.

Olesen, V., Taylor, D., Ruzek, S., & Clarke, A. (1996). Strengths and strongholds in women's health research. In S. Ruzek, A. Clarke, & V. Olesen (Eds.), *Women's health: Complexities and differences.* Columbus, OH: Ohio State University Press.

O'Neill, E. (March, 1995). *Future trends in the health care system.* Paper presented to University of California–San Francisco School of Nursing, San Francisco, CA.

Pender, N.J. (1987). *Health promotion in nursing practice* (2nd ed.). Norwalk, CT: Appleton & Lange.

Pepperdine, L., & Taylor, D. (1993). Health care crisis: Nursing solutions. *The Nurse Practitioner Journal, 18*(8), 15–25.

Pew Commission for the Health Professions. (1991). *Healthy America: Practitioners for 2005* (pp. 109–153). San Francisco: Center for the Health Professions.

Stevens, P.E., & Hall, J.M. (1988). Stigma, health beliefs and experiences with health care in lesbian women. *Image: Journal of Nursing Scholarship, 20*(2), 69–73.

Taylor, D. (1992). The nurse specialist in women's health: A model for graduate education. *NAACOG's Women's Health Nursing Scan, 6*(6), 1–2.

Taylor, D., & Dower, C. (1997). Toward a women-centered health care system: Women's experiences, women's voices, women's needs. *Health Care for Women International, 18*(4), 407–422.

Taylor, I., & Robertson, A. (1994). The health needs of gay men: A discussion of the literature and implications for nursing. *Journal of Advanced Nursing, 20*(3), 560–566.

U.S. Public Health Service. (1985). *Women's health: Report of the Public Health Service task force on women's health issues.* Washington, DC: Author.

U.S. Public Health Service. (1991). *Healthy people 2000: National health promotion and disease prevention objectives.* Washington, DC: Government Printing Office.

Woods, N.F. (1995). Women and their health. In C. Fogel & N.F. Woods (Eds.), *Women's health care.* Thousand Oaks, CA: Sage Publications.

World Health Organization (1978). *Healthy people 2000: Report of the Alma Ata world conference.* Brussels, Belgium: WHO.

14

Career Issues in Managed Care Delivery Systems

Care of the Self for the Nurse Entrepreneur

Vicki D. Lachman

Walk a mile, meditate, eat fresh fruits, get a mammogram, assert yourself—all of these behaviors require the initiative of an individual interested in taking responsibility for his or her health. Self-care is a form of conscious, deliberate action. Orem, a well-known nursing scholar and prolific writer on self-care, defines this process as "activities that individuals personally initiate and perform on their own behalf in maintaining life, health, and well-being. Self-care is an adult's personal, continuous contribution to his/her own health and well-being."[1(p.365)]

Maintaining a balanced perspective requires a commitment to the practice of self-awareness and self-care. Developing a balanced life-style means recognizing what things are important to you, evaluating what needs to be changed, and generating an action plan for change. This should not be a difficult task for the nurse entrepreneur who is both knowledgeable and assertive, or is it?

All self-care sounds this easy in theory; however, in the daily pull of work, family, community, church, etc., the nurse entrepreneur usually finds self-care practices more difficult to implement. Having practiced as a nurse entrepreneur for 23 years, listened and watched multiple other nurse entrepreneurs struggle to stay balanced, and having been an active researcher in stress management for 14 years, I've come to some conclusions as to what it takes to maintain self-care. I'll share these ideas in 19 principles that are at the heart of effective self-care, recommending specific actions for your own care plan.

1. IDENTIFY WHAT IS IMPORTANT, OF VALUE TO YOU, AND ASSESS WHETHER YOUR ACTIONS ARE CONSISTENT WITH YOUR BELIEFS.

For example, list five things you love doing. In the next column list how often you like doing them. Before you proceed, please list the five things you love doing and how often you would like to do them. In the third column, list how often you actually do them. The inconsistencies between your desired life and your actual habits can act as a trigger for you to change things. (See Figure 1.)

2. CHALLENGE THE BELIEF THAT OTHERS COME FIRST.

Patients need you, children need you, the PTA needs you; however, overinvolvement and excessive taking on of responsibility for others' happiness and welfare will lead you to burnout. Sometimes what we offer may not cure, or may not even be enough in the eyes of the other, and it takes courage to say "This is all I can do."

Nurs Admin Q, 1998, 22(2): 48–59
© 1998 Aspen Publishers, Inc.

THINGS YOU LIKE TO DO	HOW OFTEN YOU WOULD LIKE TO DO THEM	HOW OFTEN YOU ACTUALLY DO THEM
1.		
2.		
3.		
4.		
5.		

Figure 1. Things you like to do.

Using the image of a seesaw may help you visualize the importance of the fulcrum in balancing the needs of self and of others. At one end is your work and at the other end is your personal/family life. If one demands too much, we usually go to the other end for reinforcement. However, the way to balance is to use the fulcrum. This fulcrum activity is anything that fills you up, helps you stay balanced. Probably on your earlier list of five things you love doing, there was some activity that could be an example. A walk in the country, playing your guitar, listening to Mozart, are all ways that might help fill you up. You need something that is not dependent on your work or your family that helps you stay balanced. Remember, you need to give from the overflow, not from your well. It is most important to accept that you cannot be all things to all people.

3. LIVE CONSCIOUSLY; BE MINDFUL OF THE PRESENT. REMEMBER TO CHOOSE YOUR RESPONSE. THE SITUATION IS WHAT YOU THINK IT IS.

The perceptual and cognitive functions of your brain determine how you perceive an event. Your choice of response to any event depends on how you interpret the meaning of your perception. This is a key concept to remember in gaining control over your mind.

Anxiety is actually considered normal when its intensity and character are appropriate to a given situation. However, the type of anxiety I'm referring to here is not the pleasure of excitement, but the nervous tension you experience as you are responding to a perceived threat. Whether your mind is racing, confused, or scattered, you need to bring yourself back and be mindful of the present. Remember, first breathe, then ask yourself what can I do now? If nothing, refocus on what you can control in the present—i.e., ask for help, go to lunch, focus on a patient. It is key to remember that you can manage all situations with help.

Albert Ellis and David Burns describe several other kinds of errors in thinking that disrupt your ability to effectively problem solve in the present.[2,3] A few examples follow:

1. Dichotomous thinking—"I either do what they say or I lose the contract." This is either/or, black and white thinking.
2. Catastrophic thinking—"This day has started badly—the whole day will be terrible." Catastrophic thinking is viewing events as 100 percent bad.
3. Stereotyping—"Category X persons are . . . " is a standard type of stereotyping.

These are just a few of the concepts on distorted thinking. However, all of the 15 styles that Ellis and Burns list can play a significant role in decreasing one's focus on the present.

4. BE INTERDEPENDENT AND INTERDISCIPLINARY IN YOUR NATURE.

The importance of a support system has been shown over and over again. Pines and Kafry define social support systems as "enduring, interpersonal ties to a group of people who can be relied upon to provide feedback while sharing standards and values. . . ."[4(p.500)] Career and personal support are the two major focuses in an individual's support system. Support from others on the job enriches the individual's work resources. For example, a group of psychiatric clinical specialists formed a professional support group and found it useful in dealing with their frustrations from the multilevel demands for support.[5] Others have found their professional organizations as sources of support, networking with other nurse entrepreneurs to stay current and problem solve.

You can use your social support system to help support and guide you in achieving your professional and personal goals. Who can you call for emotional help at 3:00 AM? Who can provide you with consistent feedback on your consulting performance? Who challenges you to grow professionally and/or personally? A list of at least five different names should provide you with a safe buffer. If you had difficulty naming people who provide personal and/or professional support for you, take note that your support system is not solid.

5. SCHEDULE EXERCISE ON YOUR CALENDAR, UNTIL IT'S AN INGRAINED HABIT.

Activity relaxes muscles through the discharge of built-up tension. However, clubbing your "most difficult client" or your "favorite" physician is not an accepted mode of behavior in our civilized society. Swallowing the feelings of anger and frustration are acceptable; however, swallowing feelings whole is very bad for your body. As Gal and Lazarus point out, "even non-relevant activity under stress has stress reducing capabilities in that it allows for reasonable rapid dissipation of body arousal."[6(p.10)]

Cardiopulmonary or aerobic exercise is good not only for your body—surveys have shown that one of the main benefits of active participation in sports is a feeling of well-being. Choose one that you enjoy and do it three to four times a week for 20–30 minutes. Research has shown it makes a difference; by consistent practice you will know the researchers are right!

6. EATING HEALTHY IS POSSIBLE IF YOU PLAN

Habituation to processed and refined food, full of sugar and chemicals, contributes to many people using food for more than sustenance. Some people use food to numb themselves to emotional pain and then forget that the pain has anything to do with eating the food. To refresh your memory, refer to the food guide pyramid in Figure 2.[7]

Even though I find it difficult to follow this each day, I use it as my guideline for healthy eating. By including boxes of raisins, low-fat granola bars, and fresh fruits in my briefcase, I am able to many times make choices that I would have not otherwise been granted by vending machines. As a frequent flyer, it is standard for me to have low-fat diets on planes and I request them as a speaker at luncheons and dinners.

The questions of whether or not to take vitamins always arises when nutrition is being discussed. Some experts say "no," others say "yes." This expert says "yes." The amounts and types continue to be discussed in alternative medicine publications.

7. ELIMINATE, OR AT LEAST DECREASE, DRUGS LIKE CAFFEINE, ALCOHOL, NICOTINE, AND REFINED SUGAR.

Drugs are designed to alter your mental status, your emotional feelings, or your conscious experience of reality. But so can laughter, lovemaking, nature's beauty, or all of the positive addictions like running or a massage.

In order to avoid the use of artificial stimulants you will need to balance the excitement of risk taking and the stability of traditions and rituals. All humans have a need for some level of stimulation to their central nervous system; the degree of intensity and amount vary with the individual's makeup. White-water rafting, opening night at the theater, giving a surprise party, or simply trying something new all contribute to the natural excitement of life.

8. SPEND TIME IN AN ALPHA STATE EACH DAY IF YOU WANT TO BE A CREATIVE THINKER.

An alpha state is when you are awake, alert, and relaxed. Creating relaxing images in your mind, combined with a progressive muscle relaxation exercise, will essentially put you in an

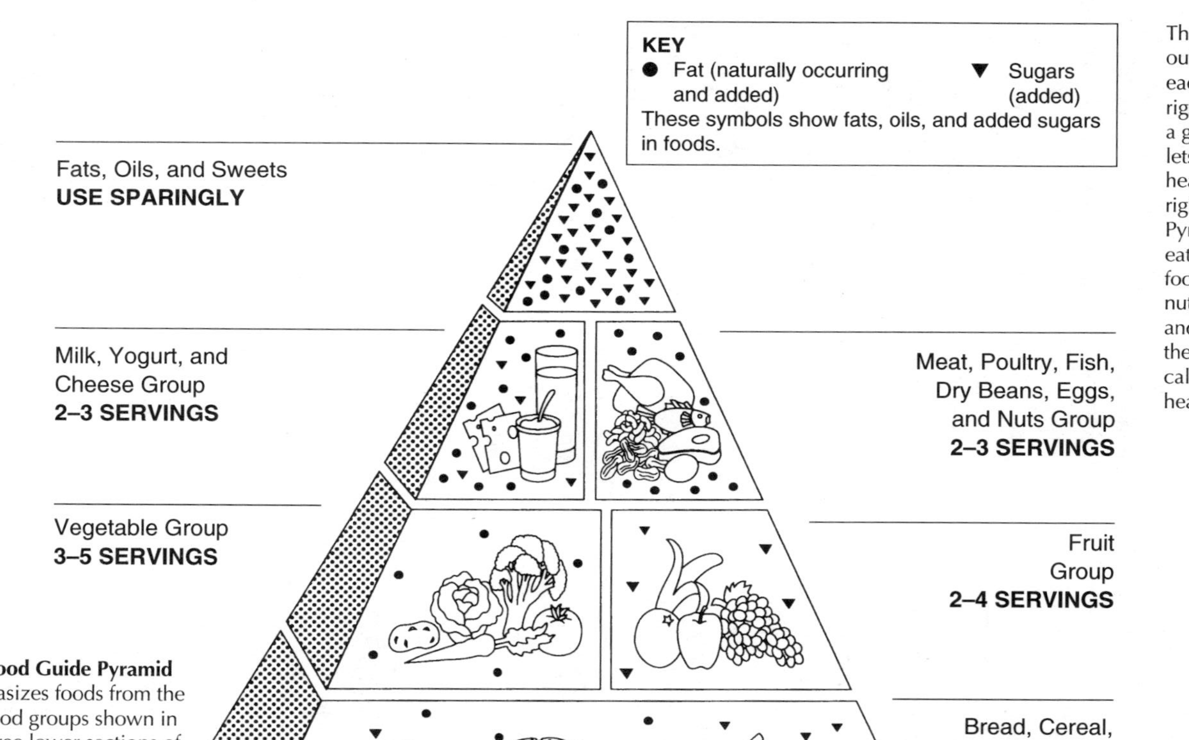

The Pyramid is an outline of what to eat each day. It's not a rigid prescription, but a general guide that lets you choose a healthful diet that's right for you. The Pyramid calls for eating a variety of foods to get the nutrients you need and at the same time the right amount of calories to maintain a healthy weight.

The **Food Guide Pyramid** emphasizes foods from the five food groups shown in the three lower sections of the Pyramid.

Each of these food groups provides some, but not all of the nutrients you need. Foods in one group can't replace those in another. No one food group is more important than another—for good health, you need them all.

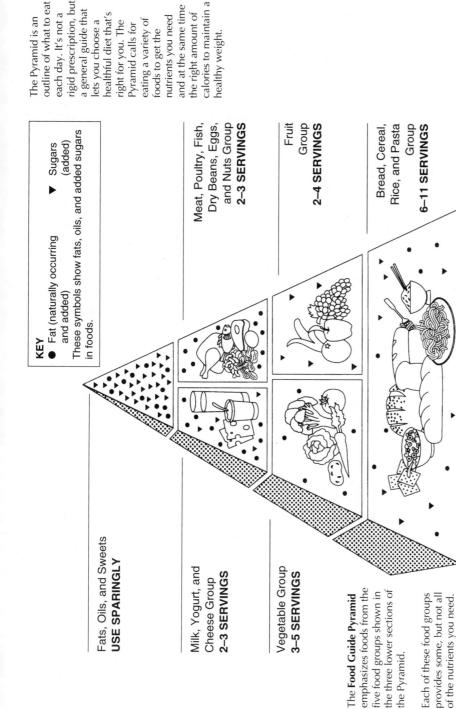

Figure 2. The Food Guide Pyramid. *Source:* U.S. Department of Agriculture/U.S. Department of Health and Human Services.

alpha state.[8] Visualization simply means creating an image or a picture in your mind's eye that offers you a sense of calmness and serenity.

Meditation can have the same effect on your body as a relaxation exercise. Your mind also becomes calm because you are focusing on only one thing. Meditation needs to be practiced at least 20 minutes daily in order for you to reap the benefits.Your goal is to concentrate on your breathing. The power of breathing as part of meditation has been illustrated by Zen monks in Japan who are able to reduce their oxygen consumption by as much as 20 percent.[9]

Hypnosis, self-hypnosis, autogenic training, and biofeedback are all based upon the premise that when muscles relax, tension is released. Massage, whether superficial or deep, creates a relax message from the outside to the inside. Listening to classical/new age music, knitting, prayer—any repetitive activity that allows you to focus, and helps your conscious mind to relax, is helpful.

9. MANAGE YOUR BOSS AND/OR WHOEVER THINKS THEY ARE YOUR BOSS.

Negotiate the priorities of your role with your boss or your client regularly to keep a clear focus. Advanced practice nurses are good at doing many things and are often asked to do projects that they are capable of doing well, but which have little relevance to their role. After many years of "helping out" in these situations, their focus becomes diluted and they become ineffective in the very thing that they are most qualified to do. This becomes especially challenging in this era of downsizing where you need to justify the value of your role. Remember though that more isn't always better, just because you do a variety of projects doesn't mean your time is being used to everyone's best advantage.

10. MANAGE THE POLITICS OF YOUR WORKPLACE.

In every organization, no matter how small, there is maneuvering for power and control. Some of the maneuvering is overt and obvious politics whereas other behavior is subversive. To operate effectively in any organization, you will need to understand what behaviors are acceptable and rewarded in the organizational culture.

Ambivalent attitudes toward power and politics, together with a lack of useful information about power breeds naive and cynical beliefs about what an effective individual must do. There are five political strategies that all individuals must have at their fingertips in order to be politically savvy.[10]

1. Coalition forming. One group teams up with another group to put pressure on a third group. For example, nurse practitioners and physicians may put pressure on administration to change their productivity standards for the practice.
2. Bargaining or trade-offs. "I'll scratch your back if you scratch my back" is seen in the daily operations of any operating room (OR). As the nurse practitioner negotiates to give up OR time in exchange for a better time schedule the following day, the OR supervisor's appreciation is well-founded.
3. Lobbying. When an advanced practice nurse lets the Medical Executive Committee know that with her privileges come patients who will need to be referred to the psychiatrist and the neurologist on staff, she is clearly lobbying for admission privileges.
4. Posturing or bluffing. It is often true that who you know is more important than what you know. There is certain power gained when you are identified

with other powerful persons. The use of effective name dropping can sometimes bring you more than your fair share of scarce resources.

5. Increasing visibility. Increasing visibility focuses on being with the right person, in the right place, at the right time. What social events are important for you to attend? Remember that using politics can help you cut through an enormous amount of bureaucratic red tape.

11. DO A YEARLY STRESS INVENTORY AND CHANGE YOUR TOP PERSONAL AND PROFESSIONAL STRESSORS.

At least once a year all individuals need to take the time to assess their present levels of stress caused by both personal and professional responsibilities. First list all the activities in your personal, as well as your professional life that create the most tension, anxiety, and frustration. What drives you crazy? For example, there might be a meeting that you are expected to attend that is always poorly run, runs overtime, and accomplishes very little. Another example might be that your child's day care does not routinely open on time and, therefore, you are at times late for your first appointment. Both of these can be major sources of stress and might be at the top of your priority list to change for the coming year. Second, prioritize your list and develop an active plan to remove the problem.

12. KNOW YOUR GENETIC VULNERABILITY AND MANAGE IT.

According to Hans Selye, all of us enter this world with an "Achilles' Heel," a vulnerability in our mind or body.[11] When we ineffectively manage stress, our vulnerability can become illness. For some of us it is our stomachs, while for others it is the ability to manage emotions. The easiest way to understand and address this issue is to complete the "Family Tree of Health Problems" shown in Figure 3.

The family tree affords you the opportunity to assess where your vulnerability is in relationship to some diseases connected with ineffective management of stress. For example, is hypertension, low-back pain, migraine headaches, cardiac disease, or cancer on your family tree? Is depression, alcoholism, or obesity a problem in your family? If you have a significant amount of low-back pain on your family tree, then there are certain things that you will need to do in your life style that can help you manage such a problem. Back strengthening and stretching exercises each morning, asking people to help you, and wearing low-heel shoes are examples of life style and support system changes to cope with your vulnerability.

13. LAUGHTER RELEASES THE ENDORPHINS AND HELPS YOU KEEP PERSPECTIVE ON THE SERIOUSNESS OF OUR BUSINESS.

Court jesters and ceremonial clowns are credited with restoring cheer and scaring off the demons of disease in the Middle Ages. In our time, Norman Cousins, the highly acclaimed writer of *Head First: The Biology of Hope and the Healing Power of the Human Spirit*, tells us how he benefited by forming a therapeutic partnership with his health care providers in using humor to cure a potentially fatal disease.[12] Stress is alleviated by humor because we know that joy and sadness cannot operate simultaneously. Furthermore, the increased autonomic activities produce relaxation and afford you the ability to see the logical and abstract nuances of the problem.[13] In addition to the increased endorphin pro-

MOTHER FATHER

GRANDPARENTS GRANDPARENTS

AUNTS AND UNCLES AUNTS AND UNCLES

BROTHERS AND SISTERS

MY HEALTH PROBLEMS

Figure 3. Family tree of health problems.

duction, there is also an increase in immune cell production, an increase in heart rate, respiratory rate, and oxygen saturation.

There are numerous strategies to improve your laugh life; the one I'm most fond of is to look at the lighter side of life. The strategies of exaggeration, mirroring reality, and reversals are the ones I find most effective.[13] Exaggeration refers to magnifying or minimizing an undesirable behavior, compared to the real behavior. For example: I'd rather go to a gynecologist 20 times than a dentist once. Mirroring reality involves looking for humor in everyday life. Reversals take the situation from "bad to reverse," providing perspective and distance. For example, I wish more people would be "inverse paranoids," people who think the world is out to do them good.

14. BE REALISTIC ABOUT YOUR ABILITY AND SET GOALS TO STRETCH YOURSELF.

Nurse entrepreneurs are high achievers and therefore have had multiple experiences in stretching themselves to reach increasingly complex goals. It is important for our mental and physical health that we focus our minds on creating pictures of what we want to have, not what we don't like about what we have. Too many people forget one of the basic laws of the universe, which is that we attract to ourselves that which we focus upon with our thoughts. Therefore, we need to focus on measurable, obtainable goals that bring us joy. For example, the goal "I will increase the number of patients in my practice by 10 percent in the following year" is a much more effective way to deal with the diminishing patient referrals in the community due to managed care, than to lament about the changing health care reimbursement system.

15. CONNECTING WITH GOD, YOUR SPIRITUALITY, OR YOUR SENSE OF WONDER WILL HELP YOU GRAPPLE WITH THE MORAL AND ETHICAL ISSUES YOU FACE.

Leaders in medicine and science point out that the movement toward health is necessarily a spiritual one. Too often the thing we budget out of our schedule is the time we need to recognize and nurture our spiritual and creative inclinations. Meditation and prayer are acts of surrender, of letting go of one's usual preoccupations. By accepting God's love, we can begin to love ourselves and, as a result, be able to reach out to others in love.[14] In accepting life, we are also accepting death because a person who truly accepts life is not afraid to die; a person who is not afraid to die can fully embrace life.[15]

16. SCHEDULE A "SABBATH DAY" OF REST AT LEAST ONCE A WEEK.

This doesn't mean do housework that day, it means rest. Rest can take the form of experiencing/interacting with nature, listening to music, spending time with enriching friends/family, reading, meditating, or best of all, just doing nothing. This will help you learn what it means to be a "human being" versus a "human doing."

In addition, take a mental health day off when you need it and schedule vacations. If you don't put vacations on your calendar well in advance, you are likely to justify your need to remain at work. Taking a long weekend on a quarterly basis can also help you keep perspective on work.

Finally, do not agree to be on-call for more than 24 hours at a time, since sleep deprivation reduces your ability to think and make effective decisions. Sleep deprivation can also occur from an overzealous work schedule. Plan your sleep renewal time, whether you need six or nine hours, because without it your body and mind cannot get the rejuvenation they deserve.

17. IF TRAVEL IS A SIGNIFICANT PART OF YOUR BUSINESS, MAKE IT USER-FRIENDLY. AIRPORT CLUBS AND AUDIOTAPES ARE PART OF THE ANSWER.

As a nurse entrepreneur who travels two or three days a week, and as one who can drive as much as five hours in one day to and from a consulting job, I feel qualified to speak about what it takes to make the travel easier. As a member of several airline clubs, I can tell you that they make check-in and waiting time in airports much easier. You have access to phones, fax machines, comfortable chairs, and friendly people to help you to your next destination. On several occasions, when I have been detained, I have even taken advantage of their couches for a brief nap.

In the past year, I have listened to tapes of five biographies, including those of Colin Powell, Lincoln, and Mother Teresa, as well as tapes on various clinical topics. Obtaining this information would not have been possible if I had counted on reading the material, since I can barely keep up with my journals at the present time. I found all of these tapes entertaining, enriching, and helpful in making the travel time more enjoyable.

18. MANAGE THE BUSINESS OF YOUR PRACTICE.

I find nurse entrepreneurs most commonly neglect the areas of finance and marketing. There are many computer software programs that can help you keep track of finances, including Quicken and Excel. You must have a competent accountant who can set up an accounting system and provide you with adequate records to help you control your budget, and prepare you for tax purposes, or possible investors.[16]

The success of a practice, as in any other business, is based on two basic issues: the quality of service/product and an effective marketing program.[17] Marketing is basically determining what your customer needs and wants, and then designing a service/product that will satisfy those needs.[18,19] Whatever promotional activities are used, the service/product needs to be positioned as first choice in the mind of the consumer as Kleenex, Coke, and Mayo Clinic are to many consumers.

19. DO THE PREVENTION AND DETECTION TESTS YOU PREACH.

Many of the "over 50" nurse entrepreneurs complain about the amount of "maintenance work" it takes to stay healthy. This includes annual Pap smears, mammograms, dental checkups, eye exams for glaucoma, colonoscopies, and prostate exams. Since the major causes of illness still remain in the cardiopulmonary and cancer realms, it is important that we complete the proper maintenance and prevention work that we preach to our clients/patients. For example, although we preach drink eight glasses of water a day, how many of you actually do it?

• • •

Each of these principles addresses some aspect of our physical, mental, spiritual, or work-related health. Please do not use this list of principles as a new hammer to beat yourself up, but as a gentle reminder to take care of yourself, so you can take care of others. Life is meant to be joyous. By focusing on what you want, rather than on what you don't have, by deliberately creating what you want and allowing others to have what they want without judgment, you will be practicing the essence of self-care. The nursing profession, with its historical roots in caring and its holistic philosophy of self-care, must serve as a leader, advocate, and role model of self-care principles to keep the stress in the professional practice environment at a productive level.[20]

REFERENCES

1. D.E. Orem, *Nursing Concepts of Practice* (3rd ed.) (New York: McGraw Hill, 1991).
2. A. Ellis, and R. Harper, *A New Guide to Rational Living* (North Hollywood, CA: Wilshire Books, 1979).
3. D. Burns, *Feeling Good: The New Mood Therapy*. (New York: Avon, 1992).
4. A. Pines, and D. Kafry, "Occupational Tedium in the Social Services." *Social Work* 23 (1978): 499–507.
5. R.M. Johnson, et al., "The Professional Support Group: A Model for Psychiatric Clinical Specialists." *Journal of Psychosocial Nursing and Mental Health Services* 20, no.2 (1982): 9–13.
6. R. Gal, and R.S. Lazarus, "The Role of Activity in Anticipating and Confronting Stressful Situations." *Journal of Human Stress* 1, no.4 (1975): 4–20.
7. U.S. Department of Agriculture and the U.S. Department of Health and Human Services, the Food Guide Pyramid, Home and Garden No. 252, (Washington, DC: U.S. Government Printing Office, 1992).
8. D. Chopra, *Ageless Bodies, Timeless Mind: The Quantum Alternative to Growing Old* (New York: Harmony Books, 1993).
9. H. Benson, *Beyond the Relaxation Response*. (New York: Times Books, 1984).
10. D. del Bueno, and C. Freund, *Power and Politics in Nursing Administration: A Case Book*. (Owings Mills, MD: National Health Publishing, 1986).
11. H. Selye, *The Stress of Life* (New York: McGraw-Hill, 1976).
12. N. Cousins, *Head First: The Biology of Hope and the Healing Power of the Human Spirit* (New York: Penguin Books, 1989).
13. M. Cohen, "Caring for Ourselves Can be a Funny Business." *Holistic Nursing Practice* 4, no.4 (1990): 1–11.
14. M.E. McGlone, "Healing the Spirit." *Holistic Nursing Practice* 4, no.4 (1990): 77–84.
15. S.R. Henderson, *Facing Life Through Death* (Staunton, VA: Full Circle Counseling, 1978).
16. G.L. Crow, "The Business of Planning Your Practice: Success Is No Accident." *Advanced Practice Nursing Quarterly* 2, no.1 (1996): 55–61.
17. G. Vogel, and N. Doleysh, *Entrepreneuring: A Nurse's Guide to Starting Your Business* (New York: National League for Nursing, 1988).
18. V. Lachman, "Positioning Your Business in the Marketplace." *Advanced Practice Nursing Quarterly* 2, no.1 (1996): 27–32.
19. A. Reis, and J. Trout, *The Twenty-Two Immutable Laws of Marketing: Violate Them at Your Own Risk!* (New York: Harper Business, 1994).
20. V. Lachman, "Stress and Self-Care Revisited." *Holistic Nursing Practice* 10, no.2 (1996): 1–11.

Floating: A Nurse's Nightmare?

Kenneth Brownson and Steven B. Dowd

The process of "floating," wherein nurses are moved from their normal assignment to an area that is short-staffed, is thought by many managers to be a cost-effective strategy for responding to workload needs. This practice is enjoying renewed favor with attempts to minimize personnel costs through "leaner" staffs. The basic assumption is that "a nurse is a nurse is a nurse" or that nurses are generalists rather than specialists.

However, surveys show that most nurses consider themselves to be specialists and that the practice of floating causes stress among staff.[1] One study of intensive care unit nurses showed that only death outranked floating as a source of stress.[2] Ornstein[3] found that 73 percent of the nurses in her study "disliked, resented, or hated" floating.

Staff nurses do not oppose floating from selfish standpoints. They worry that floating may place them in litigious situations or in vulnerable positions before state boards of nursing and, worst of all, that it makes them violate basic concepts of patient safety. Many nurses have worked hard to ensure that they understand every nuance of their specialty through experience and additional education; they fear that they may be pulled to a unit where they are no longer "competent" and in control.

Nicholls and colleagues[4] found that, although floating was stressful to nurses, the stress could be alleviated with proper orientation and management responses. This article reviews potential legal problems in floating, ethical dilemmas nurses face when asked to float, strategies nurses can use to float successfully, strategies management can use to help their staff, and the role of union contracts.

LEGAL ISSUES IN FLOATING

One of the early cases involving floating was *Norton v. Argonaut Ins. Co.*[5] A nursing supervisor assisting on a busy pediatric unit administered 3.0 ml of injectable dioxin to a child, not knowing that an oral elixir existed. The child arrested and died. A key element in the case was the nurse's lack of knowledge of pediatric medications and dosages.

In *Dessauer v. Memorial General Hospital,*[6] an obstetrical nurse was pulled from her unit to the emergency department. Based on a complaint of substernal chest pain, diaphoresis, and other signs, the emergency department physician diagnosed an acute myocardial infarction. He gave an order for 50 mg. of Lidocaine. Again, the nurse was unfamiliar with the peculiarities of doses and packaging of drugs in this particular department. She located a vial of Lidocaine, unaware that the instructions indicated that this vial was for dilution only and not for direct injection. A total of 800 mg. of Lidocaine was administered to the patient, who had an arrest and died.

Health Care Superv, 1997, 15(3): 10–15
© 1997 Aspen Publishers, Inc.

These cases may seem simplistic and solvable in hindsight. For years, however, nurses have contended that there is a special science to the practice of nursing and that each nursing specialty requires a knowledgebase of its own. There were well over 110,000 certified specialty nurses in the United States for the last year that numbers were reported.[7] Increasingly, legal opinion has indicated that nursing should be viewed as a profession, like medicine, with distinct specialties.[8,9] As Regan[10] has noted, "Indiscriminate floating in hospitals reflects an administrative mentality that still subscribes to the hackneyed notion that a license to practice nursing is a license to do anything within the legal definition of professional nursing."[10(p.1)]

Does this mean that nurses have the right to refuse to float? In general terms, the answer is no, unless specified in the employment agreement. In *Francis v. Memorial General Hospital,*[11] a nurse was fired for refusing to float from his regular intensive care unit to the orthopedic unit. He sued the hospital for violation of civil rights but lost both the case and the subsequent appeal. The court found that floating was an established hospital policy and not contrary to public policy.

However, other cases have also indicated that the practice and applicability of floating is situation specific. In *Winkelman v. Beloit Memorial Hospital,*[12] a nurse established that she was unable to perform even the simplest nursing tasks in a postoperative unit due to her 40-year history of nursery-only nursing. It was found that "a nurse isn't necessarily qualified or competent to practice in any area of nursing simply because she's graduated from a nursing school and passed the licensure examination."[13(p.66)]

THE ETHICAL DILEMMA IN FLOATING

Nurse practice acts typically contain language that make the practice of floating appear to be suspect. Also, nursing organizations tend to oppose the practice of floating. The Massachusetts Nurse Association, the New Jersey State Nurses Association, and the American Nurses Association, among others, have all indicated that nurses should have the right to accept or reject reassignment.[14,15] Many state nursing associations have also developed assignment despite objection (ADO) forms that allow nurses to document what they feel are unsafe floating practices; the right to use these is often a part of collective bargaining agreements.

The Standards of the Joint Commission on Accreditation of Healthcare Organizations (Joint Commission) have never spoken directly against floating, but they used to discourage it through some of their statements. For example, NC 2.3.3 stated that "the staff member is competent to provide nursing care to patients in each unit and/or to each type of patient."[16] Many of the Joint Commission standards for specialty units spoke of "training and experience" in the specialty area (e.g., burn care, care of high-risk infants, and renal patients). However, newer emphases on outcomes, rather than the process,[17] and the "continuum of care protocol"[18] have removed even such indirect statements, although competence and education are certainly expected.

Nurses tend to be aware of these position statements and guidelines. They also believe, as mentioned earlier, that nursing is a science that requires special skills for special situations. However, many nurses also believe that they are called upon to deliver care to any patient needing it. Beyond legal obligations, this sets up a major ethical dilemma for the nurse.[19] When one area is "overstaffed," and another "understaffed," what should the nurse do? If she does accept reassignment to the understaffed area, patient care may be compromised through the lack of available caregivers. On the other hand, if she works in the area and commits an error through lack of experience and thus jeopardizes the patient's health, what value has her "floating" accomplished?

Ethical dilemmas are particularly difficult as they provide two alternates—in this case, to float or not to float—that appear to have equal measure of pluses and minuses. As professionals, staff nurses must do what they think is right and live with the consequences. Should they decide that floating is the best solution, the next section tells them how they can do so and still attempt to provide the quality of care they do on their "normal" unit.

WHAT CAN STAFF NURSES DO?

The Florida Nurses Association has developed guidelines for nurses who are asked to float.[14] Before accepting a floating assignment, nurses should *clarify, assess,* and *identify* options. In clarification, the nurse must ensure that expectations are clear: how many patients will I be responsible for? What is their acuity level? What support services will other nurses provide?

In assessment, nurses evaluate their own knowledge and skill level and their past experiences with similar patient populations. In the previously discussed *Winkelman* case, this is exactly what the nurse did when she refused to float to a postsurgical unit.

In option identification, the nurse decides to accept or decline the floating assignment. If the assignment is accepted, nurses must remember their ethical and legal obligations to provide the same standard of care as any other nurse on that unit. If declined, it is best to do so in a way that asks for other options: Could the assignment be accepted in part by monitoring less acute patients? Could I be floated to another unit and a nurse with the appropriate skills floated to this unit? Refusal can result in termination, which may or may not be successfully fought in grievance hearings or court.

An additional step cited by Hamilton and Kiefer[20] is evaluation of thc floating experience by the nurse. What about the experience was successful? Unsuccessful? Should the nurse accept a future reassignment to that unit? If not, is it due to a specific lack of knowledge? Could this be remediated through some sort of training or educational experience?

ARE UNION CONTRACTS THE ANSWER?

Union contracts for nursing tend to include language that mitigates against floating. For example, most contracts state that, except in the case of emergency,

- PRNs will be used first.
- Rotations will be assigned as equitably as possible.
- Rotations will be to units similar to those in which employees are normally scheduled.
- Employees will not be reassigned after the first hour of the shift.
- Employees will not be required to be in charge.
- Employees will not be reassigned more than once per shift.
- Employees will not be reassigned while on overtime.[21]

It has been often stated that it is not unions that organize employees; instead it is a deficit in employee relations that drives employees to unions.[22,23] McConnell has stated that "Many employees—quite likely the majority—would prefer to be loyal to the organization, but the organization's seeming indifference to upward communication can discourage such loyalty."[24(p.292)] If management implements poorly thought-out floating policies, implements no policies at all, or does not encourage supervisors to listen to employee concerns about floating, employees will choose the option that appears to protect them and the patient—unionization.

WHAT CAN ADMINISTRATION DO?

There are few guidelines for administration on implementing successful guidelines for floating. Queensway General Hospital in Ontario developed Float Survival Kits, containing essential information for reassigned nurses.[3] Education and orientation of reassigned nurses *as well as the nurses on the units to which they are reassigned to* is also often mentioned in the literature.[4,8,19]

The notion that "a nurse is a nurse is a nurse" must be addressed. Although increasingly physicians are becoming hospital employees, there does not appear to be a similar consideration that a physician can work on any unit; also, no one would expect a radiologic technologist normally performing general radiography to perform computed tomography without appropriate cross-training. Floating is often justified on the premise that the nurse will only perform the most basic of nursing duties, those skills that all nurses possess. In reality, when patient needs arise on the unit that must be addressed immediately, and experienced staff are busy, the instruction to perform basic duties only becomes much more difficult to follow.

A currently popular notion in intra-unit assignment is self-staffing or scheduling, which delegates the responsibility for staffing to staff nurses in the unit.[25–27] Although this notion probably could not work for the hospital as a whole, the idea that nurses should have professional autonomy does. How can staff nurses become involved in the floating process? Communication and shared responsibility are the keys.

For example, New York Hospital has developed its own form for the nurse to fill out after the shift.[28] This form allows the nurse to air grievances; more importantly, it allows for the collection of data by the hospital to improve patient care and make improvements in units, in accordance with quality measures and continuum of care protocols. Staff nurses may be able to provide administration with useful guidelines in the floating process, including when it is acceptable or not acceptable and specific strategies to facilitate the process.

For facilities without union contracts, it may be advisable to develop guidelines for floating similiar to those found in collective bargaining agreements. This sends a signal to staff that administration understands their concerns and wants to come to equitable solutions without the need for adversarial relationships.

Although supervisors might feel like the "person in the middle," they can help facilitate the communication process. They can let management know of the potential dangers in floating as well as employee concerns. They can communicate management's needs for cost-effective care to employees. They can also serve as problem-solvers in such situations, and perhaps develop innovative solutions that benefit staff, management, and, most importantly, the patient.

CONCLUSION

Like any situation that involves the management of people, what appears to be a simple solution in times of need—"floating" available nurses to units that are short-staffed—is, in reality, complex. Nurses typically have a legal and ethical obligation to float, although there certainly are circumstances in which a nurse should refuse to float based on legal and ethical objections. The primary factor that speaks against floating is when it would appear that patient safety would be jeopardized. Administration must institute guidelines that facilitate the floating process for the nurse and maintain patient safety, as well as keep lines of communication open. Lack of appropriate guidelines may contribute to nursing staff considering unions as the solution, a move that typically protects them from floating, especially arbitrarily.

REFERENCES

1. Beard, E.L. "Stop Floating—The Next Paradigm Shift?" *Journal of Nursing Administration* 24, no. 3 (1994): 4.
2. Foxall, M. "A Comparison of Frequency and Sources of Nursing Job Stress Perceived By Intensive Care, Hospice and Medical-Surgical Nurses." *Journal of Advanced Nursing* 15 (1990): 581.
3. Ornstein, H. "The Floating Dilemma." *The Canadian Nurse* 88, no. 9 (1992): 20–22.
4. Nicholls, D.J., Duplaga, E.A., and Meyer, L.M. "Nurses' Attitudes About Floating." *Nursing Management* 27, no. 1 (1996): 56–58.
5. *Norton v. Argonaut Ins. Co.,* 144 S.2d 249 (La. 1962).
6. *Dessauer v. Memorial General Hospital,* 628 P.2d 337 (N.M. 1981).
7. Washington, DC: American Nurses Credentialing Center, October, 1995.
8. O'Reilly, M.E. "Floating: A Reality and a Problem." *Focus on Critical Care* 14, no. 3 (1987): 60–61.
9. Politis, E.K. "Nurses' Legal Dilemma: When Hospital Staffing Compromises Professional Standards." *University of San Francisco Law Review* 18 (1983): 109–143.
10. Regan, W. "Blockbuster Lawsuits: Nurse Defendants." *The Regan Report on Nursing Law* 22, no. 3 (1981): 1.
11. Tamello, D. "Nurse Refuses to Float: Sunk." *The Regan Report on Nursing Law* 27, no. 7 (1986): 1.
12. *Winkelman v. Beloit Memorial Hospital,* 483 N.W. 2d 211 (Wis. 1992).
13. Anonymous. "Legal Questions. Floating: Fish Out of Water." *Nursing* 26, no. 1 (1996): 66.
14. Ketter, J. "The Ethical and Legal Implications of Restructuring. Floating Without Being Properly Trained." *American Nurse* 26, no. 7 (1994): 23.
15. Anonymous. "NJSNA Position Statement on Temporary Reassignment." *New Jersey Nurse* 21, no. 4 (1991): 12.
16. Joint Commission on Accreditation of Healthcare Organizations. *Accreditation Manual for Hospitals.* Oakbrook Terrace, Ill.: Joint Commission, 1991.
17. Joint Commission on Accreditation of Healthcare Organizations. *Accreditation Manual for Hospitals.* Oakbrook Terrace, Ill.: Joint Commission, 1996.
18. Skarzynski, J. "The Continuum of Care Protocol." *The Health Care Supervisor* 14, no. 3 (1996): 64–77.
19. Donner, T.A. "Floating Out of ICU: The Ethical Dilemmas." *Dimensions of Critical Care Nursing* 11, no. 2 (1992): 105–107.
20. Hamilton, J.M., and Kiefer, M.E. "4 Tips To Take the Fear Out of Floating." *Nursing* 17, no. 2 (1987): 60–61.
21. Pennsylvania Nurses' Association Economic and General Welfare Program. *Professional Agreement Between Pennsylvania Nurses' Association and Crozer-Chester Medical Center.* July 1991–October 1993: 42–44.
22. Metzger, N. *The Health Care Supervisor's Handbook.* Rockville, Md.: Aspen Systems, 1982.
23. Henry, K.H. "Health Care Union Organizing: Guidelines for Supervisory Conduct." *The Health Care Supervisor* 4, no. 1 (1985): 14–26.
24. McConnell, C. *The Effective Health Care Supervisor.* Rockville, Md.: Aspen Systems, 1982.
25. McCoy, A.K. "Developing Self-Scheduling In Critical Care." *Dimensions of Critical Care Nursing* 11, no. 3 (1992): 152–156.
26. Hausfeld, J., et al. "Self-Staffing: Improving Care and Staff Satisfaction." *Nursing Management* 25, no. 10 (1994): 74, 76, 78.
27. Abbott, M.E. "Measuring The Effects of a Self-Scheduling Committee." *Nursing Management* 26, no. 9 (1995): 64A–B, D, G.
28. Sklar, J. "Pain-Less Floating." *Nursing Management* 23, no. 7 (1992): 104.

15

Career Development Strategies in Managed Care

Career Journeys: How To Be a Successful Clinical Nurse Specialist—Be a Willow Tree

Vivian S. Sternweiler

My motto is: "Be a willow tree." As a clinical nurse specialist (CNS) in today's ever-changing health care environment, flexibility is the key to success. Emulating the grace and flow of a willow tree is critical to survival in the marketplace.

WILLOW TREES HAVE MANY BRANCHES

A clinical specialist must have many "branches" that extend into all aspects of care provision. In my role, I maintain a caseload of patients, provide formal and informal education, participate as a leader for projects and committees, write and implement standards of care, and apply research findings to practice. These role responsibilities are typical and critical for a CNS.

In the 15 years since obtaining a master of science degree in adult acute care clinical specialty, I have held a variety of roles as a clinical or educational consultant throughout the metropolitan Boston area. For the past 8 years, I have been employed as the medical–surgical clinical nurse specialist in a large Boston tertiary care facility. Flexibility has never been more important to the success of my role as it has in the past few years.

The CNS role is inherently ambiguous and complex. Each role is designed specifically to balance the individual's strengths with the needs of the institution. As internal and external pressures continue to be exerted on the health care system, there is a greater need within institutions for multifaceted employees. The CNS is perfectly positioned—in a role that is intended to be diverse—to develop innovative and strategic opportunities for role development that meet the increasing needs of the institution.

WILLOW TREES BEND GRACEFULLY WITH THE WIND

The winds of change are constantly blowing, creating an ongoing need for flexible team players within health care organizations. A clinical specialist is often well situated to assess the organizational climate and assist in meeting the goals of the institution. Maintaining one's focus, composure, and spirit in the face of a shifting landscape is imperative for survival in an expanded role.

My clinical practice consists primarily of clinical consultation for skin and wound care. I carry a caseload of patients who may have pressure ulcers, tape tears, rashes, complex wounds, or any number of dermatological conditions. In addition to my clinical practice, I participate in many hospital or service-related projects. These projects range from new product evaluation to participating on a

Adv Prac Nurs Q, 1998, 3(4): 31–33
© 1998 Aspen Publishers, Inc.

task force to prepare for a visit by the Joint Commission on Accreditation of Healthcare Organizations (Joint Commission).

Two years ago, the tertiary care hospital in which I work was preparing for a Joint Commission visit. As one of the facilitators for the preparation process in the nursing service, I was asked by my director to assist one of the outpatient clinics that serves psychiatric patients in its preparation. The clinic was slated for a Joint Commission visit for the first time in its history. The acting manager of the clinic had recently left the institution, so there were quite a few loose ends to tie up in a short period of time. Although my specialty is not psychiatry, the clinic nurses and I pulled everything together in time for the visit, and the clinic passed with flying colors. I had established a good rapport with the nursing staff and my director gave me the opportunity to remain administratively responsible for the clinic. I had no prior experience in a management role, but knew the opportunity would afford additional learning and development opportunities. It also was a great way to demonstrate my flexibility and willingness to help meet institutional needs. I accepted the offer and have successfully added managerial duties to my clinical specialist responsibilities.

WILLOW TREES HAVE A WIDE-REACHING, BUT SHALLOW ROOT SYSTEM

The CNS is often involved in numerous projects at the same time. The CNS needs to be well grounded as a clinical leader, while working collaboratively and intricately with other members of the care team. The CNS often functions as a change agent for the institution. This role demands the ability to rearrange priorities as the need arises, either by self-assessment or by external forces. It is the ever-changing landscape of health care that is often the catalyst for change.

The need to respond quickly to the environment has been particularly important during the past year—the institution in which I work merged with another large teaching institution. Suddenly, everything had changed, and nothing was the same. Although my clinical practice and administrative responsibilities for the clinic continued uninterrupted, projects and committees that had been my focus for years were suddenly "on hold." New committees and projects arose quickly, and priorities shifted suddenly.

What a perfect time to be a willow tree with a shallow root system! Being "uprooted" with deep, entrenched roots is much more painful than having an intricate, but shallow root system. Again, flexibility is the key to success during such a period. Each day brings a new piece of information, a new perspective, a new change, a new challenge.

WILLOW TREES GROW IN CLUSTERS

Being able to function autonomously is a critical factor for a successful CNS. However, that autonomy can lead to isolation if one does not take steps to avoid it. It is necessary to establish and maintain a peer group for professional and personal support for continued professional growth.

BE A WILLOW TREE

I can honestly say that I have wanted to be a nurse for as far back as I can remember. From a very young age, I accompanied my physician father on his patient rounds every Sunday morning. I was fascinated by the hospital environment and knew from the start that nursing was my future.

So much has changed in the decades since I colored with the nurses' tri-colored pens while I waited for my father. It is often hard to remember that the central core of nursing has remained the same. There are many more options for nursing roles today. The environment demands that advanced practice nurses stay focused, develop multifaceted roles, and remain flexible. In other words, it demands that we be willow trees.

Are You Your Resumé?

Deborah A. Straka

Resumés are a significant topic for discussion and debate in this era of redesign and right sizing. Advanced practitioners in particular have found themselves caught in the frenzy of health care organizational re-engineering efforts. These efforts have resulted in job loss or lack of job security for the advanced practitioner. Both of these situations encourage individuals to think about the challenges of job hunting. For the jobless, resumé writing, of course, is a hot topic because most people suggest that resumés can be the key to finding jobs. For those who have jobs, it is important to note that there are good reasons to focus on resumé writing even if you are not looking for a job. In fact, there are at least three good reasons (Rosenberg & Hizer, 1990):

1. The majority of desirable positions are offered to individuals who are satisfied in their work and who are not necessarily seeking a new job. An updated resumé will prepare you for unexpected opportunities.
2. It can be a valuable experience to observe one's own professional career on paper. This can help you chart the path of your future career.
3. Having a resumé can help protect you from the unexpected—losing your job in an economic turndown. A well-prepared resumé can take some of the anxiety out of a job search.

A resumé is your tool to market yourself and ultimately obtain an interview. It is the marketing piece you have to get yourself in the door. The functions of a resumé can be an extended calling card, an overview of your career, an interview agenda, and a communication tool for key stakeholders who may be influential in making decisions about candidates who will have professional relationships within their health service delivery system. Quick "knockout factors" (Beatty, 1995) of a resumé, perceived by those reviewing it, can include inappropriate or insufficient educational credentials; a poorly organized, sloppy, or hard-to-read resumé; too many pages; too many employers in too short a time; and objectives or accomplishments not compatible with current openings. The work experience sections are often screened with consideration to

- sufficient years and appropriateness of experience,
- sufficient breadth and depth of technical or leadership knowledge and skills,
- a solid record of achievement,
- absence of critical skills or experience, and

Adv Prac Nurs Q, 1996, 2(1): 75–77
© 1996 Aspen Publishers, Inc.

- comparison of qualifications with others being considered, as well as past candidates.

There is nothing magical about resumé writing. It is a logical, straightforward process for the purpose of showcasing your knowledge, skills, accomplishments, and other pertinent professional qualifications. The clarity, neatness, organizational style and format, combined with your enthusiasm and the ability to convince others that you can make them more successful and profitable are key to your effectiveness. Since there are limited resources specific to advanced practice nurses (APNs) who wish to write or revise their own resumés, Ruth Theken was interviewed about the purpose and use of resumés, as well as effective strategies for developing and updating them. Ruth Theken, RN, MHA, FAAHC, is President, Founder, and Chief Executive Officer (CEO) of Theken Associates, Inc., the only nursing administration executive search firm in the United States.

***Straka:* What is the purpose of a resumé for APNs?**

***Theken*:** It is a snapshot of their career, a facilitation tool to get you invited for an interview, and most of all it is presenting yourself in written form.

***Straka*: What style of resumé is most effective for APNs?**

***Theken*:** There are really four styles of resumés: narrative, functional, curriculum vitae, and historical. The historical is the type that is accepted in health care. It is a brief snapshot of current and previous roles highlighting accomplishments. The curriculum vitae is acceptable in the academic world.

***Straka*: What are the critical elements of an effective resumé and how should they be formatted?**

***Theken*:** In terms of general information, there are six critical elements:

1. The resumé should be no longer than three pages.
2. It must be easy to read in less than 2 minutes.
3. There must be something to catch the reader's attention.
4. Resumés must be written on good bond paper of a neutral color. (Often resumés are deleted just based upon their color.)
5. A printed resumé is essential; dot matrix is not acceptable.
6. Spacing, appropriate capitalization, and highlighting are critical.

Resumé format consists of six categories that must be written in the following order:

1. *Contact Information.* This information must be presented first and be centered on the page. It should include name, title, home address, and phone number. (Include work information only if you can be contacted there.)
2. *Education.* Include your most recent education and work backward. Indicate the university or college (underline) and include the degree obtained. Do not include high school degrees.
3. *Work Experience and Accomplishments.*
   - List current position first, working back chronologically.
   - Start with the date on the left-hand side.
   - Specify name of institution, city, and state (underline).
   - Job title (bold)—include a brief description of role, accountability, and who you reported to.
   - Accomplishments—be sure they are quantifiable or qualifiable. Remember to begin with impact words, such as

"created, developed, implemented, established." *Note:* List fewer accomplishments with each past position, and, if you have a long work history, do a synopsis of early positions.

4. *Professional Committees.* Under this section include leadership abilities as an officer or official. Also include representation on any boards. Academic affiliations should be included in this section. (Underline the college or university and use boldfacing for the title.)
5. *Publications.*
6. *Honors and Awards.* List only those honors and awards of a professional nature. *Note:* It is not necessary to state that references are provided upon request. This is assumed.

Straka: **What are your thoughts about updating and revising?**

Theken: Health care is changing so rapidly, it is better to develop a standard resumé and put specific objectives in your cover letter. You should update your resumé with every job/title change. It is most beneficial to keep your resumé on disc.

Straka: **What should APNs consider when writing cover letters?**

Theken: There are really four objectives for a well-written cover letter:

1. It allows the writer to direct particular attention to specific skills pertinent to position.
2. It provides the job seeker an opportunity to target the resumé to a particular person.
3. It opens the door for future communications.
4. It enables the applicant to state why the position is of interest to him or her.

Straka: **Are there any references that might provide guidance and examples to APNs who wish additional information about writing resumés?**

Theken: There are three that would be very helpful:

1. Balles, R. (1995). *What color is your parachute?* Berkeley, CA: Ten Speed Press.
2. Rosenberg, A., & Hizer, D. (1990). *The resume handbook* (2nd ed.). Holbrook, MA: Bob Adams, Inc.
3. Deep, S., & Sussman, L. (1990). *Smart moves.* Reading, MA: Addison-Wesley Publishing Co.

Straka: **Do you have any final words?**

Theken: Just remember, there is no second chance for a first impression.

• • •

"And what about you?" Do you have that perfect resumé that will prepare you for unex-

Check Any Characteristic that Applies to Your Resumé

___ Too long—more than three pages
___ Disorganized information—hard to follow—no format
___ Poorly typed and printed—dot matrix
___ Overwritten—long paragraphs and sentences
___ Too sparse—only bare essentials of dates and job titles
___ Not oriented for results—does not show accomplishments
___ Too many irrelevancies—sex, health, marital status, etc.
___ Misspelling, poor grammar
___ Tries too hard—fancy typesetting, colored paper
___ Misdirected—no connection to the position or organization's need (A cover letter avoids this.)

pected opportunities? Using the key information provided, get started and begin to develop a dynamic resumé or aggressively edit your current one. Remember, this is the key to you marketing you. As a final exercise to review your resumé, see the box for a checklist of the 10 most common resumé-writing mistakes (Jackson, 1990). If you have checked any of the characteristics in the box, review the information from Ruth Theken and the suggested references. This process should assist you in creating a resumé you will be proud of. A good resumé can be your winning ticket to a great career path. The purpose of this article is to provide you with a format and general information that will assist you in designing your single most important self-advertisement—your resumé. This is your opportunity to really make a statement about yourself. Don't miss it.

REFERENCES

Beatty, R. (1995). *The resume kit* (3rd ed.). New York, NY: John Wiley & Sons.

Jackson, T. (1990). *The perfect resume.* New York, NY: Doubleday.

Rosenberg, A., & Hizer, D. (1990). *The resume handbook* (2nd ed.). Holbrook, MA: Bob Adams, Inc.

Your Career and Job Success

Deborah A. Straka

Achieving success in your current job is the most important aspect of developing your career. So often we focus on resume writing, networking, and so on, but you are really developing your references for the future when you focus on current job success.

The health care practitioners who manage their jobs smarter will be those who thrive in this chaotic environment. The principles that will enable you to manage smarter are based on looking forward to and preparing for events, seeking opportunities, and creating strategies to enhance your marketability. Time management and working smarter are not about learning to shuffle paper better, they are about getting focused and spending your time on priorities that produce outcomes.

This article provides a model to assist you in developing your career. According to Neubauer (1995) the four key aspects to job success are as follows:

1. Be clear about *what* you are attempting to do.
2. Have a specific action plan about *how* to complete the work.
3. Identify *who* the key individuals (stakeholders) are to assist in achieving results.
4. Know how to measure and market the *outcomes.*

These key aspects will be discussed within the context of a model (see Figure 1) that includes the what, how, who, and outcomes measurement (behaviors, processes, stakeholders, evaluation).

WHAT

The what often seems like the very obvious aspect. After all, every role has a job description. Success for the what, however, is being very clear and very specific about what you seek to accomplish. It means identifying four or five key measurable goals that are related directly to your organization's goals. The purposes of identifying only four or five goals are to: (a) provide a mechanism to focus and produce versus trying to do it all and producing very little, and (b) establish a framework for setting priorities. Identifying key goals gives you a set direction and a framework for clarifying your role and negotiating priorities. It is important to note that if your goals do not coincide with your supervisor's goals then you may have your five goals plus his or her five. Key individuals in the organization should always know your key goals for the year.

HOW

Identifying what you want to focus on is often the difficult component. Unfortunately, many great plans are never com-

Adv Prac Nurs Q, 1998, 3(4): 77–78
© 1998 Aspen Publishers, Inc.

pleted. A few suggested steps for goal achievement include:

- Be very specific about what, who, when, and where.
- Identify responsible parties and implement a process to hold them accountable (even if it is you).
- Communicate your initiative to all individuals involved.
- Set target dates or milestones along the way. Use a chart to see successes and accomplishments visually along the way.

WHO

Identifying and managing the individuals who are key to the success of your initiatives are important responsibilities. The obvious key stakeholder is your boss. Discussing priorities regularly, as well as clarifying his or her priorities, provides assurance that you are on course together. The once-a-year evaluation no longer fits in this era of high complexity and rapid change. One strategy is to write a one-page report of goal achievement, concerns, and suggestions for future initiatives each month. Use this report as a basis of discussion with your boss and obtain feedback and suggestions. Other stakeholders are equally important. As a practitioner, relevant stakeholders can include nursing leaders, nursing staff, administrators, physicians, and colleagues. It is critical to identify what roles these stakeholders will play in relationship to your initiative and how they can support successful outcomes you want to accomplish.

Developing and actively managing relationships with stakeholders can often be the key to a successful initiative. The more individuals you have working with or for you the better chance you have of achieving your outcomes.

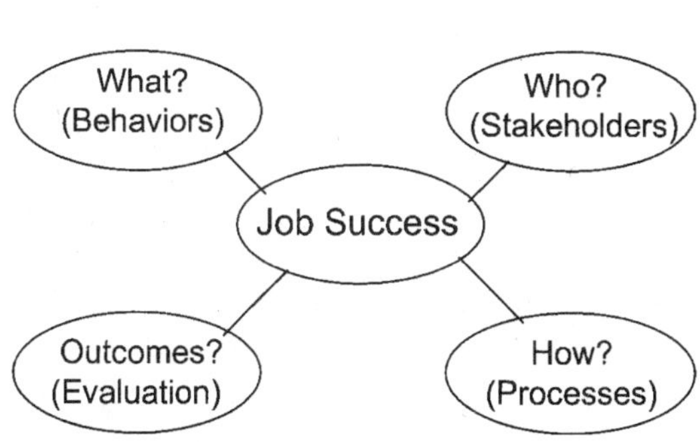

Figure 1. Job success map.

Table 1 Example Job Success

Component	*Examples*
What (behaviors)	Clinical changes, financial targets
How (processes)	Tools, teaching, facilitation, delegation
Who (stakeholders)	Executives, management, physicians, staff, other disciplines
Outcomes (evaluation)	Quality indicators, budget, satisfaction survey

OUTCOMES MEASUREMENT

How will you and others know when you have achieved your goals? From the very beginning, it is important that you identify specific measures that will determine goal achievement. Most often organizational goals are in three categories: patient (clinical) outcomes, customer satisfaction, and financial success. The most effective outcomes demonstrate quantifiable measures such as decreased length of stay, percentage increase of patient satisfaction, amount of decreased cost, and so forth. Developing quantifiable measures will assist you in two ways: (1) provide clear direction for what you want to accomplish, and (2) serve as a vehicle for communicating your success. You can revise your resume yearly noting these key achievements.

• • •

Now, you are ready to create your own job success map. Get a large sheet of paper (flip chart size) and design your success map using the model in Figure 1 and the examples provided in Table 1. Keep it where you can access it frequently and use it as a guide for how you spend your time. The best antidote to fear about job security is to be doing your job well and providing evidence of results.

REFERENCE

Neubauer, J. (1995). Thriving in chaos: Personal and career development. *Nursing Administration Quarterly, 19*(4), 71–82.

16

Nursing and Unions: Do They Mix?

Can You Create a Professional Practice Model in a Unionized Setting?

Paula Marchianno

Being the new vice president of Nursing in a long-standing unionized organization in today's rough and rugged health care environment has been a tremendous learning experience in both a management and leadership arena.

THE JOURNEY BEGINS

I accepted the position on the premise that my 25 years of clinical nursing and management background in non-union community teaching hospitals in Pennsylvania and New York had afforded me the skills to manage this new assignment. The bargaining unit environment was overwhelmingly foreign to me, particularly in terms of its impact on developing professional practice.

In my zeal to excel in my new role, I searched the literature for the wisdom and experience of those who had pioneered this endeavor. I attended conferences, seminars, and programs around the country to ascertain this new knowledge base. Surprisingly, my efforts yielded minimal information that would assist me in creating a professional practice environment in a unionized setting. Even my peers also employed in unionized nursing environments, were of limited assistance.

ENGAGING THE CULTURE

It was clear that the nursing management team and staff was grounded by core patient care values and a commitment to the provision of quality care. This was a plus and truly a head start for building a strong foundation of professional practice in nursing that currently did not exist. Very few of my colleagues were able to offer advice. The little advice they offered was most often to let the staff file a grievance and then deal with it. I quickly gained a new sense that other leaders in nursing felt this to be a nearly impossible task.

While the foundation of patient care was strong, I discovered that the goals and visions of the nursing department were not clearly defined or articulated to the managers or the staff. Furthermore, I found the environment reactive and transactional, rather than proactive and transformational. Activities and initiatives were fragmented and lacked a common thread, contributing to a sense of disorganization and lack of direction. My goal was to create a picture, along with the management team, of what nursing practice at Niagara Falls Memorial Medical Center would need to look like to meet the needs of the community of the future.

Aspen's Advisor for Nurse Executives, 1997, 13(1): 7–8
© 1997 Aspen Publishers, Inc.

Knowing that the health care environment is rapidly and constantly changing, it was necessary to create a model that was flexible and fluid. Our challenge was to design a model that defined where we were going and would serve as the roadmap for the journey; that defined the timeframes in which this would occur; and allowed for much needed rest stops along the way.

My initial assessment of the nursing organization suggested the need for me to demonstrate several essential competencies:

- recognizing and reading the culture;
- exercising flexibility to understand the environment; and
- maintaining a sense of firm leadership and direction in a non-punitive but educational fashion.

The primary thought I had to keep in mind was that the union environment was created for a reason: most likely a lack of trust in management; lack of communication, follow-up, and active listening; and the inability to work together as a team toward consensus and in a collaborative fashion. Our overall goal was the creation of a new environment in which staff felt non-compromised, satisfied, and motivated to learn new things and develop as professionals.

Although my initial interactions with the staff were positive, I could sense a deep-rooted mistrust with a pervasive "we vs. they" mentality. Obviously, I could say anything to the staff due to my position of authority; but what I needed most was to create a referent power base. There was a need to establish positive relationships with the staff that were not based on "lip service," but on demonstrated, consistent, and committed behaviors. I needed to convey the thought that "we were in this together" and to create a cohesive team.

In order to create a healthy environment, there was a need to clearly pursue caregiver and patient satisfaction, state-of-the-art financial management of the department, and a mechanism to ensure personal as well as professional growth and development. The key was to locate a model for professional practice that was pragmatic in this institution, setting, and culture.

FIRST STEPS

An assessment of where we were and where we wanted to go was the initial starting point. A two-day weekend retreat was held with the management team for the purpose of creating a vision and mission statement for the department along with defining our philosophy of nursing care. The staff members were not included in this endeavor at this point. Although we realized that their needs at that time were focused on operational issues, these issues would be addressed by their participation in a similar exercise at a later date.

In our initial research, we discovered The Transformational Model for Professional Practice in Health Care Organizations.[1] The model appeared to offer the conceptual framework and basic components for professional practice on which we could, and would, drive every initiative in the department in order to reach our vision:

- Transformational Leadership;
- Professional Growth;
- Care Delivery Systems; and
- Collaborative Practice.

STRATEGIC INITIATIVES AND OUTCOMES

Transformational Leadership

- Development of a mission/vision statement and strategic plan at both the departmental and unit-specific level.

- A decision-making committee structure composed of both councils and committees.
- Roles developed for administrative and clinical coordinators.

Professional Growth

- Created an on-site baccalaureate program provided by Niagara University.
- Certification required for each specialty for all managers, and strongly promoted and encouraged for all staff.
- An upgrade in hiring practices required a BSN as entry level for all newly hired professional registered nurses, with a MSN preferred for all middle management positions.
- With the new bargaining unit contract, the staff and management team developed a $500 perfect attendance bonus and redesigned the Nurse Preceptor Program and Clinical Ladder Advancement Program.
- The Department of Education/Staff Development created a "Lunch and Learn" program on a bi-monthly basis featuring a management and clinical topic for all hospital staff, with a self-supporting educational fund for staff.
- The nursing management team, in collaboration with the Foundation at the Medical Center and the hospital alumni, created a four-tiered nursing scholarship and loan program for nursing staff.
- Professional Nurse Week activities were enhanced to provide educational programs that featured a national speaker, an Excellence in Practice and Nurse of Distinction Program, and Shadow a Nurse/Walk in My Shoes day on all nursing units.

The Care Delivery Systems

- Primary Nursing, Case Management/ Critical Pathways implemented.
- A Patient Care Assistant Program was created to include upgraded clinical skills and commensurate pay levels.
- A state-of-the-art process for review/development of Policy, Procedure, Standards of Care, Nursing Protocols, Performance Standards, and related Nursing Competency Statements was implemented.
- Quality outcomes were identified, including patient and caregiver satisfaction.
- A solid financial management program was initiated, generating an automated template for budget development, a variable staffing plan, and a management report (featuring volume adjusted reports of required to actual staffing, hours/dollars per patient day, and parameters for productivity and performance).

Collaborative Practice

- Development of a departmental newsletter, *Nursing Center Connections,* featuring articles on professional practice, changes in the environment of health care, clinical topics, and programmatic changes.
- A Nurse/Physician Collaboration Committee was implemented to create a forum for physicians to learn about initiatives in the nursing department and promote dialogue regarding implementation of standards and regulatory agency requirements.
- A quarterly meeting of the union stewards was held with members of the nursing management team to assure proactive resolution of issues to avoid grievances well in advance. An automated event report program was created in tandem with the Information Systems Department to assure a priority focus related to high risk, high volume, high cost issues, along with the development of

action plans, and educational programs for patient falls, skin care, and medication errors.

A VISION FOR THE FUTURE

Creating a Professional Practice Model in a unionized environment is not insurmountable! However, it has not been well documented in the nursing literature. Over the past two-and-a-half years, a new foundation for the Department of Nursing has been created that will assist us as we alter the care delivery system, manage both human and material resources differently, and transition our professional practice into the community setting. Our future objectives and initiatives will continue to center around the education and development of the nursing staff, engagement of their participation and an enhancement of their accountability for practice, and expansion of the care delivery system across the continuum.

REFERENCE

1. Wolf, G., RN, DNS, FAAN, Aukerman, M., RN, PhD, and Boland, S., RN, MSN. 1995. *The Transformational Model For Professional Practice In Health Care Organizations.* The Beckwith Institute For Innovation In Nursing, Shadyside Hospital, Preservation Hall, 5230 Centre Avenue, Pittsburgh, PA 15232.

Addressing the State of the (Labor) Union

Steve Davis

"Anytime you restructure, you impact—or at least threaten—the employment security and income of your employees. That's one of the biggest problems in reengineering. Labor unions survive by the share of the market they possess. If your reengineering plan is going to cause a union to lose 100 members, they won't be very willing to participate." That's the word from Jack Dobier, labor management coordinator with Minneapolis-based Allina Health System. The health system currently employs 20,000 people at 17 locations throughout Minnesota. About a third of the employees are represented by one of six labor unions.

In recent years, progressive companies outside health care have tried to patch up the damage caused by years of adversarial relations. Mending this damage, however, can be a long and arduous process.

"Employers generally carry so many prejudices and stereotypes into relationships with the labor unions that they don't ever question what they're doing," Dobier explains. "They view the relationship as being detrimental from day one. And neither side ever tries to do anything to improve it."

Over the past 26 years, Dobier has worked on both sides of the fence. Prior to joining Allina, he spent 14 years as a representative for a labor union. He also has experience working with company management. This unique background has allowed Allina and their unions to develop an unusual, yet successful partnership.

Rather than being an employee of the company or of the union, Dobier has a dual allegiance. While his office is in a hospital, he is jointly supervised by six labor unions and management. His responsibility to each side is to advocate for the party not represented at a meeting. Today, only a handful of companies use this type of management-union liaison. Dobier speculates he is the only one currently working in a health care setting.

MENDING A BROKEN RELATIONSHIP

Like many industries in the early '80s, the relationship between hospital management and unions in the Twin Cities had traditionally been very adversarial. Unions typically proposed changes and hospital management opposed them, and vice versa. Over the years, tensions between the two sides grew increasingly fierce as conflict often went unresolved. A six-week nurses strike in 1984 worsened the management/union relationship even further. Hospital management used the strike to reexamine and eventually eliminate some positions.

Reengineering the Hospital, 1997, 3(11): 6–8
© 1997 Aspen Publishers, Inc.

MANAGED CARE—AN IMPETUS FOR CHANGE

"In the Twin Cities, we have a very competitive health care market. In recent years, we've had a number of hospital closures," Dobier explains. "Most of our business now is managed care—less than 10 percent comes from commercial payers—so we've had to adjust to survive. We knew we'd have to restructure to get cost out of the system. We also knew we couldn't successfully make these adaptations if we were fighting with our competitors in the market while we were fighting with our employees and their labor unions."

Management worked to develop a strategic partnership with their labor unions. With unions representing a third of Allina's hospital employees, such a partnership was essential. One strategy they came up with is referred to as "interest-based" or "mutual gains" bargaining—a process of identifying issues early on and brainstorming for solutions. This type of relationship, if successful, would result in a "labor peace," allowing the two sides to settle disputes without disruptive tactics such as strikes and lockouts. **Note:** Strikes—or just the planning of a strike—have a severe impact on the management/employee relationship. And the tense atmosphere created is disruptive to patient care. A work stoppage can cause bad feelings throughout the organization that take years to overcome. The loss of revenue resulting from a work stoppage has serious financial consequences throughout the entire system. It also can have a negative impact on a hospital's relationship with physicians and other providers.

GETTING EMPLOYEES INVOLVED

Several years ago, the health system was involved in a number of mergers. To cope with the changes, management periodically sought advice and feedback from various members of the business community. These businesses emphasized the importance of quality. While most hospitals have reams of data on quality, the majority of measurements are taken after care has been provided. Management at the health system realized little was being done to improve the quality of care.

"That started us on a journey," Dobier recalls. "We knew if we were going to be successful at getting ideas out of our employees, we'd have to create an environment where they wouldn't feel threatened."

Creating this type of an environment, however, meant management would have to do something they had never truly done before. Work with the unions. **Note:** The National Labor Relations Board has held that contract employee involvement committees could be in violation of the National Labor Relations Act if conducted *without* union sanction.

Early on in the process, union leaders were somewhat suspicious of management's plan to develop a partnership. Much of the mistrust, Dobier says, stemmed from past experiences unions have had with companies involved in quality improvement programs. Some programs ultimately undermined the unions.

"The early '90s in particular was a bad time for unions, so they were pretty cautious," Dobier recalls. "I heard of a plant in Tennessee where management convinced the union to get involved on the steering committee for a CQI program. To improve quality, they told the union they would video tape all the workers on their drill presses to identify improvements that could be made. Instead, the company took the tapes, closed the plant, and moved the operation to Mexico. The tapes were then used as training films for the Mexican workers."

The first matter of business was to convince the unions they would be considered as equal in the development of a CQI process. Management worked to build a reputation of being trustworthy, predictable, and consistent in dealing with union leaders and employees. The involvement of unions in the process of restructuring was essential as employee wages, hours, and conditions of employment all needed to be considered. **Important:** Using employees to undermine the position of union members with the union is considered an unfair labor practice by the NLRB.

DECISION-MAKING, COLLABORATION AND CONSENSUS

Building a strong relationship between union leaders and management is a long and difficult task. In some instances, leaders from the two sides had never met. Management had typically turned everything over to their human resource people or attorneys.

"We found union people often were never asked to sit in on meetings, or even asked for an idea. So the prospect of just sitting down and sharing information with management was a big deal," says Dobicr. "As the relationship moves forward, the union people want to get more involved and take on more extensive problems. If everyone holds onto their traditional power, working together is a very frustrating situation. We encourage the two sides to move to consensus. If it's a decision that has any impact on a member of a labor organization, then the union needs to be involved. While in some cases, we can't involve everyone in the decision-making process, we'll always seek input and feedback."

CASE IN POINT

During a 1993-94 redesign at one of Allina's hospitals, a joint labor/management committee was established to help steer the process. Together, the two sides worked to select a consultant to help in the redesign process.

"Originally, we projected we could get $10 million out of the system—within a year, we had achieved 98 percent of that goal," Dobier recalls.

The role of employees in achieving this goal was invaluable. In the early stages of the redesign, more than 3,000 ideas were submitted, and at least 400 employees served on task forces. From this came a restructured patient care delivery model. Also, the goal was achieved with no layoffs and with no negative impact on patient satisfaction levels.

"This was a highly conflictive process, but we were successful because we really honored the conflict. We posted potential problems on a board and addressed them as we went along," Dobier says. "In the past, when there was a conflict, you just stepped back and threw a grenade into the middle of it. Now both sides are involved in the problem-solving process."

Allina, Dobier says, is moving toward more of a strategic partnership. Ultimately, he expects union contracts will become simpler and more principal-based, allowing more flexibility and adaptability. He also expects to move away from the traditional 3-year contract to longer-term agreements.

10 Elements of a Strong Union/Management Relationship

1. **Recognition of legitimacy**—Both the union and management recognize the legitimate role each side has to play in the achievement of their separate goals and mutual concerns.
2. **Commitment**—A successful union/management cooperative process is one which requires an initial commitment from both parties. The significant factor correlating with success is top leadership support.
3. **Quality of initiation**—A successful union/management cooperative process depends upon the quality of initiation of the process. This must include joint, consensus-based design, ownership, control, and implementation.
4. **Vision**—Successful change depends on an accurate understanding of the status quo, the defining of a vision for the future, and the joint creation of realistic means to fulfill that vision.
5. **Human resources**—Union/management cooperation is based on the premise that the greatest assets of any organization are its employees.
6. **System integration**—Union/management cooperation should be seen as a long-term strategy designed to improve organizational effectiveness. This cooperation must be fully integrated with contract negotiations and administration. It also must include the organizational goals and values of the unions and the corporation.
7. **Role expansion**—Both parties must expand their traditional roles to include those of partner and collaborator. Neither party loses or relinquishes its existing roles.
8. **Mutual self-interest**—Both sides must recognize that cooperation is essential to the survival and growth of both groups. Union and management must be willing to adapt their values and norms to institutionalize the cooperation and participation.
9. **Power**—Cooperation involves the evolutionary aligning of the authority power of management with the influence power of unions.
10. **Relationships**—Cooperation impacts every relationship in the organization: supervisor/employee; union/management; union/union; and management/management. Standards for quality relationships are defined in terms of honesty, equality, good faith, trust, fairness, and respect.

17

Thriving in the New Environment

The Nurse as Senior Health Care Executive

Kathryn J. McDonagh

The global transformation of health care and advances in health and management sciences have certainly created new challenges for leaders in the field. Opportunities abound in this era of tumultuous change and emerging concepts of how health care should be delivered. Nurses with vision, strategic competencies, business acumen, and advanced leadership skills have a unique opportunity to play a pivotal role in the transformation of our health care system.

This has not always been the case. Although for many years nurses have represented the largest group of health care providers in the system; have played an integral role in patient care, advocacy, health education, and health policy development; and have had an important coordinating role in the complex maze of care delivery, their role has not been at a governing or decision-making level to make a significant impact on the design of the entire health care system. Much of this phenomenon is related to the role of women and the valuation of "women's work" in this culture. Nursing, like other predominantly female professions in this country, tends to make up the vast majority of the work force in the field but has a disproportionately smaller role in top executive and governance positions.

In the 1996 report on Nursing Leadership in the 21st Century published by Sigma Theta Tau International,[1] the point is made that many nonclinicians are making critical decisions about the health care system based primarily on the economic forces driving the changes. Innovative models of care delivery that meet both financial and health outcome expectations need to evolve with the input of many clinical disciplines along with the business experts. A delivery model designed to improve the health of community members is multifaceted and should not be driven by economic factors alone. "In this era of rapid, systemic change, however, those most involved and best positioned to influence the health of people, nurses, are frequently absent from the leadership and policy setting table."[1(p.14)] Some of the reasons for this include the public image of nursing which is rooted in perceptions of women and their work, male–female relationships, educational programs which have emphasized clinical management versus leadership, and an absence of a platform for preparing and positioning nurse leaders within other communities of leaders.[1]

HISTORICAL ROLE OF NURSE LEADERS

Stereotypical images of nurse leaders tend to center on the historical concept of the head nurse or director of nursing in a hospital. Although throughout the history of American

Nurs Admin Q, 1998, 22(2): 22–29
© 1998 Aspen Publishers, Inc.

nursing these nurse leaders had varying degrees of power and authority within hospitals, they were mostly perceived to have more informal authority, with administrators and physicians having the formal governing authority. With only this traditional hospital-based role as an avenue for career advancement, nurses had limited promotional opportunities in the past. If a nurse was seeking career expansion or a change in work outside of the intense, technological, clinical arena, usually teaching or research were the only alternatives. And even these options rarely went beyond the nursing sphere into other health care areas.

So, the executive advancement track was limited to the traditional director of nursing role which was usually filled by a mature nurse who was seen as controlling, autocratic, and entrenched in the bureaucratic organizational structure of hospitals. This person was typically not viewed as progressive or innovative. The mantra of management at that time was planning, organizing, controlling, and leading with an emphasis on controlling. For many nurses, an image comes to them of someone in their past who fit this stereotypical image. The traditional hierarchy of the hospital, rooted in its religious and military history, often led to territorial behaviors and the creation of fiefdoms and turfs. These spheres of influence still affect many hospitals today and are a direct cause of higher costs and barriers to teamwork and the development of multidisciplinary models of care delivery. The director of nursing was often seen as a powerful figure because of the central and integrating role that nursing played throughout the organization. Although this central, coordinating role led to a sense of pervasiveness of nursing in hospital structures, such as the fact that it comprised the largest portion of the work force and had the largest budget, nursing as a profession and the nursing leader often had little formal influence in the governance of the organization. The director of nursing was often the only female on the executive team and struggled for parity in role, recognition, influence, and rewards. These historical leaders were often only prepared academically in clinical nursing and lacked the financial and business skills necessary today for such a role. These nursing leaders were challenged by the marginality of their roles. Marginality is defined as when an individual lives in two worlds simultaneously, one of which by prevailing standards is regarded as superior.[2] Nursing leaders lived on the margins of several worlds. They were women in a male world. They were nurses in an administrative world. They were clinicians in a business world.

The challenges for these leaders were many, and unfortunately the stereotype of an ill-prepared nurse leader in health care administration has been hard to break despite the fact that the contemporary nurse executive most often has advanced academic degrees, strong business skills, and a very beneficial understanding of clinical processes, patient needs, and service and product development. The nurse executive has another advantage in that historically, the positive relationships with physicians that have been built around patient care issues, have resulted in trust and open dialogue about the complex health care issues that exist today. The ability to work collaboratively with physicians is obviously an advantage in an environment that requires both clinical and business development savvy. Martin D. Merry, MD, who writes and speaks extensively on the cultural differences between clinicians and executives, believes that true excellence in health care will require an understanding of the cultural differences between clinicians and business-oriented executives and their collaboration will be needed to create effective organizations that deliver the best of care to patients. A model of shared leadership is necessary so that leaders from both clinical and management science traditions can learn from one another to create better results than either group could achieve working alone.[3]

Margaret J. Wheatley describes this as a new awareness of the value of relationships for leaders. Leaders who value the complex network of people who contribute to organizations rather than viewing people as annoying inconveniences along the path of accomplishing tasks will be able to accomplish significant strides in the multidisciplinary world of health care.[4]

Nurse executives have often been leaders in the area of shared governance or shared leadership models as well as quality improvement programs which are vital competencies in contemporary business environments today. The bottom line is that purchasers of health care are looking for positive outcomes and satisfied customers. Evidence indicates that patient satisfaction is higher when nurses are involved collaboratively in the plan of care, and patient outcomes are improved when nurses and physicians have productive, communicative relationships. Physician satisfaction with an organization improves as well when their confidence level is high that their patients are getting excellent nursing care.[5]

So, it is important to understand the historical development of the role of nurse executives and as a leader, to be able to use the skills inherent in those roles that bring strength to the negotiation table in the current environment, such as knowledge and understanding of complex health care organizations, understanding of clinical processes, awareness of health care professional domains and issues, ability to collaborate with physicians in business and clinical issues, and sensitivity to the unique needs of patients and families. Although the negative aspects of historical stereotypes have resulted in lingering prejudices, so that it is a handicap to be a nurse in an executive role in health care, that is being eradicated as the delivery system dynamics have resulted in the need for executives with a vision for healthier communities, excellent relationships with physicians, systems perspectives, clinical process understanding, patient advocacy, and a knowledge of prevention and education as a foundation for health care delivery. These skills are competencies developed in the comprehensive and complex career paths of nurse executives.

It was once rare to see a woman or nurse in the boardroom of health care organizations, but now many opportunities exist for nurses to have an influence on how organizations are managed and the strategic direction that is taken. Opportunities have emerged as the multifaceted skills of nurse health care executives have been recognized in hospitals, ambulatory and home health agencies, consulting firms, and many other types of organizations.

The nurse must make a dramatic shift to succeed in a broader health care executive role. This mental shift involves a new paradigm that takes the important and relevant competencies learned in the nursing realm and adds other skills necessary to succeed in the emerging health care world. It means moving beyond nursing and yet bringing the valuable skills from that domain to a much larger vision that includes many other professional disciplines in the creation of models that will help improve the health of our communities. This role transition should be made with grace and aplomb and in such a way that one's nursing background is not denied, as can happen when one starts in an undervalued field or profession and progresses to one seen in higher esteem by others. An example of this phenomenon is seen when nurses move to broader executive or innovative roles and are often described as "former nurses." However, for example, when physicians or attorneys move to such roles they are not referred to as "former physicians" or "former attorneys." They are recognized for their dual areas of expertise and all the varied skill sets they bring to their role. This is because their backgrounds are valued more than nursing. The nurse is often viewed as abandoning the profession for a new one, whereas the physician or attorney are seen as bringing valuable experience and insight to a new role.

This effect can be minimized by speaking with pride about nursing as a profession and delineating to others the strengths this background brings to a new role. Fortunately, with the increasing numbers of women in professional and executive roles and the recognition of the contributions of many nurse executives in health care, this stereotypical phenomenon is changing. The values of nursing can be appropriately melded into a much broader role that envisions health care in a context quite apart from the traditional medical model. Many role models in the health care field have demonstrated this through their many professional accomplishments. Many health care executives with nursing backgrounds are successful chief executive officers, chief operating officers, and entrepreneurs of all types. In fact, a survey done by the American College of Healthcare Executives shows that many female health care executives have clinical backgrounds.[6] This may demonstrate that women are more often than men coming up through the ranks in health care and using their knowledge of clinical and operational processes to move ahead in their careers.

CURRENT OPPORTUNITIES FOR NURSE EXECUTIVES

The changing dynamics of the health care system have created many opportunities for nurse executives to advance into broader executive and entrepreneurial roles. First of all, health care is a larger business in this country than ever before. Health care now makes up close to 15 percent of the gross national product and, along with the continued aging of the population and shifting demographics, there are many opportunities opening up as long-term care, home care, ambulatory care, and managed care companies flourish in an effort to develop more community-based health care programs along a continuum of care. Health care reforms are being driven primarily by payers and employers unwilling to pay the rapidly rising costs of ineffective health care programs. Although the changes are cost-driven, the solutions arise from the shattering of the traditional paradigms of medical care which put emphasis on acute care and disease management rather than prevention, education, and health, versus disease-focused programs. Nursing provides an academic and experiential foundation conducive to development of community-based health programs. Efforts to provide equal opportunities for women and minorities in the field and a growing recognition by governing boards of the value of diversity in developing new visions and strategies have also opened avenues not available in the past. The glass ceilings that nurses and women have often experienced in health care appear to be disappearing.

Some of the characteristics of the current health care environment are creating demands on executives to operate in wholly new milieus. The competencies required in the past are quite different from those needed today for successful health care executives. That is one reason for such high turnover of executives in the last decade: as the volatility of the environment creates demands for new behaviors, not all health care executives can adapt to the changes. Yet when analyzing the changes in the health care environment, an executive with the depth and breadth of complexity and systems thinking that a clinical background requires, often does possess the talents and skills needed for the future.

CHARACTERISTICS OF HEALTH CARE TODAY

Some key characteristics of the health care system today include a movement towards managed care and increasing assumption of risk for the health of populations; more collaborative, multidisciplinary models of governance, system complexity, and interdependence; increasing impact of changing technology; the influence of human rights and an ethical orientation towards patient choices, rapidly changing environment, and the development of a comprehensive continuum of care. An analysis of these emerging health care system characteristics with a resulting executive skill requirement reveals that nurse executives have advantages from their competency portfolios as well as opportunities for skill development to ensure their success in the future.

Managed Care/Risk Assumption

As the pervasiveness of managed care increases in local markets, executives leading health care organizations will need strong business and financial skills combined with knowledge of product and service development in order to create systems that are appealing to payers, employers, and other purchasers of health care services. Assuming risk for the financial and health care outcomes of a defined population means a reversal in thinking and practice from the traditional medical model which focused on disease treatment in an acute care environment. Knowledge about developing a health and risk assessment profile of a population of members or "covered lives" will be necessary in order to understand what clinical programs need to be developed. Clinical processes will need to be refocused on education, prevention, disease management, personal health, and community health. All of this will require reengineering of clinical and business processes. This is an area in which many nurse executives have leadership experience from clinical delivery reengineering, staffing redesign, and other operational restructuring efforts.

Collaborative Models of Governance

The involvement of physicians, nurses, and other clinical knowledge workers is imperative if significant clinical process reengineering is to be successful. A leader who understands and practices principles of shared governance or shared leadership will be a step ahead of those who lack appreciation for the collaborative nature of clinical professionals. Nurse executives have been leaders in the business of management science, positively influencing many organizations with a strong foundation of shared decision making.

Systems Development

Nurse executives learn systems theory as a basis of clinical practice and then learn about larger applications of systems theory in the complex and interdependent world of health care. Any action, no matter how small, in one area of the organization can have a profound impact on the entire system. This theoretical framework plays out every day in a health care system, and experienced executives manage change and lead new program development with this in mind. The development of integrated delivery systems or networks that encompass various components of care delivery from primary care, specialty care, home care, and hospital care in a variety of settings are models requiring extensive systems theory knowledge and understanding.

Changing Technology

Advances in biotechnology, pharmaceuticals, genetics, and medical interventions have radically changed the delivery of health care globally in the last decade. Information technology is advancing rapidly and is a key integrating mechanism in the development of a health care network. An executive needs to understand the various impacts that new technologies have on systems, whether it be the shift to outpatient settings, the need for newly skilled staff, or an effort to balance the increasingly high technology approach with high-touch or compassionate, humanistic care.

Patient Choices/Consumerism

The rise of educated consumers has had a tremendous impact on the health care system. Today's patients and families expect full disclosure about their health status and want to participate with their providers in the plan of care. Nurse executives are familiar with the needs of patients to be informed, educated and active in their care since an orientation of advocacy has long been a part of the role of clinicians. This becomes particularly important as providers assume more risk for the health of their patients, since it is imperative to have patients fully participating in the process of health maintenance and prevention of disease in order to reduce expenses for treatment that could have been avoided.

Another important factor in meeting the needs of today's consumer is related to bringing caring and compassion back to the health care system. The business focus that has been emphasized of late often makes patients and their families feel lost in an impersonal system at a vulnerable time in their lives. Nurse executives, with their background in patient advocacy and compassionate care, can help bring the humanistic side back to a field that has become "big business" in this managed care environment.

Rapidly Changing Environment

Executives in a rapidly changing field such as health care need skills and experience that will enable them to handle a multitude of competing demands. Certainly nurse executives who have been responsible for operations in large, complex health care organizations have the necessary stamina, political savvy, and knowledge to manage change effectively in an uncertain environment. With the velocity of change occurring today, the executive's challenge is to anticipate the second curve, as described by Ian Morrison, which is a phenomenon that is fueled by massive forces of change over which one has no control: new technology, new consumers, and new markets. To succeed in this era of change, the visionary executive must learn to anticipate these changes and adapt the organization to them.[7]

Continuum of Care Development

In order to cost-effectively manage the health care needs of a defined population, it is necessary to provide the appropriate level of care in the appropriate setting. It is also important to purchasers of health care to have a full continuum of services for their patients depending on individual needs. So, the development of a continuum of care and integrating mechanisms that link each component of care, such as case management and information support, is an essential competency for a senior health care executive.

These characteristics of emerging integrated delivery systems make a case for executives to become transformational leaders with a plethora of skills and experiences to lead in such an environment. Other competencies required for today's health care leader include:

- Strategic planning/Vision
- Change management skills/Mastering change
- Negotiation skills
- Team building/Coalition development
- Continous quality improvement/Performance improvement skills
- Financial analyses
- Physician collaboration and partnership skills
- Systems thinking/Organizational dynamics/Reengineering
- Information technology
- Communications skills
- Operational savvy
- Policy formulation development

• • •

The expertise and background of a nurse executive are appropriate foundations for stepping into a broader senior health care executive role. The combination of clinical understanding and business savvy along with the diverse experiential base of a clinical executive make the transition a natural one. As with any role transformation, there are new notions and concepts to master as well as new competencies to learn. Nurse executives with demonstrated leadership abilities and the willingness to assume new challenges will contribute a great deal in a time of transformation that requires courageous and competent leaders.

REFERENCES

1. *Nursing Leadership in the 21st Century*, A Report of ARISTA II: Healthy People: Leaders in Partnership (Indianapolis, IN: Center Nursing Press, Sigma Theta Tau International, 1996), 14.
2. D.L. Biordi, "Nursing Service Administrators: Marginality and the Public Person," *Nursing Clinics of North America* 21 (1986): 173–183.
3. M.D. Merry, "Shared Leadership in Healthcare Organizations," *Topics in Healthcare Financing* 20 (1994): 26–38.
4. M.J. Wheatley, "Leadership and the New Science: Learning about Organization from an Orderly Universe" (San Francisco, Berrett-Koehler, 1994), 144–145.
5. K.J. McDonagh, "Saint Joseph's Hospital of Atlanta: A Decade of Success" and "Nursing Leadership in Transition: Key to a Strong Shared Governance Program" in *Nursing Shared Governance: Restructuring for the Future*, ed K.J. McDonagh. (Atlanta, GA: K.J. McDonagh and Associates, 1990), 59, 132.
6. *A Comparison of the Career Attainments of Men and Women Healthcare Executives, Executive Summary* (Chicago: American College of Healthcare Executives, 1996).
7. I. Morrison, *The Second Curve: Managing the Velocity of Change*, (New York: Ballantine Books, 1996).

Congruency between Nurses' Values and Job Requirements: A Call for Integrity

JoEllen Goertz Koerner

A discipline is distinguished by a shared belief among its members regarding its reason for being. A professional discipline is further defined by its social relevance and value orientation.[1] The value orientation within a profession specifies its domain of practice.

It is the values of each nurse that guide his or her decision making and resultant action in each clinical encounter. The type and extent of care rendered by the nurse are directly related to the value orientation of that professional. Thus, unifying core values give a normative framework for decision making across the profession, and individual values create the unique practice pattern of each nurse.

ESTABLISHING A VALUES ORIENTATION

Values stand between the inner and outer dimensions of an individual's life. Self-directed, they are the priorities by which we live, through which we select our information, and shape our consciousness. Values are an integral part of human existence; they relate to every aspect of our life. Lee[2] characterized values as the basis upon which individuals make choices about how to live their lives. Thus they are to human behavior what instinct is to animal behavior: They select and initiate the priorities actually acted upon.

Socialization is a process used to gain the knowledge, skills, and behaviors of a certain group to belong and participate. The powerful authority figures and cultural norms that surround us in childhood create the basic framework for our personal value system. Professional socialization is primarily an unconscious process through which an occupational identity is gained as values and norms of the profession are internalized.[3] A multitude of factors affect the socialization outcome of nurses, including their educational institution, faculty, classmates, family, friends, professional colleagues, other health care professionals, patients, and the general public.[4]

Cultural and group norms also have a profound impact on the values that are visibly expressed by nursing staff on various units within an organization. Peterson[5] discovered that nurses with a narrow view of health and healing limit their function to physical care, technical procedures, and the giving of medication, whereas nurses with a broader view provide more holistic care tailored to the unique needs of the individual. Her findings further suggest that nurses are sensitive to work group norms, modifying their practice to meet the expectations and unwritten rules of the unit. This study demonstrated that social orientation and cultural professional norms influence group behavior as surely as

Holist Nurs Pract, 1996, 10(2): 69–77
© 1996 Aspen Publishers, Inc.

family of origin, culture, and life style influence individual values and behavior.

DIFFERENTIATION OF NURSING VALUES

Numerous values studies have been done in the past 20 years on the collective body of nursing, treating it as a singular entity. A descriptive analysis of the values of nurses working in three distinct nursing career roles within one hospital-based nursing practice was carried out to explore a more defining question: Is there a set of common core values that appear across all role categories in the nursing profession as well as some values that are unique to each role category? A second, related question examined the congruence between the values of the nurses in the various roles and the values inherent in the job descriptions that they filled.[6]

Sioux Valley Hospital (SVH) created a care delivery model based on differentiated nursing practice: 67% of the registered nurse positions represent the associate role based on associate degree competencies; 30% are ascribed to the primary role based on bachelor level competencies; and 3%, filled by master's-prepared nurses, represent the advanced practice role. Twenty nurses working in each job category for a minimum of 3 years participated in the study. Benner[7] observed that it takes approximately 3 years to reach expert status. Each group of 20 also comprised well-performing nurses as identified by management and peers through the peer review process utilized at SVH. The investigator wanted to study optimal nursing performance.

ASSESSING VALUES CONGRUENCE WITHIN A NURSING PRACTICE

The Hall-Tonna Inventory of Values,[8] a paper-and-pencil test consisting of 77 forced choice items relating to a list of 125 values, was given to study participants. The 125 values were generated from multiple studies on 9000 individuals in 48 nations of the world by the International Values Institute. The 125 values were further grouped into 55 values-related categories. From the staff nurse responses, a computer-generated report gave information regarding the aggregate ranked values of each group as well as each individual within the group.

A second part of the study focused on document analysis of the job descriptions that guide the work of each nursing group. One can note in corporate America the growing awareness of the centrality of values and mission to the success of the business enterprise. These values and beliefs are reflected in the documents that describe the organization: corporate philosophy, mission, and goal statements; the policies and procedures that govern activities; and job requirements of those who make up the workforce. Comparison between the analysis of the job description values and the values of well-performing nurses in each role revealed the level of congruence between them.

When the groups value clusters (eg, safety/survival with security) were matched with job description values, only 2 of the top 10 values in the associate group analysis were absent: rights/respect and adaptability (Table 1). Significantly, the associate group was the only one in the study with fewer than half the subjects (30%) selecting adaptability and flexibility. It was the only group that selected obedience as a value. This may pose a major barrier for these nurses in accepting and adjusting to the radical changes occurring in the health care industry. Furthermore, it may explain the difficulty demonstrated by some bedside nurses in adapting to some of the challenges and changes occurring in this era of health care reform. It also may be the ab-

Table 1. Values congruence: Associate group

Job description	*Specific to associate role*	*Found in all roles*
Care/nurture	Care/nurture	
Rights/respect		
Accountability/ethics	Rule/accountability	
Safety/survival	Security	
Responsibility	Responsibility	
Competence		Competence/confidence
Productivity		Productivity
Adaptability		
Education/certification		Knowledge/discovery/insight
Law/rule	Worship/faith/creed	

sence of this value that facilitates the feelings of insecurity and threat identified by this group in another part of the study.[6]

When the primary role group value clusters were matched with job description values, two values remained unclaimed by those nurses: responsibility and adaptability (Table 2). Although 50% of the respondents selected adaptability, this did not reach statistical significance. Closer examination revealed that this group, along with the associate group, did not score highly on initiation/decision. These findings may describe a position of responding to the initiatives of others rather than creating them. This may reflect our history of a profession socialized to react to situations from policy and procedure rather than from initiative and creativity.

When job descriptions and value clusters of the advanced practice group were matched, there was perfect congruence (Table 3). The majority of these values reflected initiative, decision making, accountability, and internal locus of control behaviors. This pattern of performance is consistent with the expectation of advanced practice nursing roles.

A careful analysis of the job description values showed that they were quite consistent with those identified as important by the

Table 2. Values congruence: Primary group

Job description	*Specific to primary role*	*Found in all roles*
Rights/respect	Rights/respect	
Accountability/ethics	Authority/honesty	
Cooperation	Collaboration	
Research/originality	Pioneering/innovation	
Safety/survival	Self-preservation	
Competence/confidence		Competence/confidence
Education/certification		Knowledge/discovery/insight
Responsibility		
Adaptability/flexibility		
Sharing/listening/trust		Sharing/listening/trust

Table 3. Values congruence: Advanced practice group

Job description	*Specific to advanced practice*	*Found in all roles*
Knowledge/discovery/insight		Knowledge/discovery/insight
Cooperation	Community	
Corporation/new order	Corporation/new order	
Research/originality	Growth/expansion	
Accountability/ethics	Decision/initiation	
Competence/confidence		Competence/confidence
Integration/wholeness	Integration/wholeness	
Sharing/listening/trust		Sharing/listening/trust
Education/certification		Education/certification
Adaptability	Adaptability/flexibility	

nurses within those roles. This may account for the well-performing identity of these practitioners as well as the 4% turnover rate within the Department of Patient Services at SVH. Furthermore, the values of the job categories were consistent with those identified by document analysis of department and corporate expectations (Table 4).

VALUES ANALYSIS

We are called upon to look at the world in a more integrated and holistic fashion. Far too often, methods of teaching, styles of leadership, and methods of healing have been too narrowly confined to one set of skills or one set of values to the neglect of others. An examination of value patterns can reveal the degree of individual and group maturation while suggesting an approach for future growth in individuals, professions, and institutions. Thus a twofold process of values analysis and skill attainment will assist the health care industry and the nursing professional to create integrity between nurse value systems and job role requirements in a more holistic manner.

Values analysis provides a strong foundation for personal and organizational maturation.[9] Critical to the process of organizational development (academic or health care institutions) is the collection of reliable data regarding the values expressed by the institution in its documents and the collective behavior it rewards. Comparisons and discrepancies can be analyzed using a consistent methodology.[10] Document analysis includes the collection of such information from philosophy, mission, goal, and objective statements; information contained in policies and procedures from a point of view of behavioral expectations and sanctions; and attitudes and opinions gathered from students, patients,

Table 4. Corporate/environmental values

Department of patient services	*Corporate values*
Flexibility/ adaptability	Caring
Autonomous/ self-directed	Knowledge
Competence	Enjoyable
Teamwork	Collaborative
Organized/productive	Fast-paced/changing
Assertive	Flexible/diverse
Technical competence	Supportive/giving
Self-confident	Professional/ progressive
Caring	Confident
Critical thinking	Risk-taking/accepting

employees, and administrators. Such analysis will disclose the values that create and support the culture and performance of those affiliated with the institution.

Personal values inventories, such as the one used in this study, are also a rich source of information for the individual and the organization. The institution gets a clearer message as to the expectations and talents of its employees, and employees become more aware of the values and beliefs that motivate and influence their behavior and choices. This enhanced awareness is enriching for both parties.

Group value inventories can provide a profile of an entire collection of individuals, identifying their strengths and challenges. The combined group values can be used in human resource training programs or may mandate revision of philosophy statements or corporate direction. Furthermore, the data can uncover dysfunctional group behavior, which would provide an agenda for further growth and development. This systematic analysis can enhance systemwide strategic planning and development.

SKILL ACQUISITION TO FACILITATE VALUE DEVELOPMENT

Frequently a job requires values that are not fully developed in the practitioner who assumes the position. Associate nurses in this study were placed in positions requiring flexibility and adaptability, whereas the group self-reported a value of obedience. Values are related to skills; it is through skill acquisition that we advance to more complex value sets leading to higher levels of awareness, which enlarges our choices and flexibility. Although obedience is nested in skills of listening and doing the task outlined, adaptability requires skills in imagination to envision alternative ways to achieve the same outcome coupled with initiative to act on these self-determined actions.

As individuals move to more complex career opportunities, new skills are required. Hall and colleagues[10] identified four basic skill sets essential to fostering more complex value sets: instrumental skills, interpersonal skills, imaginal skills, and system skills. They noted that some level of imaginal skills is required in the development of all other skills because it is impossible to change or develop without some image of the desired future state.

Instrumental skills are task oriented. They encompass all the technical tasks necessary to get the job done. These skills contain a blend of intellectual and physical competencies that enable one to shape both ideas and the external environment. Instrumental skills in nursing include things such as manual dexterity in handling equipment and technology; reading, writing, and handling numbers; researching a topic and summarizing the findings clearly; critical thinking; and managing one's time.

Interpersonal skills have long been the hallmark of nursing care. They equip an individual to enter into deeply satisfying human relationships that widen their social circle. They require one to perceive self and others accurately and to communicate with the intent of understanding and being understood. Interpersonal competence facilitates mutual trust, understanding, cooperation, and intimacy. These skills are increasingly important as we move from an era of autonomy to one of interdependence.

There is a correlation between a person's expansion of awareness and the deepening and widening of his or her social relationships. Thus an essential value for the development of trusting and healthy relationships is empathy, "the capacity for one person to enter imaginatively into the sphere of consciousness of another, to feel the specific contours of another's experience, to allow one's imagination to risk entering the inner experiencing process of another."[10(p44)] Persons who develop this skill will develop and sustain many relationships; without it, authenticity is impossible. The development of this skill is essential to moving into broader stages of values development.

It is only after one has mastered the capacity for self-awareness that imaginal skills become more pronounced because one can now trust the intuitive promptings of which one becomes increasingly aware. Imaginal skills are a blend of internal fantasy and feeling that enables us to combine images in new ways and project them into the external world effectively in creative and relevant response to the issue at hand. It is our imaginal skills that enable us to see alternatives, to change conventional ways of doing things in a flexible and life-giving manner, to remedy deficiencies, to grasp and make sense of increasing amounts of data, and to choose and act on complex alternatives. In truth, a fertile imagination is an indispensable element in human development across the life span.

Imagination creates a synergistic interaction among one's active fantasy, emotions, and capacity for reflective intellect. The product of this thought process is something new, a product that is greater than the sum of its parts. Our emotions are critical to interpretation of the information we picked up in the environment, perceiving it as helpful or harmful, almost never neutral. Thus there is an interaction between fantasy and emotion. An imaginative mind examines and simplifies data from the lived experience by looking past the many parts to their core source. It explores the consequences of several alternatives and then creates a novel response. Our reflective intellect examines the resultant experience and attaches meaning to it. It is the meaning we ascribe to the experience that is coded into our value system.

The way in which we exercise our imaginal skills either hinders or promotes our continued development. How we use our imagination determines largely where we are developmentally. Our imagination is the primary factor in determining whether we are responders or creators in our interaction with the environment. Passive individuals are reactive, allowing others to take the initiative and shaping their activity to fit the demands of others. For imagination to be functioning, however, basic needs such as security, approval, and sense of adequacy must be minimally satisfied. It is at this point that a person can begin to explore alternative choices in his or her life style.

Most complex is the development of system skills. These enable one to see the parts in relation to the whole. They comprise a particular blend of competence, sensitivity, and imagination that gives rise to seeing the whole in a single part. This increases one's ability to plan and design change in a system, be it organizational, familial, or self. System skills depend on the development and integration of the other three skill sets, making them the last to be fully developed.

VALUES-BASED LEARNING

If we are going to facilitate nurses' career progression across the life span, we must offer continuing education that moves beyond the technical competencies so prevalent in staff development programs today. Holistic development in interpersonal, imaginal, and systems domains must also be addressed if individual value frames are to be enhanced to prepare nurses for increasingly complex work and working environments.

Hall and colleagues[10] suggest that leaders identify an appropriate pattern of values and create learning opportunities around them. Each value has basic skills within it. The following is an example:

> *Empathy*: reflecting and experiencing another's feelings and state of being through a quality of presence that enables them to see themselves with more clarity, without any words necessarily having been spoken.
>
> *Necessary Skills*: Empathy requires both imaginal and interpersonal skills, such as imagining how others see the world and being able to objectively report that to them, entering into their feelings, being able to express that to them objectively, being present to another so attentively that they are enabled to clarify their feelings.[10(p39)]

Mezirow[11] identified various learning techniques that could be used by faculty to facilitate adult transformation. Instrumental learning is all too familiar to most practicing nurses. Objectives are listed that are then transmitted through classroom lecture and measured in tests. This teaching–learning style is appropriate only for the physical sciences, such as mathematics, chemistry, and physics.

Communicative learning focuses on the dynamics of learning to understand self and others. We learn to understand what others mean while making ourselves understood as we attempt to share ideas through speech, the written word, plays, moving pictures, and the arts. Most significant learning in adulthood falls into this category because it involves understanding, describing, and explaining intentions, values, ideals, feelings, and reasons. All these things are profoundly shaped by cultural, professional, and social norms. The learner actively and purposefully negotiates his or her way through a series of encounters using language and gesture while anticipating the actions of others. The focus is to increase insight and attain common ground with others in the group. Teaching strategies include group work, dialogue, journaling, and storytelling. Evaluation is based on the demonstration of increasing depth and breadth of expression and understanding.

A final learning strategy essential for imaginal learning is play. Here the goal is to defer judgment, avoiding habitual response. The individual becomes comfortable with ambiguity, playing with a problem by looking at it from a fresh angle and redefining it in new ways. Through play one increases one's fluency in making fresh associations, perceiving connections or similarities between disparate realms of experience. Skills emerge that foster new ways to generate alternative solutions to problems, to see consequences of alternative courses of action, and to call upon a variety of alternatives in the heat of tension or conflict while facilitating others in the generation of new ideas.

Mezirow[11] distinguishes four characteristics of divergent thinking:

- *flexibility*—the ability to see with a fresh pair of eyes, to shift from one perspective to another, quite literally to move to a different standpoint
- *fluency*—an abundant flow of words, images, and ideas
- *originality*—the capacity to produce fresh responses arising out of each person's unique perspective, personal history, and reactions
- *elaboration*—the ability to develop an idea or image, to make connections, and to fill in details

Before we can begin to develop these various aspects of our being, we need to break through the barriers imposed by our internal censors and the rules of the external environment. It takes courage to be creative and authentic.

LIVING A LIFE WITH INTEGRITY

DeAngelis observed "it takes a lot of courage to release the familiar and seemingly secure, to embrace the new. But there is no real security in what is no longer meaningful. There is more security in the adventurous and exciting, for in *movement* there is life, and in *change* there is power."[12] Each time we give up a dream, idea, desire, or habit because it would not be approved of, was not expected, or just has not been done that way, we give away a piece of ourselves. When we compromise our dreams and our values for someone else's, we give away our power. The more we sacrifice our authenticity, the more disempowered and disabled we become.

Living outside our value system is exhausting; it takes much energy because our inner selves are not congruent with one another. We need to find the courage to say no to things that are not serving us well; this is the first step to personal and professional integration. The secret, however, is learning to say no without having to make what we are leaving behind wrong or make ourselves wrong for not having left sooner. Many times the leaving is a function of the right time, reflecting that we have outgrown our previous way of being.

How do we live courageous lives? By rediscovering and redefining who we are as we move through the changes that engulf us. We must redefine our values, desires, abilities, and voice, and we must live it every day. It means saying goodbye to the person others want you to be and living with integrity. It calls for educators and administrators to create environments and growth opportunities that foster the current and evolving values of all within the organization. It calls for learners (we all are learners after all) to take risks and to make a commitment to play while remembering the joy and wonder of simply being human. It calls for us all to embrace the human community with caring and commitment as we continue to facilitate our own and others' healing. In this spirit we will heal the world.

REFERENCES

1. Newman M, Sime A, Corcoran-Perry S. The focus of the discipline of nursing. *Adv Nurs Sci*. 1991;14:1–6.
2. Lee D. *Valuing the Self.* Englewood Cliffs, NJ: Prentice-Hall; 1976.
3. Pardue, SF. Decision-making skills and critical thinking ability among associate degree, diploma, baccalaureate, and master's-prepared nurses. *J Nurs Educ*. 1987;26:354–361.
4. Blatchley ME, Stephan E. RN students in generic programs: What to do with them? *J Nurs Educ*. 1984;23:351–352.
5. Peterson M. The norms and values held by three groups of nurses concerning psychosocial nursing practice. *Int J Nurs Stud*. 1988;25:85–103.
6. Koerner J. *Values: A Foundational Factor in Role Selection, Corporate and Curriculum Design for Professional Nurses*. Santa Barbara, Calif: Fielding Institute; 1992. Thesis.
7. Benner P. *From Novice to Expert*. Reading, Mass: Addison-Wesley; 1984.
8. Hall, BP. *The Genesis Effect: Personal and Organizational Transformation*. New York, NY: Paulist Press; 1986.
9. McCoy, CS. *Management of Values: The Ethical Difference in Corporate Policy and Performance*. Boston, Mass: Pitman; 1985.
10. Hall, BT, Yaylor B, Kalven J, Rosen LS. *Developing Human Values*. Fondulac, Wis: International Values Institute at Marian College; 1990.
11. Mezirow J. *Transformative Dimensions of Adult Learning*. San Francisco, Calif: Jossey-Bass; 1991.
12. DeAngelis, B. *Real Moments*. New York, NY: Delacorte; 1994.

18

Managed Care Business Skills

1995 Fast Track: Cost Reduction and Improvement

Robert J. Panzer, Deborah N. Tuttle, and Rosemarie M. Kolker

To respond to a cost reduction crisis, Strong Memorial Hospital implemented an aggressively managed program of accelerated improvement teams. "Fast-track" teams combined the application of many management tools (total quality management, breakthrough thinking, reengineering, etc.) into one problem-solving process. Teams and managers were charged to work on specific cost reduction strategies. Teams were given additional instruction on interpersonal skills such as communication, teamwork, and leadership. Paradoxically, quality improvement in our hospital was advanced more through this effort at cost reduction than had previously been done in the name of quality itself.

THE COST REDUCTION CHALLENGE

In February 1995, the leadership of Strong Memorial Hospital (SMH) faced an unprecedented financial challenge due to new state and federal reductions in reimbursement. It had already planned a three-year, $26-million cost reduction effort, of which $8 million was planned for 1995. Of that $8 million, $6 million had already been achieved, largely in concert with the budgeting process that preceded the start of the year. An early step in the three-year program was a $2-million management downsize, intentionally done first to demonstrate that the cost reduction effort was serious and to allow remaining managers to participate in cost reduction without the worry of immediate effects on their own jobs.

With the hospital's budget of over $300 million at the time, the additional $15 million cost reduction represented only 5 percent of the budget. However, the hospital was already in the middle of the three-year effort, had implemented across-the-board reductions of several percent twice in the previous seven years, and already was one of the leaner teaching hospitals in benchmarking studies.

The hospital's management team, led by our CEO Leo Brideau, held a special retreat with cost reduction as the focus. We came to a number of conclusions that guided the efforts to follow. A key decision was to recommit to a set of principles outlined prior to beginning the three-year Cost Reduction Program. Key principles included the following:

- Across the board cuts are a last resort.
- We will work to minimize layoffs.
- If layoffs do occur, we will treat individuals with consideration.
- All areas of the hospital will participate in the cost reduction effort.
- Clinical leadership will be active in both guiding and supporting cost reduction.
- We will consider the effects of any changes on quality carefully.

Quality Management in Health Care, 1997, 6(1): 75–83
© 1997 Aspen Publishers, Inc.

- We will maintain one high standard of care for all patients regardless of payer.

These principles guided our cost reduction efforts and led to specific actions described in the following sections. We set as our goal "to achieve a $15-million annual cost reduction in a way that positions us well to meet future challenges." We realized that cost reduction would likely become a way of life and that a Cost Reduction Program that reduced the quality of patient care or demoralized staff would hurt us in the long run.

THE EMERGENCY BUDGET RECONCILIATION PROGRAM

The overall effort would be called the Emergency Budget Reconciliation Program (EBRP), both to indicate the urgency of the problem and to clearly dissociate these urgent actions in response to a sudden change in external reimbursement from our planned three-year Cost Reduction Program.

Within a month we made a key decision that meaningful personal leadership from the senior management team of the hospital would be needed. As a result, we created an EBRP team composed of several members from the senior management team of the hospital with the anticipation that substantial time would be needed from each member of the team. The concept of this team came in part from the experience of Methodist Hospital in Indianapolis during its cost reduction efforts in 1994, prompted by a similar state-level Medicaid budget reduction.

The "War Room"

During March 1995, the EBRP team began its work. While its primary role was to oversee specific cost reduction activities, it also was responsible for refining the cost reduction plan, monitoring its success, and ensuring communication about cost reduction throughout the hospital.

After beginning our work with meetings lasting a few hours per day, the team arranged a one-day consultation from the human resources director at Methodist Hospital in Indianapolis. He shared the Methodist Hospital's experience in managing a similar cost reduction effort and convinced us that a more substantial block of management time would be needed. We decided to go nearly full-time in late-March, allocating six hours (9 AM–3 PM) each day for EBRP, most days delivering fully on that time commitment.

To reinforce the importance of the EBRP effort, we likened the commitment to our staffs to that of a "war room," where we needed time for all of us to work together every day to deploy and support teams, regardless of competing meetings and prior commitments. The one major exception was the hospital's senior management weekly meeting, which provided a forum for the EBRP team to provide updates on cost reduction and to catch up on other management activities. "War room" stayed on our calendars for the more than three months while EBRP meetings occurred six hours per day. Some felt that it was an inappropriate term for a health care organization's management, but others felt that it accurately described the intensity and aggressive nature of our work.

Our EBRP team was co-led by two of the four senior directors of the hospital: the chief financial officer (Michael Goonan) and director of patient care programs (Jack Olivier). The team also included the hospital's leader for Human Resources (Cynthia Beckwith, associate director within the University of Rochester HR function), an additional participant from Finance (Len Shute, director of financial operations), a nursing chief (Kathleen Parrinello, RN, now director of hospital operations), and a physician/QI leader (Robert Panzer, MD). The team received support from an administrative resident, as well as the support staffs of the team members.

Each of the EBRP team members currently has an expanded or new role in the institution, several at the medical center level. While such new transitions were not solely based on work in the Fast Track and EBRP processes, the achievement of the hospital's cost reduction goals demonstrated that we could change and adapt to our changing health care environment—success factors for both individuals and institutions.

MANAGING THE FAST TRACK

Ideas and Initiatives

To take us beyond the ideas we developed through our senior management team retreat and to involve others in the process, in mid-March 1995 we planned and coordinated a retreat for more than 30 leaders from across the hospital, including senior and middle management from clinical departments, support areas, and central administration. The ground rules for the retreat included a focus on cost reduction but asked that participants identify important ideas for quality improvement as well. At the retreat, brainstorming yielded several hundred individual ideas, with affinity diagrams of the ideas showing remarkable similarities across the three breakout groups.

At EBRP, we added the ideas from the brainstorming retreat to those already generated from previous planning activities and our own thinking as the cost reduction effort developed. We also established a hot line to allow staff to send in ideas via phone or e-mail, with a commitment to serious consideration and a personal response by an EBRP team member or hospital manager to each suggestion, indicating its status and to whom or what team it was referred.

By early-April 1995, we had identified a large number of candidate cost reduction projects. We tracked and developed these in several categories:

- personnel freeze
- wage and salary freeze
- management initiatives
- program consolidation and elimination
- Fast Track teams—We identified projects that were the right size and right focus for a team-based effort. Usually we were looking for interdepartmental, interdisciplinary issues and areas where redesign of work or a key process could achieve major savings. Ideas that fell in the category of "just do it" were handed off to managers directly.

Chartering

We identified more than 30 potential teams. We turned each of the project ideas into a specific team aim that included both the content of the team's work and its degree of empowerment, with most teams being asked to proceed to implementation. We gave most teams a specific cost reduction target, based on the likely opportunity and the method for cost reduction. Some teams had no cost reduction target of their own but supported cost reduction by reducing unnecessary work and freeing time of staff on patient care units to take on newly decentralized tasks. We expected that teams applying redesign methods could target a 15-percent reduction in cost. While we asked teams to focus primarily on cost reduction, we indicated that they could extend their work to quality improvement (and ideally readiness for our Integrated Delivery System) if they were sure that they could reach their cost reduction target.

Once we had a candidate "portfolio" of teams, we shared the list of teams and their aims with senior hospital management and clinical leaders. We also worked to identify the right members for the teams, aiming for five to six members to optimize team functioning. Recognizing that all the possible stakeholders could not be represented on a team, we encouraged teams to include focus groups or meetings with stakeholders early in their work.

We identified six teams that could do their work full-time and prepared an off-site area for them to work all day for two weeks. Most of these teams were involved in significant work or process redesign, lending themselves to full-time work away from the hospital. We also identified 22 teams that could work part-time on new cost reduction ideas and an additional three teams that were preexisting but whose work could be accelerated to provide increased or earlier cost savings.

We applied the full-time and part-time designations to describe the initial work of the teams, anticipating that later they would all simply be called "Fast Track teams." We did pay special attention to the six full-time teams, as they had more substantial targets (averaging $500,000 each) and redesign work to accomplish.

In mid-April 1995, we sent individual letters from our General Director/CEO to each of the identified team leaders and members requesting their participation and inviting them to training. We invited all team leaders to the two-day training. We scheduled a shorter (less than two-hour) orientation session for team members. Full-time team members attended a half-day session with their leaders so that they were prepared to go off-site and apply redesign approaches.

Although we provided copies of the requests to team leaders' and members' supervisors or department heads, we did not ask for their prior approval. We knew that the best participants in the cost reduction process already would be heavily committed to important activities but could find the time for cost reduction teams through reprioritizing their work. We did not have a large number of extra ideas or potential team members in waiting; thus, we did not want to ask permission in advance and risk needing to defer important teams or find alternate participants.

Monitoring

We assigned one member of the EBRP team to serve as liaison to each team, averaging six teams each. Teams did not have a formal facilitator. Instead, we gave team leaders facilitation and leadership skills via the leader training. We did assign team members who had special skills, or could facilitate team activities as a member, to critical Fast Track teams when necessary. For a few teams, we assigned a team leader from a neutral management area when no impartial stakeholder could be identified to lead.

Team leaders checked in with the EBRP liaison frequently, especially to overcome roadblocks, seek guidance, or obtain needed information. This occurred as often as daily for the full-time teams, more often weekly for other teams. Team leaders often needed to modify modestly their aim or target after their initial team meeting, though we generally kept teams challenged to hit their original target, enlarging or focusing their scope as needed.

At times, teams found it easy to lose focus and to begin taking on a bigger issue or an issue that was not originally the focus of the team's efforts. While we did not automatically stop teams from doing this, often we found that it resulted in the team bogging down or finding increased resistance; a review and recommitment to the specific original aim of the team helped frequently.

Commonly, a key stakeholder or area in the hospital questioned whether the team's solution could work. We then asked the team to proceed to its pilot and include the concerns raised in its evaluation. We let the pilot, rather than advance logic or argument, answer the questions. This was a key to overcoming organizational inertia.

TEAMS AND ACCOMPLISHMENTS

The ERBP team chartered the 31 Fast Track teams to begin work in May 1995. These teams were divided into full-time teams and part-time teams, yet each had the same focus of cost reduction and improvement. All full-time teams had a dollar or FTE target to achieve. Approximately half of the part-time teams had a targeted dollar amount, and the rest were support teams whose focus was to improve a work process and/or policies.

There were six full-time cost reduction teams. All six full-time teams met or exceeded their targets; the average savings was $500,000. Each of these teams started their work by spending two weeks off-site applying breakthrough thinking and redesign approaches. There were 22 new part-time cost reduction teams. Part-time teams with more important aims and larger targets generally met or exceeded their original targets, while teams with not as important work or smaller targets less consistently achieved a cost reduction. Commitment from the Fast Track team and EBRP was more consistent for the former teams. As a result, counter to expectations, the teams with the harder tasks were more successful.

Three hospital teams with cost reduction implications were already in progress before the Fast Track strategy was rolled out in the hospital. The EBRP team saw an opportunity to accelerate or increase the effect of their work. We asked these teams to continue their efforts with a more accelerated Fast Track mindset and then tracked their progress with the other teams. The three teams included Pharmacy (PYXIS medication system), Support Services (decentralized multiskilled workers), and Patient Access Services (hotel links).

Tables summarize the work of the Fast Track teams. Table 1 lists the full-time teams achieving significant cost reduction; Table 2 the part-time teams achieving significant cost reduction; and Table 3 those part-time teams supporting cost reduction by achieving improvement of quality or processes.

COST REDUCTION RESULTS

Overall, the Fast Track teams helped achieve roughly half of the $15-million annual cost reduction target. Most teams implemented their work with partial cost savings in 1995, with some implementing solutions that took effect in 1996.

Despite elimination of more than 100 positions through the Fast Track process, there were essentially no layoffs at our hospital. As we neared implementation of staff reductions, we created a temporary layoff pool to help individuals transition from eliminated jobs to positions that had remained empty (often to positions previously frozen by the "hiring freeze") and to positions elsewhere in the community. Only a handful of individuals entered the temporary layoff pool.

The overall Cost Reduction Program helped SMH hit its targeted operating margin for the year. Some of the actual Medicaid cuts were less than anticipated, allowing us to share cost savings with all staff affected by the 1995 wage and salary program deferral (all non-unionized staff; union staff were affected in 1996 at the end of their contract period). We shared cost savings evenly across all staff, not in proportion to salaries, ensuring that front-line staff benefited from the success. Physician house staff were included as well.

Table 1 Significant Fast Track Cost Reductions—Full-Time Teams

Fast Track team	*Aim*	*Recommendation/Improvement*	*Annualized savings*
Phlebotomy/ ECG/IV Decentralization	Design and implement a patient unit based approach to performing phlebotomy, ECG, and IV services.	• Transferred the performance of all lab specimen collection (phlebotomy), ECG testing, and IV line insertion to personnel on the nursing units. • Provided competency-based training to all nursing and Patient Care Technician (PCT) staff consistent with their new responsibilities. • Satellite phlebotomy collection stations located at the Cancer Center, Infectious Disease Clinic, Medicine Outpatient Department, and University Health Services phased out. • Supplier for disposable ECG tab electrodes changed to one that provides a comparable product at considerably less cost.	$1,240,000
Intensive Care Unit Technician/ Respiratory Therapy Redesign	Redesign respiratory care, hemodynamic monitoring processes and related equipment management activities in the Intensive Care Units to require less labor.	• Eliminated 64 FTE ICU Technician and 12.0 FTE Respiratory Therapist positions. • Cross-trained ICU staff to assume hemodynamic monitoring activities.	$700,000
Discharge Planning Integration	Achieve optimal efficiency and effectiveness for addressing patient discharge planning, psychosocial care, and community care needs.	• Phased in implementation of a Continuity of Care Program which deploys social work, community health nursing, and financial counseling to work with inpatient care coordinators to address high risk discharge needs. • Transferred 2 utilization review nurses to the Continuity of Care Program to create a multi-skilled team. • Eliminated 5 FTEs from Social Work and 4 FTEs from Admitting Office.	$420,000
Food and Nutrition Service	Design and implement changes in the food and nutrition services to reduce labor and food costs.	• Implemented limited patient menu (Chef's Choice). • Consolidated dietitian and nutrition support consultations to reduce redundancy. • Selected and promoted widespread use of generic tube feeding and nutrition supplements. • Eliminated soda as a floor stock item. • Eliminated "hot-grilled" breakfast service in cafeteria. • Reduced standard milk portions on patient trays. • Eliminated meal vouchers for patients who refuse inpatient meal selections.	$310,000
Physical Therapy Decentralization	Design and implement a unit-based approach to performing specified physical therapy activities to increase efficiency and effectiveness.	• Designed the right mix of centralized/decentralized physical therapy service for patient care units. • Assigned PTs to units requiring high levels of technical service (e.g. Orthopaedics). • Patient care technicians assumed conditioning and mobility service for patients on their general patient care units.	$150,000

Table 2 Significant Fast Track Cost Reduction—Part-Time Teams

Fast Track team	*Aim*	*Recommendation/Improvement*	*Annualized savings*
Consolidate Psychiatry and Hospital Medical Record Departments	Consolidate Psychiatry medical records processes and department into the Hospital's medical record department.	• Psychiatry and Hospital Medical Record department combined.	$120,000
ICU Pharmaceutical Protocols	Develop and implement guidelines for more selective use of expensive pharmaceuticals in the intensive care units including but not limited to: paralyzing agents, IV albumin, and IV sedation.	• Protocols developed and implemented for: sedation, neuromuscular blockades, and use of albumin.	$470,000
Nursing Recruitment	Eliminate redundancies in the operation and staff of the nursing recruitment office and university employment services.	• Recruitment processes (screening, application, interviewing, and hiring processes) were redesigned to ensure consistency with the university process. • Funds allocated for advertisement decreased. • Eliminated 1.6 FTEs	$260,000
Antibiotic Use	Develop and implement strategies and guidelines for the most cost effective use of antibiotics.	• Ciprofloxacin to ofloxacin conversion. • Ceftriaxone to cefotaxime conversion. • Surgical antibiotic prophylaxis guidelines developed. • IV acyclovir dosing changes in autologous Bone Marrow Transplant patients. • Vancomycin restriction and usage guidelines developed.	$220,000
Blood Utilization	Develop and implement strategies and guidelines to reduce expense related to blood utilization. Consider: minimize waste of blood products associated with surgical operations; selective use of leukocyte filters; guidelines for use of type and screen.	• Replaced CMV serotested blood units with components leukodepleted by filtration. • Reduced single donor platelet use. • Purchased Rapid Plasma Thawer to thaw FFP only as needed.	$230,000
Quality Management	Design and implement an integrated and streamlined approach for concurrent and retrospective management of quality and utilization.	• Reduced 6.5 FTEs primarily in Operations Management. • Replaced decentralized QA system with a program based council structure. • Developed and implemented Quality Improvement Coordination Center (QICC) approach to organize and track ongoing Fast Track efforts. • Integrated oversight of all quality and utilization concerns.	$190,000
Medication Administration Practices: IVSS to IVP, IV to Oral	Develop and implement strategies and guidelines to achieve timely conversion of medications: intravenous therapy to oral therapy; use of IV push instead of IV infusion (piggyback) when appropriate.	• H2 antagonist, fluconazole and ofloxacin are automatically switched to the oral formulation by the pharmacists when the patients meet medical staff approved guidelines. • Six drugs covering eleven dosages are dispensed in syringes for direct IV push.	$165,000

continues

Table 2 Continued

Fast Track team	*Aim*	*Recommendation/Improvement*	*Annualized savings*
PYXIS/Decentralize Pharmacists	Install and implement PYXIS system hospital-wide; decentralize appropriate pharmacist functions.	• PYXIS medication dispensing system implemented in all inpatient care areas. • Pharmacist assigned to each patient care area to ensure medication guidelines are in place.	$80,000
Admission Information Redundancy	Design and implement a streamlined admission assessment and documentation process to reduce redundancy within and across all disciplines.	• Eliminated duplicate data collection of admission assessment by nursing.	$38,000

UNEXPECTED RESULTS

We were pleasantly surprised by several unexpected effects of the Fast Track and cost reduction effort:

- Many teams were able to hit their financial target by broadening their aim at their own suggestion.
- Essentially none of the ideas given to Fast Track teams were "wrong" or harmful in the long run, although some did not move forward and some did not represent significant cost reductions.
- Creativity in small, empowered teams was high. We had talked about empowerment before but, as a hospital, had never "let go" to this degree.
- Many teams were able to improve the quality of key processes during their cost reduction effort.
- Several teams took their solutions further and redesigned processes to give both cost reduction and readiness for our developing Integrated Delivery System.
- The skills, creativity, and "can-do" attitudes of Fast Track participants spilled over into their management behaviors during and after their Fast Track participation. A number of middle managers reported being better able to solve problems after the experience, especially when working with another Fast Track participant.
- Many of the participants moved to new or expanded roles after the Fast Track process—some expectedly, as we had chosen the best individuals to help teams succeed, but others unexpectedly as individuals thrived with increased responsibility and independence.

LESSONS LEARNED

We learned a number of lessons in the process; again some were expected and some unanticipated:

- We entered the Fast Track process believing that we would need to communicate much more than before. We did not appreciate how much more communication was needed to avoid damaging rumors about the overall process or individual teams' work.
- A clearly stated aim indicating the area of the teams' work, their level of empowerment, and potential method of

Table 3 Teams Supporting Cost Reduction—Part-Time Teams

Fast Track team	*Aim*	*Recommendation/Improvement*
IV Solution Practice Changes	Develop and implement strategies for more cost-effective IV solution administration: consider type of solutions used; size of bags available; related equipment and tubing.	• Selected antibiotics are administered direct IVP over 3–5 minutes decreasing the need for IV tubing and mini-bag.
Oxygen Protocols	Decentralize and implement guidelines for service and discontinuation of oxygen.	• Fully implemented pre-existing automatic stop order for patients no longer needing oxygen based on O_2 saturation. • O_2 devices are now stocked on patient care units and directly accessible by nursing. • No delays in setting up oxygen on patients waiting for respiratory therapy.
DRG Coding	Determine the opportunities for enhanced revenue through improved coding of diagnoses.	• Verified DRG coding to be on target.
ICU Process Improvement Team	Develop and implement strategies and guidelines for optimal use of intensive care units including: appropriate triage; timely admission and discharge; effective coordination within and across disciplines and units.	• Admission/discharge criteria developed for all three adult ICUs based on priority rating system. • Daily rating of patients provide patient "profiles" for units and validated assumptions.
Centralized Education/ Training/ Orientation	Design and implement a more cost-effective approach and program for staff and management orientation, education, and training.	• Develop a centralized resource for non-clinical education Medical Center-wide called LEARN (Lifelong Education and Resource Network). • LEARN's chief function is to identify and create processes for meeting learning needs that continually align with the Hospital's strategic plan. • Developed a network of identified internal expertise to link experts with those who need to learn. • Established a database of educational resources organization-wide. • Established a process for monitoring educational expenditures and outcome measures. • Support lifelong learning and culture of learning organization.
Preferred Pharmaceutical Supplier	Fully implement a preferred provider pharmaceutical program to achieve participation of pharmaceutical suppliers in SMH cost reduction efforts. Revise SMH policies for pharmaceutical representative activities and achieve full adherence to those policies.	• Revised and implemented policies regarding pharmaceutical representatives' activities. • Guidelines being developed, in collaboration with the SMH pharmaceutical suppliers, for use of acyclovir and ampicillin/sulbactam as a pilot of the program.
Support Service Decentralization	Fully implement a unit-based approach to providing housekeeping, dietary, transport, and hospital stores activities to increase efficiency and effectiveness.	• Implemented a multiskilled worker titled United Support Assistant (USA) with patient care unit responsibilities that include housekeeping, dietary, transportation, and unit stores services. • Increased satisfaction with support services.
Expand Hotel Links	Expand links with local hotels to provide patients from outside our immediate service area with a lower-cost alternative to pre-procedure (over-night) admission.	• Implemented "Strong Lodging Program" for Cardiology and Cardiac Surgery patients. • Hospital covers the cost of hotel, food, and transportation for patients meeting criteria: for resident outside of county, hotel stay will save a day on LOS either before or after surgery.

success was critical. When teams or others questioned their purpose and work, we returned again and again to the aim statement.

- A specific financial target for cost reduction based on good knowledge of the expenses of the current system was important. While the target often was roughly 15 percent of current expenses given our beliefs about the potential of redesign, the denominator was at times problematic.
- We set a default rule that no individual should participate beyond being the leader of one team or being a member of two teams. When we violated this rule, often with the permission or at the request of the individual, meaningful participation in the less important effort tended to suffer.
- Piloting was invaluable. It allowed us to help teams move forward when key stakeholders were skeptical. We pushed hard for the teams to be allowed to pilot their solutions and answer questions. Often we had to pull the team back from attempting to implement their solution broadly without a pilot in the face of questioning from key stakeholders.
- Competition for the attention of key participants and supporters was significant, especially during the pilot or implementation phase for part-time teams.
- Teams that did their work full-time for two weeks came up with more creative, redesign-oriented solutions than teams that met a few hours per week. The longer periods of work allowed for better team development and more complete use of the breakthrough/redesign approach. However, the personal cost of such commitment and the necessary support was much higher for such teams.
- Getting ideas was not hard. Involving a broad spectrum of clinicians and nonclinicians, ranging from department heads to front-line workers, gave us more creative and more specific cost reduction ideas.
- By going "faster" in the Fast Track process, we designed, piloted, or began implementing solutions that were imperfect and needed to be fixed. However, we accomplished much more than we would have had we carefully worked out all the contingencies for each idea and sought the understanding and approval of each and every stakeholder.
- Looking back on problematic Fast Track teams, we wished that all members of some teams had had full training in key improvement tools and behaviors. Those already familiar with work in small teams and quality tools were more effective.

Perhaps most important in this process is having a dedicated team leader who serves to keep the team on task, serves as a champion for the team's work as it goes to key stakeholder areas for support, and follows through to ensure that implementation occurs and that the gains remain over time.

• • •

The 1995 Fast Track team experience was a "pilot" for the work to follow in continuing cost reduction, building our integrated delivery system, and adapting to true managed care. Our commitment to Fast Track went from a small senior management "war room" strategy to a medical center–wide initiative in 1996. As teams complete their work, most leaders and members move on to the next team initiative needing their expertise. In the past an employee may have referred to improvement teamwork as an "add on" to his or her job; however, today the culture at Strong Memorial Hospital is one where we understand that Fast Track *is* a key part of the work, whether through teams or individual management action. Fast Track has helped us transform both our quality culture and our ability to become cost competitive. Our hospital and medical center are more confident that we can meet the challenges for each of our missions (patient care, teaching, and research) and respond creatively to the changing demands of the health care environment.

19

Nurses as Political Health Care Activists

Nurses Can Influence Public Health Policy

Maureen Whitman

Health care policies are frequently made by public officials without the benefit of nursing influence. Nurse leaders may know what health care policies are needed, yet not have the knowledge and skills necessary to influence public decisions. Many nurse leaders have not been exposed to policy or political analysis, either in their nursing education or their practice. Those with graduate education in nursing administration may have had some exposure to analysis of public institutions but they, too, lack the skills to take a leadership role in the development of public policies favorable to nursing practice and to the health of clients.

At a time when health care is literally changing before our eyes, it is more important than ever for nurses to become involved in efforts that make a difference. One way to make a difference is to influence policy makers through involvement in politics. Political involvement for the purpose of having a say in matters of health policy is water that many nurses have been reluctant to tred. For some reason, many nurses feel that politics is a dirty word and not a worthy endeavor for a professional nurse. Today's nurses who do not want to think of themselves as involved with politics are either very shortsighted or have selective attention—or both. Politics is central to, not peripheral to, nursing practice.

Politics is everywhere and, as the largest group of health care providers, nurses must become the watchdogs over our practice—in the work setting, in the community, and in the entire health care setting. If there is anyone out there who has never been involved in politics, may I ask the planet from which you hail?

As a teen-ager, or the parent of a teen-ager, were you ever involved in negotiations about the use of a car? Have you ever been involved in trading days off with a colleague? What about that policy in your workplace that you were involved in getting changed? Those and many other examples of negotiation and horse trading describe just how often we are all involved in politics. The principles involved in approaching elected officials for the purpose of effecting political change are the same as in the above examples.

PRINCIPLES OF POLITICS

Friends or Enemies: Know the Difference

Regardless of the subject matter of the issue in which you are involved, there are some things you need to do in preparation. Do an assessment of all the groups you can think of who might take an interest in this subject (or candidate) and determine where they will fall out in this case. Make a list of those who will be your friends, those who will be your enemies, and those who will not care or who will remain neutral.

Adv Prac Nurs Q, 1998, 3(4): 67–71
© 1998 Aspen Publishers, Inc.

Be sure to do this for each issue, as the same group may be your friend on one issue, your enemy on another issue, and neutral on a third. You cannot depend on friends following you from issue to issue because they like you.

But, do not discount the importance of someone liking you—they may change jobs. By liking you, I mean respecting your ability to do the job, even if you sometimes or often end up on separate sides of the debate. These individuals can sometimes be your biggest allies in a pinch. In lobbying for a bill related to prescriptive privileges for nurse practitioners, which I will discuss later, an employee of the Oregon Medical Society was my enemy, but she liked me. She later took a position for a rural health care association, where she had more freedom to be an ally on future issues.

Collaboration versus Turf Protection

Collaboration is the effort in which groups or individuals can accomplish something that neither, on their own, could accomplish. One of the things that is the hardest to do when a group or individual is invested in a project is to give any of it up, even if the desired outcome is getting help, money, and so on. In some instances, protecting one's turf becomes the project, and the cause is lost because of pride. With resources becoming more and more scarce, collaboration is becoming more important than ever.

Collaboration depends on interest, motivation, and commitment between more than one individual or group of individuals who are willing to share resources toward a common goal. Empowerment of the collaborators is possible when the group has a clear goal in mind and a definite work plan that spells out the responsibilities of everyone involved. Again, just because you are in a collaborative relationship with a group around one issue does not mean that the same combination will work for another issue.

The "Camel's Nose under the Tent" Theory

There are times when you will have to be willing to settle for less than your ultimate goal. Particularly when the time is right, you have your players all identified and categorized, your coalition is in place and functioning, and things are happening. You can settle for part of your goal, knowing that you will have to do it all over again in a few weeks, months, or years to get the rest. At least you will have been through it all once and know the steps. Also, you will be aware of the pitfalls and can start to keep data on any of the areas where there was doubt (dissension, opposition).

In 1979 nurse practitioners in Oregon lobbied for, and achieved, a law that allowed them to have prescription privileges and third-party reimbursement. This collaborative group launched an impressive campaign and achieved the necessary legislative support. They came to a place, however, where they had to make a decision to continue and risk losing everything or settle for most of what they wanted. It became clear that to reach their overall goal, it would be necessary to negotiate about having the formulary located in the Board of Medical Examiners (the legislature wanted to have nurse practitioner certification there, also, but the group would not consider that option). The decision was made to accept that solution and collect data. Eight years later, the group was able to go back to the legislature, present the data, and have the formulary moved to the Board of Nursing.

One physician had accused us of getting our "nose under the tent" by wanting to prescribe. He added, "If you get this much, you'll want to get the whole camel in." Nurse practitioners have been practicing in the tent for nearly 20 years, thank you, owing to our ability to launch a successful collaborative effort and strive for our goal. The president of the Oregon Medical Society also accused me of being a "thorn under the skin of society," which I consider a personal high.

PRINCIPLES OF CHANGE

Another consideration for successful involvement in the political process is change. If one is expecting to change something, it is important to understand what change is and how it affects us.

Some people with vision will change with an idea; some will change if the entire process is spelled out; and some will not change, no matter what. Change is hardest when you are the one being changed against your will. Those who are part of the process have the easiest time changing (and the most fun). You can be an agent of change. But, there are considerations that cannot be overlooked. One of the first is to identify barriers that may get in your way. The second consideration is knowing how to avoid barriers, use them, or remove them.

The following process is useful for analyzing the political environment for any situation needing change, identifying barriers that are likely to impede progress toward that change, and planning for the situations and issues to which opposition is likely:

- What is the present policy (or practice), and what is the proposed change? What issue does it address?
- Which "actors" will be concerned about the proposed change?
- How can each of the actors be expected to view the proposed change?
  - Will change increase or decrease the size of turf?
  - Will change increase or decrease decision-making power?
  - Will change increase or decrease fiscal resources?
  - Will change be consistent with the values and beliefs of the community?
  - What is the relative power of each of the actors?
  - Which actors should be selected for which intervention strategies?
  - What is the potential threat or boost associated with the proposed change that will be perceived by each of the actors in regard to turf, power, and money?

Once the potential barriers and actors have been identified, start to formulate a strategic plan for how to overcome, use, or remove the barriers in order to achieve your goal.

People will endure change better, and more wholy, if they feel safe and have energy. You can put energy into supporting people, making them feel safe, and giving them an ally and support network. When some people see the change process starting, they try to avoid it. Pain and stress are sometimes signs that a window is about to open, and they are not willing or able to accept it. Many people will hold on to a position, relationship, plan, or issue until it is worthless, either to themselves or anyone else. One nurse practitioner in Oregon was so afraid that physicians would be "mad" if the law on prescription privileges and third-party reimbursement passed, she was actually going to testify against the bill. The group was able to defuse the potential threat of perceived division by convincing her to do nothing.

If people on your planning group cannot handle risk or change, work as a group to develop small steps with which everyone can be comfortable. Then every member of the group can have some success. An attempt to take steps that are too large may set the project up for failure.

INVESTING IN A PROCESS IS SAFER AND MORE LIKELY TO BE SUCCESSFUL THAN INVESTING IN A GOAL

The following steps constitute a process for formulating and reaching a goal by removing, getting around, or using barriers:

- Be sure you are very clear about what everyone in the group considers the goal to be. Be as specific as you possibly can. Remember that the barriers may be slightly different if one or two elements are added or left out.
- Know the arena.
  - Who are the players? What are their strengths? How can everyone's energies be used in order to enhance a successful change?
  - What resources already exist, and how can they be included in the planning or as part of the goal? This approach represents one potential source of support. If an existing entity can be built into the goal, and the current actors do not perceive the change as competition, those involved may be counted on to support the effort.
- Be alert to the stages of the change process (Jones, 1989):
  - *The window of opportunity.* Notice, recognize, and decide whether or not to do something about (take advantage of) it. To respond, you must slow down, relax, take a big breath, and be rational about making a move. If you want windows open, you must clear a space; to open windows for others, send them information and give them support.
  - *Exploration.* Be ready for when the window opens. Have your team, goal, and plan in place; gather resources and information. When you are ready and make a commitment, the world moves!
  - *Integration.* Take the time to compare the opportunity with the concepts of your goal. Take the information, get up on a windowsill, and make a decision as to whether or not to go through. (These three steps are necessary for readiness, and they should not be confused with finding excuses for not moving forward.) This stage is something like a neutral zone, and no one likes to be in neutral. Change does not happen in a straight line. It is more like "the dance of life," or "zig-zagging" through life.
  - *Tumble.* Let go and tumble through the window when you are feeling safe enough. There may be a moment of shock and feeling sorry the moment you tumble, but it will pass.
  - *Land.* Be thrilled when you have made it. This tumble might not work out right, but you have proven that you can take a risk and still remain whole.
  - *Talk about it.* Share feelings, and regroup. At this point, some team members might drop out. This situation is not a negative; it just is not the right time for them. (They might become a barrier if forced to stay.) Most people who get through the change process feel good about it—even though someone else has initiated it—as long as

they feel they have had a part and were listened to when they had ideas, questions, or concerns.

By facing the worst, sometimes a way out can be found. Have alternatives for where a way out can be found. And remember some people will create a crisis just to feel alive again! Crisis decisions are usually unnecessary unless someone is dying, so the group should think carefully before responding to a crisis unless that is the case. With careful identification of barriers, actors, a goal, and the steps of the desired change, crisis decisions should never be necessary.

THE DECADE OF THE NURSE?

In this the computer age, nurses are still very much in demand for assessing and hands-on intervention. Computers can take a history, of course, but they cannot give the assurance of the warm and personal touch. Likewise, policy makers need personal, hands-on attention.

In order for us to have an impact, it is necessary for nurses, both individually and as part of a group, to face those who are in a position to pass the laws and make the policies that affect our practice. If they know you, they know who to call when they have questions.

Secretary of Health and Human Services Lewis Sullivan, during the introduction of the *Healthy People 2000* health objectives, encouraged us to consider the ripple effect of our actions. He stressed that three main concepts are:

1. building a culture of character,
2. finding ways to extend benefits of good health to the most vulnerable, and
3. finding ways to contain and reduce costs of sick care in order to introduce more dollars into prevention.

In order to achieve these goals, each individual nurse must be involved, contribute, volunteer (both money and time), organize, keep informed, and vote.

CLOSING

In closing, the following fable seems appropriate.

> There was a child walking along the beach and, suddenly, she came upon a bunch of starfish that had been washed up by the tide. Unfortunately, they had been washed up so far that the waves did not retrieve them when the tide went out, and they were in danger of drying out. She felt sorry for them and, one by one, started carrying them back to the water so that they could have moisture and life. Soon, a macho jogger came running along the beach and, when he saw the child carrying the starfish down to the waves, he laughed and said: "You'll never be able to carry them all down to the water, kid, you might as well give up—you can't make a difference here!" Unimpressed, the child kept walking down to the water as she responded: "I may not be able to help them all, but for the ones I get back into the water, I'll make a difference."

So, that is what we must remember as we take our tired bodies out of the house to spend a few hours working on a campaign for a candidate who can help us make a difference for the disenfranchised, vulnerable patients who cannot advocate for themselves: We cannot make a difference for the whole population, but for those we do help we make a difference.

The following quote about risk is worth sharing:

- "Those who run the world are the ones who show up" (Salmon, 1993).

REFERENCES

Jones, J. (1989, May). Positive vision for nurse managers conference, Ashland, Oregon.

Salmon, M. (1993, May). One hundred years of public health nursing celebration, Portland, Oregon.

The Nurse Executive as Health Policy Champion

Judith G. Berg

New political forces are needed to influence the direction and scope of health care delivery systems in our nation. Nurse executives who are knowledgeable across the continuum of health care services are *a crucial force* in influencing decisions made in both the formal and informal policy arenas.

Today's nurse executives must be knowledgeable concerning the economic, social, and political factors that affect health care, and have a willingness to work to change those factors in order to obtain better health care for all.

HEALTH CARE DELIVERY, POLITICAL PROCESSES, AND THE NURSE EXECUTIVE

Nurse executives offer a unique blend of special skills and expertise that can be used individually and collectively to express important perspectives. Nurses can also educate, motivate, and mobilize people within their community who are recipients of health care services.

It is imperative that nurse executives enlarge their roles in health policy-making by increasing their legislative expertise and activity. To increase nursing's effectiveness in competing for scarce resources, the number of politically active nurse executives simply must increase.

The connection between political processes and health care delivery continues to grow, with public pressures for cost-effective, accessible, and high-quality health care services converging in the political arena. Federal, state, and local fiscal crises have necessitated increased government involvement in the provision of health care in order to control spending for public health programs.

In addition, the government has stepped in to assure that fiscal constraints faced by health care providers do not deny access to care for individuals in need. As issues such as the effectiveness and quality of care increase in importance, the government will become even more involved in the future.

From a public policy perspective, the health care system is increasingly fluid because of the interaction between government-prescribed changes to the system and larger economic and demographic changes. As a result of these forces, more and more interests are competing for limited resources at the state, federal, and local levels.

Nongovernmental factors are also changing the environment. The number of uninsured (currently 41 million) and underinsured individuals continues to rise, adding to the strain on the health care system in the form of uncompensated care. An aging population, higher costs of labor, new medical technolo-

Aspen's Advisor for Nurse Executives, 1997, 12(4): 1–4
© 1997 Aspen Publishers, Inc.

gies, and aggressive competition are additional factors affecting the current health care arena.

WHAT WE CAN EXPECT

The public policy debate on health issues will continue to rage nationally. In the short term, Medicare and Medicaid must change. The Medicare Hospital Insurance Trust Fund will be depleted by the year 2001. In 1935, the ratio of contributors to recipients under government/social security programs was 17 to 1; today, it is 4 to 1; by 2025, it will be slightly more than 2 to 1.[1] When one-third of the population is being sustained by the remaining two-thirds, the social structure of the nation is in danger of collapse.

In the next four years, there will likely be policy changes in the Medicare program to either decrease eligibility for this program, increase contributions to the trust fund, or perform some combination thereof. The Medicaid program will also have changes involving per capita grants to states, and most probably there will be a continuous stream of incremental changes on the national health scene. It is further likely that most of these incremental changes occurring through bills enacted into law will focus on the delivery side of the health care system.

HOW PUBLIC POLICY IS CHANGED

Health policy changes occur in both orderly and chaotic ways. Some processes are formal; some are informal. Changes within the marketplace reflect informal policy changes occurring in a chaotic environment. In fact, more changes have occurred during the past decade as a result of private sector influences than can be attributed to law makers.

These changes have included mega-mergers within the physician sector, as well as within hospital and related service sectors. Regional oversupply of hospital beds and physician services has encouraged the growth of managed care insurance products and services.

In most acute care organizations, length of stay is dropping dramatically and care is shifting to nontraditional settings. As these market forces continue to develop, associated issues with cost and quality of care are beginning to emerge in the public policy arena.

Formal public policy is established through legislation, regulations, and court actions. In this area, we can expect a continuing series of incremental adjustments and alterations. *Approximately 2,500 health-related bills and resolutions are introduced during every two-year congressional session.* Although only 2 percent are enacted into law, many have the potential to affect patient care and the practice of nursing.

Public policymakers respond to real or perceived needs and desires of the electorates. Consequently, the directions of change will continually shift. However, legislators' personal interests will always be factors. Influencing legislators directly and clearly is essential in determining the outcomes of legislative processes.

FIVE STRATEGIES FOR PARTICIPATING IN THE LEGISLATIVE PROCESS

1. Learn about the Issues

Core to being successful in influencing health care policy decisions is understanding the issue(s). This can be done in a variety of ways, such as by reading the lay press as well as professional journals. Another key way to get information is by participating in a professional organization that represents your concerns.

The American Organization of Nurse Executives (AONE) is an organization dedicated to the stewardship of health policy and to the professional development of nurse leaders functioning in a dynamic environment. Many organizations, including AONE, have grassroots networks formed specifically for the purpose of keeping members informed regarding health care policy issues and their potential implications.

2. Educate the Decision Makers

Influence and the access it brings come from developing personal relationships with those making the decisions. The most powerful influence occurs when citizens with first-hand experience and personal involvement in issues communicate with elected and appointed officials.

Nursing leaders can and should play an active role by engaging in efforts to educate and inform public policymakers. The most accessible means of legislative involvement is writing letters and sending telegrams. An effective letter should have an individual and positive approach. It does not need to be lengthy. The checklist in the box provides guidelines to consider when writing letters to legislators.

Occasional visits to legislators are important, particularly when you need to educate or inform the politicians on a specific piece of legislation, or when it is important to get to know your legislator and offer assistance to him or her. When making a visit to a legislator, the following key considerations are important to remember:

- *Know your subject.* Refer to talking points issued by professional associations. You may want to leave briefing documents with the legislator, or use the documents yourself so you are sure you covered all the key concepts.
- *Tell your story.* Once you are prepared on the issue, personalize it to your own experience. Always let the legislator know you are a nurse, what your background is, and the organization you represent. Relating specific examples as to what this bill would do in real-life terms is helpful to educate the member as well as illustrate the point.
- *Never, ever lie.* If you don't know the answer to a question, don't guess. It is acceptable to explain that you don't

A Checklist for Strong Policy Communications

- *Use your own stationery.* A letter is better than a postcard or telegram. Make your letter creative and original. Do not fax your letter, and be sure the correct address is on the letter as well as the envelope.
- *Identify your subject clearly.* State the name of the legislation for which you are writing.
- *Be brief.* State your position on the legislation. Explain how the issues would impact you, your profession, and your community. Give examples.
- *Know the committees in which your legislators serve* and indicate in the letter if the bill is being brought before any of those committees.
- *Sign your name with RN.*
- *Be courteous and complimentary.* A rude letter neither makes friends nor influences the legislators. If you can, express appreciation for past decisions, a favorable vote, or leadership on a committee.
- *Timing is important.* Try to express your position while the bill is in committee. Your legislators will probably be more responsive to appeal at this time rather than when the bill has already been approved in committee.
- *Limit your letter to one issue* and do not write more than once on the same subject.
- *Follow up with a thank you letter* if the legislator takes the action you requested.

know but will get back to them at a later time. But, you must be sure you do get back to them — don't forget.

- *Never argue with a member.* Sometimes a legislator will have his or her mind already made up and will want to argue with you. However, always be polite and respectful, even though it may be difficult.
- *Keep it simple.* Remember that most legislators are not from the health care field. Use plain English and simple concepts to explain the impact of any legislation.
- *Be on time.* You may have to wait for your appointment with a legislator. However, he or she will not wait for you. If for some reason your meeting is cut short, ask if you can meet with him or her again, or with the staff person assigned to the bill.
- *Meet with the legislator's staff.* Often, the staff member who works in the legislator's office is your best contact to determine the bill status or the member's position. Sometimes, it is impossible to get time with a legislator, but meeting with the appropriate staff member can be just as useful because the staff prepare the legislator's briefing on all bills.
- *Be available for follow-up.* At the conclusion of the meeting, leave documents that have been prepared ahead of time, as well as information on how the member or staff can reach you or someone from the organization if future questions occur.

3. Participate with Time and Money in Legislative Activities

Influencing the public policy process takes a well-rounded effort. Another important component is to support elected officials with your time and money as they campaign for future offices.

Involvement in campaigns through personal efforts is a very powerful "door opener" to establishing access and the ability to influence issues related to health care policy decisions. Although this is a relatively new component of influencing health care policy for many nurse executives, it is equally important to educating law makers on the issues.

4. Participate in Advisory Groups and Task Forces

Occasionally, elected officials will constitute locally based, topic-specific advisory groups that are intended to provide feedback and discussion opportunities with the elected official on issues of concern. By establishing linkages with the staff members and legislators, these groups will become opportunities to influence the health care process in a very tangible way.

Typically, advisory groups and task forces are used at local levels as well as state and federal levels. They provide opportunities for nurse executives to influence the structure of health care delivery systems as well as the components of service.

5. Start Now!

The most challenging aspect of being a participant in the exciting arena of influencing health care policy is getting started. Although it may seem overwhelming at first, you can start with incremental efforts and build to levels of personal comfort.

- Choose one or two issues of personal concern. These may be local issues, neighborhood/community health issues, or state and/or federal issues.

- Become knowledgeable in those one or two areas by using the resources of a professional association and the professional journals you are already reading.
- Write one letter to one elected official on a topic of personal concern to you.
- Make a donation to one candidate who most closely represents your views on that particular topic.

You will be surprised how these small beginnings gradually position you to be an effective advocate for improving the health care status of your community.

REFERENCE

1. Donner, C. D. September, 1996. Impact of public policy on health care in the future (Letter from the President). *The California Health Care Newsletter,* p. 2.

Policy Imperatives for Nursing in an Era of Health Care Restructuring

David Keepnews and Geri Marullo

The forces shaping health policy in the United States, particularly as they affect nursing and its place in the health care system, have changed drastically over the past two years. The health policy environment facing nursing in 1995 and 1996 is virtually unrecognizable when compared to that of 1993 and 1994.

In 1993 and 1994, nursing was in a largely "proactive" stance as it worked with a new political leadership in Washington, one elected with a commitment to sweeping health care reform that promised to include some of nursing's most cherished goals: a system based on universal access, equity, primary care, prevention and wellness, and a recognition and fuller use of nursing's role both in health care delivery and in shaping a dynamic new health care system. Debates within nursing centered on exactly what to ask for in sweeping health care reform and how to achieve it—how to ensure the fullest possible use of nursing's contributions; how best to break down barriers to practice and payment; how to provide for new entitlement programs for nursing education; how to ensure consumer choice of type of provider (including advanced practice RNs); and how to ensure that nurses could best be prepared to take their proper role in emerging practice settings as the health care system moved to emphasize primary and preventive care based in communities, workplaces, schools, and homes. For many, the mere fact that nursing was being listened to as health care reform proposals were being formulated (while organized medicine fumed at its seeming isolation from the process) in itself represented a notable accomplishment.

In 1995 and 1996, the environment is radically different for nursing and for all other players in health care policy. The defeat of comprehensive health care reform in the 103rd Congress and a much-changed political environment in Washington (and in many state capitals) have been accompanied by massive changes in the settings in which most RNs practice as the health care industry fundamentally reorganizes its structures, its business, and its clinical operations. Nursing finds itself focusing much of its energies on defending past gains and protecting patient safety and nursing practice in a health care environment that seems increasingly to shift its emphasis from patients and quality care to utilization control, cost, and profit. Furthermore, these changes occur in a political environment that is increasingly hostile to government regulatory intervention and friendlier to market-based approaches such as those in whose name these changes are being made.

Nursing has responded to changes in the outside world by restating and refocusing its policy priorities. In this article, the authors identify some of those changes and priorities

Nurs Admin Q, 1996, 20(3): 19–31
© 1996 Aspen Publishers, Inc.

and the strategies that are being developed to respond to them in order that nursing can progress toward its goal of a health care system that prioritizes safe, quality services, even in an era of cost containment.

HEALTH CARE RESTRUCTURING AND COST CONTAINMENT

Efforts toward comprehensive federal health care reform in 1993 and 1994 occurred in the context of a health care system that was taking up greater and greater portions of federal and state budgets and personal expenditures but that seemed to be delivering less and less for the money that was put in it while leaving tens of millions of Americans uninsured.[1] To be sure, different players identified vastly different interests in the achievement of a new health care system, and by no means did all of them concentrate singly on cost containment. Nursing made its goals clear in *Nursing's Agenda for Health Care Reform*,[2] a document that had the support of the majority of nursing organizations. That document stressed a simultaneous focus on access, quality, and cost. What most captured the imagination of nurses and many other proponents of health care reform was the goal of a health-oriented, equitable, and just health care system, not a single-minded focus on cost containment. Nursing understood that the social goals of health care reform were inextricably linked to the goal of cost containment. That recognition, however, should not obscure the pivotal role of cost containment as a driving force in health care reform.

CHANGES IN SYSTEM PREDATED CLINTON PLAN

Efforts toward major change in the health care system did not begin with the development of health care reform legislation in the 103rd Congress. Managed care was continuing to grow at an accelerating pace in markets throughout the country. Mergers and consolidations among hospitals and between hospitals and other providers had been in evidence for some years preceding. State-based efforts at reform, particularly in state Medicaid programs, were becoming increasingly popular as well. In some markets, particularly those where managed care had achieved significant market penetration, efforts had already begun in earnest to employ "creative" models of care that involved replacement of registered nurses with semiskilled, low-paid, unlicensed personnel (models that appear so ubiquitous today and that, in many areas, are already being abandoned).

Far from initiating the transformation in U.S. health care, comprehensive federal reform held the promise of providing a regulatory structure for changes in the health care system, of providing some degree of planning and rationality, for shepherding changes based on a careful evaluation of the nation's health care needs, and for constraining industry action that was adverse to the nation's health care goals and priorities.

The failure of the 103rd Congress to pass health care reform gave a signal to the health care industry that attempts to shape changes in the health care system were not likely to come from the federal government at any time soon. For the industry, this promised a measure of freedom from government "interference" through the impositions of new regulatory schemes, structures, or standards.

Restructuring in the Health Care Industry

The health care industry is in the midst of a far-reaching, basic transformation in how its structures are configured and its operations conducted.[3] Health care facilities and services are forming broad, integrated health delivery systems that offer a continuum of health care services. Hospitals are merging, consolidating, and often closing. More and more patient care is moved out of acute care settings and into clinics, practitioners' offices, the home, and long-term care facilities. The financing of health care is changing dramatically with the increasing dominance of capitated payment mechanisms and the consolidation of the managed care industry into a handful of increasingly large and powerful corporations.

The health care industry has increasingly sought to mimic the restructuring moves of other industries, often without enough discrimination to weed out some of their worst features. The emphasis more and more is on the financial bottom line. Hospitals and health systems increasingly seek to improve their own competitive postures—to capture bigger and bigger market shares, to secure managed care contracts, and to attract a larger patient base.

If only in theory, many aspects of this restructuring appear either unremarkable or may even appear to bring with them some of the things that nursing has been advocating for some time. For instance, nursing has been talking for years about the need to integrate and coordinate health care services and to provide a continuum of services as seamlessly as possible. Nursing certainly cannot object to the concept of hospitals and health systems running as efficiently and wisely as possible, to minimize wasted health care dollars.

The Underlying Motives

But while many of these concepts may superficially appear nonobjectionable, they are shaped and implemented with the goal not of improving patient care, but of improving systems' competitive posture—by maximizing revenue and decreasing expenses, to generate profit that can be used for further expansion, to fund more mergers, or, for some for-profit entities, to provide a return on investment. Where they involve changes in an organization's clinical operations, these changes are often largely untested and are employed with little or no outcomes data to attest to their impact on patient care.

An intimately related phenomenon is that the changes that are made to fund this restructuring often involve drastic cost-cutting maneuvers. Too often, these are made at the expense of safe, quality patient care. In its testimony to the Institute of Medicine (IOM) Committee on the Adequacy of Nurse Staffing, the American Nurses Association (ANA) referred to this phenomenon as "Cutting Costs at Any Cost."[4] Many hospitals and health systems, looking for budgets to cut, have all too often looked first and foremost at their labor budgets and zeroed in on nursing labor expenses as one of the biggest and seemingly easiest targets for cost cutting. As a result, facility after facility has seen layoffs, frozen positions, and replacement of RNs by assistive personnel.[5,6]

These changes come at a time when utilization of RNs in health care delivery is more critical than ever to maintain patient safety and quality of care. Hospitalized patient populations are sicker than ever, their stays shorter than ever, and, therefore, their needs more intense than ever, and their nursing care needs more intense than ever.[7] As patients who would previously have been hospitalized are cared for instead in long-term care facilities, outpatient settings, and at home, the acuity of patients in those settings has also risen. It is estimated that "the cumulative real case mix change in hospitals has been on the order of a 20 percent growth in complexity between

1981 and 1992."[8(p.319)] Attempts to provide patient care with fewer professional staff, and to fragment care and assign most patient care tasks to non-RNs seem especially ill-timed.

Layoffs and replacements of RNs may have helped some institutions to cut their operating budgets in the very short term, but in the long term they are unlikely to prove beneficial to either patients or the industry itself. ANA has argued that removing RNs from patient care deprives patients of the level of professional caregiving they require, and deprives health care systems of the comprehensive, cost-efficient services of professional RNs.

One of the important lessons for nursing from the institution of the prospective payment system (PPS) for Medicare in 1983 is the impact of cost restraints on utilization of nursing. When the PPS system was introduced, many predicted dire reductions in the use of RNs, since hospitals would want to deliver care as cheaply as possible. Initially, it did appear that many hospitals did move to cut their RN staffs. The industry, however, soon realized that replacement by lesser-trained personnel did not yield a saving.[9] These ancillary personnel could not do as much, could not provide adequate patient assessment or detect complications or other problems at an early stage. The years following introduction of the PPS system saw a large increase in use of RNs (although, significantly, not a rise in labor costs as a percentage of overall spending). The ratio of RNs to patients increased by 26 percent between 1982 and 1986.[10] Those years also witnessed a large and prolonged undersupply of RNs.

The ANA has strongly advocated that nurses be at the table when hospitals restructure.[4] In some instances, state nurses associations (SNAs) have found some success in negotiating involvement in staff redesign decisions and in providing for retraining of nurses displaced from inpatient units.

SAFETY AND QUALITY CONCERNS COME TO THE FORE

Nursing's Agenda for Health Care Reform[2] identified three defining principles for a new health care system—access, quality, and cost containment. Indeed, nurses and other supporters of health care reform recognized that no one goal could be achieved to the exclusion of the others. While cost containment concerns provided much of the imperative for health care reform, the need for wider access to coverage and services, and how to achieve that goal, drove much of the public debate on reform. The need to maintain and even improve the quality of services in the face of expanded coverage and effective cost containment provided a third, anchoring principle for health care reform. As patient advocates, and as the practitioners most directly entrusted with protecting patient care quality and patient safety, nurses attached particular importance to this principle.

Increasing Emphasis on Cost Containment

Currently, both market-based and public sector initiatives have centered in large part on control of costs. The reasons behind this are several. As discussed above, it was cost containment that was the driving force behind the effort for federal reform and, in a much more clearly evident way, has driven most state-based efforts for health reform. Within the private sector, transformations that have been at play for some time have been largely cost driven. Managed care, which long held the promise of a more tightly organized, wellness and prevention oriented system of health care delivery, has increasingly been centered on management of cost. In addition to the financial pressures created by the growing influence of capitated payment systems, competition among both insurers and institutional providers has led to tighter attention to costs, profit margins, and the ability to fund acquisitions that hold the promise of capturing greater and greater market share.

It is in the context of this increasing focus on cost that nursing has identified its growing concern that patient care quality, including the fundamental principle of protecting patient safety, is being compromised in the process of a unilateral drive to cut costs. Of particular concern to nursing has been the industry's efforts to cut utilization of RNs and to replace nursing staff with lower-paid, unskilled substitutes. These concerns are based not only on previous data that suggest a close link between RN staffing and patient care quality[11]; increasing anecdotal evidence has also pointed to growing problems in patient care safety and quality as a result of the slashing of staffing levels. An important review of the literature addressing the links between nurse staffing and skill mix and patient outcomes is provided by Prescott.[11] A review is also contained in the ANA's *Nursing Care Report Card for Acute Care.*[12] Reports from individual nurses on patient care problems resulting from decreased staffing have been collected by the ANA and by state nurses associations, including the California Nurses Association (CNA), which was then affiliated with the ANA. CNA had collected these as part of public testimony on proposed changes in state hospital regulations; these were submitted to the California Department of Health Services and also, by ANA, to the IOM Committee on Adequacy of Nurse Staffing.

Current mechanisms to ensure patient safety and quality of care have proved inadequate to address the current changes in nurse staffing. The standards of the Joint Commission on Accreditation of Healthcare Organizations (Joint Commission) provide conditions in several areas, but none measures safe staffing levels or occupational mix per se. Patient classification systems are intended to provide a guide for hospital staffing. There is little uniformity among them, however, as different hospitals opt to use different systems. Most significantly, widespread reports from nurses indicate that in many instances patient classification systems are commonly manipulated to yield results that meet budgetary needs rather than patient care needs. Medicare's Conditions of Participation (CoPs) give little specific guidance beyond this to evaluate the adequacy of staffing levels and occupational mix.

These mechanisms for quality enforcement may have been adequate in years past. Until recently, the assumption that hospitals and health facilities would, with rare exception, staff at safe levels and would prioritize patient care needs may have appeared to be a safe one. In an era when a restructuring health care system stresses cost and revenue as its central priorities, this assumption no longer appears so safe. Many hospitals and facilities may be able to maintain their Joint Commission and Medicare accreditation despite slashing their nurse staffing levels because they maintain technical compliance with the letter of Joint Commission and Medicare standards. That they maintain such accreditation may speak more to the skill of their risk managers and to the adequacy of current standards than to the actual state of care in those facilities.

Challenges to the Role of Regulation in Protecting Safety and Quality

While the logical places to turn for assistance in remedying growing concerns over safety and quality are federal and state regulatory agencies, the viability of this option is threatened by the current political and policy environments. The defeat of comprehensive federal health care reform was seen by many as a rejection of new regulatory frameworks for addressing problems with the health care system. Indeed, regulatory intervention would seem to compromise the current freedom of the industry to devise the "market-based reforms" that are transforming the system.

Moreover, Congress and many state governments are currently in the grip of a pronounced antiregulatory fervor that argues for a diminished government presence in many areas of American life. Proposals that involve the imposition of new regulatory schemes, even in an area as critical as health care, may face particularly sharp challenges in this climate.

This antiregulatory sentiment, in fact, may clear the way for new challenges to nursing, even in areas where they may not have been previously expected. Nursing has turned to regulatory bodies at the state level (where the power to regulate the provision of health services, along with the exercise of other powers to protect the public health, safety, and welfare has traditionally rested) to argue its case for restrictions on facility discretion in the area of staffing levels or of inappropriate or unsafe use of assistive personnel. Among these regulatory bodies, nursing has traditionally found a hearing from state boards of nursing. These boards are empowered with licensing nurses and regulating the practice of nursing. In a great many states, their nurse and consumer members are particularly aware of the need to address the unauthorized practice of nursing, including the institutional use of unlicensed personnel to provide nursing care. Some state boards of nursing have sought to address this practice directly. (In one state, concerns voiced by consumer members of the board of nursing moved the state attorney general to take action on the unsafe use of unlicensed personnel.[13])

Some attempts to reduce the power of the boards of nursing to exert such authority have begun to surface. In Oregon, the state hospital association and the state affiliate of the American Organization of Nurse Executives (AONE) sponsored a legislative proposal (H. B. 3045, 1995) that would have diluted the authority of the Board of Nursing to regulate the use of unlicensed personnel. Among other things, this bill would have imposed a distinction between "nursing care services" and "patient care services"; the nursing board's power would have been limited to regulating "nursing care" as narrowly defined by the bill. That bill drew significant opposition from nursing, spearheaded by the Oregon Nurses Association, and was defeated. (A subsequent attempt to restrict the power of health professionals' licensing boards to issue rules that affect the workplace was later amended into a piece of technical legislation that passed but was vetoed by the governor.[14])

Other voices have begun to advocate one form or another of institutional licensure, or of health system licensure, in which the institution or system would determine the training and practice of its employees based on its own determination of its needs. Still others have questioned the efficacy of health professions' regulatory boards to protect the public, despite the more favorable record of many nursing boards in disciplining their licensees who practice unsafely. The Task Force on Health Care Workforce Regulation of the Pew Commission on the Health Professions released its report and recommendations on health professions' licensure in December 1995 and included a number of far-reaching proposals for changing state health care regulatory mechanisms. Advocates of changes in the way health professions' licensure boards are configured, and the powers they exercise, are likely to win a broad hearing in many state legislatures this year, particularly as many of their arguments build upon a growing public distrust and skepticism of government regulation.

STRATEGIES AND SOLUTIONS ON SAFETY AND QUALITY

Recognizing both its historical commitment to quality care and patient safety and the direct relevance of these issues to current changes in nursing practice and the health care system, ANA has taken up a broad initiative to address the issues of safety and quality in patient care.

Nursing Report Card

Fundamental to this initiative has been a recognition of the need to establish understandable, objective measures by which to measure quality in nursing care. Defining and measuring quality has, of course, been a confounding issue for virtually everyone in health care. ANA's effort seeks to build upon work that has already been accomplished and has used a "report card" approach, which identified specific quality indicators by which performance can be rated.

The initial results of that effort are published as the *Nursing Care Report Card for Acute Care*.[12] It is based on work done by ANA and Lewin-VHI, Inc. The development of the quality indicators included identifying an initial set of 71 nursing indicators, which was narrowed to 21 with the strongest, established, or theoretical link to the availability and quality of professional nursing services in hospital settings. Those indicators have been further refined to include: patient satisfaction; pain management; skin integrity; total nursing care hours per patient (case/acuity adjusted); nosocomial infections (urinary tract infection [UTI] and pneumonia rates); patient injury rate; and assessment and implementation of patient care requirements.

Much work remains to be done in this area, not the least of which is piloting the use of the report card. Work has recently been completed on uniform definitions for each of seven indicators (work in which AONE, to its credit, is participating) and to develop an educational program for RNs on the use of quality indicators and clinical outcomes in their work settings. Identification of institutions interested in piloting the report card is also proceeding, with the participation of the AONE.

An important goal here is not just to add a new entry to an already crowded field of report cards, but also to work to incorporate the elements of the Nursing Report Card into existing and developing quality measurement tools.

Other Important Voices on Quality

Nursing's efforts on quality measurement dovetail with those of other groups. The Health Plan Employer Data and Information Set (HEDIS), developed by the National Coalition for Quality Assurance (NCQA), has come into increasing use as a standard means of measuring managed care plan performance and accrediting those plans. As the use of managed care in both Medicaid and Medicare grows, HEDIS is being adapted to reflect care for those populations.

In July of 1995, a number of public and private groups met to take up the issue of quality in managed care and formed a new initiative, the Foundation for Accountability (FAcct). Much of the talk at the meeting, as reported, centered on the idea that, as costs are coming under control, more attention now needs to be paid to quality.[15] Participants in this initial meeting included large corporations; federal and state agencies that administer health insurance programs, including the Health Care Financing Administration and the California Public Employees Retirement Board; union purchasers of health insurance; and NCQA. Estimates are that the groups who make up FAcct represent 80 million insureds.[16]

Notably, this meeting was convened by the Jackson Hole Group and included the active participation of Dr. Paul Ellwood of that group, whose work had provided much of the foundation for what later became the Clinton health care reform proposal. The work of this group appears to mesh with some of the refocused priorities enunciated by the Jackson Hole Group.[17]

This new initiative may indeed prove significant, not only because it is a public–private initiative of unprecedented magnitude but also because it offers the possibility of an outcomes approach that measures patients' response to interventions performed by providers under those plans.

Accountability

Closely tied to the need for more and better data and clearer outcomes measures is the goal of public accountability for health care delivery. Holding performance of plans and institutions out for public scrutiny is important not only because, as many would argue, the public has a right to know (and, conversely, providers have a duty to disclose) but also because public disclosure itself can potentially influence consumer choice and encourage competition based on performance. An ANA-commissioned Gallup survey found that 84 percent of respondents would choose a hospital with smaller patient–nurse ratios than one with larger ratios.[18] At the Jackson Hole meeting, Dwight McNeill, information manager for the GTE Corporation and co-chair of FAcct, stated:

> What we want to do is [to] have information out there in the marketplace on performance and outcome measurements. If consumers and purchasers have information on both outcome and cost, it drives market share toward that vendor that has the best value, and, surprisingly, we haven't got that as yet.[19(p.1)]

As part of its efforts on public accountability, ANA has advocated public disclosure by health care institutions regarding staffing levels and patient outcomes data. ANA has advocated that such public disclosure be part of the Medicare Conditions of Participation for hospitals and also supports legislative efforts to require such disclosure for health care institutions. ANA is also advocating that proposed mergers and acquisitions of health care facilities, as part of their regulatory review, be assessed for their potential impact on patient safety and quality of care.[20]

Consumer Education

A key part of moving forward nursing's policy agenda on health care safety and quality is to educate consumers and establish close working ties with consumer organizations. ANA's public education campaign has been conducted around the theme "Every Patient Deserves a Nurse," and has involved extensive distribution of an educational brochure, work with local and national media, and other educational efforts. ANA cosponsored the March 1995 Nurses' March on Washington, which sought to bring public attention to the issues of patient safety and quality of care. In addition, ANA is seeking active partnership and coalition with consumer groups around these issues. These efforts seek not only to educate consumers, but also to help create a consistent consumer demand for RN services.

Reasserting Nurses' Role as Patient Advocate

As conditions for RNs and their patients change, nurses' role as advocate for their patients (a key ethical precept for the profession[21]) becomes increasingly important. Threats to nurses' ability to fill that role have recently emerged. In *NLRB v. Health Care & Retirement Corp.* (114 S. Ct. 1778 [1994]), the U.S. Supreme Court found that nurses who direct the work of less-skilled aides are supervisors and therefore not entitled to protection under the National Labor Relations Act (NLRA). That protection includes not only the rights to organize and to bargain collectively (rights that have provided nurses with important tools with which to protect patient care and nursing practice), but also to speak out on issues relevant to their employment and working conditions, including patient safety concerns. ANA is pushing to amend the NLRA to clarify that nurses who direct the work of ancillary personnel are not outside the NLRA's protection. ANA has held that this is a critical issue for patient care and for the nurse's ability to meet her or his ethical obligations.[22,23]

In addition, ANA is supporting efforts to enact federal whistle-blower protections for nurses who report unsafe patient care conditions.[20]

Breaking Down Barriers to Full Utilization of Nurses

Ensuring full use of RNs in meeting the country's health care needs, including breaking down barriers to nursing practice and payment for nursing services, remains an important policy imperative for nursing. Some important progress continues to be made in breaking down legislative and regulatory barriers at the state level, particularly as they apply to advanced practice RNs (APRNs). At the federal level, nursing continues to push for Medicare and Medicaid payment for all APRNs, regardless of specialty, practice setting, or geographic area. Coverage of APRN services, long an important goal of nursing, may prove particularly important in ensuring that nurses, including APRNs, are used as fully as possible in a changing health care system.[24] In addition, Medicare payment is needed in order to allow for the generation of important data; currently, because the services of nurse practitioners and clinical nurse specialists are generally billed under physicians' or clinics' provider numbers, Medicare has virtually no information on the services provided by these nurses.

With the growth of managed care plans, APRNs in many areas have encountered the problem of exclusion from provider panels. Even in states with relatively few regulatory barriers to practice, exclusion from such plans has restricted the ability of these nurses to receive payment for their services. A closely connected problem has been that, with the growth of managed care Medicare and Medicaid programs, many APRNs face similar restrictions. Many states operate Medicaid waiver programs that use a primary care case management (PCCM) mechanism, whereby each patient is assigned to a primary care provider who serves as "gatekeeper" for other health services. In some states, the PCCM role has been limited to physicians; nurses are excluded from this role either through the state Medicaid agency's plan itself, or by the private insurance companies that administer the plan.

The American Medical Association (AMA), long adverse to efforts to ease state restrictions on nursing practice, solidified that position at its 1995 House of Delegates meeting.[25] Among other things, the AMA delegates supported giving more assistance to state medical societies in opposing efforts to remove barriers to nursing practice.

Nursing will also need to pay closer attention to methods of valuing its contributions to inpatient care and seek to establish means of building on existing payment methodologies to demonstrate the importance of adequate nurse staffing in the financial well-being of health care institutions.

THREATS TO PUBLIC PROGRAMS

Numerous public programs of great importance to nursing face increased threats during the 104th Congress. Nursing is working to preserve funding for nursing education, research, and health and safety. In addition, nursing is working to prevent crippling cuts in Medicare and to preserve its character as an affordable and accessible social program. Similarly, nursing is working to protect Medicaid and its ability to provide services to low-income individuals. While the future of these programs will likely be settled by Congress for this season by the time this article is printed, these issues will undoubtedly continue to recur for some time.

THE NEED FOR CONTINUED PROFESSIONAL UNITY

During its efforts on federal health care reform, nursing achieved an unprecedented degree of unity within the profession in identifying common goals and strategies. Most nursing organizations showed an earnest willingness to compromise where needed, or at a minimum to keep its debates internal.

As nursing faces different challenges in a much-changed health care environment, can this unity be replicated? If so, on what should it be based? These are issues that cannot be settled in this article, but that nursing will need to confront as it faces growing challenges to its practice and its professional survival.

A traditional role for nurse managers and nurse executives has been to serve as patient advocates within hospital administration, to advocate for nursing's concerns within the organization. Among other things, their placement within health care organizations provided an important opportunity to play that role. This role is threatened in many organizations and systems as operational decisions are taken out of the hands of nursing, as midlevel nursing managers are replaced by nonnursing managers with nonclinical backgrounds, and as, in many hospital chains and health systems, key decisions that affect patient care are made outside of the institution. Moreover, many nurse managers and executives face pressures to conform to newly enunciated institutional values.

At the same time, staff nurses feel intense pressures to provide quality care to their patients with smaller, and often inadequate resources. In a recent survey, 58 percent of nurse respondents identified "cost containment issues that jeopardize patient welfare" as a "priority" ethical issue.[26]

Nurse managers and executives share a common interest with staff nurses in focusing attention on the issues of safety and quality and in protecting patients through ensuring nursing's continued role in patient care (although their placement within health care organizations, and the current pressures of a volatile health care environment, may not always allow them to voice these issues in the same manner). Should it surprise anyone that some institutions have lost sight of the value of nurses in midlevel management positions when they are losing sight of the value of nurses at the bedside?

A great many nurse managers and executives have continued to recognize the interests that they hold in common with all nurses, and to use their positions to fulfill their roles as patient advocates. Some have continued this commitment in the face of risk to their own current positions.

If the current environment calls for more aggressive action in some spheres, such as the March 1995 Nurses' March on Washington, or the negotiation of clearer patient care standards through collective bargaining, it does not require the disintegration of the unity that nursing found during its efforts on health care reform. The things that brought nursing together at that time—a common appreciation of the unique and critical role of nursing in health care, and of the overriding goal of serving and protecting health care consumers—will be critical to keep closely in mind as nursing continues to confront major challenges in the days and years ahead.

REFERENCES

1. Clinton, W. "Letter to the American People," November 2, 1993 (introducing the Health Security Act).
2. American Nurses Association. *Nursing's Agenda for Health Care Reform*. Washington, D.C.: ANA, 1991.
3. Shortell, S., Gillies, R., and Devers, K. "Reinventing the American Hospital." *The Milbank Quarterly* 73, no. 2 (June 22, 1995): 131–55.
4. Written Testimony of the American Nurses Association before the Institute of Medicine Committee on the Adequacy of Nurse Staffing, pp. 14–17. Washington, D.C.: ANA, September 16, 1994.
5. American Nurses Association. *1994 Layoffs Survey*. Washington, D.C.: ANA, 1994.
6. Service Employees International Union. *National Nurses Survey*. Washington, D.C.: SEIU, 1993.
7. Aiken, L. "Implications of Changing Hospital Employment Trends on Basic Nursing Workforce Requirements." Paper presented to Conference on Strategies for Health Workforce Research, March 10, 1995.
8. Aiken, L., and Salmon, M., "Health Care Workforce Priorities: What Nursing Should Do Now." *Inquiry* 31, (1994): 318–29.
9. Shindul-Rothschild, J., and Gordon, S. "Health Care Reform: A Political Economy Analysis," unpublished manuscript.
10. Aiken, L. "Nursing Shortage: Myth or Reality?" *New England Journal of Medicine* 317, no. 10 (1987): 641–45.
11. Prescott, P. "Nursing: An Important Component of Hospital Survival Under a Reformed Healthcare System." *Nursing Economics* 11, no. 4 (1993): 192–99.
12. American Nurses Association. *Nursing Care Report Card for Acute Care*. Washington, D.C.: ANA, 1995.
13. "Carter Raises Patient Care Issue; Attorney General Warns Public That Unlicensed Hospital Workers May Be Giving Medical Treatment." *Indianapolis Star*, March 24, 1994, p. D1.
14. "Oregon Governor Signs Death-Knell for Anti-RN Legislation." *The American Nurse*, September 1995, p.23.
15. Winslow, R. "Major purchasers of health serv-ices form alliance to evaluate HMO care." *Wall Street Journal*, July 3, 1995, p. A3.
16. Noble, H. "Quality is focus for health plans." *New York Times*, July 3, 1995, p. 1.
17. Ellwood, P.A., and Enthoven, A. "'Responsible Choices: The Jackson Hole Group Plan for Health Reform." *Health Affairs* 14, no. 2 (Summer 1995): 24.
18. Gallup survey on consumer perceptions of nursing staff, conducted for the American Nurses Association, 1994.
19. *New York Times*, July 3, 1995, p. 1.
20. American Nurses Association. *Legislative and Regulatory Initiatives for the 104th Congress*. Washington, D.C.: ANA, 1995.
21. American Nurses Association. *Code for Nurses with Interpretive Statements*. Washington, D.C.: ANA, 1985.
22. American Nurses Association. *The Supreme Court Has Issued the Ultimate Gag Order for Nurses*. Washington, D.C.: ANA, 1995.
23. American Nurses Association. *Can Your Nurse Still Speak for Your Needs?* Washington, D.C.: ANA, 1995.
24. Keepnews, D. "The Role of Nurses in the New Health Care Marketplace." Letter. *Health Affairs* 14, no. 3 (Fall 1995): 280–81.
25. "AMA Calls for Stronger Supervision of Nurse Practitioners/Physician Assistants." *BNA Health Care Policy Reporter*, June 26, 1995, p.4.
26. Scanlon, C. "Survey Yields Significant Results." *Communique* (American Nurses Association Center for Ethics and Human Rights), 3, no. 2 (1994): 1–3.

20

Is Your Organization Managed Care Friendly?

Readiness, Action, and Resolve for Change: Do Health Care Leaders Have What It Takes?

C. David Hardison

From Hippocrates to Florence Nightingale to the caregivers of today, "to serve and to heal" have special meaning. These values appear to be under constant assault when management's minds are on the latest deal or they are proclaiming yet another cost-cutting initiative. Much of the conflict, tension, and strained relationships that exist because of the apparent differences in values are unnecessary, as demonstrated by the great efforts of the participants in the Interdisciplinary Professional Eductation Collaborative. The integration of continuous quality improvement (CQI) principles into the education and training of physicians, nurses, and administrators provides hope that these enduring values will be preserved while, simultaneously, maintaining the economic viability of health care organizations.

THE CQI TRANSFORMATION

The integration of continuous improvement into health professions education requires that both educational institutions and the participating service delivery organizations candidly assess their readiness for change. As with change in any organization (see box titled "Some Practical Tips for Facilitating Change and Dealing with CQI Myths"), this is a process, and the model that was developed years ago by Kurt Lewin and refined by the early pioneers of CQI (see box) and is relevant to assessing and managing the process. As described in Figure 1, the model identifies three stages of the change process: the present state, the transition state, and the desired state.

To assess the situation, both parties need to describe each phase and compare their responses. Past experiences suggest amazing agreement in the two lists. As you read the following descriptions, think about your organization and which characteristics and phase bests fit your circumstances.

The present state is one of high uncertainty, curiosity, and skepticism, lack of sta-

The author would like to acknowledge the HCA Quality: Focus on Continuous Improvement Design Team: Tom Stalnaker, assistant administrator, and Nancy Hilton, RN, director of education, HCA Trident Regional Medical Center, Charleston, SC; Linda Mild, RN, vice president of nursing, and Anita Dorf, PhD, director of education, HCA Wesley Medical Center, Wichita, KS; Ron Sepielli, director of human resource development, Memorial Medical Center, Inc, Savannah, GA; Katrina Smith, RN, consultant, University of Tennessee at Knoxville; Major Chuck Boone, PhD, US Air Force Research Associate, Nashville, TN; Jan Shepard, director, HCA Management Development/HRD, and Harry Hollis, PhD, manager, HCA Management Development/HRD, Nashville, TN; Tom Meachum, consultant, HCA Hospital Operational Support Services, Nashville, TN; David Hardison, PhD, Tom Gillem, and Paul Batalden, MD, HCA Quality Resource Group.

Quality Management in Health Care, 1998, 6(2): 44–51
© 1998 Aspen Publishers, Inc.

When asked to write about the challenges of implementing CQI in a changing delivery organization, I recalled working with Paul Batalden, MD, on the same topic 10 years earlier. In late-1986, Paul began looking for hospital CEOs in Hospital Corporation of America who would volunteer to learn about what became known as the HCA Quality Improvement Process (QIP). I had the privilege of joining the HCA Quality Resource Group shortly thereafter and the rest, as they say, is history. In 1988 alone, Paul and I conducted 33 workshops, each of three days duration, called "HCA Quality: Focus on Continuous Improvement." The workbook that we used for what we fondly called Q101 was created by a Design Team consisting of staff from three HCA hospitals and the corporate office. The material presented in this article is based upon the last day of the Q101 workshop that we took across the country a decade ago. I am reminded of the French proverb, "The more things change, the more they stay the same." You decide if our message is still relevant today.

bility, perceived ambiguity and inconsistency, emotions running high (stress, excitement, conflict, etc.), unclear direction or focus, an increased need for power, control and/or dependence. Old ways become "cherished" and threatened, self-esteem and self-confidence are questioned and reassessed.

During the transition phase, you will find new external allies, mixed signals everywhere, both short-term and long-term foci, an unbelievably strong commitment to the status quo, employees that are confused, employees that are resisting, leaders that are tired, a new mission/purpose identified, new communication efforts, critical mass building, champions of the change come forward, encouragement and control are frustrating, premature "refreezing" on the new way, surprise support, new leaders emerge, some people leave, confusion over roles begins to clear.

In the new preferred state, people work together more efficiently, and a common language evolves related to mission, customers, and daily organizational life. Standards are never enough; the status quo is never good enough. People work smarter and often harder, listening to customers drives the organization and productivity continually increases. Every worker is important, involved, and making improvements. Leadership/management becomes a new, exciting, and continual learning opportunity. A more complete understanding of the long-tem creates short-term resiliency and responsiveness. Employees become fiercely loyal and excited about their work, and customers sense the enthusiasm, excitement, and freshness in the organization and its interest in them. Good employees are attracted to the organization; customers seek out the organization.

IMPACT OF TRANSFORMATION ON PEOPLE

Both university and service delivery personnel need to think about the impact of this transformation on different groups of people in the organization. For example, "In this time of organizational change, what should

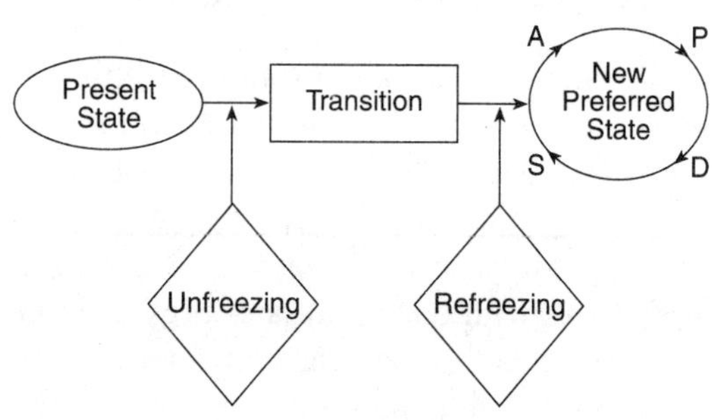

Figure 1. The three stages of the change process: the present state, the transition state, and the desired state.

Some Practical Tips for Facilitating Change and Dealing with CQI Myths

The term *organization* is used here in its most general sense. An organization might range from a legal entity to a temporary team called together to work on improvement. The defining characteristics are that the collection of people have a common purpose (though it may not be stated or well understood), are interdependent, have expected and perceived roles, and, hence, form a social system. The Lewin model and the principles of managing change apply. This also invites the question about whether the approach to transformation should be top-down or bottom-up. I think that the answer is both; however, I have yet to see an example of successful large-scale change effort that did not have the active participation and leadership of the CEO.

The literature on the subject of change is very rich. The issues are also very complex. Thus, I do not pretend to comprehensively cover "change," though I offer some tips that I have found to be useful in practice. In addition, a number of myths about CQI have emerged over time. I offer some responses that may be helpful.

Creating widespread buy-in to change. Let people know that you understand and care about their concerns at their level, i.e., demonstrate empathy. Be genuine or people will see right through it. This means actively listen to people. Try to understand their point of view even if you do not necessarily agree with it. Try to walk in their shoes. View change as a journey to take together to a desirable destination. You must create a picture of a future that is better than the status quo. However, many of us view change as painful. Therefore, the pain of staying the same must exceed the perceived pain of changing. Remember that it is our nature to put our own self-interests first or, to say it another way, our internal radio is preset to station WIII-FM (What Is In It For Me?). Until this basic need is addressed, we will not listen to another station even if there is a compelling reason.

Break down barriers among administrators, physicians and nurses. In the name of professional allegiance or downright stubbornness, we often miss tremendous opportunities to make improvements. How many times have you heard "It's not my job, it's ____'s job." or "It's not my fault, it's ___." ? While we are finger pointing and denying our interdependencies, the needs of our patients and their families go unmet. So how to we attack this problem? Start with a flowchart. The most underrated tool in the CQI arsenal is the flowchart. The deployment flowchart[1] is an especially useful version of this tool because it highlights relationships among process stakeholders in addition to workflow. I have seen many barriers (and egos) melt away by the mere act of creating a flowchart by asking questions like: "Who do you depend on? For what? What happens first? What happens next?" This "catwalk"[2] of a process can focus the energies of very smart and capable people on working together to better serve our customers. At an organizational level, nothing works better than creating a picture of your organization as a system to illustrate and begin to understand macro relationships with suppliers, customers, the community and the system of production.[3–6]

CQI takes too long. Many factors contribute to this perception of CQI. In an effort to "ease into CQI," a team will be formed to work on improvement with meetings scheduled for one hour every other week. This is a recipe for waste because the first 15 to 20 minutes of each meeting is spent reconnecting with the last meeting. That represents 25 percent to 33 percent of valuable group time engaged in rework. This, of course, is a conservative estimate since it assumes that the meeting started at the scheduled time. One study of teams estimates that the time wasted in is closer to 50 percent.[7] Other common problems include poorly focused team charters, "What are we trying to accomplish?", and the lack of specific homework assignments between meetings, "Who is going to do what before we get together again that will increase our knowledge about what changes we can make that will result in

continues

improvement?" Several excellent sources exist that describe proven strategies for improving the efficacy and speed of improvement efforts.[1,8,9] Forming a team is a business decision and the bottom-line is that the real work of improvement does not occur in meetings. As Tom Nolan, PhD, says, "Eliminate meeting room analysis. Go out and run a test!"

CQI is nice theory but it is not practical. The Plan-Do-Study-Act cycle is the most practical approach to learning and improving that exists. Unfortunately, people use the theory thing as a cop out, as an excuse to not think critically and examine their assumptions, and as a way of clinging to the status quo. The best way that I have found to pierce the veil of the status quo is to use the three key improvement questions[10] and rapid cycles of PDSA:

1. What are we trying to accomplish?
2. How will we know a change is an improvement?
3. What can we change that will result in improvement?

Improvement requires change but not all change results in improvement and, in the context of applying PDSA cycles, no action and no learning!

CQI requires a team for every improvement effort. Teamwork (not a team) is necessary because all work is a process with many people depending upon one another to produce results. Organizing a team to work on improvement is often necessary because people lack teamwork skills, knowledge of the interdependencies in a process and improvement knowledge. As people become more adept at teamwork and acquire more process knowledge and improvement knowledge, temporary structures like teams become less necessary. In fact, the goal is self-forming, self-managing teams PRN.

CQI requires every decision to be made by consensus. A leader has choices. He or she can decide with input (consultative), without input (command), or can let a group decide (consensus). All three are necessary and have different advantages and disadvantages. Followers expect leaders to make decisions; however, leaders should declare the choice at the beginning of a decision-making process versus during the process (i.e., after getting frustrated).

top leaders be prepared to do? What should middle managers be prepared to do? What should front-line workers be prepared to do?" Ask yourself these questions, then compare and contrast your responses against those below.

Top leaders are obligated to send symbolic messages supporting the "new way," to teach and reinforce new behaviors, to question past and present practices, to illustrate benefits of the new way, to ensure understanding of the need for change, to adapt systems and processes, to gain maximum input and involvement from people, to design and communicate an action plan, to provide feedback and coaching. The advantages of leading the transformation in these ways are a greater likelihood of success. Genuine commitment on the part of everyone concerned is more likely. Costs (financial, technical, and human) of change are minimized. The integrity of technical and human sides of change will be maintained.

All managers of people at other levels of the organization are obligated to take responsibility for leading CQI in their functional areas; to support top leadership, peers, and subordinates in initiating and sustaining CQI; to provide coaching within their departments and functional areas to foster improvements in process through use of CQI strategies and tools; to provide feedback to ensure that CQI is initiated and sustained and to recognize and reward achievements; to show initiative by participating in CQI workshops and serving on project teams; and to provide direction for CQI by articulating and reinforcing the organization's action plan.

All personnel are obligated to demonstrate involvement in CQI by participating in workshops and serving on teams, to take initiative to identify opportunities and offer suggestions for the improvement of processes, to serve customers to the best of their abilities with a goal of meeting the customers' judgments of quality, to study processes and improve them by participating on teams, and to take pride in their work with the goal of continuous improvement.

ROLE OF CEO

The role of the CEO is critical to the change process, and it is important that the CEO follow 10 prerequisites for successfully leading an organizational transformation:

1. Dissatisfaction with present conditions and willing to learn.
2. A solid understanding of the changing demands placed upon the organization, its systems, and its people.
3. A growing awareness of the increased expectations placed upon the organization by its customers (internal and external).
4. A clear vision of a better, more effective way of doing business.
5. Experiencing or anticipating a weakening, uncertain, or unsatisfactory competitive edge.
6. Observation that the organization is stagnant or not advancing rapidly enough to meet the new demands and expectations.
7. Awareness of an opportunity for significant improvement.
8. A belief that the organization is doing well but could continually do better.
9. A belief that organizations and their people have a tremendous capacity for withstanding and fostering positive change.
10. An ethical conviction that an organization has a moral obligation to better society through the development of its people and its customers.

In addition, it may be helpful for the CEO to reflect on these prerequisites using a self-assessment exercise with the following preamble: "Research has shown that all, or a combination of many, of the 10 factors were deeply felt by CEOs before leading a major organizational transformation."

This is why the factors are referred to as "prerequisites" to CQI transformation. If the feelings described are unfamiliar to you, you probably are not currently ready to move forward with the CQI. If you do believe that many of these feelings describe your current situation, you may be ready.

The following exercise is intended to help assess the degree to which you are feeling the need to launch an organizational transformation. It will identify your primary motivator, which may be driving your need to begin.

Many CEOs acknowledged how helpful this exercise was to them and to the work of transformation. It helped them assess their readiness to embark on this long journey.

ORGANIZATIONAL READINESS

Similarly, leaders must reflect on the readiness and preparation of their organizations to undertake this task. The Appendix presents an excerpt of a tool and process to assess the readiness of an organization to undertake the CQI transformation. Once completed, the work provides a useful starting point for developing an action plan.

Considerations and Strategies for the Transformation

As a planning tool, take a look at how "ready" your organization appears to be for the organizational transformation. The model presented in the Appendix addresses organizational dynamics and change requirements. If any organization is to successfully initiate CQI, this model should be kept in mind. From this model, a change strategy unique to your organization can be built.

To ensure that the transformation will be able to flourish in a fertile environment, this model addresses

- the organizational side of change,
- the systems and structures that support change,
- the human side of change, and
- the strategies that support change.

This model allows you to initiate actions promoting movement away from the present state (unfreezing), while providing structure, guidance, confidence, and trust within the organization. Movement occurs more easily and throughout the organization with the collective efforts of the people within the organization.

Under each of the 10 considerations are questions. These questions, and the considerations themselves, are very similar to, and in some cases, the same as those we covered earlier:

- organizational transformation,
- characteristics of the CQI process,
- CEO roles, and
- prerequisites to change.

You will see common themes recurring that serve to underscore their importance and illustrate how all pervasive they are in CQI. Examples of common themes are vision, leadership, and commitment.

Take a few minutes to consider each of the 10 items listed in the Appendix. Read the questions under each. They should be thought provoking and provide you with information to assist you in planning a change strategy. Jot down brief reactions to each question. Once you have done this, refer to the 10-item rating scale. You will be rating your organization, as it is now, in relation to each consideration. You will be rating your organization on two elements:

1. Where your organization stands presently.
2. Where it should be, ideally, for a successful CQI process.

For each consideration, rate where your organization presently stands with a (P) and where it needs to be for CQI with a (Q). Is there a difference (gap) between where the organization stands now (P) and where it should be (Q) to move into CQI? What does this gap signify? How do you plan to move your organization more toward the "Q"?

CONCLUSION

Unfortunately, parts of an organization and individuals do not move in lock step through major change. Different components of the organization may simultaneously be in different phases of change. This is certainly true for different people. Managing this variation provides additional complexity and, with it, challenges. Daryl Conner states that what matters most when pursuing any fundamental change "is not the degree of reason or emotion involved, but the level of resolve."[11] Dr. W. Edwards Deming declares that the first of his 14 obligations of management is "to create constancy of purpose toward improvement of product and service, with the aim to become competitive and to stay in business, and to provide jobs."[12] He also states that this is the hardest management obligation to achieve. Why? Why is it so difficult to embark on a journey that so many agree makes sense? I am reminded of a conversation that I had with Dr. Vin Sahney about this. When Henry Ford Health System initiated their CQI transformation in

1989, he remarked that so much of CQI is just common sense and then began laughing. He then asked me if I knew what Mark Twain said about common sense. He said, "It is the sense that is not commonly applied." There are no barriers to access the knowledge for improvement that makes so much sense.[8,10,13–15] The major barriers to overcome are to take action to apply CQI to real work and to have the patience to stick with it as we move up the learning curve. Let us hope that we have the courage and conviction to prove Mark Twain wrong.

REFERENCES

1. Scholtes, P. *The Team Handbook.* Madison, WI: Joiner, 1988.
2. Hardison, C.D. "Applying Systems Thinking to Health Care." Keynote speech. Quorum Network Meeting, March 1992.
3. Hardison, C.D. "Applying Knowledge of Systems to Health Care." One-day pre-conference mini-course. National Forum on Quality Improvement in Health Care, December 1992.
4. Hardison, C.D. "Appreciation of an Organization as a System." Invited workshop. National Forum on Quality Improvement in Health Care, December 1992.
5. Batalden, P.B., and Mohr, J.J. "Building Knowledge of Health Care as a System." *Quality Management in Health Care* 5, no. 3 (1997): 1–12.
6. Early, J.F., and Godfrey, A.B. "But It Takes Too Long. . . ." *Quality Progress* 28 (July 1995): 51–55.
7. Caldwell, C. "Accelerated Cost Reduction Strategies." Post-conference mini-course. National Forum on Quality Improvement in Health Care, December 1996.
8. Langley, G.J., Nolan, K.M., Nolan, T.W., Norman, C.L., and Provost, L.P. *The Improvement Guide: A Practical Approach to Enhancing Organizational Performance.* San Francisco: Jossey-Bass, 1996.
9. IHI Breakthrough Series.
10. Langley, G.J., Nolan, K.M., and Nolan, T.W. "The Foundation of Improvement." *Quality Progress* 27 (June 1994): 81–86.
11. Conner, D. *Managing at the Speed of Change: How Resilient Managers Succeed and Prosper Where Others Fail.* New York: Villard Books, 1993.
12. Deming, W.E. *Out of the Crisis.* Cambridge, MA: Massachusetts Institute of Technology, Center for Advanced Engineering Study, 1986.
13. Deming, W.E. *The New Economics for Industry, Government, Education.* Cambridge, MA: Massachusetts Institute of Technology, Center for Advanced Engineering Study, 1993.
14. Batalden, P,B., and Nolan, T.W. *Knowledge for the Leadership of Continual Improvement in Health Care.* Gaithersburg, MD: Aspen Publishers, 1993.
15. Strickland, R.W., and Hardison, C.D. "Transforming the Hospital Department." *Quality Management in Health Care* 2, no. 1 (Fall 1993): 46–56.

Appendix

Ten Considerations for the Transformation: An Organizational Assessment

1. **Vision**—Common Purpose and Goal
   A. How clear, current, appropriate are your organizational . . .
      - mission?
      - values?
      - philosophy?
      - goals?
      - purpose?
   B. How well focused are they upon, and consistent with, the new vision?
   C. How well communicated, modeled, and understood is the **vision**?
2. **Leadership**
   A. Who is driving this process with a passion?
   B. Who is designing and supporting a long-term leadership strategy to sustain the effort? What does it look like?
   C. Is the top leadership leading the way . . .
      - visibly?
      - symbolically?
      - consistently?
      - passionately?
      - with their actions and behavior?
   D. Is all leadership aware of, practicing, and communicating common values and direction?
   E. Do you have sufficient support and coaching in this quest?
3. **Organization Structure**
   A. How supportive or adaptive is your organizational structure to CQI?
   B. How will you operate to accomplish your goals and lead the CQI journey?
   C. What impact upon the organization will this change have?
4. **Training and Support Mechanisms**
   A. What initial education on the new vision is needed?
   B. What new knowledge and skills are now needed?
   C. How supportive of CQI are your training strategies?
   D. How well provided to the organization are logistical, administrative, economic, and human resources?
   E. How well provided is accurate/timely information?
5. **Genuine Commitment**
   A. How skilled are your leaders in managing the human side of change and gaining genuine commitment?
   B. How clearly understood and accepted by your people is . . .
      - the need for change?
      - the benefits of change?

6. **Reinforcement, Recognition, and Reward**
   A. What reinforcement exists to foster the new climate and develop the new behaviors?
   B. What incentives exist that reward the new behaviors?
   C. Is the new way favored and encouraged over the old in a clear, consistent, and frequent manner?
7. **Internal Empowerment**
   A. Is the process self-sustaining from within the organization?
   B. Are the leaders and the people at all levels of the organization equipped with the necessary knowledge and skills to sustain the CQI transformation?
   C. How dependent is the organization upon outside assistance and "prescription" from others? Why? For how long?
8. **Multiple Entry/Critical Mass**
   A. Has change been introduced into several key areas of the organization?
   B. Has a strong and building trust been developing throughout the organization?
9. **Champions and Chance for Success**
   A. Are there obvious "champions" surfacing from all levels of the organization in support of CQI? How are they recognized? How are they supported?
   B. Have individuals taken responsibility to maintain the integrity of CQI and realize tangible successes?
   C. Has CQI had an initial introduction where a series of small victories been won?
   D. Are successes visible, communicated, and illustrated throughout the organization?
10. **Monitoring, Follow-Up, Support**
    A. Is there a feedback mechanism built into the CQI Process which . . .
       - allows for the celebration of success?
       - identifies pitfalls and failures?
    B. Are there periodic reviews and evaluation sessions built in to monitor progress?
    C. Is this information being acted upon to make changes and continuous improvements?

RATING YOUR ORGANIZATION'S READINESS FOR THE TRANSFORMATION

P—Where your organization stands presently?
Q—Where it ideally needs to be for a successful CQI Process.

Consideration	**Low**				**High**
1. Vision	1	2	3	4	5
2. Leadership	1	2	3	4	5
3. Organizational Structure	1	2	3	4	5
4. Training and Support Mechanism	1	2	3	4	5

5. Genuine Commitment	1	2	3	4	5
6. Reinforcement, Recognition, and Rewards	1	2	3	4	5
7. Internal Empowerment	1	2	3	4	5
8. Multiple Entry/Critical Mass	1	2	3	4	5
9. Champions and Chance for Success	1	2	3	4	5
10. Monitoring, Follow-Up, and Support	1	2	3	4	5

Index

D

O

P

Q

R